# Familiar Strangers

# Familiar Strangers

## The Georgian Diaspora and the Evolution of Soviet Empire

ERIK R. SCOTT

OXFORD
UNIVERSITY PRESS

# OXFORD

UNIVERSITY PRESS

Oxford University Press is a department of the University of Oxford. It furthers
the University's objective of excellence in research, scholarship, and education
by publishing worldwide. Oxford is a registered trade mark of Oxford University
Press in the UK and certain other countries.

Published in the United States of America by Oxford University Press
198 Madison Avenue, New York, NY 10016, United States of America.

Library of Congress Cataloging-in-Publication Data
Names: Scott, Erik, 1978–
Title: Familiar strangers : the Georgian diaspora and the evolution of Soviet
empire / Erik R. Scott.
Description: Oxford : Oxford University Press, 2016. | Includes
bibliographical references and index.
Identifiers: LCCN HYPERLINK "tel:2015037325" \t "_blank" 2015037325 |
ISBN 978–0–19–939637–5 (hardcover : acid-free paper)
Subjects: LCSH: Georgia (Republic)—Relations—Soviet Union. | Soviet
Union—Relations—Georgia (Republic) | Georgians (South
Caucasians)—Migrations—History. | Migration, Internal—Soviet
Union—History. | Cultural pluralism—Soviet Union—History. | Soviet
Union—Ethnic relations. | Soviet Union—Territorial expansion. | Soviet
Union—Economic conditions.
Classification: LCC DK676.9.S65 S36 2016 | DDC 305.899/9690470904—dc23 LC
record available at http://lccn.loc.gov/2015037325

3 5 7 9 8 6 4
Printed by Sheridan, USA

*To Keeli and Sabina*

# CONTENTS

# ACKNOWLEDGMENTS

My fascination with the Georgian diaspora began during my first visit to Moscow as an undergraduate student, when I was struck by the profoundly multiethnic character of the former Soviet capital. Clearly, there was more to Russia than ethnic Russians, and, among non-Russians, Georgians stood out in intriguing ways. The irresistible appeal of Georgian cuisine and a retrospective of Soviet Georgian films at Moscow's Museum of Cinema only deepened my interest. While this book is a historical study of migration and diaspora, it is also the product of my subsequent travels in Russia and Georgia in pursuit of this interest and the relationships forged along the way.

Even before graduate school, I was fortunate to have a wonderful series of mentors. At Brown University, Pat Herlihy introduced me to the major questions of Russian and Soviet history, including the "national question" that preoccupied nineteenth-century intellectuals, was forcefully addressed by Bolshevik revolutionaries, and remains at the forefront of Russian politics today. In Washington, DC, Martha Brill Olcott shared her knowledge of the Caucasus and Central Asia, and Louise Shelly gave me an unforgettable opportunity to work in Georgia from 2002 to 2004.

Informed by these experiences, this book took shape at the University of California, Berkeley, where it began as a dissertation. I owe a debt of gratitude to my committee: Victoria Frede, Leslie Peirce, Stephan Astourian, and Victoria Bonnell. I am particularly indebted to my adviser, Yuri Slezkine. Rather than limiting my study to Georgian political networks, Georgian food, or Georgian success in the Soviet marketplace, he encouraged me to examine the Georgian diaspora in all of its diverse

ix

forms over the entire Soviet period. His commitment to addressing the big questions of history continues to inspire my work. While at Berkeley, I was lucky to have been a part of a number of overlapping intellectual communities: the Russian history *kruzhok*, the Central Eurasia Working Group, and the Georgian-language program led by Vakhtang Chikovani and Shorena Kurtsikidze.

I am truly grateful for all of the colleagues and friends in Russia, Georgia, and the United States who helped me carry out my research. In Russia, I would like to thank the staff of the State Archive of the Russian Federation, the Russian State Archive of the Economy, the Russian State Archive of Literature and Art, the Russian State Archive of Contemporary History, the Russian State Archive of Socio-Political History, the Central State Archive of the City of Moscow and its Division for the Preservation of Audio-Visual Documents, and the Russian State Archive of Film and Photo Documents. I am also grateful for the assistance rendered by Nona Matua of the Union of Georgians in Russia in arranging interviews, and would like to thank everyone who took the time to meet with me. In Georgia, I wish to extend my gratitude to the Archive of the Ministry of Internal Affairs of Georgia and its director, Colonel Omar Tushurashvili. I would also like to thank the archivists of the National Archive of Georgia, particularly the staff of the Central Archive of Contemporary History, its Department of Literature and Art, and the Central Archive of Audiovisual and Film Documents. I am grateful for the assistance provided by Timothy Blauvelt, Giorgi Kldiashvili, Sasha Kukhianidze, Shalva Machavariani, Berdia Natsvlishvili, Ketevan Rostiashvili, and Anton Vacharadze in helping me carry out my research in Tbilisi and also for Tamriko Bakuradze and Shota Papava's help in deciphering the handwriting of early Georgian revolutionaries. In the United States, I would like to thank the Hoover Institution's archivists and the staff of the European and African and Middle Eastern Reading Rooms of the Library of Congress.

I was fortunate to have many friends and colleagues who offered valuable input on my project at critical stages in its development. A good number of people, including Sergei Arutiunov, Jeffrey Brooks, Bob Crews, Beshara Doumani, Bob Edelman, Charles King, Peter Rutland, Ned Walker, Amir Weiner, and the late Gregory Grossman, provided insights and responded to queries as I completed my research. Ron Suny, a pathbreaking scholar in Soviet and Georgian history, generously shared his knowledge and his latest research on the young Stalin. As I wrote, Tom Liles assisted with editing; Vitaly Chernetsky, James Heinzen, and Jeff Sahadeo were kind enough to read selected chapters; and Alexis Peri and Victoria Smolkin graciously agreed to read the entire manuscript. In revising, I was guided by the thoughtful comments of two anonymous reviewers. At Oxford University Press, Susan Ferber expertly guided the book's development from proposal to publication, Anne Sanow refined the text, and Lori Hobkirk and Maya Bringe skillfully supervised production.

While I bear sole responsibility for the final product, this book would not have been possible without the support I received from the Berkeley Department of History, the Berkeley Program in Eurasian and East European Studies, the Department of Education's Foreign Language and Area Studies Fellowship, the Alan Sharlin Memorial Award, the Fulbright-Hays Doctoral Dissertation Research Abroad Grant, the Mellon/ACLS Dissertation Completion Fellowship, the National Council for Eurasian and East European Research's Title VIII Travel Grant, the American Philosophical Society's Franklin Research Grant, and the Vice Chancellor for Research Book Publication Award of the University of Kansas. A postdoctoral fellowship at Georgetown University's Center for Eurasian, Russian, and East European Studies and a Title VIII Research Fellowship at the Kennan Institute gave me the time I needed to revise my manuscript. Since arriving at the University of Kansas in 2012, I have been surrounded by supportive colleagues who have helped me develop as a historian. I am particularly grateful to Luis Corteguera, Sheyda Jahanbani, and Nathan Wood for their guidance, advice, and mentorship. I would also like to thank Jon Giullian of the University of Kansas Libraries and Darin Grauberger, Travis White, and the University of Kansas Cartographic Services for the maps.

Before my travels even began, my parents nurtured my intellectual interests, and my grandparents gave me an intimate understanding of our own family's experience of migration and diaspora by sharing stories of their life in a small Italian village. Later on, my family supported my decision to go to graduate school, and my parents, grandparents, sister, and brother-in-law did everything they could to help me along the way. I owe the deepest gratitude to my wife, Keeli. She was my true companion at every stage of this book's long journey. Throughout, she was a source of support and inspiration, offering a fresh perspective on my research and a steady reminder that there was so much more beyond it. This book is dedicated to her and our daughter, Sabina.

# NOTE ON TRANSLITERATION
## AND DATING

In the interest of simplicity, I use a modified version of the Library of Congress system to render Georgian names and words in Latin characters. I forego diacritics and special characters in the hope that the resulting transliteration will be more easily pronounced by non-Georgian speakers but still recognizable to those familiar with the language. Although Georgian does not use capital letters, I have capitalized personal names while transliterating them from their original language (rather than from their Russianized version). Accordingly, Stalin's given name appears as Ioseb Jughashvili rather than Iosif Dzhughashvili.

In transliterating Russian names and words, I adhere to the Library of Congress system, with the exception of recognizable names in general usage (e.g., Trotsky rather than Trotskii). For the sake of brevity, I often refer to Soviet republics by their shortened name, which reflects contemporary usage (e.g., Georgia rather than the Georgian Soviet Socialist Republic). While the official name of Georgia's capital changed from Tiflis to the more Georgianized Tbilisi in 1936, I use the latter name throughout.

Dates are given in their chronological and geographic context. Events taking place in Russia and Georgia before February 1, 1918 are provided in the Julian calendar (thirteen days behind the calendar used in the West); those occurring afterward are given in the Gregorian calendar.

# Familiar Strangers

The Georgian Soviet Socialist Republic

The Caucasus in the Soviet Union

# Introduction

If any single moment can be considered the high point of Soviet history, it occurred when Soviet soldiers raised the Red Flag over the Reichstag on May 1, 1945. The event signaled the defeat of German fascism after a costly war and portended a new era of international relations redefined by the Soviet Union's emergence as a global superpower. Two soldiers in particular were credited with this defining achievement, their images appearing in Soviet newspapers and subsequently reprinted in school textbooks. The Russian Mikhail Egorov represented the largest nation in the Soviet Union, while the Georgian Meliton Kantaria stood for the victory of a multiethnic state and society.[1] Yet this was not the only historical juncture at which a Georgian appeared at the forefront of Soviet life.

Georgians occupied a central role at each stage of the Soviet Union's evolution, from establishment to dissolution. Joseph Stalin, born Ioseb Jughashvili, was just one of a group of Georgian revolutionaries who came to power in the early years of Soviet rule and directed the development of the new state. After the socialist state was established Soviet citizens sought new opportunities for leisure and consumption, and they found them at the Georgian restaurant, where they adopted the distinctive rituals of the Georgian table. During the "Thaw" that followed Stalin's death, Georgian cultural entrepreneurs embodied the era's spirit of spontaneity as popular though recognizably ethnic entertainers specializing in song and dance. As official life grew stagnant under Leonid Brezhnev, Georgians thrived in the burgeoning informal economy. Finally, with the advent of Mikhail Gorbachev's reforms, it was a

Georgian film, *Repentance* (*monanieba*), that explored the furthest limits of allowable expression, calling into question the very legitimacy of Soviet power.

Georgians were the multiethnic Soviet empire's most familiar strangers. They moved beyond their native republic in the Caucasus to gain imperial prominence in Moscow, yet remained a distinctive national community. They were a diaspora defined by ethnic difference, yet one internal to the Soviet Union. Georgians employed strangeness in ways that met the demands of the Soviet state, but they did so largely for their own benefit. They succeeded because their cultural repertoire emphasized recognizable difference, because their networks stretched beyond the Georgian Soviet Socialist Republic (SSR) to intersect with central institutions, and because their homeland was firmly within Soviet borders, able to provide a steady supply of ideologically sanctioned cultural and material resources. Georgians had a distinct set of skills and a cultivated mythology that fit those skills. The Soviet authorities used, promoted, and sometimes resented Georgian success, while Georgians capitalized on it, negotiating between imperial prominence and local self-assertion.

At first glance, this story of Georgian diasporic success might seem unlikely. After all, Georgians were one of over one hundred officially classified Soviet nationalities. Numbering just under four million, they made up less than 2 percent of the overall Soviet population.[2] Their homeland, the Georgian SSR, was a small territory located far from Moscow, beyond the towering mountains of the Caucasus range. While the Georgians were historically Orthodox Christians, for most of their history they had been more closely linked to the Ottoman and Persian empires than to Russia. Their non-Slavic language was completely unrelated to Russian and written in a unique alphabet indecipherable to most Soviet citizens. Yet these factors make the prominence they achieved in the Soviet context even more intriguing.

This book's premise is that the history of the Georgian diaspora cannot be understood without a thorough reconceptualization of the Soviet empire. While previous scholars have made a convincing case for understanding the Soviet state as an empire because it expanded across vast territory, exerted its authority over an ethnically defined periphery, and

*Figure I.1* Georgian soldier Meliton Kantaria (left) holding the Soviet Banner of Victory alongside Russian soldier Mikhail Egorov (right) after the pair raised the flag over the Reichstag in Berlin. Russian State Archive of Film and Photo Documents.

ruled through difference, the Soviet Union was not simply a federation of nationalities confined to titular republics. Instead, it was an empire of mobile diasporas that transcended the borders of the republics, inter-mixed, and helped construct a truly multiethnic society. The state's treat-ment of its myriad nationalities was rarely equitable, but non-Russians could and did exploit the state's dependence on national difference. By reimagining the Soviet Union as an empire defined by its diasporas, this book recasts imperial subjects as imperial agents.

It also makes the case for a broader understanding of diaspora, a term describing an ethnic community that lives beyond its homeland yet maintains a collective sense of identity over time.[3] Departing from prior scholarship on diaspora and the established trends of Soviet his-toriography, this book contends that homelands can also be internal to empire and expands the concept of diaspora to include nationalities in the Soviet Union living beyond their titular republics.[4] It argues that by enabling the internal migration of diverse populations but upholding a system in which national identity was based on descent, the Soviet Union engendered and perpetuated a diverse range of diasporic groups who were seen, and most often saw themselves, as nationally distinctive even as they remained Soviet citizens. While some scholars have argued for a more limited application of the concept of diaspora, there is no other term that so clearly underscores the fact that life as a member of one of these communities was shaped by the experience of being, at least in some sense, a stranger.[5]

These internal groups differed from more commonly studied diasporas in important ways, suggesting the need for a new typology. Unlike Jews or Armenians, Georgians were not heirs to a long diaspora tradition. They were rapidly transformed from rooted agriculturalists into mobile urban specialists within the context of the Soviet empire, and their dispersal arguably had more to do with imperial opportunity than national trauma. While Georgian migrants drew on preexisting cultural practices and pursued their own interests, the Soviet state helped fund and produce their diasporic identity. In contrast to more typical diasporas, Georgians and other groups that this book describes as familiar strangers tended to place greater emphasis on the outward performance of national difference, using otherness as a strategy to manage the terms of their imperial integration.

Although the Georgians described in this book came from diverse backgrounds, held divergent opinions, and did not always think of themselves as a unified community, all of them came to the fore as Georgians beyond Georgia and performed their own nationality at important moments in Soviet history. Their Georgianness was a historical artifact: a visible, audible, and edible repertoire of familiar strangeness forged at the intersection of national and imperial culture. This repertoire, composed of practices, symbols, texts, and modes of self-presentation, was the subject of internal debates among the diaspora even as it was externally oriented for the purposes of Soviet empire. Admittedly, this book does not look equally at all Georgians but focuses on those who gained widespread prominence in Moscow as a way of explaining the leading role that non-Russian diasporas played at the heart of the Soviet empire.

Beginning in the final years of imperial Russia and continuing through the collapse of the Soviet Union, this book uses the Georgian story to explore the evolution of the multiethnic Soviet state and the accompanying transformation of Soviet society. Chapter 1 provides the theoretical framework and discusses the historiographical consequences of this *longue durée* approach, reimagining the Soviet Union as an empire of diasporas, examining the Georgians in comparison with other diasporas within and beyond Soviet borders, and describing the creation of a domestic internationalism that brought opportunities as well as risks for groups like the Georgians. Subsequent chapters proceed chronologically, each looking at Georgian prominence in a different realm of Soviet life at a time when that aspect of Soviet life was most relevant. These chapters should be understood as episodic, rather than comprehensive, though together they offer a perspective on Soviet history as a whole.

Chapter 2 traces an entire generation of Georgian revolutionaries from the late nineteenth century to the 1930s, following their advancement from the Caucasus to the Kremlin. Looking at how the Russian Revolution was made largely by non-Russians, the chapter brings to light the so-called Caucasian group, of which Joseph Stalin was the leading member. In so doing, it considers what made Georgian political networks different and in some ways more effective than those of other groups competing for power in the Soviet state. Chapter 3 continues this examination from a culinary perspective, looking at Stalin as a Georgian *tamada* (toastmaster)-in-chief who conducted business around banquet tables in the Kremlin laden with the food and drink of his homeland. It follows the dissemination of Georgian dishes and wines, accompanied by distinct dining and drinking rituals, from the upper echelons of Soviet power to the broader Soviet public. It tells the story of the creation of a multiethnic Soviet diet and explains how it was that of all the diverse cuisines in the Soviet Union, Georgian food and drink went farthest in conquering the Soviet table.

Chapter 4 looks at the redefinition of Georgian culture after Stalin's death. Freed from Stalinist constraints but benefiting from several decades of institutional development, Georgian artists and entertainers seized upon new opportunities for cultural entrepreneurship created by the Thaw. Shifting to the subsequent period typically characterized as one of stagnation (*zastoi*), Chapter 5 looks below the surface to consider the vital role Georgians played in the expanding informal economy. In this sphere the Georgian diaspora was a numerically small but dominant group, ubiquitous in markets throughout the Soviet Union yet rooted in the increasingly assertive Georgian SSR. They provided the goods necessary for the continued functioning of the Soviet economy, but had an uneasy relationship with the imperial state.

Chapter 6 explores how Georgian success bred discontent with the restrictions that Soviet rule placed on professional advancement and cultural expression. While the preceding chapters consider skillful performances of Georgian otherness, this chapter reveals the Georgian intelligentsia's mastery of the universal language of Soviet high culture and their emergent critique of the limitations of Soviet empire. Of all Soviet cinematic traditions, Georgian film perhaps best portrayed the stifled sentiments of late Soviet intellectual life. Although they had been nurtured by the Soviet state, the ambitions of Georgia's sizable intelligentsia eventually provoked a forceful movement against the empire by the end of the 1980s.

While many Georgians embraced independence in 1991, the Georgian diaspora succeeded not despite, but because of the relatively closed, domestically diverse nature of the Soviet empire. With the empire's collapse, Georgians faced new dilemmas as they were transformed from an internal Soviet group into a transnational population living across state borders.[6] The story of their success and its limitations illuminates the intertwined history of empire and diaspora, both in Eurasia and beyond.

# 1

# An Empire of Diasporas

Over one thousand miles lay between the expansive balconies and tiled roofs of the Georgian capital of Tbilisi and the walls and towers of Moscow's Kremlin. The most direct path led past the ancient city of Mtskheta and the medieval fortress of Ananuri, then along a winding road reaching from verdant valleys to the slopes of snow-capped Mount Kazbek, and finally through the Darial Gorge, where the powerful Terek River cut through the Caucasus mountain range and imperial Russia had moved earth and resettled populations to complete its Georgian Military Highway. As Russia consolidated its rule over the Caucasus in the nineteenth century, tsarist officials, administrators, and soldiers from the north traveled the Georgian Military Highway. So, too, did imperial Russia's leading literary figures—authors such as Alexander Pushkin and Mikhail Lermontov—rendering the picturesque and polyglot Caucasus on the page for millions of Russian readers.

The road also brought visitors from the south. Following the absorption of their homeland into the Russian Empire, a new generation of Georgians traveled the Georgian Military Highway to pursue education in Russian universities. They were known in Georgian as the *tergdaleulebi*, "Terek-drinkers," who crossed the mighty river and returned home having imbibed the latest intellectual currents of Moscow and St. Petersburg.[1] Future generations followed their path northward, though by the late nineteenth century they were more likely to return home as committed socialists. They crossed and recrossed the mountainous Caucasus, cultivating a distinctive national identity in a Russian context and seeking the transformation of their homeland upon return. For Georgians, Russia became a pathway to European modernity; it provided models and categories that could be applied to Georgian realities and integrated with preexisting Georgian practices, producing a conception of nationality and a repertoire of cultural performance that fused national consciousness with imperial awareness.

In 1921, after a short period of independence, Georgia was invaded by socialist Russia's Red Army, with a coterie of Georgian Bolsheviks leading the charge. Under Soviet power, the distance separating the two nations in effect grew smaller. It was traversed by new roads and tunnels dug through the mountains, serviced by expanded ports and ferry lines on the Black Sea, and connected by railroad tracks and flight paths. More significantly, Soviet rule entailed changes in ideology as well as infrastructure. In pursuit of its socialist mission, the Soviet Union sought to

*Figure 1.1* A photograph taken along the Georgian Military Highway in the late nineteenth century, showing the Darial Gorge and the Terek River. This narrow mountain pass was the main crossing between Russia and Georgia. Library of Congress.

thoroughly transform the relationship between the metropole and the peoples of imperial Russia's former colonies.

While other empires relied on diasporas, Georgians achieved exceptional prominence in the Soviet Union because they were able to exploit the needs of a unique state that ruled through nationality (*natsional'nost'*) and defined itself as presiding over a multiethnic country (*mnogonatsional'naia strana*).[2] An internal Georgian diaspora skillfully navigated between the Caucasus and the Kremlin, blending the national and the imperial in ways that spoke for a diverse polity. Their arrival in the center of Soviet life reflected the revolution's dramatic mobilization of non-Russian nationalities and the new opportunities Moscow offered for advancement. Among non-Russian residents in the Soviet capital Georgians were far from the largest group, but their overrepresentation in important political, cultural, and economic roles gave them a prominence far beyond their numerically small population, which at its high point in 1989 officially reached only 19,608. By contrast, there were 252,670 Ukrainians, 174,728 Jews, 73,005 Belarussians, 43,989 Armenians, and 20,727 Azeris living in Moscow by that time.[3] Granted, tabulating official registration in Moscow was only one way of counting communities that were highly mobile and did not always take up permanent residence or register with the relevant authorities.[4] However, it was also important that in the roles they came to occupy Georgians tended to perform their national repertoire loudly and colorfully, coming to the fore as pan-imperial specialists of otherness.

The vast literature on Soviet nationalities has tended to overlook their mobility, focusing instead on nationality and nationalism within national republics. This tendency is perhaps understandable, since historians focused their attention on the importance of non-Russian populations around the time of the collapse of the Soviet Union into fifteen independent national republics.[5] New histories were written for the emergent post-Soviet nations; at the same time, nationalism and the nation-state were the subjects of widespread scholarly inquiry.[6] As nationality was examined in a variety of national contexts, scholars reached a new understanding of the Soviet state as a maker, rather than a breaker, of nations.[7] They began to describe this state as a peculiar type of empire, a centralizing polity that nevertheless promoted non-Russian nations in earnest. Terry Martin considered the administration of what he termed the "affirmative action empire," mainly from the perspective of policymakers in Moscow.[8] Drawing on the theories of Benedict Anderson, Francine Hirsch examined how ethnographic knowledge was employed by the state to organize and rule the Soviet "empire of nations."[9] These works reflected a broader historiographical fascination with empire that had its parallels in the study of Russia's imperial past, where scholars attempted to place the tsarist empire in the context of European colonial empires.[10] Framing the history of nationalities in a broader imperial setting, it seemed, was a way of moving away from separate historical accounts written for each nationality, a welcome departure from what Benjamin Nathans justly criticized as the "one people after another approach."[11] Yet these studies of multiethnic empire continued to highlight the way the Soviet state grounded nationalities in titular republics by language, cultural institutions, and the process of local cadre promotion known as *korenizatsiia*. These were important factors, to be sure, but their emphasis obscured the extent to which the Soviet Union also stimulated movement across the internal borders of the national republics. Left untreated was the diasporic experience that defined life for millions in the Soviet empire.

The Soviet state contained a broad array of diaspora populations. Some, like the Germans, Greeks, or Jews after the establishment of Israel in 1948, were linked in real or imagined ways to homelands abroad and were viewed with ideological suspicion.[12] Others, like the Kurds and Roma (Gypsies), had ethnic ties to communities in neighboring states but no internationally recognized homeland, existing uneasily in the Soviet context without a clear territorial basis.[13] A third category, one that has received almost no attention, consisted of internal diasporas, nationalities with assigned territories in the Soviet Union who traveled outside their titular homelands and often gained prominence in the center.[14] This category encompassed a diverse set of communities, including an Armenian population that was already widely dispersed in 1917, but also Ukrainians, Kazakhs, Tajiks, and others who left their homelands for the first time to serve in the Red Army, work at industrial sites, and settle in Russian cities. To varying degrees, internal diaspora groups maintained distinctive identities, yet their members remained integral citizens of a larger multiethnic state.

Internal diasporas differed from other types of diasporas in ways that illuminate the politics and practice of nationality in the Soviet Union. Members of these communities left their homelands and crossed republic-level borders without leaving Soviet territory; as a result, they could move back and forth with ease between homeland and host society. Yet while their ethnic distinctiveness was officially promoted, they were generally prohibited from organizing politically as diasporas beyond the borders of their native republics.[15] Lacking official representation as communities beyond their homelands, they were not classified by Soviet bureaucrats as diasporas, and they were only obliquely noted in census records as nationalities residing outside their titular republics; for these reasons, they have generally been ignored by historians. However, the presence of these outsider communities was felt in every aspect of Soviet life, from the marketplace, to the theatrical stage, to the restaurant menu. While some scholars have called for an approach to empire that "transcends ethnicity," a glimpse at the history of internal diasporas reveals that nationality in the Soviet Union was far more than a fixed administrative or ethnographic classification confined to the national republics.[16] National categories transcended territory, interacted, and in some cases blended together. Rather than casting nationality aside because of the limited ways it has been studied, the concept needs to be reconsidered and set in motion.

This chapter argues for internal diaspora as a way of exploring the mobile dimensions of nationality within the Soviet empire and introduces three related concepts to reimagine the internal diversity of the Soviet state in a global comparative context. The first, the idea of the Soviet Union as an empire of diasporas, looks at the Soviet state in comparison with other empires; the second, the notion of the Georgians as familiar strangers, describes the range of cultural strategies available to diaspora populations and places the Georgians alongside diasporas within and beyond the Soviet Union; the third concept, domestic internationalism, provides a perspective on the evolving dialogue between the Soviet empire and its diverse populations.

## The Soviet Union and Other Empires

The Soviet Union was rather a peculiar imperial state; it was avowedly anti-imperialist in its ideology, and its leaders often denounced racial and ethnic hierarchies.[17] Yet the Soviet state ultimately privileged the center over the periphery, and a politically enlightened Communist Party, with its central institutions in the capital, over the rest of society. It was a state heavily engaged in what historians Jane Burbank and Frederick Cooper call the "politics of difference," an imperial mode that contrasts with the nation-state's emphasis on homogeneity and lateral ties.[18] Like other empires, the Soviet Union ruled through hierarchically organized heterogeneity, expanded to absorb new territories, and subordinated an ethnically defined periphery to the metropole.[19] However, the Georgian experience suggests that the Soviet Union was a state where the periphery may have been defined ethnically, but the national core was ambiguous and poorly articulated. At its center was not a single nation, but rather a mixture of diasporas.

In this sense, the Soviet Union was never truly a Russian empire. While Russian was the Soviet Union's default language and Russians gained a representational prominence after the Second World War, Russians were neither the most prosperous, nor the most educated, nor most successful group in the USSR.[20] While there were more Russians than other nationalities, they still made up only 50 percent of the Soviet Union's overall population.[21] The Russian Soviet Federated Socialist Republic (RSFSR) notably lacked the trappings of statehood accorded the other republics. It was the only Soviet republic that did not have its own Communist Party and Academy of Sciences, and, as a federation, it was composed of a patchwork of regional and ethno-territorial units inhabited by groups as diverse as Tatars, Chechens, and Finns.

The heart of the Soviet empire was Moscow, an imperial rather than a national capital. In the Soviet period, the Russian city was reinvented as a self-consciously multiethnic metropolis. Its streets were marked with the names and heroes of the non-Russian socialist republics, and a Georgian visitor could find the familiar in a visit to Moscow's historic Georgian Square, or a drive along the capital's Rustaveli Street.[22] The city played host to countless political gatherings, cultural events, youth festivals, and academic conferences that showcased internal diasporas from the national republics. Moscow's own political elite was multiethnic and composed of upwardly mobile cadres from the periphery; its culinary tastes favored a multiethnic smorgasbord of national cuisines; its cultural life celebrated the art, music, and theater of the national republics; and its marketplaces featured their goods, often sold by conspicuously non-Russian traders. Political, cultural, and economic life in the Soviet metropole was constructed out of a mixture of national cultures drawn from the Soviet periphery. The Kremlin and Red Square evoked the city's Russian past, but Moscow stood for many things: Russia, certainly, in its various historical incarnations, but also the peoples and places of a diverse empire.

*Figure 1.2* The unveiling of the monument to Russian–Georgian friendship in Moscow in 1983, photographed from a nearby balcony. The monument featured intertwined Georgian and Russian letters and towered over a central Moscow neighborhood, marking the Soviet capital as a multiethnic space. Central State Archive of the City of Moscow, Division for the Preservation of Audio-Visual Documents of Moscow.

The Soviet Union was by no means the first empire to grant a prominent place to its diasporas, though perhaps no other empire was so thoroughly defined by its ethnic minorities. The Byzantine Empire, like most
imperial states before it, relied on ethnically distinct outsiders to bolster
its military.[23] The Spanish Empire employed Swiss mercenaries, along
with German technicians, Maltese merchants, and Genoese sailors,
and was ruled at its height by the Hapsburgs, a supranational Catholic
dynasty.[24] The creation of Britain entailed the absorption of Scottish
and Welsh populations, who often maintained their distinctive identities and professed unique religious denominations even as they came
to serve as the empire's leading military officers, administrators, educa-
tors, and industrialists.[25] Britain, like many other empires, also relied on
a host of local intermediaries and service minorities in the new areas it
conquered, among them polyglot Parsi traders in Hong Kong and peri-
patetic Greek merchants in the Levant.[26]

All of these empires created opportunities for specialized diasporas,
who pursued their own agendas within an imperial framework. Empires
facilitated widespread migration, not only horizontally between metropole and colony, but also laterally from one colony to another. The
Catholic Irish, though arguably colonized at home, traveled in large
numbers to India, as well as to North America and the West Indies,
almost immediately after these territories came under British rule.[27]
Racial ideology deprived Indians of many rights and played a key role
in the exploitative use of Indian labor in eastern and southern Africa;
however, once transported to British-controlled Africa, Indian migrants
established themselves as a critically important commercial community
and preserved Hindu and Muslim religious traditions in diaspora.[28]

Like the Spanish Empire, Britain had a monarch at its center, though
after the French Revolution, dynastic empires had to contend with
calls for popular sovereignty, both from their core and from the furthest reaches of their imperial domains. One strategy of multiethnic
states in the modern age was to promote an assimilationist concept of
imperial citizenship, as France did, which held the promise of universalism, even if in practice it partially or fully excluded groups on the
basis of race and gender.[29] Another strategy was to simultaneously tolerate and constrain nations within imperial borders, as was undertaken

in nineteenth-century Austria-Hungary. There, the Hapsburg dynasty strengthened its central bureaucracy and brandished its Catholic identity, while at the same time cultivating ties with Protestant, Orthodox Christian, and even Jewish populations.[30]

The Soviet Union was not a dynastic empire, though it bore a special resemblance to the past empires of Eurasia, a broad but interconnected geographic area.[31] Eurasian empires excelled at ruling religiously and ethnically diverse populations, and many of them encompassed the same national groups that the Soviets would later govern. They were not maritime empires, like the vast British overseas empire, but land empires, where borders were not so easily defined geographically, and the separation between center and periphery was even more difficult to establish. To a greater degree than empires based in Western Europe, Eurasian empires lacked a clearly defined ethnic and racial core; as a result, they typically created as many opportunities in the center for skilled outsiders as they did for members of their numerically dominant nation. As the preeminent historian of imperial Russia, V. O. Kliuchevskii, famously noted, colonization may have been "the basic fact of Russian history," but the history of Russia was that of "a country that colonizes itself."[32]

The Soviet Union was in many ways similar to the Russian Empire that preceded it, and not only because both shared roughly the same borders and occupied the same position on the Eurasian landmass. Both were expressly multiethnic states with a universalizing ideology, rather than a nation, at their center. The Russian Empire, which some proclaimed as the "Third Rome," accorded a privileged place to Orthodox Christianity and sometimes promoted Russification, but also accommodated religious and ethnic diversity and was ruled by a transnational dynastic elite.[33] The Soviet Union's inheritance from the state that preceded it was not merely geographic; it also included longer-term practices of imperial management and established repertoires of national distinctiveness.

Imperial Russia's Eurasian neighbor, the Ottoman Empire, followed many of the same practices. The Ottoman state did not define itself as Turkish, but proclaimed an encompassing dynastic and Islamic identity while granting protection and reaching a range of special deals with religiously and linguistically diverse populations living in the sultan's domain.[34] As was the case with Russians in the Russian Empire, Turks in the Ottoman Empire were the numerically dominant nationality, yet they had no trappings of national statehood. Both Russians and Turks were predominantly rural and in many cases underrepresented in key areas of imperial life, including commerce and imperial administration. Instead of displaying the dominance of a core nationality, Eurasian empires featured a range of ethnically distinct imperial specialists. The Ottoman Empire had its Armenian, Greek, and Jewish commercial elites, and its imperial bureaucracy and military were staffed by descendants of slaves taken from the Balkans and the Caucasus.[35] In the same fashion, the empire of the tsars relied on Old Believer and Tatar merchant networks, Baltic German bureaucrats and scientists, and Jewish industrial barons.[36] Ottoman imperial diversity could even be seen in the composition of the "Young Turks" who sought to reform the empire and ended up calling for a more nationalist state. Among the founders of the organization that became the nucleus of the Committee of Union and Progress, there was not one ethnic Turk, but an Ottoman Albanian, two Kurds, and a Circassian.[37]

While its neighbors splintered into nationally exclusive states, the Soviet Union found new ways of enduring as a multiethnic empire in twentieth-century Eurasia. Unlike the Ottoman Empire, Austria-Hungary, or even the Fourth French Republic, it effectively fashioned itself as a self-consciously anti-imperialist entity. It more emphatically expressed its multiethnic identity and more thoroughly pursued its internationalist vision, at least within state borders, than any empire had before it. If the Soviet Union can be said to have had a *mission civilisatrice*, it was not about turning Uzbeks into Russians, but rather about making both better communists. This mission was applied with equal zeal to Russian peasants and the pastoral nomads of Central Asia. Moreover, this mission was not simply led by Russians from Moscow; it was embraced by radical communists of diverse ethnic backgrounds. In the Soviet Union, internal diasporas were not simply compradors or imperial intermediaries; they were often the very builders of empire.

The Soviet empire of diasporas was ruled from Moscow, but it was not, contrary to what many historians have argued, merely constructed by the center. The Soviet Union was formed as a federative state following the absorption of Ukraine, Belarus, and the countries of the

South Caucasus, all of which experienced brief periods of independence after the collapse of the Russian Empire.[38] Although the Soviet Union became a highly centralized federation that accorded each republic the same types of national forms, the degree to which nations were granted cultural autonomy varied, based on demography and the perceived need to accommodate local elites. In republics with large Russian populations, like the Kazakh SSR, Russian and the local language were accorded equal status, while in republics with a numerically dominant titular nationality, like the Georgian SSR, the local language retained primacy.[39] In addition, the treatment of local elites initially depended on the way republics were incorporated into the Soviet Union. After the Red Army's invasion of Georgia, for example, Lenin stressed the need for a conciliatory approach.[40] Although Stalin ultimately pursued a ruthless policy of political centralization in his homeland, Georgian national expression in the Soviet period was promoted by Georgian institutions that were established in the imperial period, and had begun developing their cultural repertoire before the Soviet state came into existence.

While the circumstances of nationalities in the Soviet Union were in part made by the nationalities themselves, policies in Moscow created a framework for interactions and gave the Soviet state a crucial role in classifying, sorting, and managing its diaspora populations. As committed socialists, the Bolsheviks judged all nationalities based on their perceived level of development, as understood in Marxist terms. Following Stalin's formula, nations were defined as "historically evolved" communities based on language, territory, economic life, and "psychological make-up"; some, by virtue of high literacy rates, territorial consolidation, economic development, and ideologically sound intellectual production, were judged to be more evolved, and thus closer to socialism, than others.[41] As will be seen, this approach imbued nationality with some of the same characteristics as class, with important consequences for the domestic internationalism that took root within Soviet borders. Yet the state's framework for managing diversity proved remarkably durable. Although there was sometimes an undercurrent of racial thinking that informed popularly held beliefs about supposedly uncivilized "peoples of the East" or hot-tempered southerners, such concepts tended to remain in the background.[42] Instead, diasporas were more likely to be represented and to represent themselves by Soviet national categories, such as Georgian or Uzbek, or, if one were to generalize, by region, such as Caucasian or Central Asian.

Since building socialism meant advancing the interests of the socialist state, the hierarchy of Soviet nationalities, and, in turn, Soviet diasporas, was based on the interests of state centralization and perceptions of state loyalty. By the mid-1930s smaller, nontitular nationalities had been "consolidated" and a process of downgrading autonomous regions had begun, essentially prohibiting the expression of identities deemed subethnic, like that of Mingrelians in Georgia, and constraining the institutional resources available to diasporas whose homeland was placed in another Union republic, as occurred when the Abkhaz Autonomous Soviet Socialist Republic was subsumed under the auspices of the Georgian SSR.[43] An emphasis on otherness by diasporas with homelands abroad became riskier as cross-border populations, such as Finns, Iranians, Koreans, and Poles, faced deportations away from the Soviet Union's external boundaries.[44] Loyalty came to be defined as the lack of potential foreign allegiances and, especially after World War II, the perception of a nationality's heroism or collaboration in the elemental struggle against Fascism. In the context of the Great Patriotic War, national populations viewed as ideologically suspect, like Chechens, Ingushetians, and Crimean Tatars, were labeled as "enemy nations" and forcibly resettled, with the taint of alleged collaboration following them into exile.[45] Yet the notion of collective responsibility could also bestow benefits, with favored nationalities based in a Union republic welcomed across Soviet territory as socialist "friends" and "brothers."

While it is common to speak of the colonization of the periphery by the center, the Soviet state in some cases allowed and even encouraged certain representatives of the periphery to colonize its institutions in multiethnic Moscow. The ascent of Stalin and the "Caucasian group" to the Kremlin is the most striking example of this phenomenon, though by no means the only one. Describing the Soviet Union as an empire of diasporas complicates the typical division between center and periphery, and colonizer and colonized, that guides most scholarship on empire. It brings into view the diversity of the Soviet multiethnic state in a way that the story of nationalities is not simply one of their suffering under Russian domination, pointing to the fact that some groups could achieve success in an imperial context by performing otherness.

## Diasporas Between Strangeness and Familiarity

Diaspora, as theorist Khachig Tölöyan has argued, is not so much a "fixed concept and social formation" as it is a "process of collective identification" that draws on aspects of the homeland's culture.[46] The cultural repertoire of a diaspora might employ a distinctive language, shared texts and symbols, social practices, and norms that evoke or appeal to the homeland, whether that homeland is real or imagined, a distant memory or a future possibility. Yet the cultural expressions of diasporas are always shaped by the context of the host society as well as their connection to the homeland. Those seeking to articulate a diasporic identity must navigate between these two poles: the host society, which might attract or constrain migrants with its political and cultural framework, and the homeland, which might beckon with the call of kinship or be criticized for alleged cultural backwardness.

The strategies that diaspora communities employ to negotiate the terms of their identity are conditioned by divergent histories, diverse state contexts, and distinctive cultural repertoires. Rather than attempting to place these strategies on a spectrum between outright assimilation and full-scale ethnic mobilization, it is better to think of two basic genres of diasporic performance: the first characterized by acting within the host culture, and the second by making a spectacle of group otherness. These are of course ideal types; in practice, diasporas might strike different balances in different contexts, or view both options with ambivalence. The scholarly literature on diaspora, however, tends to focus on the first, emphasizing the pressures of assimilation and the dangers of maintaining a diasporic identity. In so doing, it overlooks the fact that a number of groups have sought and achieved success by performing their own ethnic difference. Groups like these are best described as familiar strangers, and their experiences expand our notions of the possibilities and risks of diaspora.[47]

Until very recently, the word "diaspora" was capitalized in most dictionaries. Jews were seen as the paradigmatic Diaspora, and generalizations proceeded from the Jewish case. Emphasizing their traumatic dispersal, their longstanding diaspora tradition, and their persecution, sociologist Robin Cohen characterized Jews as a "victim diaspora."[48] Certainly, they were more than mere victims, even in Cohen's view, but the term neatly described a large body of literature on the Jewish experience. Recent scholarship on Jews in Soviet history has complicated this conception, though the Jewish embrace of revolutionary universalism was fraught with the threat of "unmasking" and explicitly Jewish cultural production generally ended with the closure of Moscow's Yiddish theater under Stalin.[49]

Influenced in part by Jewish historiography, scholarly accounts of the African diaspora have similarly placed traumatic memory at the heart of collective identity and emphasized the risks of otherness.[50] However, the terms of the Jewish experience do not hold for all diasporas. An important counterpoint can be found in the literature on "middlemen minorities" and "trade diasporas."[51] These terms have most commonly been used to describe Greek, Armenian, and overseas Chinese communities, though they have also sometimes been applied to Jews. Such groups may have been dispersed traumatically, but they also profited from their otherness. In general, though, these groups have been depicted as incapable or unwilling to form lasting or meaningful relationships with the host society. Sometimes described as "professional boundary crossers," their economic role might be likened to the cultural niche ascribed to Roma, particularly in Russia.[52] Like economic middlemen, Romani entertainers specialized in providing a product considered transgressive by the host society.[53] Scholars may have underestimated the extent to which Roma were in fact integrated into the culture of the host society, but the fact remains that they were generally perceived as potentially dangerous and ideologically problematic outsiders.[54] Their risqué social position may have gained imperial Russia's Gypsy choirs a place on the stage, but, for the most part, Roma continued to be seen as strangers apart, their prominence confined to exoticized musical theater.

Unlike Jews and Africans, Georgians migrated out of opportunity and, in contrast to Greeks and Roma, they did not possess such a longstanding tradition of dispersal. Their central importance calls to mind sociologist Georg Simmel's discussion of strangers who stay, but more than other stranger communities, they integrated and came to the fore in Soviet imperial culture while remaining noticeably national, comfortably combining the familiar and the strange.[55] They were not confined to a single role but performed their otherness in a variety of settings: as non-Russian experts in the "national question" when it came to politics, as pioneers of a distinctly multiethnic diet in the Soviet kitchen, as interpreters of national culture on the Soviet stage, and as intellectual critics equally comfortable espousing national revivalism and pan-imperial idealism. In a state where nationality was balanced by a multiethnic socialist identity, the Georgians succeeded as Soviets without shedding their national accent.

As strangers who integrated by remaining, in some sense, apart, and as former agriculturalists who specialized in modern urban fields like entrepreneurship and entertainment, the Georgians were similar in some ways to the Lebanese in Latin America, though they had even more in common with Italian migrants in the United States.[56] As familiar strangers, these groups occupied a liminal social position. If they were Christians transplanted to predominantly Christian societies, they tended to have their own distinctive religious traditions—Georgian Orthodoxy, Maronite Catholicism for many Lebanese migrants, and an ethnically defined Italian American Catholicism whose places of worship architecturally evoked or even replicated village churches back in Italy. In the United States, where race was usually the primary means of sorting migrants, Lebanese and Italians straddled the boundary between black and white; in the Soviet Union, Georgians (along with Armenians) were at the easternmost fringe of nations classified as "Western," and thus seen as more advanced and European than their Azeri neighbors, to say nothing of the supposedly backward nations of Central Asia.[57] All familiar strangers maintained roots in a home territory even as they were physically dispersed. Italian migration, like Georgian migration, was far more circular and multidirectional than the American "immigrant paradigm" suggests.[58] Many Italians in the United States dreamed of imminent return and remained tied to extended family and home village-based networks for generations.[59] While Lebanese were less likely to actually return home, they funded the reconstruction of family homes, economically supported their native villages, and forged alliances with politicians in their homeland.

The success of familiar strangers depended on the extent to which they could manage the terms of their self-presentation in the host society. While the exoticized representation of the "other" is typically identified as a linchpin of imperialist domination, these groups were able to employ ethnic difference as a form of cultural capital, adapting national repertoires for a broader audience while still using them to mark the contours of group identity.[60] In part, the effectiveness of this strategy depended on the demands of the host society and the extent to which ethnic and racial hierarchies were employed to constrain outsiders. The "double consciousness" that literary scholar and theorist Paul Gilroy describes among the African diaspora, for example, proceeded from the more rigid and enduring nature of racial barriers and the resulting sense of alienation from the host society. Although it was widely popularized, cultural production by the African diaspora in the United States was often appropriated by others, resulting in a loss of control and the expropriation of profit.[61]

Even if they succeeded in translating their otherness without losing authorship, a diaspora community's ability to gain prominence as familiar strangers also depended on the cultural repertoire available to them. Though national culture may be socially constructed, it is not made from scratch. Cultural idioms and practices arise in specific historical circumstances and differ across space and time; they are in turn reinforced or readjusted in different ways by social and state institutions. The cultural repertoires of nations are seldom interchangeable, since, to be successful, a cultural repertoire must convince those inside a group of belonging and those outside it of difference. Georgian culture in particular was recognized by insiders and outsiders as having some distinctive features: a long history of imperial adaptation, a strong but flexible sense of linguistic community, and a tendency toward public display. It is worth looking at how these factors arose and came together in the Soviet context.

The Soviet period was not the first time that local Georgian cultural practices were articulated in a broader imperial framework. In the territories that came to comprise modern Georgia, cultural distinctiveness

endured even as Georgian elites demonstrated flexibility in integrating with foreign imperial structures. In some cases, absorption into the
Ottoman and Persian empires led to the conversion of leading Georgian
noble families to Islam; yet these families frequently remained ethnically recognizable among the Ottoman and Persian service elites and
stayed connected to political events in their homeland.[62] Under Russian
tutelage, the formerly Persianized Georgian elite of Tbilisi eagerly joined
the Russian court and soon dressed in the latest European fashion at
balls organized by Russian administrators.[63] At the same time, Russian
rule stimulated the development of nationalism in the second half of the
nineteenth century, though Georgian nationalism generally meant cultural autonomy within the Russian Empire rather than political sovereignty, at least until 1917.[64]

In the Soviet period, as had been the case for centuries under imperial
rule, the Georgian effort to preserve a sense of national distinctiveness
centered less on formal political organization than it did on the maintenance of cultural practices among a dispersed population, especially the
use of the Georgian language. With its own distinct alphabet and historical connection to the Georgian Orthodox tradition, Georgian was
in some ways a sacred language, famously praised by the tenth-century
Georgian monk Ioane Zosime, who, as an expatriate in Sinai after fleeing the Arab conquest of Georgia, wrote that "every secret is buried in
this [the Georgian] language."[65] A language with a high-culture literature as well as a language associated with folk culture, it was also indeed
a good language for "burying secrets." Unlike many other languages in
the Soviet Union, it was virtually unintelligible to outsiders. This reinforced a sense of belonging by including Georgians who were in on the
conversation, while excluding—sometimes purposefully—others who
lay outside the community. Yet bilingual, bicultural, and experienced at
moving between nation and empire, members of the Georgian diaspora
generally did not hesitate to switch between the language of their homeland and the imperial tongue to present their otherness in an accessible
manner.

Georgians were not only willing to adapt their national repertoire,
but they were also able to convey it in a convincing way that resonated
widely. Although all identities, national and otherwise, are, in a sense,

performative, Georgian culture placed a particular emphasis on nearly constant public performance. In Georgian society, social bonds were affirmed openly and often, personal loyalty prized above and often intertwined with institutional affiliation, and social status highly unstable, based on a constant game of showmanship for men and the maintenance of an imperturbable poise for women.[66] Georgian performance was not just explicitly visible, but also expressly lyrical. It involved rituals of singing and dancing, with established roles for both men and women, though it accorded the highest prestige to men who could compete for status while carrying one part of a polyphonic tune or offering a tasteful and appropriate toast around the table. The culture of oration that celebrated the Georgian *tamada* engendered skillful politicians, just as the pervasive Georgian emphasis on lyricism created an artistic milieu that lent itself to skilled self-representation. Interestingly, similar qualities were ascribed to Lebanese, Italians, and other migrants from the Mediterranean basin, a region linked to Georgia by cultural associations and historical connections.[67] Whether such cultural qualities were real or imagined, they were frequently appropriated and employed by members of these diasporic communities.

Familiar strangers occupied a special place in societies interested in multiethnic representation, and, in this regard, Georgians in the Soviet Union and Italians in the United States encountered similar contexts. Though ideological opponents, both the Soviet Union and the United States were civic communities with a global reach, yet surrounded by borders and moral boundaries.[68] Just as being Soviet also meant being national, by the twentieth century being American often entailed having a "hyphenated identity" and living in a society at times envisioned as a "nation of immigrants."[69] While nativists feared that difference would erode American values, immigrants were also valorized for their potential contributions to the United States, much as Soviet nationalities were supposed to contribute their unique skills and cultures in building a socialist society.[70] Immigrants culturally and physically transformed American cities with festivals that celebrated their homelands and statues erected to ethnic heroes, just as internal diasporas helped redefine Moscow as a multiethnic space. While the United States and the Soviet Union had different political systems, both saw the rise of ethnic political networks, with immigrants giving shape to the voting-bloc patterns that structured the modern American political campaign.[71]

Although economic incentives, the acquisition of English, and intermarriage encouraged assimilation, otherness was an important path to integration for Italians in the American context. Their difference defined them as a diaspora, even as it was made more approachable and marketable. Italian neighborhoods in American cities were built around ethnic and village ties, but their restaurants, pizzerias, and cafes came to serve as popular sites of consumption for non-Italian diners, just as the Georgian restaurant became a pan-Soviet institution.[72] Like Georgians in the Soviet Union, Italians in the United States had access to a colorful repertoire that was ethnically distinctive but accessible to the masses, perhaps best displayed by Italian American crooners of the 1950s and 1960s who sang American jazz standards but employed Italian ethnicity as part of their romantic allure.[73] Like Georgians, Italians could claim status as heirs to a longstanding European high culture tradition, an inheritance visibly expressed by Italian American cinematic auteurs who chronicled the Italian migrant experience, but did so in dialogue with Italian and American artistic and cinematic traditions.[74] In representation and sometimes in reality, Italian American film directors and singers were linked to an "Italian Mafia," whose heavily mythologized prominence paralleled that of informal Georgian trade networks in the Soviet Union.[75]

Yet particularly in a twentieth-century context, where state intervention and control over migration was the norm, it remained significant that the Georgian performance of otherness occurred in the context of one state.[76] For political figures, a homeland in the Soviet Union provided a power base for broader ambitions and offered a steady supply of loyal cadres to serve those already in Moscow. For culinary specialists, Georgia supplied recipes and ingredients otherwise unavailable to the Soviet palate. For cultural entrepreneurs, the Georgian republic was home to institutions that specialized in the performance of national culture for a Soviet-wide audience. For Georgian traders, the homeland provided marketable goods like fruit, flowers, wine, tea, and tobacco. The resources of the Georgian republic were not simply human, institutional, and physical; they were also highly symbolic, in that their distinctiveness was widely known, officially celebrated, and emphasized by Georgia's diaspora.

Even among Soviet nationalities with a titular republic, not every group preserved or saw it in their interest to maintain a sense of difference over time as much as the Georgians. While some blended in, others remained inscrutable strangers. Differences among Slavic nationalities, who, like Georgians, also came from a predominantly agricultural context, were expressed by a closely related set of songs, symbols, and languages that were distinctive, yet mutually intelligible. Perhaps as a result of this cultural closeness, separate Slavic national identities were not always maintained beyond the borders of their titular republics; by the 1937 census, many Ukrainians and Belarusians residing in the RSFSR who previously claimed ethnic distinctiveness came to identify themselves as Russians.[77] Over time, most Slavic migrants seemed more familiar than strange.

By contrast, the cultural differences expressed by Central Asian diasporas were sometimes more exotic than understandable, or alternately seen as inauthentic creations of recent Soviet vintage. While Soviet culture was supposed to be "national in form, socialist in content," an interchangeability of form was required so that, for example, every republic could have its national opera and its national epic, preferably written by a national author. Georgian culture, though non-Slavic, offered a recognizable counterpoint to Russian national forms. Its literary high culture was embodied by the twelfth-century Georgian poet Shota Rustaveli, and its links to the classical world ran deeper than those of Russia itself.[78] The required forms were harder to find in Central Asia, which was not only non-Slavic, but informed by a historical legacy of seminomadic pastoralism.[79] Either Central Asian epics were passed down orally and lacked a clear author, or they were pan-Islamic and insufficiently national.[80] As a result, the appropriate forms had to be imposed on the region, sometimes under Russian direction. By the post-Stalinist period, there were important Central Asian figures who fluently combined national themes with universal Soviet concerns, such as the Kyrgyz author Chingiz Aitmatov. However, their work reached pan-Soviet audiences later, after the general mold of Soviet multiethnic culture had been set. By that point the Central Asian presence in the Soviet capital was sometimes associated with unskilled *limitchiki* (temporary workers) from the region who were largely confined to living in shared-room hostels, which further emphasized their separateness.[81]

Long-term patterns of mobility and imperial integration also set Georgians apart from their neighbors in the Caucasus. In contrast to Azerbaijan, Georgia was, like Russia, a historically Orthodox Christian nation. In fact, the founding of Georgia's national church predated Russia's by several centuries.[82] Georgia also possessed a sizable aristocracy at the time of Russia's expansion in the Caucasus, one that because of its religious affiliation, social standing, and high rate of literacy was able to join the imperial Russian court and participate in imperial Russian society in ways that were often not possible for Armenian merchants and Azeri notables, to say nothing of Chechen highlanders.[83] As a result, modern Georgian culture developed in intimate contact with imperial Russian high culture, nurtured by imperial institutions like Tbilisi's opera house, which was established in the middle of the nineteenth century.[84]

While some Armenians also embraced Russian high culture, the highly dispersed nature of the Armenian diaspora and its complicated relationship to the Armenian SSR made it rather different from the Georgian diaspora and more akin to conventional diasporas. Like Jews, Armenians were members of far-flung community whose members maintained boundaries of separation but often sought prominence by performing in the language and culture of the host society, sometimes at the expense of their own linguistic and cultural distinctiveness. There were important Armenian artists and intellectuals who appealed to the national while reaching a pan-Soviet audience: the composer Aram Khachaturian, for example, or the filmmaker Sergei Parajanov. Both, it might be noted, were born in Tbilisi, just as the first film made in the Armenian language, *Pepo*, was set in the Georgian capital. While Tbilisi was indeed a vital and historical center of Armenian cultural production, the fact that it lay beyond the Armenian SSR is indicative of the broader contours and constraints of the Armenian diaspora. Many Soviet Armenians had only the shallowest of roots in their titular republic, instead arising from longstanding Armenian settlements in the Caucasus and southern Russia or arriving in the Soviet Union after fleeing genocide in the Ottoman Empire. Although the Armenian SSR had its own mythology, with much of the historic Armenian homeland lying beyond Soviet borders it never acquired the institutional, economic, and symbolic resources of Georgia.[85]

As a result, many Armenians gained imperial prominence by mastering the cultural repertoires of other Soviet nations: Tamara Petrosian, better known as Tamara Khanum, was the first woman to publicly perform Uzbek dances; Artavazd Kefchiian gave one of the best-known performances of Georgianness in the 1939 film *The Tractor Drivers* (*Traktoristy*), his character waxing rhapsodic about the wonders of his Georgian homeland.[86] Armenian success in the context of Russian culture was even more common. Armenians were more likely than Georgians to consider Russian as their native language (though significantly less likely than Jews), and they more frequently Russified their last names.[87] An informative study conducted in the late Soviet period suggested that many members of the Armenian diaspora in Moscow aspired primarily to an urban, pan-Soviet identity.[88]

In the sense that Georgian difference was seen as stemming from a relatively advanced, if distinctive, European civilization grounded in a specific territory, one might expect commonalities among Georgians and internal diasporas from the Baltic states. Yet artists from the Baltic republics joined the Soviet state later, and their institutions were never as integrated with the center. Lithuanian writers and artists, for example, were less likely to participate in creative unions and the Moscow-based cultural establishment than their Georgian counterparts.[89] This tendency likely bespoke a lack of enthusiasm, and many Baltic intellectuals were probably strangers by choice who elected to remain silent.[90] By contrast, Georgian artists and intellectuals took part in the revolution from the outset and, at least until the late Soviet period, were comfortable operating in a Russian context. The native intelligentsias of Estonia, Latvia, and Lithuania, because of history, geography, and a relatively lengthy period of independence in the interwar years, yearned to participate directly in European artistic and intellectual life without Russian mediation. While Baltic distinctiveness was sometimes simply not on offer for imperial use, Georgian artistry was matched with a Soviet state ready to fund it, regardless of the cost.

Among the Soviet Union's many diasporas, some were so familiar that they ultimately blended into the host society; some aspired to the universal but were still marked as different; others remained little-noticed strangers, either by choice or because of cultural distance. As a prominent group that was at once familiar and strange, the Georgian diaspora showcased the opportunities as well as the limitations of the multiethnic Soviet empire.

## Domestic Internationalism and Its Consequences

As is well known, the Bolsheviks initially hoped to lead an international revolution but eventually settled on building socialism in one country. What has been overlooked is how the Soviet emphasis on political and economic self-reliance intersected with a push for domestic ethnic diversity and cultural self-sufficiency. By introducing the concept of domestic internationalism to describe these related processes and exploring its development in Soviet politics, economics, and culture, this book offers a different understanding of Soviet multiethnicity than past studies of the "friendship of the peoples" (*druzhba narodov*), which have generally treated the Soviet Union's explicit emphasis of its multiethnic character as an ornamental cover for Russian domination.[91] The logic of domestic internationalism was central to the governing ideology of the Soviet state; it had official and unofficial forms, intended and unintended consequences, and created novel opportunities for internal diasporas like the Georgians.

Even after the Bolsheviks retreated from the pursuit of international revolution to build socialism within sovereign borders, socialism and internationalism were not so easily separated. This was particularly the case in the diverse territory the Bolsheviks inherited from the tsars, where the socialist movement was eagerly joined by a range of nationalities. Marx and Engels's call for proletarians of all countries to unite became the Soviet state motto, appearing in the titular languages of the constituent Soviet republics on the official emblem of the USSR. Nationalities placed their cultural repertoires in service to the socialist cause, out of sincere belief or in pursuit of imperial prominence, and the empire's core became a dynamic space of cultural syncretism.[92] The hierarchically organized "friendship of the peoples," which positioned the Russians as "first among equals," was only one of many potential configurations possible among the multitude of nationalities found within Soviet borders.

The internal borders that ran throughout the new socialist state reflected the dynamics and contradictions of its domestically defined internationalism. Depending on the circumstances, these borders could be emphasized or ignored by the state and the Soviet citizens who moved across them. On the one hand, the policy of *korenizatsiia* clearly lent political importance to internal borders, defining the spaces in which titular nationalities could claim certain advantages over other ethnic groups. On the other hand, internal borders sometimes seemed like a mere formality; they could be crossed without a passport and were transcended when central authorities advanced cadres from the republics to Moscow, set economic plans and production targets, or funded and promoted Union-wide tours of national song and dance ensembles. While porous, the persistence of these internal borders and the national distinctions associated with them meant that a sovereign system of recognizable nationalities centered in Moscow, rather than a domestic transnationalism of blurred identities and lateral ties, remained the dominant structuring principle for state and society.[93]

The national distinctiveness defined by internal borders was intended to serve the interests of state-led socialism. Because of the frequent movement of internal diasporas, however, political networks and cultural production spilled across internal borders in unpredictable ways. So too did economic activity; despite the efforts of central planners to set prices across eleven time zones and fifteen republics, the existence of unevenly distributed economic opportunities created different regimes of value among the republics, giving diasporas with access to high-demand goods in their native republics lucrative opportunities for trade.[94] While forced labor directed by the state was an important aspect of the Stalinist economy, the system remained surprisingly dependent on informal exchange and voluntary migration to get goods and labor where they were needed.[95] Although a legal framework regulated residence in the Soviet capital, there was a good deal of irregular, illegal, temporary, and circular migration to Moscow.[96] As diasporas gathered and interacted in the Soviet capital, they began to forge a cosmopolitan imperial culture with a more tenuous relationship to the Soviet state.

When describing manifestations of domestic internationalism, it is important to remember that the Soviet Union was never entirely autarkic, nor was it a closed cultural universe. At home, the cultures of Soviet nationalities, propagated by internal diasporas, substituted for and sometimes referred to selected aspects of foreign culture. The importance of substitution in Russian and Soviet history has been stressed by economists like Alexander Gerschenkron, who argued that the Russian state served as a substitute for private industry, and by political scientists like Ken Jowitt, who claimed that the Soviet political system substituted Leninist neotraditionalism for capitalist modernity.[97] In some sense, nationality substituted for class in ordering the Soviet empire, a trend that was not entirely surprising since Stalin's own definition of a nation acknowledged the existence of varying levels of historical development and recognizable distinctions among nations in terms of "economic life."[98] In turn, the goods and cultures of domestic nationalities frequently served as replacements for their foreign, bourgeois counterparts.[99] Internal diasporas from the Soviet periphery occupied the place once held by tsarist bureaucrats in running the state, Georgian food replaced French food as the cuisine of sophistication, and, on stage, Soviet internal diversity was substituted for foreign internationalism, even as performers selectively drew upon trends arising beyond the Soviet Union. Foreign influences ebbed and flowed, particularly with the establishment of socialist governments in Eastern Europe after the Second World War, though nationalities contained within the state's borders remained at the heart of Soviet life.

Domestic internationalism could entail an imperial synthesis of all Soviet nationalities, or emphasize the ethnic distinctiveness of each. It found expression in state-sanctioned displays as well as the informal culture of everyday life, and the two were often closely related in the way that internal diasporas were perceived and in turn promoted themselves among the broader population. The "friendship of the peoples" was the most familiar paradigm of domestic internationalism endorsed by the state, famously represented by the fountain at the Exhibition of

Economic Achievements (VDNKh) in Moscow, which featured statues of each of the main Soviet nationalities, each with its own individual features. VDNKh itself was divided into pavilions for the constituent republics: each had its respective national goods and examples of national costume and culture. Visitors saw depictions of Uzbeks cultivating cotton and cheerfully weaving it into colorful textiles; they learned about the stoic lifestyle of Kyrgyz shepherds and heard performances of their traditional songs played on the fretless *komuz*; they viewed displays of Ukraine's wheat harvests and witnessed enthusiastic performances of Ukrainian folk dancers dressed in colorfully embroidered blouses. In this idealized microcosm of Soviet empire national distinctiveness took on a celebratory feeling, defined by what each nationality contributed to the larger Union.

Outside VDNKh, however, the formation of stock characters based on stereotypes of ethnic traits intersected with the state-authorized emphasis on national difference. Each nation not only had its own official national dress, dance, language, and food, but also had its own tacitly understood characteristics and personality traits, both positive

*Figure 1.3* Georgian dancers performing at Moscow's VDNKh in 1967. The Friendship of the Peoples fountain, its distinctive statues representing the titular nationalities of the Soviet Union's republics, is visible behind the assembled crowd. Russian State Archive of Film and Photo Documents.

and negative. These differences were represented and reproduced in children's books, museum exhibits, travel brochures, and films that demonstrated how the vastness of Soviet territory was populated by a panoply of diverse peoples, each with their part to play in the building of socialism.[100] The Soviet imagination came to be filled with a collection of generalizations that often reflected, however distortedly, the realities of cultural difference among diverse nationalities and the respective political, economic, and cultural niches found by these nationalities as they arrived in the Soviet capital. The fact that Georgians were officially celebrated as flamboyant entertainers made it relatively easy to imagine them as gregarious tricksters and speculators who brought their distinctive style of performance to the marketplace. Official and unofficial representations also informed popular understanding of what constituted typical and atypical specializations for an ethnic group. Soviet citizens traded jokes about clever Jews and Armenians, taciturn Baltics, naive but crafty Georgians, and benighted Chukchi. Unexpected roles were as important as expected ones. Just as one might be surprised to encounter an Estonian toastmaster, one might not anticipate meeting a Georgian janitor.

Ideally, the roles ascribed to the various nationalities were meant to complement one another and form a harmonious whole. Certainly, this was the model of domestic internationalism depicted in popular films like *The Tractor Drivers*, in which the differences among a Russian, Ukrainian, and Georgian cement their friendship, or the 1950 film *The Fall of Berlin* (*Padenie Berlina*), where a multiethnic collective of Soviet soldiers fight together to defeat the Nazis. In practice, ethnic specialization could indeed be complementary, though complementariness did not necessarily mean equality. When it came to socialist politics and economics, there were times when the entrenchment of ethnic networks led to some diasporas having greater influence, or greater access to scarce resources, than others.[101]

Finally, the notion of domestic internationalism reveals the unique forms of cosmopolitanism tolerated and sometimes encouraged within Soviet borders, especially in Moscow, the capital of the multiethnic Soviet state. Scholars have uncovered transnational linkages between Stalinist intellectuals and European cultural figures that were maintained across state borders as late as the 1930s; however, processes of cross-cultural engagement, translation, and appropriation also occurred across the internal national boundaries of the Soviet empire, which, after all, were more frequently crossed by Soviet citizens than external ones.[102] Moscow was a mecca for the international socialist movement, but perhaps more effectively, it functioned as the center of a domestically oriented cosmopolitan culture that drew heavily on the national republics. In Moscow, non-Russian nationalities encountered the ideas of European socialists and studied the classics of European literature, typically through the imperial medium of the Russian language. Intellectuals and cultural entrepreneurs from the non-Russian republics avidly translated the works of national poets into Russian for a pan-Soviet readership, informed imperial tastes by contributing recipes to Soviet cookbooks, staged song and dance performances for audiences beyond the boundaries of their native republics, and eagerly participated in the defining debates of Soviet intellectual life. Their diverse contributions combined to create a Soviet political, artistic, and intellectual culture that was cosmopolitan in that it aimed to build a multiethnic socialist future for all humanity, yet grounded in a sovereign state.[103]

While Stalin's campaign against "rootless cosmopolitans" targeted Soviet Jews who had integrated into the Soviet elite while masking their "true" national identity, charging them with the promotion of a borderless and transgressive culture inimical to the clearly demarcated nations of the socialist state, the rooted cosmopolitanism of internal Soviet diasporas was generally permitted.[104] The state welcomed the efforts of national intellectuals to bridge internal cultural differences and funded their efforts as a way to achieve the eventual "coming together" of Soviet nationalities and the creation of a "Soviet people."[105] Domesticated but never fully controlled by the Soviet state, cosmopolitanism rooted in Soviet territory attracted its enthusiastic adherents and opportunistic entrepreneurs. Eventually, however, it posed a challenge to the existence of Soviet diasporas and the perpetuation of Soviet empire.

The pursuit of pan-Soviet prominence was not without its risks. At its heart, domestic internationalism was an ongoing dialogue between an imperial state and its nationalities, though this dialogue was rarely carried out on equal terms. While diasporas like the Georgians performed national difference as a way of achieving a preferable position in an expressly multiethnic polity, the imperial state regulated and reined in national expression, seeking to place national repertoires at its disposal. Among political networks national allegiances could become a liability, since Bolshevism ultimately trumped national loyalty. National dishes were brought to the Soviet table in blander form, and supposed national culinary secrets were expected to belong in the public domain. The performances of national song and dance ensembles had to conform to audience expectations, and their choreography reflected the influence of Russian ballet. In the Soviet economy, cultural differences were transformed into commodities to be sold in the imperial marketplace. Ideally, national intellectuals could embrace Russian as a means of universal communication without forsaking their native language. However, while Russian was taught in the national republics, instruction in national languages was restricted in Russia itself.[106] A life physically and symbolically spent between a host society and a homeland fostered a remarkably creative tension, but it also risked undermining the national distinctiveness that diasporas needed to succeed in the Soviet state.

Subsequent chapters explore the dynamics of domestic internationalism and the evolution of Soviet empire from the vantage point of the Georgian diaspora. They tell a story not only of imperial and national continuity, but also of radical change. The story begins in late imperial Georgia, a place of fervent socialist politics, rapid economic modernization, rural unrest, and, at the same time, cultural renaissance. This landscape was inhabited by rebellious seminarians, an emergent working class, peasants striving for educational opportunities, and disenchanted nobles. It was at the center of political debates over the proper course of socialist revolution in a multiethnic context and artistic and cultural experimentation among poets, playwrights, and musicians interested in combining national, imperial, and European forms, or surmounting them altogether.

As the Bolsheviks came to power, this revolutionary upheaval in the Caucasus reached and transformed the Soviet capital. A migration of

Georgian people, goods, and ideas that began in the imperial period gathered steam as the Soviet Union took shape. The patterns of mobility that drew the Georgian diaspora to Russia persisted across political changes in the Soviet Union, with success building on success, before eventually turning into discontent with the empire they had helped to build.

# Between the Caucasus and
# the Kremlin

On September 29, 1913, the Georgian Bolshevik Grigol "Sergo" Orjonikidze wrote to his brother from the confines of the Schlüsselburg prison, an island fortress in St. Petersburg.[1] At twenty-nine years old, "Comrade Sergo," as he was known among his fellow radicals, was already a veteran revolutionary. Born to an impoverished noble family in a small village in western Georgia, he first joined the Bolshevik wing of the Russian Social Democratic Labor Party (RSDLP) at seventeen, while studying to be a doctor's assistant in Tbilisi. Trading his nascent medical career for the passions of the radical socialist underground, he agitated for revolution abroad and at home under a series of false passports. This was not his first time in prison; he had been arrested for gun-running along the Black Sea coast in 1905 and for helping organize a May Day parade in Baku in 1907. In a Baku jail he befriended Ioseb Jughashvili, the man the world would later know as Joseph Stalin.[2]

His ideological commitment to socialism matched by a willingness to carry out the dangerous work of fomenting revolution, Sergo Orjonikidze personified the qualities Lenin was looking for in his effort to recruit non-Russians to the radical cause. Having come to Lenin's attention, Orjonikidze was invited to attend the Prague conference of the Russian Social Democratic Labor Party in 1912, where the Bolsheviks decisively split from the Mensheviks and formed their own party organization. At the conference, Lenin spoke about the need for the diverse ethnic groups of the Russian Empire to join together in revolutionary struggle.[3] While Lenin criticized the failure of the Jewish *Bund* and the Polish and Latvian Social Democrats to coordinate their efforts with the party's central authorities, he looked more favorably on Georgian Bolsheviks like Orjonikidze. Although the Georgian revolutionary movement sprang from a distinctive cultural milieu, Georgian radicals, both Mensheviks and Bolsheviks, showed a commitment to the broader struggle for socialism across the Russian Empire.

Following the conference, Orjonikidze was sent to Petersburg to organize the Central Committee's Russian bureau and soon attracted the scrutiny of the tsarist authorities. While being held at the Schlüsselburg prison, he faced an impending transfer to eastern Siberia. His prison correspondence reveals how radical networks ran within families, as well as among tight-knit groups of Georgian revolutionaries. For underground radicals like Orjonikidze, the risk of arrest meant that loyalty was prized and the danger of betrayal always present.[4] For these reasons, ideological commitment was wedded to a symbolic—and sometimes genetic—sense of fraternity among the predominantly male socialists of the Caucasus, a region where idealized male friendship was celebrated in poetry and practices of adoptive kinship were deep-rooted.[5] These sentiments were openly expressed in the ideological and familial appeal he now made to his brother, Papulia, who was also active in the revolutionary movement, and in the note he asked his brother to pass on to Nikoloz "Karlo" Chkheidze, a prominent figure among the Georgian Mensheviks and a representative to the State Duma. Despite the factional difference that separated Orjonikidze from Chkheidze, the networks of Georgian Bolsheviks and Mensheviks were intertwined, since they both sprang from the burgeoning Georgian intelligentsia. And so Orjonikidze appealed to Chkheidze in a Georgian-language note as a coethnic with shared acquaintances and a common background.

The archival record does not indicate Chkheidze's response, but Orjonikidze's hope of avoiding exile was not to be realized. As the First World War engulfed Europe he remained locked in the Schlüsselburg prison, and in 1915 he was sent to Iakutiia. Like other Bolsheviks of the period, he used his time in prison to prepare himself for the revolution through careful study. A glance at his prison diary reveals that in addition to his willingness to pursue violent revolution, he possessed the voracious reading habits of someone who sought to expand his education far beyond that of a doctor's assistant in rural Georgia. In addition to the classics of Georgian literature he consumed the heroic tales of Jack London, the romantic poetry of Lord Byron, and the novels of Dostoyevsky. As befitted a future manager of the Soviet economy, he pored over statistics and perused the details of meat, milk, and grain production in Russia.[6] His notes reveal a profound interest in Russian history, the French Revolution, and, of course, Marx and Engels. Like other Georgians, he was particularly concerned with what the revolution would mean for the empire's non-Russian nationalities. His diary is a record of the cosmopolitan intellectual and cultural currents that swept him and so many other Georgians into the Russian Empire's revolutionary movement.

The revolution in Russia was made by outsiders like Orjonikidze: impoverished aristocrats, provincial intellectuals, and ethnic minorities from across the vast Eurasian empire. Revolutionary fervor was often greatest among groups for whom class revolution and national revolution coincided, and the so-called Russian Revolution in fact encompassed a series of national revolutions.[7] Jews, Latvians, Poles, and Georgians all joined the socialist cause with exceptional enthusiasm.[8] As the revolution was institutionalized, members of ethnic diasporas were overrepresented in very visible positions of power throughout the new Soviet state.[9] Historians have devoted considerable attention to the special role played by Jews in the early Soviet Communist Party, and chronicled the rise of the Latvian Riflemen as Lenin's Praetorian Guard.[10] However, in power few groups so visibly affirmed their membership in an ethnic diaspora— through appearance, shared rituals, and linguistic ties—as did the Georgians. Their revolution had rural roots and empire-wide aspirations; it was driven by national and social grievances against tsarist authority.

The rapid rise of Georgians throughout the various branches of the revolutionary movement was stunning. Georgian Mensheviks initially headed the Petrograd Soviet and rose to key positions in the Provisional Government, while Georgian Bolsheviks accompanied Lenin back to Russia on his sealed train and helped him seize power in the Russian capital. After October 1917, Georgian Mensheviks established an independent social democracy in their native country, while Georgian

Bolsheviks ultimately led the Red Army's invasion of Georgia in 1921 and were critical to establishing Soviet power throughout the Caucasus. The revolution pitted Georgian against Georgian, yet from the turmoil of the Civil War a core group of Georgian Bolsheviks emerged, assuming leadership positions in Moscow and leading the way forward during the Great Transformation. They ascended with Stalin in the 1920s, sharing his cultural background and ideological dedication; these, along with Caucasian bonds of loyalty and friendship, made them highly effective foot soldiers in the revolutionary underground. The same qualities proved well suited to their eventual careers as managers of a Soviet state in which the personal was political and politics itself was often personalized.[11]

Orjonikidze's career illustrates the remarkable ascendance of Georgians in the revolutionary movement and the place they took at the helm of the early Soviet state. Released from prison in 1917, he helped launch the Bolshevik takeover in Petrograd, led the violent struggle during the ensuing Civil War as commissar for Ukraine, and returned to Georgia at the front of the invading Red Army. He became Stalin's most trusted deputy, a member of the Politburo by 1926, and the first Commissar of Heavy Industry in 1932. A product of a Georgian revolution within the Russian revolution, he was well prepared to administer a multiethnic state and skillfully relied on an intimate circle of trusted friends—many of them fellow Georgians—to accomplish his goals. He owed much to his personal connection to Stalin, yet he also served as patron to upwardly mobile party cadres, often handpicked from his native Georgia. The success of Orjonikidze and other Georgians lent a Caucasian coloring to Soviet political life in the 1930s, bringing the periphery to the heart of a reconstituted Eurasian empire.

There has been an abundance of literature on Stalin and his circle, its contradictions reflecting the complexity and historical significance of the dictator himself. The Great Leader has been presented as a despotic tyrant, but also as a committed Bolshevik; he has been described as a man driven by a deeply troubling psychopathology, or a cunning master of bureaucratic politics and a *khoziain* (manager) of the economy; some have maintained that he was unmistakably shaped by the allegedly violent culture of the Caucasus, others have claimed that he progressed from a cultural Georgian identity to a political Russian identity, or that the geopolitical situation of the Soviet state ultimately guided his actions.[12] Much has also been much written about the importance of informal ties, patronage, *blat*, and personal networks in the Soviet state, although the scholarship on ethnic networks tends to focus on the late Soviet period.[13] These two bodies of literature—the first on the person who headed the state, the second on the informal bonds that ran through it—have never really been connected.

This chapter argues that ethnic networks were in fact critical in the late imperial and early Soviet period, and were a pathway for young Georgian Bolsheviks to advance their careers and achieve high-ranking positions in the Soviet state. These networks emerged from the revolutionary underground and the Civil War and were composed of highly literate and mobile specialists, often drawn from the Soviet Union's internal diasporas, who filled the state's bureaucracy and were the ideal representatives of a new, consciously multiethnic political order.

From this perspective, Stalin can be understood as a member of a Georgian-dominated network from the Caucasus, a tightly bound group of revolutionaries held together by shared history, revolutionary beliefs, and fluency in a common culture. This network was not simply defined by its members' propensity for violence, but also by their high degree of ethnic awareness and their intellectual and cultural aspirations, which derived from Georgia's revolutionary context and appear so clearly in Orjonikidze's correspondence and prison diary. Rather than engaging in essentialist debates about whether Stalin was a "good Georgian" or a national traitor, this chapter looks at the various performances of Georgianness by Stalin and the revolutionaries from the Caucasus who surrounded him. An examination of Stalin's correspondence reveals someone who did not abandon his Georgian background over time but instead appealed to it at different moments, in public and in private, though he was ultimately willing to sacrifice his ethnic loyalties for revolutionary goals. As he made his political ascent he continued to receive and write letters in Georgian, and as someone who was heavily invested in managing his public image, cultivated and sought to control its Georgian aspect.[14] Accordingly, this chapter places Stalin in the context of his network and tells the larger story of the political ascent of the Georgian diaspora.

Following a generation of Georgian revolutionaries from the late nineteenth century to the 1930s, the chapter begins by situating Georgian radicals in the historical and cultural context of late imperial Georgia. It then tracks Georgian revolutionary networks as they expanded, first beyond Georgia as the vanguard of a multiethnic political movement in the Caucasus, and finally reaching the imperial center at the start of the Bolshevik Revolution. The chapter reveals how Georgian Bolsheviks disdained the traditions of their homeland and oversaw the violent Sovietization of Georgia, yet remained bound by explicitly Caucasian practices of friendship and mutual obligation. Their close personal bonds became a critical political asset, though ultimately these bonds would be tested as the balance shifted from horizontal friendship circles to the vertical imposition of power in the mid-1930s. By the end of that decade Orjonikidze would commit suicide, his trusted cadres would be imprisoned or shot, and most of Stalin's longtime Georgian comrades would be swept up in the purges that decimated the ranks of the Old Bolsheviks, shattering the lives of the generation who had made revolution.

## Educating Georgian Socialists

Late imperial Georgia was an incubator for radicals across the socialist spectrum. Among the diverse and often divided Georgian socialist movement of the late nineteenth and early twentieth century, Georgian Bolsheviks represented a distinct strand that went the furthest in uniting local grievances with the desire for empire-wide transformation. Although they sought destruction of the old order in their native land, the rooted revolutionary cosmopolitanism that they espoused had its origins in the intellectual world of the nineteenth-century Georgian intelligentsia.

Following their incorporation into the Russian Empire, Georgia's sizable nobility lost its political autonomy but found success in its new role as Russia's imperial service elite. They were subjects of the tsar, but also the tsar's agents: ethnographers and generals who mapped and led the expansion of the Russian Empire throughout the Caucasus.[15] Yet their imperial participation was not without its ambivalences, and the empire of the tsars not without its limitations. By the 1860s, Georgians who pursued their education in St. Petersburg found themselves at the center of a state undergoing rapid and potentially destabilizing social transformation. Rather than choosing careers in the tsarist bureaucracy, some were drawn to revolutionary appeals for imperial change and national renewal. St. Petersburg became more than the seat of Russian autocracy; it was, in the reminiscences of one Georgian student, the place where all of Russia's "intelligence and talent" gathered, the "heart" of a "new movement."[16] Yet Niko Nikoladze, the scion of a privileged Georgian family who would come to be seen as a founding figure of Georgia's socialist movement, recalled that even as Georgian students eagerly socialized with Nikolai Chernyshevksii and other Russian radicals in St. Petersburg, they lived and studied apart in their own *zemliachestvo* (informal regional association) and became engrossed in issues concerning the development of their homeland. *Zemliachestvo* members frequently debated the political situation in Georgia and took to performing Georgian plays and folk dances, both among themselves and as a way of demonstrating their national culture to the other students.[17] A Russian education opened up new opportunities, but also inspired Georgian students to seek the transformation of their native Georgia and the renewal of its national culture.

By the late nineteenth century, the drive for learning had spread from the elite to broader sections of Georgian society, making Georgians among the most educated populations in the Russian Empire.[18] As it did among the empire's Jewish population, education transformed Georgian society and challenged traditional social relations, stirring the particularities of nationalist sentiment as well as driving the search for universal solutions to local problems.[19] Educational opportunities in Georgia were available for impoverished nobles and persons of mixed social rank (*raznochintsy*), as well as the children of priests, peasants, and craftsmen. By the late nineteenth century, the conflict between a rapidly growing intellectual class and a reactionary educational policy turned tsarist schools of higher learning into ideal centers for the recruitment and training of radicals.[20] The frustrated aspirations of the new intellectual class led many to socialism and its promise of a radical egalitarianism. This phenomenon could be observed throughout Russia, but in the non-Russian regions of the empire the suppression of local languages and the close involvement of the central authorities in the administration of local educational institutions placed the "national question" at the forefront of the socialist platform. Socialist ideas grew to be especially popular among nobles from the impoverished estates of western Georgia, a rural society strikingly altered by the advance of international capitalism and the establishment of empire-wide markets for goods.[21]

Georgians who sought upward mobility but possessed lesser means were more likely to pursue education not in St. Petersburg and Moscow, but rather in provincial universities, trade schools, and seminaries. Sergo Orjonikidze left his village in western Georgia to study medicine in Tbilisi, just as the future Bolshevik Tengiz Zhghenti left his nearby western Georgian village to study at Tbilisi's Teaching Institute.[22] Both came from families so impoverished as to be virtually indistinguishable from the surrounding peasantry save in name, and, most likely, a deep sense of shame over their declining position in noble society. In Tbilisi, they found themselves in the administrative center of Russian rule over the Caucasus and in an economically dynamic, multiethnic regional capital. They likely could not help but notice that in Georgia's largest city, Russians occupied the highest posts of regional administration and the bourgeoisie was overwhelmingly Armenian.[23] As a result, many young Georgian students came to believe that socialism would entail national liberation from the intertwined forces of imperial rule and economic exploitation.

Students rallied against teachers and exchanged allegiance to their parents for fraternal bonds with one another. Radical student groups sprang up throughout Georgia, even outside Tbilisi. The Kutaisi Gymnasium had a thriving secret reading circle where students read and discussed radical literature that was smuggled into the country or printed by a growing number of underground presses in Georgia. By the early twentieth century, the regional school even had its own Georgian-language socialist periodical that students printed themselves on an illegal press.[24] Shalva Eliava, Mamia Orakhelashvili, and Ilia Mamulia, all future

Bolshevik party leaders, participated actively in the gymnasium's clandestine reading circle. The Kutaisi Gymnasium's student files reveal the concerns of the school's authorities about these students. Orakhelashvili was reprimanded for several outbursts against his instructors, while Eliava, it was noted, did well in his classes but had a tendency to "lie." Still, the authorities did not suspect the extent to which these students were already involved in a socialist movement of secret cells and underground meetings that ran throughout the Caucasus.[25] Orakhelashvili and Eliava graduated versed in the arts of concealment, and were drawn together in friendship and ideological dedication through their participation in illicit political activity.

There was perhaps no greater center of Georgian radicalism, however, than the Orthodox seminary in Tbilisi. Throughout the Russian Empire, the clerical estate was in turmoil and radicalism was especially widespread among clergymen's sons.[26] Georgian seminaries were further radicalized by the policy of Russification, as Russian authorities continued to restrict the autonomy of the Georgian Orthodox Church, discouraged distinctive Georgian church rituals, limited the use of the Georgian language, and painted over ancient church frescoes in a country whose Orthodox traditions preceded Russia's by more than six centuries. Seminarians resented the restrictions on Georgia's religious expression, even as radical ideas they encountered amidst a harsh institutional culture of rigid hierarchy and corporal discipline converted many into nonbelievers. The future Georgian Bolshevik leader Pilipe Makharadze characterized the Tbilisi seminary he attended as a "kingdom of scholasticism, lying, and hypocrisy." He wrote: "Before admission to the seminary I was a gentle and obedient student, a model for the seminary fathers . . . Few would believe that only one year later I would become, first of all, an outspoken opponent of those who kept strict order in the seminary, and, secondly, an atheist."[27] Some student protests against the seminary's rigid code of discipline ran violent: in 1884, Silva Jibladze, the future Menshevik, physically assaulted the rector, and two years later, a seminarian from Gori stabbed the rector to death.[28]

In the wake of these protests, Ioseb Jughashvili, another seminarian from Gori, arrived to study in Tbilisi in 1894. One year later, influenced by the intellectual ferment that infused student life in the city's seminary, the sixteen-year-old student composed and published a poem in Georgian that spoke of national liberation, albeit through the pursuit of education:

> Flower, oh my Georgia!
> Let peace reign in my native land!
> And may you, friends, make renowned
> Our Motherland by study![29]

The poem reflected a growing Georgian nationalist sentiment, though one linked to more universal concerns. Like other groups in the Russian Empire, Georgians resented the restrictions on the use of their native language; unlike many other national groups, however, Georgians like the young Jughashvili continued to embrace Russian as a universal language of learning alongside their native Georgian. The Georgian intelligentsia, which had arisen at the intersection of local and imperial culture, sought mastery of both. Many, including Jughashvili, eventually became enamored of socialism as a way of eliding local and imperial grievances. By the late nineteenth and early twentieth century, activists from the Russian Social Democratic Labor Party began forging contacts with Jughashvili and other rebellious seminarians. In Tbilisi, reading circles brought seminarians together with technical students and skilled workers like Abel Enukidze, the son of a peasant family from western Georgia and a future Bolshevik party figure.[30] Seminarians from rural Georgia who were expelled for revolutionary activity, like Mikha Tskhakaia, another future Bolshevik leader, remained active figures in Tbilisi's radical underground.[31]

As they faced expulsion, imprisonment, and exile, students and seminarians banded together in their struggle against political injustice and economic inequality. Their circles were defined by Caucasian standards of friendship, but were also reinforced by new intellectual currents. Their socialism was about "leveling" old hierarchies, and this ideological proclivity was reflected in the lateral ties they established with one another even as they rebelled against parental, educational, and tsarist authority.[32] The leaders of Menshevism and Bolshevism in Georgia—and ultimately, the leadership of the Soviet Union—arose from these intimately bound radical circles on the empire's periphery.

## Radicalism Reaches the Countryside

Georgian radicals no longer fit into the world they left behind when they went to school. They were seminarians who were not going to be priests, nobles in name only, frustrated white-collar professionals, and the upwardly mobile children of peasants. They found ignorance in their native villages and economic exploitation in the emergent industrial sites that dotted the Caucasian landscape by the late nineteenth century. Traveling throughout Georgia and the Caucasus, they distributed banned literature and agitated among workers and peasants. Even as they made inroads among workers and published their articles in the Georgian socialist journal *kvali*, run by Jordania, or the even more radical *brdzola*, led by Jughashvili's close friend Lado Ketskhoveli, this mobile group of agitators and publicists sought—with varying degrees of success—to bring about the transformation of rural Georgian society.

Radicalism made substantial inroads into rural families as Georgian students returned home. Shalva Eliava may have succeeded in concealing his political activities from his teachers at the Kutaisi Gymnasium, but he was subsequently expelled from St. Petersburg's law academy for open participation in a student strike in 1903. After his expulsion, he returned home to seek change in rural western Georgia. Eliava's relative, Putsu Dgebuadze, recalled an interesting episode that occurred shortly after Eliava's return. The young socialist started making eloquent speeches to the local peasants, who, according to Dgebuadze, took to calling him the "limping committee." The term referred to Eliava's leg, hurt in a childhood injury, but also may have been a mild form of mockery at the political terminology employed by the ambitious St. Petersburg law student in his local speeches.[33] His mother, who had taken charge of managing the family's affairs after his father's death, had long resisted peasant demands for greater use of her land. After calling the whole village together for a meeting, Eliava posted a proclamation on a nearby tree, unilaterally announcing that the peasants could harvest his mother's cornfield according to the divisions he marked.

In the sense that Eliava's socialism was in part a rebellion against parental rule, it should be mentioned that many Georgian Bolsheviks emerged from homes where traditional patterns of Georgian patriarchal

authority were called into question. Eliava's father had died at a young
age, leaving his mother as head of the household; Orjonikidze's father,
a man of proud aristocratic lineage, was unable to obtain the funds to
maintain the family home and was forced to eke out a living hauling
manganese ore to the Black Sea port of Poti; Jughashvili's father, who
courted his mother as an upwardly mobile craftsman, became an abusive
alcoholic and an economic failure, leaving the family to work in a shoe
factory in Tbilisi and losing the respect of the local community.[34] In
the latter two cases, crises of patriarchal authority were bound up with
experiences of economic dislocation under Russian imperial rule; the
response of the sons was to reject traditional family hierarchies, but also
to assert a fraternally oriented Georgian masculinity aimed at overturn-
ing the economic and political order.

Intimate bonds and ideological ties among these radicals were often
reinforced by lateral family relationships and local affinities. While most
Georgian Bolsheviks were men, socialism also attracted the interest of
rebellious daughters. Eliava's sister, Maro, died in 1907 while engaged in
underground political work, and his other sister, Shushana, was expelled
from class for revolutionary connections.[35] In many cases Georgian
Bolsheviks were not just ideologically intimate, but were actual brothers: Abel Enukidze, who operated underground presses throughout the
region, joined the movement along with his brother and cousin; Sergo
Orjonikidze's two brothers, as well as his nephew, Giorgi Gvakharia,
followed the future Bolshevik leader into the party ranks; and the brothers Shalva and Mikheil Okujava joined the revolutionary movement in
close succession while studying at the Kutaisi Gymnasium.[36] Rather
than serving as a deterrent, imprisonment by the tsarist authorities further radicalized Georgian family networks. After Ivane "Vano" Sturua,
an older Bolshevik who had recommended young Ioseb Jughashvili for
party membership, was imprisoned for revolutionary activity in Tbilisi's
Metekhi Castle, his brothers, Giorgi and Vasili, both villagers who
worked on the railroad, joined the socialist movement.[37]

Rural life in Georgia had some unusual features compared to the
rest of the empire that made the region especially fertile ground for
socialism. Georgia's relatively high literacy rate meant that more peasants could read the revolutionary literature produced by underground

presses in the Caucasus. The small size of Georgia, combined with the densely networked nature of the Georgian extended family, meant that information traveled quickly and developments in urban areas reached villages swiftly.[38] In addition, the social distance between peasants and minor rural nobles was often less noticeable than in Russia, facilitating the development of national revolutionary networks.[39] Finally, rural Georgians were more likely to have had exposure to the multiethnic life of regional towns, many of which had substantial Armenian, Jewish, Russian, Greek, and Muslim populations. These factors combined to infuse peasant unrest with new intellectual currents and broader imperial concerns.

Nowhere was this more true than in the western Georgian region of Guria, which saw a major uprising in the early twentieth century and produced numerous future revolutionaries. In 1903, tsarist authorities lost control of the region as Gurians ignored the official courts, carried out public works projects on their own, and shunned their appointed governor. By early 1905 peasant leaders proclaimed the establishment of the Gurian Republic, run by village committees and defended by armed peasant detachments.[40] Developments in Guria captured the attention of socialists everywhere and launched Georgian radicals to international prominence. While the Italian journalist Luigi Villari, who traveled to the region in 1905, commented on the high literacy rates and political sophistication of Guria's villagers, Russian radical Alexandra Kollontai praised Gurian women for taking an active part in village tribunals. She noted that the region's female peasants "defended their rights with particular vigor" and praised Gurian women for adopting "resolutions demanding political equality with men." Young Ioseb Jughashvili watched developments in the region with close interest; years later, as Joseph Stalin, he was overheard at a Kremlin reception explaining the inherently political nature of the Gurian peasant: "All Gurians are involved in politics. There, no one lacks a party affiliation, and everyone is literate. All of them read and write, and everyone reads the newspaper ... When you get two Gurians together, they'll inevitably start a discussion about Marx's *Kapital.*"[41]

The short-lived Gurian Republic revealed the spectacular advances of the socialist movement in a rapidly changing Georgian countryside. It came more than a decade before the self-proclaimed Iskolats Republic in Latvia, where organizers similarly fused socialist ideology with nationalist rhetoric in a rebellion of the local—and largely rural—Latvian population.[42] While seen as a success in terms of spreading the message of socialism, the rebellion and its aftermath also exposed and deepened differences between Georgian Mensheviks and Bolsheviks. Although the rebellion, and its eventual suppression by Cossack troops sent in from Russia in early 1906, made Social Democrats out of a surprisingly large number of Gurians, Mensheviks outmaneuvered their Bolshevik counterparts and forged closer links with the peasantry by promoting an explicitly Georgian vision of revolution that was more in tune with rural sentiments.[43] These same Georgian Mensheviks subsequently joined the Duma while their Bolshevik opponents boycotted participation in the institutions of the tsarist regime. Georgian Bolsheviks sought an immediate end to autocracy and a more radical transformation of Georgian society. They increasingly looked for allies among alienated workers in multiethnic urban areas throughout the Caucasus, where, according to them, developments more closely fit the contours of socialist theory.

Nevertheless, unlike the radicals who joined the Jewish *Bund*, the nationalist Armenian *Dashnaktsutiun*, or the Polish Socialist Party, Georgian socialists, Mensheviks and Bolsheviks alike, still remained factional members of an empire-wide, multiethnic organization, the Russian Social Democratic Labor Party.[44] If, almost a century earlier, Georgian nobles had joined the Russian ranks as an imperial service elite, Georgian revolutionaries across the political spectrum now aspired to be at the center of another empire-wide movement.

## Georgian Revolutionaries Beyond Georgia

By 1907, the Bolsheviks were effectively shut out of Georgia by tsarist repression and Menshevik political advances. Some left Georgia, many to pursue party work in Baku. In the words of Bolshevik Pilipe Makharadze, Baku was the "bastion of Bolshevism for all the Caucasus," because "nowhere else could one find such a strong proletariat."[45] In Baku, Georgian Bolsheviks encountered a growing working class that was multiethnic, yet in some cases divided by ethnic strife, as was evident in the clashes between the city's Muslim and Armenian populations in 1905.[46] Removed from their native context, Georgian Bolsheviks in Baku began to dream of a truly international revolution as the only comprehensive solution to the empire's social and ethnic grievances. They cast themselves as leaders of an effort to launch a multiethnic, Caucasus-wide revolution and rose to high-ranking positions in the Bolshevik party's central organs as experts in carrying out agitation among an ethnically and linguistically diverse population.

Georgian Bolsheviks proved able to negotiate ethnic difference with remarkable skill. While the dominance of Armenian merchants caused tension in rural Georgia, outside their native land Georgian Bolsheviks found common cause with Armenians who forsook the nationalist *Dashnaktsutiun* for participation in an international Bolshevik movement.[47] In some cases they found allies among Armenians who had come to Baku from Georgia, like Stepan Shaumian, who was born to an Armenian merchant family in Tbilisi but joined the international revolutionary movement after studying in St. Petersburg, Riga, and Berlin.[48] The Georgians also built ties with the somewhat smaller number of Muslims in the movement, including Nariman Narimanov, who was born in Tbilisi and educated there at the Teacher's Institute before traveling to Baku for work. As outsiders in Baku, Georgian Bolsheviks could work as mediators between Armenian and Muslim workers and revolutionaries. Fluent in Russian, they also established close contacts with Baku's Russian workers, as well as with a number of Russian revolutionaries who resided in the city.

Abel Enukidze was among the first of the Georgian radicals to arrive in Baku, moving there in 1898 to work as an assistant engine machinist for the railroad.[49] Enukidze helped build the RSDLP's organization in Baku with the help of fellow Georgian Lado Ketskhoveli and established an underground printing press that disseminated revolutionary literature in a variety of languages. He forged links with the party's Central Committee as a specialist in spreading the message of revolution and was eventually transferred to St. Petersburg by the party in 1903. Enukidze's early work in Baku launched his party career; he later recalled this pivotal period in his 1930 memoir, *The Illegal Bolshevik Press*.[50]

Enukidze's cousin, Tripon "Simon" Enukidze, followed a similar path. Arriving in Baku to work as a mechanic in 1900, he joined his cousin in setting up and operating the underground press. In 1905, the party requested that Simon travel to Moscow to help establish a secret press closer to the party's center. Housed in central Moscow in a shop with a sign outside that read "Kalandadze: Trader in Fruits from the Caucasus," Simon Enukidze worked with Russian, Armenian, and Georgian conspirators to print the radical newspaper *Rabochii* on a concealed press in the shop's hidden cellar. The plan was hatched by Simon Enukidze himself, who registered the shop in the name of a Georgian porter then residing in Moscow. The shop's fruit displays concealed a major operation that supplied and distributed revolutionary literature, one carried out within close distance of one of the city's main police headquarters and the nearby Butyrskaia prison.[51] Giorgi Sturua, another participant in running the secret press, recalled how Simon Enukidze coordinated publication with the party's Central Committee through regular meetings held at the Moscow apartment of the socialist author Maxim Gorky.[52] While it closed in 1907, the operation demonstrated how Georgian Bolsheviks could build on their successes in Baku to gain prominence at the center of party life. It also pointed to a high degree of ethnic self-awareness on the part of Simon Enukidze, who used the believable stereotype of the Georgian fruit trader as a cover for his revolutionary activities.

The work of Georgian Bolsheviks in multiethnic Baku attracted the attention of party leaders at the highest levels. While living in Geneva, Lenin organized a meeting with the Georgian Bolshevik Malakia Toroshelidze, who worked for the party in Baku. Toroshelidze subsequently returned to the Swiss city for second meeting with Lenin, this time accompanied by Sergo Orjonikidze.[53] A few years later, after leading protests in Baku during the 1905 Revolution, Ioseb Jughashvili was elected to represent the Caucasus at a party conference in Finland in early 1906, where he met Lenin for the first time.

Although he still went by "Koba," a nickname inspired by a classic of Georgian literature, Jughashvili had become a committed internationalist. He moved his wife, Ekaterine Svanidze, and his young son, Iakob, from Tbilisi to Baku.[54] He began to correspond and publish more frequently in Russian, and even studied Esperanto in hope of mastering a truly international language.[55] After attending a party congress in London in May 1907, he returned again to Baku. Describing the London meeting in the underground newspaper *Bakinskii proletarii*, he claimed that the Bolsheviks represented the interests of laborers, a vanguard linked to industrial development in central Russia, while the Mensheviks who dominated Georgia did so only because of the "backward and petty bourgeois" nature of his native land.[56] Although shaped by his youth in Georgia and surrounded by fellow Georgian revolutionaries, he saw the future of international revolution taking shape beyond the confines of his rural homeland.

Jughashvili and his Georgian comrades were also carried far beyond Georgia by the tsarist criminal justice system. All the Georgian Bolsheviks who would eventually lead the revolution spent time in prison, exile, and emigration. Banished to small villages and provincial towns in southern Russia and Siberia, many encountered Russian life firsthand. In this sense, imprisonment outside the Caucasus was a formative Russian education for Georgian revolutionaries. At the same time, tsarist persecution only strengthened their reliance on the fraternal and ethnic bonds that united them.

Sergo Orjonikidze was but one Bolshevik exiled to the far reaches of the empire. Abel Enukidze was arrested in 1911 and exiled, first to southern Russia, and finally to Yeniseisk, a region near the Chinese frontier, following a second arrest.[57] Simon Enukidze was arrested in 1912, one year after his cousin, and exiled beyond the Caucasus for three years.[58] While punishment scattered this group of Georgians, they were able to correspond with each other, depending on ethnic, family, and party networks to exchange information. Prison also mixed Bolsheviks from across the empire together. Galaktion Vashadze, a former student of the Kutaisi seminary, was arrested for carrying out Bolshevik party work in the Georgian mining town of Chiatura. In Siberian exile, he encountered Russian revolutionaries from Moscow and St. Petersburg who impressed him greatly.[59] Spending years in the far-flung corners of Russia, Georgian socialists established personal relationships with Russians and embraced an internationalism informed by the vastness and diversity of the tsarist empire. In Iakutiia, Orjonikidze met his Russian wife, Zinaida Pavlutskaia. Jughashvili was exiled to the frozen expanses of Kureika, a settlement close to the Arctic Circle. In later years, he recalled fondly his daily exchanges with the villagers, both Russians and ethnic Kets.[60]

When possible, Georgian revolutionary figures sometimes sought to escape the police by traveling abroad, and they emerged as prominent figures in emigration. Mikha Tskhakaia, one of the group's older members, was imprisoned in 1906 after helping organize the Baku Soviet. Making it to London for the Fifth Party Congress in 1907, he remained in Europe, living in Switzerland in close proximity to Lenin from 1907 to 1917. While abroad, he recommended many of his Georgian comrades personally to Lenin, and published radical articles in Russian and Georgian under a series of Russian and Georgian-sounding pseudonyms for distribution across the Russian Empire.[61] Lenin was greatly impressed by the multiethnic sensibility and multilingual work of Tskhakaia and other Georgian publicists, and in an article published in 1913 he wrote: "The work of the Social Democrats in the Caucasus should be an example for us all."[62]

It was little surprise, then, that when the revolution arrived suddenly in February 1917 following Tsar Nicholas II's unexpected abdication, Georgian revolutionaries appeared at the center of Russian political life, prominent among both Mensheviks and Bolsheviks. They returned from exile, prison, and emigration, hastening to implement their socialist vision in Petrograd and in their native Georgia. The bonds among Georgian revolutionaries, and their skill in representing a multiethnic movement, had proved to be valuable assets in the revolutionary underground and would be just as indispensable in the pursuit of revolution.

In Siberian exile, the Menshevik Irakli Tsereteli received news of the government's collapse through his network of Georgian associates. Almost immediately, he was summoned by Gerasim Makharadze, another Georgian member of the Second Duma living in exile, and the two traveled to Irkutsk together.[63] By March, Tsereteli had reached the Russian capital, where he accepted a post in the Provisional Government, first as Minister of Posts and Telegraphs, later as Minister of the Interior in Alexander Kerensky's cabinet. A Russian newspaper article from the period wryly noted that Tsereteli was the first minister in Russia's history to report to his position from prison.[64] However, he was far from the only Georgian on the new political landscape. At the Menshevik Congress of the RSDLP in 1917, the party's Caucasus organization, the majority of whom were Georgian, made up one-fifth of the mandated delegates.[65] In the words of Menshevik politician Noe Jordania, Russian Social Democracy had a "Georgian face."[66]

As Georgian Mensheviks joined the Provisional Government, Georgian Bolsheviks began to organize in Petrograd. Mikha Tskhakaia returned from emigration with Lenin in the sealed train, accompanied by Davit Suliashvili, a former seminarian from Tbilisi who had lived in exile among the Bolsheviks in Switzerland.[67] As they massed in the Russian capital, they sensed the excitement of revolutionary change. Galaktion Vashadze, returning from exile in Siberia, recalled the "grandiose" expressions of "enthusiasm and happiness" he encountered at the time of his release, accompanied by singing, dancing, and feasting.[68] Abel Enukidze, pressed into military service in 1916, happened to arrive with his Siberian division in Petrograd on the day of the tsar's abdication, on his way to the front. He remained in the capital, carrying out revolutionary activity along with his cousin, Simon Enukidze, who had promoted the socialist cause among the workers of the Siemens factory in Petrograd since 1914.[69] Wherever the revolution found them, Georgian Bolsheviks began to organize immediately. Sergo Orjonikidze first served as a member of the Executive Committee of the local Soviet in Iakutiia, where he had been in exile, before becoming a member of the Petrograd Soviet in July 1917, shortly after his arrival.[70] Fellow Georgian revolutionary Shalva Eliava assumed a leadership position in Vologda, where he had been under police supervision.[71]

While Georgian Mensheviks dominated the official political scene in early 1917, the Bolshevik seizure of power in October forced them out of their positions in the Russian government. Many returned to their native Georgia, where on May 26, 1918, amidst the chaos of the revolution and the ongoing First World War, they proclaimed an independent Democratic Republic of Georgia. Although they had lost control of an empire-wide movement, the Mensheviks attracted the attention of intellectuals throughout Europe by implementing an alternative experiment in social democracy in Georgia, a gradualist approach that contrasted with the radical revolution being carried out by the Bolsheviks in Russia. The prominent German Marxist Karl Kautsky visited the Democratic Republic of Georgia in 1920 and praised the advances made by Mensheviks in "little Georgia." Impressed by the Georgian Mensheviks' conciliatory approach to implementing socialism in a predominantly agrarian society, he wrote that Russia would "only be able to prosper when it is animated by the spirit that inspired Georgia."[72]

Bolshevik theorists thought otherwise. In a 1922 publication, Leon Trotsky derided Georgian Mensheviks for their "southern sensitivity and adaptability."[73] Referring to an already established trope of flamboyant Georgian performance, Trotsky sarcastically noted how these passionate orators had seamlessly shifted from internationalist aspirations to nationalist rhetoric, which he saw as a cunning way of clinging to power in their native Georgia. Many Georgian Bolsheviks actually shared Trotsky's sentiment, defining their ideological steadfastness in juxtaposition to the Mensheviks' purported flexibility and criticizing showy Georgian performances and flowery speeches that allegedly lacked substance. In a satirical novel published shortly after the demise of Menshevik Georgia, the author Mikheil Javakhishvili chided his fellow Georgians for these alleged flaws, which he linked to the degrading opportunism of the Georgian aristocracy under Russian imperial rule. His novel's eponymous hero, Kvachi Kvachantiradze, was a "circus acrobat" of rhetoric, a showy dilettante of revolution, and a "living barometer" who had a keen sense of social change, and accordingly shifted his self-presentation to his own advantage.[74] Such tendencies were viewed with disgust by Ioseb Jughashvili, though he himself was deeply involved in fashioning his own public image. His first nickname, Koba, had been inspired by a steadfast highlander from Georgian fiction; his second nickname, Stalin (from the Russian word for "steel"), proclaimed him unbending where his fellow countrymen were weak. Emerging from the ethnically diverse Caucasus, Stalin was appointed Commissar of Nationalities, tasked with addressing the "national question" in the multiethnic empire inherited by the Bolsheviks, including in his native Georgia.[75]

# A Bolshevik Homecoming

In February 1921, Georgian Bolsheviks returned to their homeland alongside the invading Russian Red Army. Lenin had been reluctant to authorize the military occupation of Georgia, but had finally been persuaded to endorse it by Stalin himself. A Georgian-language letter from Stalin to Sergo Orjonikidze likely written just weeks before the Red Army's invasion conveys the peculiar combination of national sentiment and socialist dedication common among those Georgian Bolsheviks who now saw their native territory from the perspective of the center. Contrary to the views of contemporaries and subsequent scholars, Stalin had not altogether cast off his Georgian identity; instead, he continued to perform Georgianness, but did so in pursuit of revolutionary aims and the radical remaking of his homeland.[76] Addressing Orjonikidze in his letter as a "fellow countryman" (*chveneburo*), Stalin wrote in an intimate and conspiring tone, relaying that those around Lenin who opposed the idea of moving the Red Army into Georgia had been defeated; according to Stalin, "Trotsky's group" was "very much weakened" and Bukharin's opposition had "collapsed like a pile of rice." Insisting that the moment the Georgian Bolsheviks had waited for was now at hand, Stalin wrote: "*Piter* [Petrograd] and Moscow are on our side . . . Let's try not to fail in the Caucasus . . . The Georgian question will be solved in the next few days." Viewing Georgia from the outside but still operating within a Georgian cultural context, Stalin closed his letter by asking Orjonikidze for a favor, requesting that he assist two Georgians who were on their way to Russia, the literary critic Geronti Kikodze and Aleksandre Giorgobiani, an engineer. He signed the letter in endearing terms: "A kiss to you. Your Soso."[77]

Once the invasion was underway, Lenin had little say over the actions on the ground of Sergo Orjonikidze and other members of the Revolutionary Military Council of the Caucasus. Despite a telegram sent by Lenin to Orjonikidze shortly after the invasion calling for a "special policy of concessions toward the Georgian intelligentsia and small traders" rather than a blind application of the "Russian pattern" of War Communism, Georgian Bolsheviks were ruthless in ushering in their vision of a socialist Georgia. Even those Georgians who did not accompany the Red Army into their native land took a personal interest in events there. Pilipe Makharadze, who headed the newly established Georgian Revolutionary Committee, received constant direction and advice from the Georgian Bolsheviks Abel Enukidze and Alesha Svanidze in Moscow.[78] Stalin personally monitored Makharadze's efforts to combat Menshevik propaganda among the Georgian population, taking Makharadze to task for inadequately responding to charges that Georgian Bolsheviks were simply "agents of Moscow."[79] The dispersal of Georgian Bolsheviks throughout Russia's socialist underground had placed them at the center of the revolution, but also meant that they were sometimes seen as Russian operatives in their native land.

The battle for the future of Soviet Georgia reached a decisive phase during the Georgian Affair of 1922. Orjonikidze, as head of the Caucasian Bureau of the Russian Communist Party, sought to integrate Georgia into the Soviet Union as part of a politically and economically unified Transcaucasus Federation that would also include neighboring Armenia and Azerbaijan. Again, Lenin urged caution, but Orjonikidze forged ahead with Stalin's backing, purging Georgian officials who did not support his position. Among the tightly networked community of Georgian Bolsheviks, these new political divisions were taken personally. The matter became a full-fledged controversy when Orjonikidze publicly slapped another Georgian Bolshevik who opposed his plans. Those Georgians who had long lived beyond the confines of Georgia— like Stalin, Orjonikidze, and Enukidze—sought complete integration of their native republic into a centralized Soviet state, leading Lenin to accuse these non-Russians of "Great Russian chauvinism."[80] However, it is perhaps more accurate to say that this group of Georgian Bolsheviks, rather than being chauvinists, were especially committed to the radical, rapid, and uncompromising transformation of their native land into a socialist society.

In particular, Georgian Bolshevik leaders had little patience for the habits and customs of rural Georgia. Although they sought to swell the party ranks by recruiting Georgian peasants as part of the "Lenin Enrollment," the Georgian Bolsheviks still had difficulty winning support in the Georgian countryside. In 1924 they faced a major armed rebellion in western Georgia, which they only suppressed by resorting to violent reprisals.[81] As chairman of the Council of People's Commissars in Georgia in the wake of the revolt, Shalva Eliava led the effort to remake rural Georgian society, attacking longstanding hierarchies and patterns of personalized ties. In a meeting of the Georgian Central Committee held on June 5, 1925, Eliava railed against the feudal nature of rural Georgian society, and warned that a new feudal mentality might reemerge, even under Soviet rule. He stated:

> Georgia is a feudal country, built on feudal principles. Soviet power has of course destroyed the basis of feudalism here, yet a new sort of feudal aristocracy—if one might describe it as such—has emerged, especially in the countryside, of people who do not consider themselves accountable to anyone and for anything.[82]

Elsewhere, Eliava criticized Georgian culture itself, railing against the pervasive establishment of "personal fiefdoms" within Soviet institutions and complaining that the anarchic tendency of every Georgian to consider himself "his own boss" extended "throughout society."[83]

According to his own daughter's account, Stalin, too, "could not stand the displays of feudal loyalty and honor" that he witnessed when he visited his native land.[84] Speaking at a closed meeting of the Central Committee's Orgburo on October 19, 1931, Stalin lamented: "I have the impression that there are no real party organizations in the Transcaucasus." Instead, Stalin claimed that local "chiefs" in the region promoted an aspirant through the party ranks solely based on matters of personal loyalty, concerned with questions like: "Whose person is he? Whom will he fight? Whom will he drink with? Whom will he visit as a guest?"[85] Yet in his own political practices, Stalin surrounded himself in Moscow with loyal comrades from the Caucasus and forged highly personalized relationships. As much as they spoke critically about Georgian culture, he and Eliava were veterans of a revolutionary movement from the Caucasus that was infused with Georgian cultural practices of friendship, patronage, and mutual obligation. The cultural connection alone was not sufficient to establish solidarity among all Georgians, but proved to be a powerful adhesive among the diaspora of Georgian Bolsheviks when paired with ideological devotion. As Stalin ascended to the highest levels of Soviet power, he was followed and supported by a core group of loyalists from his homeland. The Georgian revolution, which had begun as part of a broader process of upheaval in the tsarist empire's periphery, traveled with him to Moscow.

## The Caucasian Group in the Kremlin

By the early 1930s, many in the party referred to Stalin and those around him as the "Caucasian group."[86] The group included fellow Georgians like Sergo Orjonikidze, the Commissar of Heavy Industry, and Abel Enukidze, the Secretary of the Presidium of the Central Executive Committee, as well as the ethnic Armenian Anastas Mikoian, educated in Tbilisi, and the Russian Sergei Kirov, considered an honorary "Caucasian" because of his longtime party work in Azerbaijan.[87] Just a decade after the violence of the Civil War and the turmoil of establishing Soviet power in the Caucasus, this group of revolutionaries had emerged from the mountainous periphery of the former Russian Empire to lead the Soviet Union. All except Kirov spoke accented Russian, and most spoke Georgian. They affirmed old bonds by socializing with one another, vacationing together, and sharing Georgian food and wine at a nearly endless succession of Kremlin feasts. Membership in the Caucasian group required fluency in the region's culture and came with the privilege of intimate access to Stalin.

Personal networks were as vital to survival and success in the turbulent world of the Soviet state as they had been in the revolutionary underground. In the early Soviet Union, institutions arguably mattered less than factional and ideological loyalties.[88] The correspondence of top Bolsheviks from this period reveals that networks of trusted associates were essential for obtaining resources, building political support, and advancing one's career. Not all political networks were ethnic in nature. Factions were held together by bonds forged in prison and exile, by Civil War ties, and by regional affiliation. These factions, however, were smaller and more fluid, and group membership lacked an enduring cultural and linguistic dimension. In a world of personalized politics, networks created in the Caucasus, bound by shared experiences and cultural norms, proved especially resilient.

The Caucasian group was dominated by Georgians and reflected their political ascent in the ethnically diverse region. However, Georgians were certainly not the only non-Russian nationality overrepresented in the new Soviet state. Jews had also risen rapidly to positions of power, but generally did so in pursuit of internationalist goals beyond Judaism.[89] While most Jews left the trappings of their parents' culture behind, Georgians celebrated and affirmed their ethnic otherness in visible ways that affirmed a shared Caucasian kinship. Because they were non-Slavic, Georgian networks were more distinctive and more likely to be commented upon than Ukrainian networks; and unlike Latvians, Georgians were not confined to the military and security services, but instead could be found in different roles throughout the new state. Georgian Bolsheviks moved between the Caucasus and the Kremlin, going from periphery to center and back, and linking the two inextricably together.

As Commissar of Heavy Industry in the 1930s, Sergo Orjonikidze relied on Georgian networks in his massive effort to industrialize the

*Figure 2.1* The Caucasian group in 1926. Stalin sits in the middle, flanked by Anastas Mikoian (left) and Sergo Orjonkidze (right). National Archives of Georgia.

Soviet Union. In fact, Orjonikidze's methods of industrial organization revealed that some of the same "feudal" tendencies that Georgian
Bolsheviks decried in their native country—namely, a tendency to
establish "personal fiefdoms" based on patronage—were practiced at
the highest levels of Soviet power. Patronage was a widespread tendency
in the Soviet Union, but Georgian-style patronage was more effective
and more adaptable because clients and patrons shared a common set
of cultural expectations, and every client served as a potential patron to
those below him. In Georgian culture the principles of friendship and
reciprocity could be more elaborate and extensive, and more openly
appealed to.

Orjonikidze had risen to power as Stalin's trusted lieutenant. A loyal
friend, he supported Stalin in his disputes with political opponents
Grigorii Zinoviev and Lev Kamenev in the 1920s. He was called up by
Stalin from Tbilisi to Moscow in 1926 and placed in charge of the party's
Central Control Commission, which played an important role in expelling and arresting members of the "Trotskyite-Zinovievist Opposition."[90]
As head of the Central Control Commission, Orjonikidze gained
a reputation for ruthless effectiveness and was praised as a talented
Soviet manager. By the early 1930s, the Central Control Commission
declined in administrative importance since major opposition to Stalin
had been eliminated in the party.[91] In 1932, Orjonikidze was removed
from his old position and placed in charge of the newly created People's
Commissariat of Heavy Industry (NKTP). The Commissariat was
now of prime importance, as Stalin was poised to launch the Second
Five-Year Plan, a blueprint for economic development that emphasized
heavy industry as the means to transform rural Russia into a modern
socialist power.

As the boss of a newly created and strategically vital agency,
Orjonikidze enjoyed a great deal of autonomy. He owed his position to
Stalin, but oversaw economic development by relying on his own personal
network, whose members he promoted through the ranks of the NKTP.
Orjonikidze's management style was frenetic and confrontational, and
he had a reputation for his fiery temper, which contemporaries ascribed
to his being a "true Georgian."[92] At the same time, he was an ideal patron,
demonstrating fierce loyalty to the personnel he supervised, defending

them on numerous occasions against dangerous political charges, and in some cases protecting them from Stalin himself.[93]

As befitted a member of an internal diaspora dominant in Soviet politics, Orjonikidze's leadership of the NKTP demanded a high level of geographical mobility. Archival records show that he constantly shifted a core group of personnel to positions around the country and carried out the affairs of the NKTP wherever he traveled, hastily dispatching instructions and orders by telegraph. Whether inspecting an industrial plant or on vacation in the Caucasus, he ran the Commissariat by telephone, post, and often from a train car.[94] The Commissar, his Commissariat, and his trusted cadres were constantly in motion. It was imperative that Orjonikidze appear routinely at construction sites and factories throughout the Soviet Union, both to ensure that work was completed in the absence of other accountability mechanisms and to generate favorable coverage of the Soviet industrial effort for the pages of *Pravda* and *Izvestiia*.[95]

The personnel Orjonikidze relied on in his effort to oversee Soviet industrial development were not exclusively Georgian, though being so could certainly be an advantage. In general terms, industrialization created a strong demand for specialists. While the "bourgeois specialists" relied upon in the 1920s were no longer available, preference was given to ambitious Bolsheviks with technical training and managerial skills, and this new stratum of talented party managers was one in which literate, mobile ethnic groups excelled. Among those ethnic groups who achieved prominence during the Soviet industrialization drive, Georgians were best suited to establish a close relationship with Orjonikidze by appealing to old bonds and a common culture. Nowhere do the mechanisms that these ethnic specialists drew on to establish themselves stand out as clearly as in the patron–client relationships that were established in the NKTP.

Even before Orjonikidze assumed his position as Commissar of NKTP, many old Georgian comrades sought out his assistance. Shalva Eliava was an example of a Georgian Bolshevik who successfully appealed to Orjonikidze for political support. Their paths had diverged in the mid-1920s, when Orjonikidze pursued his career in Moscow and Eliava remained in Georgia. Eliava's prospects hit a low point in 1931,

*Figure 2.2* Sergo Orjonikidze warmly receives a political delegation from the Caucasus in Moscow in 1925. Shalva Eliava stands second from the right. Russian State Archive of Film and Photo Documents.

when he was sent by the party to supervise an economic project in the Kazakh SSR. He took issue with the posting, thinking it a waste of his energy and skills. Matters took a turn for the worse when his wife fell ill and was unable to receive proper medical care. Finding himself in a desperate position, Eliava decided to write to Orjonikidze for help.

In a letter dated March 11, 1931, Eliava informed his old comrade and potential patron that he had been sent to work in the Kazakh SSR on a matter that he "could not understand and even now can understand only poorly." He sought the support of his "dear Sergo" as a friend and protector: "I appeal to you as a person who has always played an intimate role in my fate. I am sure that you will not consider it awkward to consider my request, though it be made from afar and in writing." The paragraphs that followed can be seen as a typical example of "speaking Bolshevik."[96] Writing in Russian, Eliava expressed his dedication to the party and his willingness to accept criticism for any past failings in his service to the state. However, in the final paragraph of the letter, Eliava switched to Georgian and wrote in a strikingly different tone. At this point, Russian was the official language of correspondence among state employees at the Union-wide level, and both Eliava and Orjonikidze wrote and spoke fluent Russian. However, Eliava engaged in "code-switching," appealing to his patron in Georgian as a way to affirm a joint identity and, along with it, a shared sense of ethnic solidarity and mutual obligation.[97]

After describing in detail the state of his affairs in the Kazakh SSR, Eliava wrote in Georgian: "Such are the state of things, my dear Sergo. If you have not forgotten me and can offer me help—good. If not, what can I say! Be healthy, and let happen what will happen to me." He closed by sending his regards to Orjonikidze's wife Zinaida, and noted that his own wife sent her regards too, though she was "seriously ill" and confined to "lying down in her train compartment."[98] Orjonikidze was not able to resist this appeal as a patron who could offer help and as a fellow Georgian. Based on Orjonikidze's notes in the margins, it is apparent that he forwarded the letter immediately to Stalin. Later that year, Eliava was appointed Deputy Commissar of Foreign Trade of the Soviet Union.

In Eliava's case, a shared background and a mutually intelligible appeal in Georgian were essential for his transfer. Although Soviet leaders were committed to socialist ideology and well versed in "speaking Bolshevik," the national language they expressed themselves in very much mattered. Georgian, like other languages and other "national forms" more generally, was a semiotic system that appealed to a set of emotions and expectations familiar to the speaker and his audience.[99] As a Soviet "code language," Georgian was ideal: it was virtually unintelligible to outsiders yet recognized as an official state language with well-established high culture credentials. It could be used without suspicion or shame, not only in correspondence, but also in side conversations held among Georgian Bolsheviks at official events. The correspondence of top Jewish Bolsheviks, by contrast, reveals no trace of Yiddish or Yiddishisms; unlike Georgians, Jews were more likely to cast aside their nationality in pursuit of universalism and, as eager "converts" to the "Pushkin faith," seek expression solely through Russian language and culture.[100]

As the head of a new ministry with vast powers, Orjonikidze found that even more Georgians sought his patronage, many of them newly educated and eager for work within the Soviet state. Most of these Georgian specialists were trained in Moscow, though some were sent abroad to study the latest methods of industrial organization. Returning from Germany in

1932, A. Cheishvili, a Georgian engineer, asked for Orjonikidze's support in a letter. He recalled that his delegation had once met Orjonikidze at a railway station in the North Caucasus town of Gudermes. Now back in Moscow, he appealed to "Comrade Sergo" for advice on how he could further his "career in the international workers' movement."[101] Among aspiring Georgians like these, Orjonikidze was well known as a high-ranking but accessible party figure. When the young Grigori Mamatsashvili, who left Georgia to study engineering in Moscow in the late 1920s, strove to make connections in the Soviet capital, he called upon Orjonikidze, whose wife, Zinaida, arranged a Kremlin pass for the Georgian student, allowing him to make the acquaintance of top Soviet officials.[102] Here, as elsewhere, is evidence of the discreet but critical role women played as gatekeepers to their husbands' networks. Since many wives in the Caucasian group were, like Zinaida Orjonikidze, non-Georgian, they could skillfully mediate between the demands of Georgian culture and the norms of the host society. The ability to allow or deny access to political aspirants often rested with them.

*Figure 2.3* Sergo Orjonikidze posing for a photograph with his Russian wife, Zinaida Orjonikidze (née Pavlutskaia). National Archives of Georgia.

In his more public role as a male Georgian patron, Sergo Orjonikidze was frequently called upon to meet cultural and familial obligations. His support was critical for securing a position for his younger brother Papulia with the Transcaucasian Railway. He thus helped the same brother whom he had turned to for assistance while a prisoner in 1913.[103] His correspondence suggests that he intervened directly to support the appointment of his nephew, Giorgi Gvakharia, to direct the massive Makeevskii Metalworks in eastern Ukraine's heavily industrial Donbass region.[104] He also extended support to the children of old comrades, like Elena Japaridze, daughter of Alesha Japaridze, a Georgian Bolshevik from Baku who had been among the city's twenty-six Commissars executed by British forces during the Civil War. Elena Japaridze trained as an engineer and was posted to Magnitogorsk, a massive new industrial city near the Ural Mountains and the center of Soviet steel production.[105] She frequently corresponded with Orjonikidze about working conditions in Magnitogorsk and met with him when he visited the steel mill, providing him with valuable information on the factory's day-to-day operations. Japaridze's unpublished recollections of Orjonikidze reveal how closely personal, political, and professional relationships were intertwined in this period. Japaridze recalled that when she arrived in Moscow for a party congress, she had only to phone Zinaida Orjonikidze. The instant Zinaida heard Japaridze's voice on the line, she invited the young Georgian engineer over for dinner.[106] Once she was welcomed into the Orjonikidzes' home, standards of Georgian hospitality informed Sergo Orjonikidze's paternalistic relationship with the daughter of his fallen comrade.[107]

As a good patron, Orjonikidze rewarded the loyalty of his more valued associates, even risking his own career to defend them against political accusations. His deputy in the NKTP was Georgii Piatakov, whose standing in the party had been tarnished by an open disagreement he once had with Lenin. Although Piatakov was from Kiev, not the Caucasus, he sought to establish a personal bond with Orjonikidze. He did so in an expressive manner that alternated between loyal subservience and fraternal affinity, perhaps an effort to emulate Georgian patterns of patronage. In a letter to Orjonikidze, Piatakov wrote: "It is because you are not only a boss and *senior* comrade, but also a man whom

I have always regarded with the deepest love and respect, that your leadership was, and is, for me not only the formal tutelage of a superior, but also the leadership of a comrade whom I personally respect deeply."[108] Orjonikidze stood by Piatakov, despite the latter's damaged political reputation.

A few years earlier, Orjonikidze had extended himself politically to help Beso Lominadze. An ambitious young Georgian promoted from party secretary in Tbilisi to the Comintern in Moscow in the late 1920s, Lominadze had been accused of "left deviationism" by Stalin himself for opposing the party's position on the Chinese Revolution. Orjonikidze reportedly concealed from Stalin correspondence written by Lominadze that would have incriminated the young Georgian radical.[109] In 1934, Lominadze, as party secretary of the industrial city of Magnitogorsk, once again appealed to Orjonikidze for support after coming into conflict with the head of the Magnitogorsk Metallurgical Combine, Avraamii Zaveniagin. Lominadze wrote to "Comrade Sergo" using the informal second person and declared his opponents to be "idiots" and "fools." Emphasizing that his situation arose from an overabundance of loyalty to Orjonikidze, he wrote that his associates "cruelly punished people" for not carrying out Orjonikidze's orders, and "did so correctly." He added: "Now all know the value of Orjonikidze's directives." Aware of Lominadze's link to Orjonikidze, Zaveniagin sought to clear his name. Using the formal form of address, he wrote to the Georgian head of the NKTP: "I know you have good relations with Lominadze and, obviously, with Comrade Stalin. Therefore, it is all the more unpleasant for me to raise these questions with you. However, it would be worse to bury this matter and thus destroy our entire enterprise."[110] Called into the fray between two clients, one of them Georgian, Orjonikidze pressured both to resolve their differences while drafting a Politburo resolution that protected them from party discipline. However, Lominadze had by now attracted the scrutiny of Stalin, who ordered the People's Commissariat of Internal Affairs (NKVD) to begin investigating him and his associates in Magnitogorsk.[111]

As the leader of the Soviet Union, Stalin was the supreme patron. He ruled by balancing and playing political factions off one another. But as a Georgian Bolshevik, Stalin was more than simply a "machine politician."[112] Among the Caucasian group, patronage relations were more flexible and less hierarchical. In part, these distinctions were due to shared revolutionary experiences in the Caucasus. Sergo Orjonikidze still corresponded with Stalin using the informal form of address and peppered his Russian-language letters to Stalin concerning official matters with Georgian phrases, greetings, and personal appeals.[113] Stalin's old ally, Abel Enukidze, known around the Kremlin as "Uncle Abel," also addressed the Soviet leader in familiar terms and occasionally in Georgian, reflecting a decades-long friendship and the fraternal spirit of the Georgian revolutionary underground.[114]

While shared personal history and seniority helped determine the tenor of patronage relations, the social distance between patron and client was generally closer for Georgians, perhaps a feature of Georgian culture but also a result of their tendency to band together as a diaspora. Beso Lominadze carried out a prolonged exchange of letters directly with Stalin. Although Lominadze, Stalin's junior by almost twenty years, addressed the Soviet leader in polite terms, he wrote with surprising directness. In 1928, Lominadze wrote Stalin to complain bluntly about being posted to rural Russia, stating: "I am completely unfamiliar with the Russian countryside (I have never been there in my life) and with the lifestyle and living conditions of the Russian peasantry."[115] While such frank comments may have been characteristic of Lominadze's brash personality, it is also possible that he hoped Stalin would be sympathetic to his views on the Russian countryside as a fellow outsider in a foreign host society. The two were bound not only by shared cultural affinities, but also by their status as members of a diaspora living beyond its native land.

Stalin's patronage was also sought by Georgians back home, even those outside the party.[116] Although he seldom traveled to Georgia, he occasionally wrote to his old friends in Gori and once wired money when one of them was in need.[117] He was contacted by people who had assisted him in the revolutionary underground, and one childhood friend in particular asked that Stalin send a plane so he could see the "Kremlin and the other sites of Moscow" before dying.[118] Stalin also received more pointed requests for meetings in Moscow and financial assistance from family members in Georgia. One cousin, Epimia Gveseliani,

proved remarkably persistent in contacting him, sending Stalin numerous letters over the course of several years and at one point asking him
to support her son's efforts to receive an education abroad. Her correspondence indicates that Stalin actually met with her twice, in 1941 and
1946. When Stalin was unable to see her during a visit to Moscow in
1947, she brazenly appealed to his sense of family obligation by writing
in Georgian: "I know that I am bothering you . . . but you must forgive
me for just wanting to see you. Fulfill this, my heart's only desire. I am
thinking of returning to Tbilisi, please do not let me leave without seeing you."[119] It is unclear whether Stalin met with her on this occasion,
though it is apparent that the "meetings" were filled with thinly veiled
requests for additional assistance.

Interestingly, some of Stalin's most intimate family obligations,
including those to his mother, were not handled by the Soviet leader himself. Until her death by suicide in 1932, Stalin's second wife, Nadezhda
Allilueva, often wrote to Stalin's mother on his behalf using Georgian
greetings, reporting that her "Soso" was healthy but very busy with
the affairs of state.[120] After his wife's death, Stalin brought Aleksandre
Egnatashvili, a childhood friend from Gori, to Moscow to look after his
affairs. Part of Egnatashvili's responsibilities included supplying Stalin's
mother with meat and other scarce foods through NKVD channels.
Egnatashvili also took it upon himself to update Stalin's mother on the
leader's health, writing to her approvingly that "Soso" had "put on some
weight" and had not seemed so healthy in years.[121] Egnatashvili personally distributed special rations to other members of Stalin's family,
including the persistent Epimia Gveseliani.[122]

Having risen to high positions in Moscow, revolutionaries from the
Caucasus brought their distinct practices of hospitality with them.
Although they were in some sense ethnic guests, they became the
supreme hosts of the new state. Participation in Georgian-style feasts
and other social rituals renewed old bonds and proved vital to the
political advancement of younger party members. Prior to her death,
Nadezhda Allilueva often played the role of hostess at these social gatherings in the Kremlin. Although from a predominantly Russian family,
she had grown up in a Georgian cultural environment, her father a met-
alworker and party activist in Tbilisi. She was particularly close with

Abel Enukidze, whom she had known since childhood as her godfather. Nikita Khrushchev remembered her warm hospitality with fondness, noting that she always greeted visitors with food and kind concern. As Stalin's wife, Allilueva played an even greater role in building and maintaining social networks among the Soviet elite than Zinaida Orjonikidze. Khrushchev credited Allilueva, who studied with him at the Industrial Academy in Moscow, for introducing him to Stalin.[123]

Elaborate feasts begun in Moscow continued along Abkhazia's Black Sea coast at Kholodnaia Rechka, Stalin's dacha complex. A solid stone structure perched on a cliff near the resort town of Gagra, Kholodnaia Rechka was where Stalin held huge dinners, participated in hunting expeditions, and tended his own grove of orange trees. While Stalin rarely returned to his native Gori or even Tbilisi, he recreated the atmosphere of a Caucasian gentry estate at Kholodnaia Rechka. Dining and vacationing with Stalin at Kholodnaia Rechka gave Caucasian Bolsheviks political access that was unobtainable for regional party officials elsewhere in the Soviet Union.[124] In Abkhazia, Stalin was especially close with Nestor Lakoba, another former student of the Tbilisi seminary and, in the 1930s, the Communist party chief of the autonomous republic. At dinners held at Kholodnaia Rechka, the Soviet leader would defer to Lakoba, allowing the Abkhaz native to serve as *tamada* for their Georgian-style feasts. Eager young party members in Georgia sought introductions to Stalin and his circle while the leaders vacationed. On the grounds of his dacha, Stalin met the youthful and energetic Lavrenti Beria, a meeting arranged by Lakoba.[125]

The social and political networks that linked Georgian party leaders in Moscow with party officials in Georgia were bidirectional; patrons in Moscow helped advance the careers of clients in Georgia, and clients in Georgia offered favors in return as part of a reciprocal arrangement. As Deputy Commissar of Foreign Trade, Eliava forged a close relationship with Nestor Lakoba in Abkhazia. In a letter to Lakoba dated November 16, 1931, Eliava noted his obligation to Lakoba in advance and offered him his support in foreign trade matters. He graciously invited Lakoba to come to visit him in Moscow. In return, Eliava asked Lakoba to personally host the Minister of Trade and Industry of Mongolia in Abkhazia, saying that the Minister was a "needed person" who should be shown the "maximum attention" and provided with the best accommodations.[126] Wherever they found themselves, Bolsheviks from the Caucasus articulated a shared group identity. Shortly after Orjonikidze was promoted from Tbilisi to Moscow in 1926, he wrote to Lakoba, his comrade in the Caucasus, telling him: "Drink and shoot as much as you like, the TsKK [the Central Control Commission, which Orjonikidze headed] is now in our hands." In the same letter, he also informed Lakoba that Viacheslav Molotov, a close ally of Stalin, would be coming to Abkhazia and noted that he should be looked after. Orjonikidze closed his letter by inviting Lakoba and his family to visit him at his new home in Moscow.[127]

The Russian and Georgian-language correspondence of the Caucasian group shows they gathered together frequently for birthdays, celebrations, and cultural events. Abel Enukidze composed a very personal letter to Stalin on the Soviet leader's fiftieth birthday, celebrated in the Kremlin on December 21, 1929. While Enukidze acknowledged Stalin's importance to the international socialist movement, he devoted a great deal of attention to his own decades-long friendship with "Soso."[128] When Enukidze's own birthday came, his old comrades Shalva Eliava, Sergo and Zinaida Orjonikidze, and Galaktion Vashadze wrote a spirited birthday greeting to him on Shalva Eliava's letterhead.[129] The same group of Georgians attended performances together when Tbilisi's Rustaveli Theater came to Moscow.[130]

The group's children grew up together in close proximity to the Kremlin. Aleksandre Egnatashvili's daughter recalled many hours spent playing with Stalin's children, with whom she formed lasting friendships. Her family spoke mainly Russian at home, because Egnatashvili's wife was not Georgian, but in other ways they kept a Georgian house and ate mainly Georgian food.[131] Like other children of the Caucasian group, their social and cultural world was imbued with socialist ideology, but retained a strong regional flavor. Bulat Okujava was born on Moscow's Arbat to a Georgian father and an Armenian mother, both fervent revolutionaries who had come to study in the Soviet capital. His father, Shalva Okujava, later returned to Tbilisi before being posted to Nizhnyi Tagil to supervise a train car construction facility operating under the auspices of Orjonikidze's Commissariat of Heavy Industry. When she arrived with her husband Lavrenti in Moscow in the late 1930s, Nina

Beria evinced a more overt sense of ethnic solidarity, hoping that her son, Sergo, would marry a Georgian girl, and even finding a fiancee for him from a "good family."[132] Growing up among the children of the new Soviet elite, he ended up marrying the granddaughter of Maxim Gorky. Although members of an ethnic diaspora whose Caucasian cultural ties were visibly affirmed, the children of Georgian revolutionaries eventually noticed that their parents spoke strongly accented Russian, while they spoke like native Muscovites. After studying in Moscow and working in Magnitogorsk, Elena Japaridze remarked that Stalin's accent was thicker than she expected when she finally heard him speak at the Seventeenth Party Congress in 1934. Her surprise was perhaps a logical outcome of the expanded educational opportunities made available to her and other young Georgians after the revolution.[133]

## Stalin and the Politics of Georgian Representation

Stalin's audible Georgian accent and the presence of so many Georgians in visible positions of authority made the representation of Soviet power a politically sensitive subject and brought special attention to the state-sponsored production of Georgian culture. One unofficial anti-Bolshevik poster compared the Georgian Bolsheviks to Jews in top political positions. On one side of a river, the poster showed a Jewish group led by Trotsky, Kamenev, and Zinoviev, and on the other side a Georgian group featuring Stalin, Orjonikidze, and Enukidze. Below the image, an inscription read: "And the Slavs fell into dispute about who was to rule in Old Russia."[134] Representations of influential Jewish cliques and cabals were not new in Russia; the fabricated *Protocols of the Elders of Zion* was, after all, a Russian imperial document. While Jews faced accusations of concealed identity and hidden conspiracies, as familiar strangers the Georgian Bolsheviks stood out because of their accents, their appearance, and their distinct cultural rituals, which were visibly performed and publicly celebrated even as the national culture of minorities not rooted in national republics was increasingly restricted.[135] They had been too radical for the politics of their homeland, yet were still the product of a Georgian revolution with distinctly national contours and remained committed to Georgian cultural development. Also, Georgian political prominence was not altogether unprecedented, as it was for Jews, because Georgians had been visibly present as nobles and generals in the old imperial court. Georgian identity could be openly affirmed even more than before, especially since Moscow was now officially depicted as an international capital of revolution. The presence of these desired ethnic outsiders was often cast as a sign of the new socialist internationalism, rather than an affront to Russian identity.

Georgia and its national culture were further promoted thanks to the prominence of Georgian Bolsheviks. This was particularly true of Stalin, whose cult established him as an ever-present and all-powerful Georgian-accented figure in everyday life. While all Soviet citizens were taught that Stalin was Georgian and told about his homeland, knowledge of other Caucasian ethnic groups was generally less emphasized. Georgians could be classified as the dominant element in the Caucasian group, but at other times Soviets simply spoke of Georgians in power, counting Armenians, Abkhaz, and other Caucasian Bolsheviks among them and using "Georgian" as an overarching ethnic category. Although Stalin himself rarely visited Georgia, the republic was celebrated throughout the Soviet Union as Stalin's homeland. The Georgian pavilion at Moscow's All-Union Agricultural Exhibition (VSKhV, which later became VDNKh), opened in 1939, greeted visitors with a sign reading: "Georgia—homeland of the Great Stalin, flowering under the sun of the Stalin Constitution."[136] Official images of the multiethnic Soviet population showed a harmonious and diverse group of national representatives working together, though the exceptional prominence of Georgians was occasionally acknowledged by the decision to position Georgians spatially and rhetorically at the forefront, alongside Russians and Ukrainians and ahead of other non-Slavic nationalities.

For some Georgians, having their coethnic at the helm of the Soviet Union imbued the cult of Stalin with national and personal meaning. Citizens across the Soviet Union wrote letters of appeal to Stalin and other top Soviet leaders, but Georgian letter writers often cast their pleas in particularistic ethnic terms. When F. Kalandadze traveled to Moscow from Tbilisi, he sought Enukidze's help on an important matter, likely relating to his health. While apologizing for being a nuisance, he felt that if he did not "bother Orjonikidze, Stalin, or Enukidze"—all fellow Georgians—"nothing would come of things."[137] This sense of having a direct ethnic link to the Kremlin integrated some Georgians more fully into the Soviet system; though Stalin at times treated his native country without mercy, his ascent became a source of national pride.

As a Georgian Bolshevik at the head of the Soviet Union, Stalin had to steer between politically expedient and potentially damaging displays of Georgian culture, as well as between a system based on personalized patronage and the interests of state-building. While Stalin continued to correspond closely with his comrades from the Caucasus, in November 1925 he drafted a memo that took aim at the constant use of non-Russian languages within the Central Executive Committee, then led by Enukidze. Stalin noted with concern that in daily committee affairs, "there often circulated all manner of notes in the languages of national minorities ... without any accompanying translation into Russian." Reining in the multiethnic cosmopolitanism of the early revolution, Stalin declared that committee business needed to be carried out in Russian, or at least translated into Russian for the official record. Letters written to Enukidze from Georgian Old Bolsheviks showed discomfort over this change in language policy. Some lower-ranking party members were already dismayed that as the Soviet bureaucracy took shape they could no longer meet with Enukidze directly, but had to go through his secretary. One Old Bolshevik begrudgingly wrote a note to Enukidze and Stalin in Russian, but explained that he was only doing so "because someone might unseal and inspect the letter and thus delay its delivery."[138] Stalin and many of his Georgian associates continued to write in Georgian in their personal correspondence, which, though unofficial, was nevertheless critical to the functioning of the Soviet state. While Georgian Bolsheviks relied on their native language to affirm common bonds, Stalin recognized the need for a unified state language and sought to avoid the appearance of full-scale ethnicization of official state business.[139] The move signaled the coming shift to a more hierarchical organization of Soviet nationalities and also represented the first step in transforming a set of personalized patronage networks into a bureaucratic state apparatus. Both of these efforts would accelerate rapidly in the 1930s.

While Stalin listed "Georgian" as his nationality in government documents and Georgia was officially celebrated as his homeland, the Soviet leader carefully managed his public image and sought to control the terms of his representation as a non-Russian. He paid particular attention to publications on his Georgian youth. When novelist Evgenii Fedorov's fictionalized account of Stalin's childhood was nearly published by a Leningrad printing press in 1940 without his knowledge, Stalin was outraged. Fedorov's *Kartalinskaia povest'* (*A Kartvelian Tale*) depicted young Soso Jughashvili as a precocious boy growing up in a loving Georgian family, though one strained by his father's treatment at the Adelkhanov shoe factory in Tbilisi. The novel set its characters against a background of stock images of the picturesque Georgian countryside, and sprinkled its dialogue with Georgian expressions, songs, and the inevitable toast. Although the novel reveled in Stalin's Georgian identity, it made clear that there were "good" Georgians and "bad" Georgians. In the novel, young Soso railed against Georgian Mensheviks like Irakli Tsereteli and Noe Jordania, who thought that "all Georgians" were "brothers"; the astute child observed that the capitalists who ran the Adelkhanov shoe factory were no brothers to him or his family. Stalin's notes on the manuscript show that he read Fedorov's novel carefully, even correcting the name of his former teacher at the Tbilisi seminary.[140]

Stalin, as it turned out, was not amused by Fedorov's attempt at a Georgian-themed biography, nor did he approve of efforts to translate a similar biography by Georgian author Konstantine Gamsakhurdia into Russian. Gamsakhurdia's *beladi* (*The Leader*) had been published in Georgian in 1939 in honor of Stalin's sixtieth birthday and was an important source of inspiration for Fedorov.[141] In a hastily written note sent in September 1940 to Andrei Zhdanov, Stalin's trusted deputy on cultural matters, the Soviet leader angrily condemned Petr Pospelov, the party historian who had sanctioned Fedorov's project, and sharply criticized the new book:

> Comrade Pospelov has acted stupidly and improperly, ordering the printing of Fedorov's book without my approval (and guidance). Fedorov's book should be liquidated as the work of a literary hack and Pospelov punished.[142]

In a second note, Stalin asked that the Russian translation of Gamsakhurdia's biographical work be banned.[143] While it may have been expedient to emphasize Stalin's nationality for a Georgian audience, he grew increasingly wary of stressing the fact too strongly before the broader Soviet public, particularly as he began to balance affirmations of the Soviet Union's multiethnic identity with limited expressions of Russian nationalism on the eve of the Second World War.[144]

Yet Stalin's patronage of Georgia's culture and its national cultural institutions built them up in ways that would prove enduring. The leader spent considerable time editing Konstantin Bal'mont's translation of Shota Rustaveli's medieval Georgian epic, *The Knight in the Panther's Skin*, for Soviet publication.[145] The work was central to Georgian national mythology and became even more so after Rustaveli was placed alongside Pushkin in the pantheon of Soviet high culture with Stalin's endorsement. According to Stalin's daughter, Rustaveli was the only poet the Soviet leader truly enjoyed reading.[146] The Georgian bard's epic poem celebrated warriors bound together in oaths of eternal friendship, "brothers more close than two friends, friends more dear than two brothers."[147] Not only was the poem a demonstrable achievement of Georgian high culture, it also likely had personal meaning for a group of Bolsheviks from the Caucasus held together by fraternal ties.

Stalin was also closely involved in the development of Soviet cinema, and he took a special interest in Georgian films that reached a wider Soviet audience.[148] Between 1938 and 1940 he helped handpick a screenplay for Georgian director Mikheil Chiaureli's film, *Giorgi Saakadze*.[149] Although the film celebrated the importance of political unity in the face of external enemies, a critical theme before the Second World War, its eponymous hero, a figure from seventeenth-century Georgian history, had particular resonance for Stalin and other Georgian Bolsheviks. A Georgian military leader, Saakadze converted to Islam and served with distinction in the Persian court of Shah Abbas, eventually assisting the Shah in leading the Persian military's invasion of Georgia. Once he returned to the soil of his native land, however, Saakadze changed course and set about uniting the feuding Georgian principalities, managing to drive the Persians—temporarily—from Georgia. Saakadze personally led the resistance against his former master, Shah Abbas, despite the fact that Saakadze's son, Paata, remained a hostage in the Persian court and was eventually put to death for his father's rebellion. Stalin's notes suggest that he appreciated the film because it showed Georgia to be a land too divided to rule itself and underlined the need for a strong central government to defend against external powers.[150] In this sense, Georgia, as a divided country in need of a strong leader, symbolized the entire Soviet Union. However, the complex historical figure of Giorgi Saakadze had deeper meaning for Stalin, who, like Saakadze, had directed the invasion of his native country in service to a larger entity. The comparison was not without its ambiguities. As a Georgian leader of the Soviet Union, Stalin could be cast as a military strategist who united a divided people, like Giorgi Saakadze, or a powerful centralizer who extended imperial rule over diverse nations, like Shah Abbas. Stalin once even asked Beria provocatively, "Do you think I am like the Shah?" In a private conversation, Beria confided to his wife that Stalin might very well "seize the son of one of his circle, have him beheaded, and send the head to the young man's father," as Shah Abbas had done to Georgi Saakadze.[151]

## The Death of a Political Generation

The Great Purges that swept the Soviet Union from 1936 to 1938 were presaged by earlier ideological battles and past uses of terror, but their sudden arrival after the triumphant adoption of the 1936 "Stalin" Constitution caught most party members off guard.[152] In retrospect, it is easy to point out that the Old Bolsheviks were no strangers to violence; they were a hardened group that had faced betrayals in the revolutionary underground, fought a bloody Civil War, and exiled and eliminated their political opponents. Yet before the purges, few predicted that these comrades-at-arms would turn on each other and that the style of politics in the Soviet state would undergo an important shift. The purges signified the replacement of lateral, often personalized ties among comrades with a more anonymous, vertically organized bureaucracy composed of replaceable officials. Decades-long friendships and alliances were destroyed as some of the Soviet Union's most prominent Old Bolsheviks were charged with conspiracy, espionage, and treason. The Great Purges decimated the ranks of those who had launched the Bolshevik project, while new cadres came to the fore as the revolution consumed its children. Stalin, however, remained, guiding the purges and emerging from them even stronger.[153] A committed revolutionary, he was perhaps prepared to go the furthest in casting aside the old bonds of family, friendship, and ethnic affinity in the singular interest of building a powerful imperial state.

This level of dedication was already evident in Stalin's correspondence with Sergo Orjonikidze in October 1931. In a series of letters exchanged about the formation of the state's industrialization policy, Stalin took Orjonikidze to task for failing to differentiate between political imperatives and personal feelings. While Orjonikidze had written a fraternizing letter addressed to "Soso" that included a Georgian-language aside about Molotov, whom Orjonikidze felt was impeding his industrialization efforts, the Great Leader responded with a more formal typewritten letter in Russian that he signed as Stalin. In his letter, Stalin temporarily set aside their friendship and ethnic affinity and assumed the role of political instructor, writing: "You have not yet learned to abstract yourself from the personal element in your relationships with other political leaders. This is not good. The personal (gripes and insults) should never eclipse the needs of the public, it must not blind a political leader . . . For this reason, I feel it is my duty to warn you that I cannot be your comrade in this matter."[154] While Stalin continued his pattern of intimate socialization with Orjonikidze and other Georgian Bolsheviks after composing this letter, he was clearly prepared to sacrifice the personal for the political. The achievement of state goals and the affirmation of ethnic bonds could be mutually reinforcing, but the two could also come into opposition. In his letter, Stalin made it clear which side he would favor if that occurred.

To a large extent, the purges took aim at the entrenched Soviet patronage networks that had accompanied Stalin in his rise to power. Given the initially low capacity of the Soviet state outside the center, at first it made sense to rely on trusted, skilled people to obtain resources and operate more or less autonomously, as had been the practice in the revolutionary underground. But by the late 1930s, it became clear that a short-term solution to low state capacity had become a long-term impediment to the construction of a bureaucratic state apparatus. The internal diaspora of Georgian revolutionaries that helped build socialism had outlived its usefulness and could be discarded. This was part of a larger effort to formalize the Soviet bureaucracy while strengthening Stalin's position, eliminating personalities, rivals, and all other brakes on state power.[155] It also paralleled an attempt to consolidate Soviet nations deemed politically loyal and to punish those who did not neatly fit within Soviet borders as disloyal. Hereafter, Soviet nations would be ranked in a more hierarchical fashion, with Russians praised as "first among equals," though still placed under the rule of a Georgian leader.

Because of the particularly close cultural, familial, and ethnic links among the Caucasian group, the purges hit this community with exceptional force. Abel Enukidze, one of the group's older members, was among the first to fall. "Uncle Abel" came under scrutiny for his lavish lifestyle, easygoing character, and relatively tolerant ideological outlook, the same traits that made him such a popular figure in the social life of the Soviet elite. The first accusations against him did not concern his administrative work, but instead his treatment of the shared history of the Caucasian group. Enukidze's account of the first Bolshevik underground printing presses in the Caucasus, issued in 1930, was republished in 1934.[156] While Stalin had apparently overlooked the book's initial publication, he eventually came to see it as a challenge to his image as the Soviet Union's most distinguished Bolshevik. Enukidze had arrived in Baku to set up the party organization before Stalin began working in the city and he was, in a sense, Stalin's revolutionary senior because he had collaborated closely with Stalin's late mentor, Lado Ketskhoveli. As a Georgian, Stalin was personally concerned with representations of his Caucasian past; as undisputed leader of the Soviet Union, he demanded recognition as the unrivalled frontrunner of the Caucasian group. Stalin covered page after page of Enukidze's manuscript with critical comments and incredulous exclamation points.[157] The criticism of Enukidze from other quarters soon followed, although with the exception of Stalin, Georgian Bolsheviks refrained from overt criticism. On January 6, 1935, Lev Mekhlis, the editor of *Pravda*, issued a detailed denunciation of Enukidze's account, accusing the Old Bolshevik, who chronicled the close ties among Georgian socialists before the party split, of "liberalism" in his treatment of Georgian Mensheviks.[158]

That same year, with Stalin's tacit approval, Nikolai Yezhov, soon to be head of the NKVD, led an investigation that charged Enukidze with the careless supervision of his employees in the Kremlin service administration, several of whom stood accused of participating in a "terrorist group" allegedly linked to Sergei Kirov's mysterious assassination.[159] After frantically trying to defend himself and personally pleading with Stalin, Enukidze was expelled from the party on charges of political abuse and private immorality. Significantly, Enukidze proved unwilling to prostrate himself before the party and admit his guilt in the fantastic plot of which he was accused of taking part. There is evidence that Stalin initially wavered in taking the drastic step of expelling an old member of the party, though he ultimately approved Enukdize's arrest and his eventual execution on dubious charges of espionage in 1937.[160] Enukidze's cousin, Simon, who once operated the Bolshevik underground press in Moscow, was executed a few months later. The downfall of Abel Enukidze, whose life and career was intertwined with the leader's family, was a personal matter for Stalin; after all, Enukidze was the godfather of Stalin's second wife and employed the sister of Stalin's first wife, Maro Svanidze, as his personal secretary. Only a few years before, in September 1933, Stalin had written to Enukidze in exceptionally tender and familiar terms:

> What is keeping you in Moscow? Come to Sochi, bathe in the sea and give your heart a rest. Tell Kalinin [the Chairman of the Executive Committee, and Enukidze's superior] that he is committing a crime if he does not let you take a vacation, if only for a few weeks. You could live with me at the dacha, where—after Svetlana's [Stalin's daughter's] departure I am sitting all alone, like an owl.[161]

Enukidze's fall from grace was a stunning turn of events that sent shockwaves throughout the diaspora of Georgian Bolsheviks.

Political repressions subsequently began to encroach on Sergo Orjonikidze, another longtime Stalin ally. In January 1935, Orjonikidze's political client in Magnitogorsk, Beso Lominadze, committed suicide in the vain hope of sparing his family from political persecution. A devout believer in socialism to the end, he left a note for his patron, writing: "I die fully believing in the victory of our cause."[162] In 1936, Orjonikidze's trusted deputy at NKTP, Georgii Piatakov, was arrested on charges of belonging to a secret Trotskyite cell engaged in industrial sabotage. Orjonikidze likely recognized that the many challenges faced by heavy industry were not the result of "wrecking," but nevertheless was unable to intervene to save his longtime associate, who was tried and executed. In October 1936, around the time of the celebration of his fiftieth birthday, Orjonikidze learned that his brother Papulia had been arrested in Georgia. Evidence suggests that Stalin also began to look disapprovingly at the eulogistic publications on Orjonikidze's revolutionary career that appeared in honor of the Commissar's birthday.[163] Orjonikidze could do nothing as some of his oldest colleagues and associates from Georgia were arrested. On February 18, 1937, the day before a Central Committee plenum at which Orjonikidze had been asked to deliver a speech on "sabotage" in heavy industry, the Commissar of Heavy Industry shot himself in his apartment.[164] According to the account of a contemporary, hours before his suicide Orjonikidze exchanged heated insults in Georgian with Stalin on the telephone, irate that his apartment had been searched by the NKVD and adamantly refusing to be intimidated.[165] On February 19, 1937, Soviet newspapers solemnly announced that "Comrade Sergo" had tragically died of a sudden heart attack.

After the death of their patron, Orjonikidze's remaining clients and comrades were quickly consumed by the purges. Orjonikidze's brothers were executed, as was his nephew, Giorgi Gvakharia. His wife, Zinaida, was sentenced to ten years in prison. Shalva Eliava, whom Orjonikidze had helped promote to the Ministry of Foreign Trade and later the Ministry of Light Industry, was arrested and executed in December 1937. Mamia Orakhelashvili, who had worked with Orjonikidze to orchestrate the Red Army's invasion of Georgia and once served as deputy chairman of the Soviet Council of People's Commissars, was executed the same month. Shalva Okujava was arrested in Nizhnyi Tagil, near the massive industrial site he supervised, and shot; Okujava's wife was sent to the Gulag.[166] Their son, Bulat Okujava, the future Soviet poet and bard, had to be raised in Tbilisi by relatives. A generation of Georgian Bolsheviks who grew up together in the fraternity of late imperial Russia's revolutionary underground, including Malakia Toroshelidze, Galaktion Vashadze, Tengiz Zhghenti, and Shamshe Lezhava, perished in 1937 and 1938. Entire families were destroyed as relatives and spouses were arrested and children separated from their parents.

Few remained of Stalin's original comrades from the Caucasus. Of the most prominent Georgian Bolsheviks, only the aging Mikha Tskhakaia and Pilipe Makharadze survived, both largely retired from Soviet political life. Anastas Mikoian, Stalin's junior by nearly two decades and one of the younger Old Bolsheviks, continued to join Stalin for the sumptuous feasts held by the Soviet leader. However, unlike the spontaneous celebrations of the early 1930s, an atmosphere of fear and paranoia characterized these dinners. Bolsheviks fully subordinate to Stalin were terrified of crossing the Great Leader, while Stalin was suspicious of his food being poisoned.[167] The performance of Georgianness among the political elite was no longer spontaneous but curtailed and restricted, though it did not disappear altogether.

Lavrenti Beria was a new figure at these banquets, having been called up to Moscow in 1938 to head the NKVD. In the Soviet capital, well-founded rumors spread concerning the leading role played by Beria in arresting and executing scores of prominent Georgian Old Bolsheviks.[168] Even as he helped bring down the original Caucasian group, Beria actively sought to forge a culturally and politically intimate relationship with Stalin. While based in Tbilisi, Beria had collaborated closely with Stalin to write a history of the Bolshevik party in Transcaucasia that set aside the "falsehoods" of Enukidze's account and cast Stalin in the leading role.[169] Second to Stalin, Beria posed as the authoritative expert on the history of the Bolshevik movement in the Caucasus, even though he wrote of events that occurred before his birth in 1899.

According to the memoirs of Nikita Khrushchev, who blamed Beria for the worst excesses of high Stalinism, the Georgian NKVD chief sought to further ingratiate himself by serving as a *tamada* for Stalin's feasts. Krushchev recalled:

When no one wanted to drink and Beria saw that Stalin had a need for a drink, Beria immediately organized a round of toasts;

he would think up all sorts of pretexts and act as ringleader. . . .
People were literally becoming drunkards, and the more a person became a drunkard, the more pleasure Stalin got from it.[170]

Beria reportedly surrounded Stalin with Georgian waiters and wait-
resses around the table and Georgian servants at home. According to
Khrushchev, even Stalin grew suspicious of all of the Georgians among his
staff. At a dinner, he suddenly asked: "Why are there so many Georgians
around; where have they come from?" Beria replied that "these are people who are loyal to you." To which Stalin angrily responded, "What are
you saying? That Georgians are loyal and Russians are not?" The next
day, dinner was served by an all-Russian staff, and at least for a while,
the Georgian servants were hidden from view.[171] Nevertheless, Beria's
rise demonstrated that knowledge of Georgian culture, and expertise in
the party's roots in the Caucasus, could still be an asset in serving Stalin.
Although the aging dictator had sought to transcend his Georgianness,
at other times he fell back upon it. As long as Stalin was in power, the
complete depersonalization of politics was impossible. His efforts to
construct a bureaucratic state were ultimately undermined by a system
that gave him absolute authority and opened up specialized opportunities for those subordinate to him.

    Although lateral circles of friends around Stalin had been eliminated,
close-knit ethnic networks proved tenacious in an uncertain and often
arbitrary political environment. Like the Georgian Bolsheviks before
him, Beria brought his closest associates from the Caucasus with him
when he was promoted to Moscow. One deputy, Stepan Mamulov, an
Armenian from Tbilisi, was appointed to administer the Gulag system. Another Tbilisi Armenian, Bogdan Kobulov, later helped organize NKVD-orchestrated ethnic deportations in Crimea and the North
Caucasus. Operating under Beria's direction, Vladimir Dekanozov
(Dekanozishvili) carried out purges in the Red Army and in 1940 supervised the forcible incorporation of Lithuania into the Soviet Union.
Beria's associates from Georgia were promoted to leading posts across
the Soviet Union. Among them were Sergo Goglidze, who became the
head of the Leningrad NKVD; Lavrenti Tsanava, appointed to lead the

NKVD in Belarus; Grigol Karanadze, in charge of the NKVD in Crimea; Aleksi Sajaia, heading the NKVD in Uzbekistan; Mikheil Gvishiani, running the secret police in the Russian Far East; and Amaiak Kobulov, Bogdan Kobulov's brother, in charge of the NKVD in Ukraine.[172] A generation of Caucasian Bolsheviks had perished, but under Beria a new one rose to take its place. Leading the secretive NKVD in posts across the Soviet Union, Beria's group was not as visible, but was no less influential in administering the Soviet state.

However, the differences that distinguished Beria's network from those that preceded it were emblematic of broader political changes. Too young to have taken part in the revolutionary underground, they were a professional class for whom state service offered the possibility of career advancement.[173] Most were educated in the institutions of the new state and ascended through the ranks of the state's expanding police force. Subordinates rather than comrades, bureaucratic enforcers instead of state-builders, they rose in influence as Stalin turned to the police, rather than the party, to rule in the wake of the purges.[174] Like the Old Bolsheviks before them, they accepted that violence was sometimes necessary to accomplish socialist aims, yet they were less likely to be restrained by notions of friendship, brotherhood, and honor, seeing them as antiquated concepts associated with the old regime that had helped bring about the downfall of the prior generation of party leaders in the purges.[175]

Georgians were not alone in seeking advancement through the state's security apparatus, and a variety of other ethnic networks could be identified in the NKVD. However, the new police networks tended to reflect the emergent hierarchy of Soviet nations. If the Old Bolsheviks arose from a revolution of outsiders that placed a diverse array of mobile nationalities in prominent positions of power, then the new police clans favored Russians as well as members of internal diasporas from constituent Soviet republics. Poles, Latvians, and Germans, now deemed "foreign nationalities," all but disappeared from the leadership of the NKVD by 1939. From 1937 to 1939, the number of Jews in top NKVD posts was cut from 42 to six, while the number of Russians and Ukrainians in leadership positions nearly tripled, and the number of Georgians more than doubled.[176] Since the state had proclaimed its triumph over class-based enemies like kulaks, the foremost measure of ideological loyalty now became nationality, and those without a defined place on the Soviet map were considered untrustworthy.

Until the end of Stalin's reign and even amidst his "anti-cosmopolitan campaign," internal diasporas from Soviet republics were promoted to prominent political positions. Indeed, after weathering an attack on his network that accused its members of a subethnic and regional Mingrelian allegiance rather than a more clearly defined Georgian and Soviet loyalty, Beria nearly succeeded Stalin as undisputed leader of the Soviet Union by exploiting his position as police chief.[177] Shortly after Stalin's death in 1953, however, Beria and his closest associates were hastily tried and executed by a group of Bolsheviks fearful of their own safety. It was the Soviet Union's last episode of violence among party members and reflected the potential risks of consolidating power in a police force that many in the party—and among the population—believed had grown too strong.[178] After Stalin and Beria, the Soviet Union saw the rise of a postwar elite that was predominantly Slavic and more comfortable appealing to the state's Russian majority. There would be no more Georgians in top political positions until the appointment of Eduard Shevardnadze as Minister of Foreign Affairs in 1985.[179] Yet even as the state began to look more like a Russian empire, Soviet culture was imbued in ever more inventive ways by networks of Georgian culinary specialists and cultural entrepreneurs.

# 3

# Edible Ethnicity

It is little surprise that one of Joseph Stalin's most famous speeches was given in the form of a toast. On May 24, 1945, the leaders of the victorious Red Army were received in the Kremlin's expansive Georgievskii Hall and seated at heavily laden tables beneath sparkling chandeliers.[1] Thirty-one toasts were drunk that evening, but the last was the most memorable. Stalin stood up from his chair in the center of the main table and asked permission to say the final toast, drawing frenzied applause from the assembled officers. Raising his glass, he began predictably: "As the representative of our Soviet government, I would like to propose a toast to our Soviet people." Then, unexpectedly, he added: "And, in the first place, the Russian people." The crowd began to wildly cheer "hurrah!" Stalin thanked the Russian people for their unfailing "trust" and drank to their health, amidst applause that, according to the transcript of the event, was loud and prolonged.[2] The toast was reprinted the next day on the front page of the newspaper *Pravda* for all Soviet citizens to read.[3] Its assertion of Russian primacy has earned it a central place in historiography charting the rise of state-sponsored Russian nationalism.

While the speech's content has been frequently analyzed, its form has generally been neglected.[4] The form of a toast allowed Stalin to combine confessional candor with the spirit of jubilation required for the occasion.[5] As a Georgian, Stalin was likely seen by the guests as a natural *tamada*, a Georgian term that had become an official part of the Russian vocabulary a few years earlier.[6] Arguably, only a non-Russian could propose a toast to the Russian people. Spoken by a Russian, the

toast would violate the norms of Soviet domestic internationalism and
the rules of ritual; it would seem chauvinistic to single out one's own
people for praise and self-congratulatory to raise a glass to oneself. The
toast instead was given to the largest nationality in the Soviet empire by
an ethnically distinct admirer whose life had long been intertwined with
Russia.

Stalin ruled the Soviet Union as he governed the table; as chief
*tamada*, he was an authoritarian speechmaker, an observer of human
character and its weaknesses, and the king of an imperial court composed of competing factions and eager aspirants.[7] As Stalin toasted
the Russian people and the Georgian practice of having a *tamada* lead
festivities became a Soviet institution, it was increasingly likely that
the Soviet table was laden with Georgian cheese pies (*khachapuri*) and
spicy Georgian soup (*kharcho*), accompanied by Georgian wines and the
Georgian mineral water Borjomi. Although Stalin raised his glass to the
Russian people, the fact that he gave his speech as a Georgian-style toast
shows that Soviet culture continued to be constructed by the contributions of non-Russians.

An examination of the evolving Soviet empire from a culinary perspective reveals the extent to which the state remained committed to
promoting its brand of domestic internationalism in the everyday lives
of its citizens. Beginning in the 1930s, this effort entailed the creation of
a consumer culture based on the domestic production of cheaper copies of foreign luxury goods, on the one hand, and the state's elevation of
domestic national traditions of the Soviet peoples to the realm of high
culture, on the other.[8] Soviet planners not only began to produce their
own "Soviet champagne," but they also sought to create a multiethnic
cuisine that privileged the culinary practices of the non-Russian national
republics. The effort to construct an imperial cuisine had its parallels
among other empires: Dutch colonists embraced the *rijsttafel* (rice table)
as a way of showcasing the abundance and diversity of the Dutch East
Indies in one elaborate spread; British rule over India popularized the
use of chutney throughout the empire and eventually fostered the development of hybrid dishes like creamy chicken tikka masala. Unlike curry
houses in Britain, however, national restaurants in the Soviet Union were
tirelessly promoted by the state itself.[9] As in Mussolini's Italy, another

twentieth-century empire bent on rapid modernization, the Soviet state sought to reach into the home and transform the everyday habits of its citizens through food and drink.[10] However, while the Fascists emphasized an austere diet to engender lean and healthy bodies, the new Soviet diet offered a taste of a bountiful socialist future, served in a multiplicity of national forms.

In creating a cuisine that would be "national in form" and "socialist in content," the Soviet state funded the large-scale domestic production of national ingredients and vigorously endorsed the recipes of its internal diasporas. The new Soviet diet included not just Russian cabbage soup, but Ukrainian *borshch*, Uzbek *plov* (pilaf), melons from Central Asia, and oranges from the Caucasus. Vodka arguably remained Russia's national beverage, but Soviet consumers also drank Georgian wine, Armenian cognac, and eventually liqueurs from Tallinn and Riga. Far from being simply an administrative category, ethnicity itself became edible, and Sovietness something one could consume around the table.

Some nations had more to contribute to the state-funded development of multiethnic Soviet culture than others. While the ideology of the "friendship of the peoples" reserved a place at the Soviet table for the cuisine of each titular nationality, the ideological connotations and intrinsic versatility of Georgian food proved to be to its advantage. Although ethnically exotic in its appeal, with its elaborate rituals and vast range of dishes, it was seen not as a peasant food, but instead a refined cuisine appropriate for the Soviet middle class that emerged in the 1930s.[11] It also helped that the iconography of the Georgian table, celebrated by prerevolutionary Georgian artists like Niko Pirosmani, fit perfectly with the new emphasis on socialist abundance.[12] With its dishes pushed up against one another, offering eaters a range of choices and courses served simultaneously, and drinking horns filled to the brim with Georgian wine, the Georgian table was a stunning cornucopia that best embodied the socialist realist dream of imminent utopia.

Soviet multiethnicity around the dinner table was largely concocted from preexisting ingredients. Soviet planners did not create Georgian dishes from scratch, nor the rituals of the Georgian table that accompanied them as they were popularized. Indeed, Georgian food and drink were the focus of practices that predated Stalin and came to shape broader Soviet consumption habits. Georgian feasts were lavish and highly ritualized affairs, obligatory festivals of consumption used to mark birthdays and funerals, to celebrate reunions, and to establish and demonstratively affirm social ties and business partnerships. The quality and quantity of food and wine at a Georgian feast reflected the honor of the host, and Georgian tables groaned under a dazzling variety of dishes that were endlessly replenished. The feast (*supra*) was led by the *tamada*, who was more than an average toastmaster; he (at a Georgian table, the *tamada* was always a man) was an orator, a mediator and peacemaker among guests, and a demonstrative host.[13] A good *tamada* skilled in the arts of *tamadoba* (leading a table in toasting) needed to sense and direct the moods and desires of his guests, from jubilation to nostalgia, yet also had to maintain self-control in the face of copious amounts of wine drunk down in one shot from a glass, a drinking horn, or a large vessel. Dining in Georgia was a highly regimented affair in which the number and nature of toasts were known by all, and gender roles, as well as the respective roles of host and guest, were carefully inscribed. As a sophisticated cuisine whose ethnic distinctiveness was emphasized by the state, Georgian food and drink were believed to be best enjoyed in tandem with some of these elaborate Georgian toasting rituals, and soon Russians were not only consuming the food of the periphery, but also toasting one another in the Georgian manner.

In its promotion of multiethnic culture the state was forced to rely on ethnic specialists drawn from its internal diasporas, who capitalized on state promotion to pursue their own agendas. The state's endorsement of Georgian cuisine opened up new opportunities beyond the Georgian SSR for Georgian chefs, restaurateurs, and other culinary experts. Migrating from the Caucasus to Moscow, the Georgian diaspora connected the culture of the state's periphery with the tastes of its center. The history of Georgian cuisine's ascendance reveals how the agendas of official Soviet institutions were shaped by the diasporic networks of national experts they depended upon.

This chapter explores how the multiethnic fabric of Soviet society manifested itself in the realm of material culture and everyday life around the dinner table. Here the multiethnic nature of the Soviet

*Figure 3.1* A posed photograph from the late nineteenth century depicting a group of Georgian men at a *supra*. Library of Congress.

Union was expressed deliberately, but played out beyond the full control of the state. In a manner that recalled the diffusion of norms of personal conduct central to sociologist Norbert Elias's "civilizing process" yet involved a much greater degree of state promotion, Georgian food and drink were introduced in Stalin's court before percolating downward to the elite restaurant, the worker's cafeteria, and the private kitchen.[14] The consumption of Georgian food and drink became a practice of social distinction for upwardly mobile Soviets in part because Georgian dishes were known to be favored by Stalin himself, and because in partaking of a non-Russian cuisine, Soviets diners endorsed the state's policy of a "friendship of the peoples."[15] Yet Georgian food's popularity outlived Stalin, and was introduced to the broader Soviet public as an established form of cultural sophistication under Khrushchev. Importantly, even as Georgia's rich culinary culture was adopted by citizens across the Soviet empire, the readily identifiable otherness of Georgian cuisine also made it central to new forms of distinction separate from, and sometimes in opposition to, official life.

# Georgian Cuisine and the Rise of the Soviet Middle Class

The development of fine dining in the Soviet Union had its roots in the mid-1930s, when the new Soviet middle class of managers, bureaucrats, NKVD officers, engineers, and privileged workers began to develop an appetite for a more sophisticated cuisine.[16] Culinary opportunities were just one of the novel forms of consumption created as the state sought to develop appropriate material rewards for its loyal cadres. Production lines were constructed to produce new Soviet suits and dresses, along with Soviet perfume, luxury cars, sofas, and lampshades. In 1934 the Eliseev Store, Moscow's lavish prerevolutionary food emporium, reopened as Grocery Store No. 1, offering thirty-eight kinds of sausage, three kinds of cheese, two hundred kinds of candies and pastries, fifty kinds of bread, meat in refrigerated glass cases, and live fish in tanks.[17] The material benefits enjoyed by the elite and accompanying depictions of material abundance were held to represent the promise of socialism for all Soviet citizens, and they embodied Stalin's oft-repeated public claim of the era: "Life has become better, life has become more joyous."[18]

The new Soviet consumer society was driven both by the aspirations of the *arriviste* Soviet elite and the state's effort to cultivate an ideologically correct sense of *kulturnost'* (cultured behavior). As a replacement for European fine dining, Georgian food was seen as a suitable substitute for the French fare previously served in tsarist Russia's finest restaurants.[19] Just as the new Soviet "champagne" was produced with grapes grown in southern Russia and Armenian "cognac" replaced its French counterpart, so too did Georgian cuisine represent a domestic and readily available alternative. Unlike other substitutes for prerevolutionary luxuries, however, Georgian food was not a second-rate replica but the genuine article, a culinary tradition with an established repertoire of dishes.

The bold and subtle flavors of Georgian cuisine conveyed the Mediterranean sensibilities of the republic's warm climate and allowed it to fill the vacuum created by the disappearance of French cuisine. Georgian dining appealed to the Soviet palate with a range of highly developed and recognizable tastes: roasted, grilled, and stewed meats, complex seasonings composed of coriander, saffron, and other rare spices, and subtle sauces combining sweet and savory flavors with the taste of pomegranates, walnuts, and tangy plums. Some of these tastes and flavor combinations were seen as uniquely local, while others were exotically linked to the longstanding influence of Persian and Turkish foodways in the Caucasus. However, the Georgian cuisine encountered by the Soviet state had taken shape in the cosmopolitan environment of prerevolutionary Tbilisi and also reflected nineteenth-century European and Russian dining trends. The first major Georgian-language cookbook, published by Barbare Jorjadze in Tbilisi in 1874, was in fact modeled on Elena Molokhovets's popular Russian cookbook *A Gift to Young Housewives*, written thirteen years earlier. Jorjadze's recipes included Georgian, Persian, and Turkish dishes, but also Russian *zharkoe* (beef stew) and fashionable French-style deserts such as blancmange.[20]

The repertoire of modern Georgian cuisine was forged in the restaurants and taverns that became popular in late-nineteenth-century Tbilisi. Under Russian imperial rule these establishments became important spaces of socialization, moving the *supra*, which literally means "tablecloth," indoors. Rather than reclining on a cloth spread on the grounds of one of Tbilisi's outdoor gardens, urban diners sat around a restaurant table.[21] Georgian dining practices also underwent a significant shift in this period, with longer and more formalized toasts led by a *tamada* celebrated as an explicitly national practice, even if it had little precedent before the nineteenth century.[22] Tbilisi's restaurants aided in the development of a self-consciously national cuisine, bringing the diverse flavors of Georgia's regions together in an urban context, matching tasty food with vintage wines and brandy, and formalizing the dining experience.

Georgian cuisine was not altogether unfamiliar to the Russian palate at the start of the Soviet period. According to historian Louise McReynolds, by the end of the nineteenth century, most major Russian cities "had at least one dining spot named for somewhere in the Caucasus or Central Asia."[23] As in other European metropoles, novel dishes and spices from distant territories allowed those in imperial Russia's center to tour and taste the empire without leaving the comforts of home. *Shashlyk*, the grilled meat from the Caucasus, had appeared on Russian menus in the nineteenth century, following Russia's expansion into the mountainous region, and Georgian meat stew (*chakhokhbili*) was already in circulation at the establishment of Soviet power.[24] Helping promote these recipes, Georgian chefs could be found working in restaurants in Russian cities or serving food along imperial Russia's railway networks.[25] Accordingly, at the outset of the state's promotion of multiethnic cuisine, Georgians were arguably better established in Moscow than culinary specialists from the other national republics.

The Soviet context, however, opened up a new infrastructure for the dissemination of Georgian cooking. Of primary importance was the establishment in 1931 of Obshchepit (Obshchestvennoe pitanie), the state-sponsored Public Food Service, which performed the dual function of responding to popular demand while cultivating public taste.[26] Recipes and dishes adopted after careful deliberation by Obshchepit in Moscow immediately appeared in cafeterias and dining establishments everywhere from Tallinn to Tashkent. In its formative years Obshchepit was presided over by Anastas Mikoian, who had received his education in Tbilisi, and its activities were closely supervised by Stalin himself.[27] In the 1920s, Obshchepit saw debates between "futurists," who argued for scientific means of meeting the needs of public nutrition, and "traditionalists," who called for the popularization of prerevolutionary bourgeois cuisine.[28] The plans of the futurists, including their promotion of factory-produced vegetarian substitutes, came under fire from Stalin for failing to take into account popular tastes, while the traditionalists' promotion of prerevolutionary recipes was untenable because the necessary ingredients, sometimes scarce and of foreign origin, were no longer available.[29] Responding to the ascent of the new middle class, Obshchepit settled on a socialist realist menu of dishes that celebrated material abundance and the idea of eating for pleasure, but were made from domestically produced ingredients.

In contrast to other imperial settings, where the food of the periphery was merely meant to embellish the core diet of the center, the new Soviet cuisine was to be based entirely on the meeting and mixing of national cuisines on equal terms, an idealized reflection of the federal structure of the Union of Soviet Socialist Republics. In its introduction, a major Soviet cookbook did not single out one national cuisine as its main component but instead lavished praise equally on Russian *zakuski* (appetizers), Ukrainian *borshch*, and Uzbek *plov*.[30] The Soviet state even briefly promoted the development of a domesticated Jewish cuisine—though as one historian points out, an officially endorsed recipe for matzo ball soup made without matzo did not exactly smack of authenticity.[31] More enduring was the state's promotion of the cuisine of nationalities rooted in titular republics, where internal diasporas enjoyed access to supply chains that linked restaurants and cafes in the center with republic-level suppliers of key ingredients.

Of these domestic national cuisines, Georgian cuisine was the most favorably positioned, the most energetically patronized by the Soviet Union's Caucasian leadership, and the most appealing to popular tastes. As familiar strangers in the Soviet kitchen, the Georgian diaspora helped spread the distinctive culinary traditions of their homeland and carved out a niche for themselves as bearers of specialized knowledge about Georgian cooking. Their participation in the creation of a multiethnic Soviet diet brought professional and material success, but sometimes meant altering national recipes to suit imperial demands.

## Providing For Stalin's Table

The state's promotion of Georgian feasting practices first began in the halls of the Kremlin, around Stalin's own table. Meals with Stalin were coveted opportunities for political access, as well as dangerous occasions fraught with competitive drinking and toasts filled with threatening insinuation. Those close to Stalin might have done well to heed the warning of Lenin, who, when speaking of the Georgian revolutionary, allegedly stated: "That cook will concoct nothing but peppery dishes."[32] While the taste and range of Georgian cooking were appealing on their own, the desire to please Stalin made Georgian food and drink necessary components of any elite gathering. During Stalin's long rule supply chains were established to provide Georgian food and drink for the Kremlin table, administered by Georgian culinary specialists often selected by the Great Leader himself. Stalin's taste preferences and personal support helped set a fixed menu of culinary options for Soviet society that was notably Georgian in character.

Distinctive practices of consumption had in part defined the "Caucasian group" that accompanied Stalin in his rise to power. Appointed to high positions in Moscow, revolutionaries from the Caucasus brought their eating habits and their regional traditions of feasting and hospitality with them. Based in the Kremlin in the early 1930s, Abel Enukidze would stop by Stalin's office with baskets full of Georgian wines and tangerines, prompting spontaneous feasting celebrations at which Georgian songs were sung until dawn.[33] Group members bonded over stories of their revolutionary careers in the Caucasus shared around the table. For Stalin and his revolutionary companions food and drink were more than sustenance; they were vital components for intimate rituals expressing loyalty and affirming political and personal relationships.

Beginning in the early 1930s, a vast infrastructure of feasting was set up, stretching from Moscow to Georgia, to provide for the appetites of these top Soviet officials. The provision of supplies for Kholodnaia Rechka, Stalin's dacha on Abkhazia's Black Sea coast, was a matter of state concern that brought leading officials into the business of supplying foodstuffs. Helping supervise construction work at Stalin's dacha, Giorgi Sturua, the Deputy Commissar of Justice of the Transcaucasus Federation, personally saw to it that fifty orange trees were planted on the grounds.[34] Stalin loved to cultivate his own oranges and lemons, and helped promote the development of citrus production in the Caucasus, placing Mikoian in charge of distribution in the hope that the region's fruits could be sold throughout the Soviet Union.[35] Delegations from the region's local party leadership visiting the dacha brought gifts of food and wine, since dining with Stalin could make a party activist's career. Nestor Lakoba, the Communist Party chief of Abkhazia, performed the crucial role of overseeing the autonomous republic's network of resorts, where other political figures vacationed nearby. Photographs taken of Stalin at his Black Sea dacha show him seated at a dining table, working amidst stacks of files against a lush background of subtropical vegetation.[36] For Stalin and others in positions of leadership, work and leisure, dining and the affairs of state, were fused together.

Stalin's patronage helped spur the development of Georgian food and drink networks that linked specialized Georgian producers to elite political circles in Moscow. Stalin loved the wines of his native Georgia, particularly the semisweet Kindzmarauli. In such matters, the Great Leader was more than just a connoisseur; in 1936, Stalin's personal intervention had been crucial in launching the production of Soviet champagne.[37] With Stalin's tacit approval, the Georgian Ministry of Food Production opened a Moscow branch of the Georgian Union of Wine Producers, which shipped grapes from Georgia for wine and cognac production in the Soviet capital. A variety of wines and spirits were supplied directly to the Kremlin, including Stalin's beloved Kindzmarauli, along with cases of the Georgian mineral water Borjomi, the Georgian cheese Sulguni, and the distinctive Georgian herbs and spices necessary for preparing Georgian dishes in Moscow.[38]

A number of Georgians from Stalin's hometown of Gori arrived in Moscow to oversee food production for the Georgian feasts held in the Kremlin and at Stalin's dacha, all of them hand-picked by the Soviet leader for their combination of personal loyalty and expertise in Georgian cuisine. The first to arrive was Aleksandre Egnatashvili, Stalin's boyhood friend and a former owner of a chain of restaurants in Baku and Tbilisi, who in 1934 became an NKVD officer and deputy chief of Stalin's personal security service in charge of household affairs.[39] Under Egnatashvili's supervision, a facility was constructed at Zarech'e, outside Moscow, to supply the Kremlin's tables directly. This production base included a turkey farm to raise fowl for the Georgian dish *satsivi* and a greenhouse full of vegetables and herbs needed to cook Georgian food. Zarech'e also had its own wine cellar, run by Pavle Rusishvili, a friend of Egnatashvili's who had known Stalin as a schoolboy and for a time operated a restaurant in Georgia. Like Egnatashvili, Rusishvili was promoted to the post of officer in the NKVD and tasked with the shipment of wines and food supplies from Georgia. He also supervised the provision of meat for the Kremlin, sometimes even arranging the shipment of choice mutton directly from Georgia for the preparation of *shashlyk*. To help him run the operation, Egnatashvili brought in two more friends from Gori, one to help Rusishvili with wine shipments and another to assist with production.[40]

The services provided by these Georgian culinary specialists gave them unprecedented access to Stalin, alarming others who vied for the leader's favor. The appointment of Egnatashvili and Rusishvili to top positions in the NKVD particularly dismayed Nikita Khrushchev. In his memoirs, Khrushchev was critical of the ascendance of Egnatashvili, who rose through the ranks as Stalin's food supplier and was eventually promoted to lieutenant general during the Second World War. Emphasizing the righteousness of his own path as a revolutionary, Khrushchev expressed dismay that Egnatashvili, a former Georgian "tavern owner," now sat with him at the same table and addressed him as an equal.[41] While Egnatashvili's rapid professional advancement was remarkable, it was not entirely unusual that he and Rusishvili attained positions within the NKVD. Because state trade—of which food distribution was an important part—was both critical on a practical level and viewed with ideological suspicion as a source of potential corruption, the NKVD played a leading role in supervising trade operations, especially in the Soviet capital.[42] The NKVD may also have been so intimately involved in culinary practices because Stalin's fear of being poisoned made food supply a matter of state security. Even as he was promoted within the NKVD, Egnatashvili earned the dubious nickname of "the rabbit," since Stalin also forced him to serve as a personal food taster.[43]

Stalin played host at elite gatherings around the table, pronouncing his food preferences and dictating his choices to those around him. In his memoirs, Mikoian recalled that Stalin loved to think up and then specially order dishes of his own creation for his dining companions. The Soviet leader created a dish that combined eggplants, tomatoes, potatoes, black pepper, bay leaf, and pieces of lamb, which he adorned with cilantro and named "Aragvi," after the famous Georgian river. Mikoian admitted that the Georgian-inspired dish was actually quite tasty.[44] Stalin's dinners were typically punctuated with Georgian-style toasts and sometimes concluded with Georgian songs and dances.[45]

Dining with Stalin was vital for political access, but it required participating in Caucasian rites of the table. Such rituals continued even after the demise of many Georgian Old Bolsheviks in the purges, though the behavior of the diners shifted from celebratory camaraderie to sycophantic competition. As someone from the Caucasus who survived the purges, Mikoian was not as disoriented by the ongoing Georgian-style feasts in the Kremlin as were others from outside the region.

The Armenian revolutionary was not surprised that Lavrenti Beria ate fresh greens with his hands, as was customary in the Caucasus. Similarly, though appalled with the rising level of alcohol consumption at these gatherings, Mikoian was not particularly concerned by Stalin's admission that his father had taught him to drink as a child by dipping his finger into a glass of wine and having him suck on his finger. Khrushchev, unfamiliar with the Caucasus and its traditions of viticulture, was disgusted by Beria's table manners and thought that the father's giving wine to his young boy had led to Stalin's heavy drinking later in life.[46] However, Khrushchev and the rest of Stalin's inner circle did their best to imitate Georgian-style practices of dining when sharing meals with the Great Leader.

Foreign visitors traveling to Moscow were shocked at how central these endless feasts had become to the operation of the Soviet state. The Yugoslav Communist Milovan Djilas described elaborate dinners lasting six or more hours, from late in the evening to four or five in the morning. Recalling the experience, he wrote:

> One ate and drank slowly, during a rambling conversation which ranged from stories and anecdotes to the most serious political and even philosophical subjects. Unofficially and in actual fact a significant part of Soviet policy was shaped at these dinners.[47]

According to Djilas, Stalin was a consummate toastmaster. The Soviet leader used toasts to flatter, cajole, and chide, as well as to express personal nostalgia and address political issues. A rift with the Yugoslav party was temporarily mended when Djilas agreed to drink to the Red Army, though as a Georgian, Stalin found it problematic that Djilas drank the toast with beer.[48] Molotov told Djilas of how Stalin's toast to secret agents at a wartime dinner with Winston Churchill had been a subtle jab at the British leader, who in Stalin's view had lost the battle at Gallipoli because he lacked sufficient information.[49]

Under Stalin, toasting became a form of speechmaking adopted by the Soviet elite. Elaborate toasts incorporating political themes were even made at intimate family gatherings held at the dachas of Soviet party leaders. Svetlana Allilueva, Stalin's daughter, recalled how Kliment

Voroshilov, an important Politburo member, used to stand up at small dinners with her, his wife, and his family and make long, formal toasts, and she remembered Nikolai Shvernik, the Chairman of the Presidium of the Supreme Soviet, doing the same.[50] Such toasting continued after Stalin's death.

Stalin's support helped launch Georgian culinary practices into the broader Soviet culture, lending a distinctly Georgian flavor to the Soviet kitchen. Reflecting its favorable status among the Soviet leadership, a Georgian cookbook was among the first of the national cookbooks published by the Soviet state; consisting of one hundred recipes, it was twice as long as the other national cookbooks published around the same time.[51] By the end of the 1930s, Georgian food and drink had gained a prominent place in Moscow's restaurants and specialty stores. As a result, aspiring members of the Soviet elite were offered a taste of the dining practices of Stalin's Kremlin. At the same time, Georgian culinary specialists sought out new opportunities in Moscow as they took advantage of state support and growing popular demand.

## Dining Out in the Soviet Capital

In a Soviet-era joke, two Georgians walk out of the Aragvi, the Soviet Union's most famous Georgian restaurant, located in the very center of Moscow. Noticing the monumental statue outside the restaurant's entrance, one turns to the other and says: "*Genatsvale*, who is that handsome and impressive man sitting on the horse?"[52] The other replies: "Do you really not know? That's Yuri Dolgorukii, the founder of Moscow!" In response, the first Georgian exclaims: "What a remarkable man! He built a lovely city around our restaurant."[53] Georgians' Soviet-era reputation for self-aggrandizement aside, the restaurant Aragvi, first opened in 1940, in fact predated the famous statue of Dolgorukii by fourteen years. During the Stalinist refashioning of the Soviet capital in the late 1930s, a prime, two-story location was found for the restaurant along Gorky Street, Moscow's main thoroughfare.[54] After World War II and especially during the Thaw years, it became a model for Soviet fine dining and a center for the diffusion of Georgian cuisine among the broader Soviet elite.

Upwardly mobile party members passed through the Aragvi's doors to see a lavish reproduction of Georgia, vividly rendered in socialist realist style for a pan-Soviet clientele. Gigantic frescoes adorned the walls, richly depicting the southern republic's agricultural abundance and instructively detailing the rituals of the Georgian table. The restaurant was composed of two main halls: an Eastern Hall, decorated with Georgian national motifs, and a Marble Hall, often used for official ceremonies.[55] Guests were entertained by a roving band of Georgian musicians and, on special occasions, a Georgian dance ensemble.[56] An ornate balcony ran along the second level of the Marble Hall, with a view over the tables below. The Aragvi was both a place for the new Soviet elite to engage in ideologically sanctioned conspicuous consumption and an ideal location for private meetings. While the main level was open and those dining along the Marble Hall's balcony could observe the customers below, the top level had a number of tables located in hidden recesses and several private rooms, including one frequented by Lavrenti Beria.[57]

The restaurant itself was an extension of the sumptuous Georgian banquets held at the Kremlin and at Stalin's dachas. The Aragvi's director, Longinoz Stazhadze, a native of the Georgian region of Racha, had previously cooked for Stalin.[58] Like others responsible for Stalin's food supply, Stazhadze was promoted through the ranks of the NKVD, eventually attaining the post of colonel.[59] Given these ties with the Kremlin, diners seated in the main halls enjoying their meals might have wondered which members of the Soviet leadership were then gathered in the private rooms or observed them unseen from the balcony above. While the restaurant's architecture reminded diners of important hierarchies within the party and the watchful gaze of those at the top, proximity to power was also one of the Aragvi's main attractions. Moreover, when it opened, there were only a handful of restaurants operating in the capital, and the Aragvi was one of the few places the *arriviste* elite could enjoy the fruits of their labor for the party while articulating their new social position through the cultivation of appropriately sophisticated tastes.[60]

Although it served the Soviet capital, the restaurant technically operated under the auspices of the Ministry of Trade of the Georgian SSR.

*Figure 3.2*  A chef sets the table for an elaborate banquet at the Aragvi, 1965.
Central State Archive of the City of Moscow, Division for the Preservation of
Audio-Visual Documents of Moscow.

While archival sources in both Moscow and Tbilisi are silent concerning
the degree of initiative institutions in the Georgian SSR may have had in
launching the restaurant, they do reveal that Georgia's Ministry of Trade
oversaw the Aragvi's supply of wine, cheese, meat, vegetables, mineral
water, herbs, and spices, all of which were shipped specially from the
southern republic.[61] They also indicate that a broader effort was underway to formalize trade in these goods between Georgia and Russia, with
a 1941 directive issued by the Georgian Ministry of Trade requesting
that local Georgian producers not send their own representatives to
Moscow, but instead work through the ministry's network of officials.[62]

In the context of this assertive trade policy pursued by a republic-level institution, the restaurant effectively became a representative branch of Georgia's trade ministry in the Soviet capital and a showcase used to market Georgia's agricultural abundance to the Soviet public.

Moscow's demand for Georgian food was eagerly met by Georgian culinary experts who took up work at the Aragvi. Stazhadze, the restaurant's director, was assisted by Vladimir Jishkariani, a native of western Georgia, who served as his deputy.[63] The restaurant's team of chefs also came from Georgia. The head chef, Nikolai Kiknadze, originally from a small village in western Georgia, had made his career working in restaurants in Kutaisi and Tbilisi before coming to Moscow to work at the Evropa (Europe) restaurant.[64] Leaving the Evropa to cook the food of his native Georgia at the Aragvi, he became the driving force in the culinary development of the restaurant and, as will be seen, a leading figure in the broader dissemination of Georgian cuisine through the state-run system of Obshchepit. It is interesting to note that Stazhadze, Jishkariani, and Kiknadze had all come of age before the revolution and had likely worked in the restaurants and cafes of the NEP (New Economic Policy) era of the 1920s, if not those of the tsarist age, gaining experience in both Georgian and European-style cooking. All three took up permanent residence in the Soviet capital.[65]

As the Soviet Union's first national-themed restaurant, the Aragvi led the way in the rapid development of the Soviet Union's restaurant culture after the Second World War.[66] A number of other republics followed Georgia's example in Moscow: the Armenian SSR opened the Ararat, the Azerbaijani SSR the Baku, and the Uzbek SSR the Uzbekistan restaurant. Modeled in part on the Aragvi, these national restaurants provided visitors with recognizably ethnic forms of entertainment; as they dined, "national ensembles" played, waiters dressed in "national costume" served them, and they were surrounded by elaborate decorations evoking "national themes." Reproducing the logic of a Soviet state that elevated its internal diasporas, these restaurants turned ethnic guests into hosts in the imperial capital. Serving up imperial diversity, they reproduced each republic in miniature for display in the Soviet metropolis. They were also crucial to establishing Moscow as an international destination for foreign visitors in the ensuing Thaw years, when the state

rushed to construct showcases of Soviet achievement for tourists arriving for events like the Sixth World Festival of Youth and Students, held
in Moscow in 1957. Continued state support for the multiethnic culture forged in the Stalinist period and the relative scarcity of alternative
options meant that the Argavi maintained its enviable niche even in a
politically turbulent time.

The Aragvi accordingly survived the death of Stalin and the wave
of de-Stalinization that followed, though not without major changes
in its management. Stazhadze, the director who had once been Stalin's
personal chef, was first demoted and finally arrested on charges of corruption, as was his deputy.[67] Nikolaev, the new ethnic Russian director,
brought up the issue of closing the restaurant's private rooms, previously
the haunt of Beria and others from Stalin's inner circle, though they
ultimately remained open.[68] The restaurant's links with the Georgian
Ministry of Trade were also called into question, as the Union-wide
direction of wine production launched a major audit of the Georgian
Union of Wine Producers and its Moscow branch, finding numerous
instances of improper oversight and technical violations.[69] In late 1959
the Aragvi was finally separated from the Ministry of Trade of Georgia
and placed under the control of Mosrestorantrest (Trest moskovskikh
restoranov), which supervised over seventy restaurants in Moscow,
including the capital's other national restaurants.[70] The Aragvi's transfer
to Mosrestorantrest undoubtedly weakened its autonomy and its connection with suppliers in Georgia. As a crucial specialist in Georgian
cuisine, however, Nikolai Kiknadze, the restaurant's head chef, held on
to his position and saw his influence grow within the Obshchepit system.

While the restaurant's past associations with Stalin's Kremlin became
a liability in the Khrushchev years, the Aragvi remained exceptionally
popular, even among the growing constellation of restaurants in the
Soviet capital. Its success was in large part due to the lasting influence
of head chef Kiknadze, who perfected a host of new Georgian dishes
to meet the rising public demand for dining out. While Nikolaev and
a string of subsequent Russian directors managed the restaurant's relationship with Mosrestorantrest, Kiknadze remained the heart of the
operation. He was best known for his trademark chicken *tabaka*, a dish

in which a young chicken was flattened and then fried under a heavy weight. Adapting the recipe to Russian tastes, Kiknadze spared the hot pepper used in his native western Georgia and more often than not served the fried dish with *tqemali*, a Georgian sour plum sauce, rather than the more traditional Georgian garlic sauce, *niortsqali*.[71] According to Nikolaev, by early 1960 the restaurant was serving up to eight hundred portions of the chicken dish per day.[72] In the words of Kiknadze, the city of Moscow was "basically fed" on chicken *tabaka*.[73] There were other popular items as well; one Soviet journalist could barely contain his delight when he described the more than thirty different dishes available at the Aragvi, writing: "And who doesn't know the pleasure with which Muscovites eat its famous *shashlyk* or its chicken *satsivi*, its skewered sturgeon or its Sulguni cheese?"[74] Each day, long lines formed outside the restaurant before guests were seated for lunch and dinner.[75] By 1962, the restaurant was averaging a turnover of almost two million rubles per year.[76] Out of a side store, the restaurant sold *shashlyk* as take-out for customers who could not get a seat.[77]

At the Aragvi, Kiknadze helped train an entire generation of Russian chefs to prepare Georgian food.[78] Following his retirement in the early 1960s, these chefs took over for him. However, despite the transfer of the restaurant to the control of Mosrestorantrest and the transfer of knowledge from Kiknadze to his Russian disciples, the restaurant's fate remained connected to Georgia. For some items, the restaurant could rely on facilities outside Moscow that supplied meat and vegetables and a special factory outside Ryazan that made Sulguni cheese for them. The Aragvi still depended, however, on a steady supply of Georgian wine, mineral water, and spices shipped through Georgian networks.[79]

Georgian specialists and Georgian supplies were similarly required at other newly opened Georgian restaurants, which sought to mimic the Aragvi's success and based the preparation and presentation of their dishes on the models established by the Aragvi.[80] Georgian chefs were brought in to develop Leningrad's Kavkazskii (The Caucasian) and Moscow's Kura, which, like the Aragvi, was named after a river in Georgia.[81] Some of the Aragvi's signature dishes, like chicken *tabaka* and the spicy Georgian soup *kharcho*, were so popular they migrated to the menus of other, non-Georgian restaurants in the capital. While not every restaurant in Moscow had a Georgian chef, Georgian dishes required special supplies; without connections to Georgian producers, lamented the director of the restaurant Sovetskii (The Soviet), their *kharcho*, prepared without cilantro and *tqemali* from Georgia, was at best a "parody" of the genuine article.[82]

Georgian wine and mineral water were among the most popular beverages produced in the Soviet Union and were seen as necessary components of any Georgian restaurant meal. While the Soviet state had initially discouraged alcohol, Georgian wine was increasingly praised at the highest levels of power. Speaking at a 1960 meeting in Tbilisi, Khrushchev proclaimed: "Wine is an adornment of the table and we need to produce more of it, though it should be drunk, of course, in moderation."[83] Wine bottles from the southern republic were decorated with lavish images of the abundant Georgian countryside and a stylized script evocative of the distinct Georgian alphabet, a reminder that a connection to the Georgian land marked Georgian cuisine as authentic and that the "Georgian brand" was defined by the specific *terroir* of the southern republic.

As their Soviet hosts were quick to notice, foreign visitors gravitated toward the Aragvi by choice and seemed genuinely impressed with Georgian cuisine. Dining at the Aragvi back in 1947, John Steinbeck had written that "the food was the same as in Georgia—for our taste, the best in Russia."[84] The restaurant was subsequently profiled in a 1950 *Time* magazine article entitled "Russia: Where to Dine." The article's author noted that among Moscow's ethnic restaurants the Aragvi was still the best, and the others, like the Baku, the Ararat, and the Uzbekistan, were but "imitators" of "Communist Moscow's original luxury restaurant, the Aragvi."[85] International visitors' appreciation of Georgian food registered with Soviet officials. Nikolai Kiknadze was chosen to represent the Soviet Union at the 1958 Brussels World's Fair (Expo 58), a vast stage for the competition in living standards between the capitalist and socialist camps. Brought in to head the team sent from the Rossiia (Russia) restaurant, Kiknadze's array of Soviet food, presented with a Georgian accent, won his team a grand prize.[86] Georgian food became a staple of

*Figure 3.3* Women at a Georgian winery take part in the production of Georgian wines for the Soviet table, 1970. National Archives of Georgia.

the Soviet fare served to foreign guests, an edible reminder of the Soviet policies of tolerance and friendship among the nationalities and diasporas that made up the Union.

While the state showcased Georgian cuisine for its own purposes, it could not fully control the way the Aragvi's customers interpreted the lavish experience of dining at the restaurant. By the late 1960s the restaurant had become a "cult spot" and a favorite hangout among actors from the Moscow Art Theater. The actor and bard Vladimir Vysotskii, according to the restaurant's former Deputy Chef, was a near "permanent" fixture among guests at the restaurant.[87] Vysotskii, like other members of the Soviet intelligentsia at the time, was enamored of the festive atmosphere and traditions of toasting that he found around the Georgian table, recalled fondly in his nostalgic poem "Teper' ia budu sokhnut' ot toski" ("Now I Will Wither Away from Longing").[88] It was little surprise that the restaurant was chosen as the location for a 1979 party given by the Association of American Publishers and attended by leading Soviet intellectuals and dissidents—including Andrei Sakharov, Vasilii Aksenov, Vladimir Voinovich, and Raisa Orlova.[89]

Despite its Stalinist past, the restaurant's unmatched luxury, the privacy afforded by its dark corners and separate rooms, its popularity among the Soviet Union's artistic elite, and its vibrant, celebratory Georgian atmosphere lent it a bohemian feel that at times seemed vaguely un-Soviet. It was a place where generals rubbed shoulders with artists and, in the Brezhnev era, the "black marketeers" who gathered in the restaurant's back rooms.[90] In some ways the restaurant's changing clientele reflected the accompanying evolution of the Soviet elite, many of whom sought to define themselves as separate from—if not in opposition to—state authority. Virtually alone in a culinary scene too often defined by bland tastes in cold, institutional settings, the exceptional development of Georgian cuisine endowed it with a rich set of practices and symbols that could be appropriated by restaurant patrons of diverse backgrounds and imbued with new meanings.

Significantly, though, the halls of the Aragvi remained closed to most Soviet citizens. Not only were dinners there expensive, but the restaurant was also so popular that according to its former deputy chef, "it was almost impossible to get a table around the holidays unless you knew someone or could rely on connections."[91] Moscow's network of restaurants may have grown dramatically in the postwar period, but still lagged behind popular demand in a city of millions. The Aragvi catered to the changing Soviet elite, but remained out of reach for most. Nonetheless, thanks in part to the efforts of its Georgian head chef, Nikolai Kiknadze, the restaurant became the inspiration for the mass popularization of Georgian food through Obshchepit, the state-run food service.

## Georgian Meals for the Masses

Even as the Aragvi's opulent dining experience was imbued with new meanings by well-connected artists and intellectuals in the Soviet capital, a major state-led effort was underway to democratize Soviet fine dining. In the postwar period, and even more so in the Khrushchev era, quality of life became an increasingly important arena of Cold War competition.[92] The Soviet state needed to demonstrate that it could keep up with the capitalist West in terms of making new opportunities for consumption available to the masses, not just the elite. With its system of workers' cafeterias and food stores, Obshchepit had succeeded only at the most elemental level of providing for basic nutritional needs, and even then the institution was characterized by shortages, poor service, and the dull repetition of dishes. State officials showed a heightened sensitivity to the grievances of Soviet diners, expressed in complaint letters and comment books. In their effort to satisfy public tastes they turned to Georgian cuisine, with its established repertoire of dishes and developed supply chains. The niche first created for Georgian culinary specialists in the 1930s was significantly expanded, as Obshchepit officials sought to make the Georgian dining experience available on the mass level. The renewed promise of the socialist "good life" meant that everyone would soon dine like the Soviet elite, and this elite had a distinct taste for Georgian food.

From a culinary perspective, there are a number of striking continuities between the Stalinist and post-Stalinist periods, with the effort to democratize fine dining under Khrushchev entailing not the repudiation of the practices of the Stalinist elite but instead their broader dissemination. As before, Soviet cuisine was imagined as expressly multiethnic, and being "cultured" still meant a well-informed appreciation of the cuisines of Soviet nationalities. As it had been in the restaurant, the emphasis on a nationally diverse menu in the worker's cafeteria was also a practical way to increase assortment based on available ingredients, since the culinary resources of the national republics could be marshaled to meet the demands of domestic consumption and international display. Preparing to address the 1957 conference of Obshchepit workers and managers, the Deputy Minister of Trade wrote: "Soviet cuisine is unusually rich and diverse. A vast array of world-famous dishes is in its arsenal, including Russian appetizers and *pirogi*, Ukrainian *borshch*, Georgian *shashlyk*, Azeri lamb stew [*piti*], Uzbek *plov* and many other national dishes." Addressing those assembled for the meeting, he called on them to "exalt the accomplishments of Soviet cuisine!"[93]

Once again, Georgian cuisine emerged as first among its supposed national equals at the Soviet table. Not only was it the favorite of the elite who dined at the Aragvi, it was also indisputably Soviet. While the mass promotion of Chinese food was considered for a time, the risks involved in promoting the cuisine of a nation outside the Soviet Union but inside the communist camp became evident after the Sino-Soviet split.[94] During the Thaw and afterward, Obshchepit became a de facto platform for the popular dissemination of Georgian food, drawing on preexisting supply chains and diasporic networks of expertise that had previously been utilized to serve Georgian cuisine to Moscow's elite. Accorded a special role on account of their specialized knowledge, Georgian chefs and food service professionals worked within the Obshchepit system to promote their own vision of Georgian cuisine for the masses, and Georgia, as before, served as a critical production base.

Although their menu bore the noticeable imprint of the Stalinist period, Obshchepit's Thaw-era planners emphasized the virtues of "modern, advanced technology" and the techniques of mass production to develop Georgian food as a popular cuisine and bring material abundance to the masses.[95] They began with *shashlyk*, a dish from the Caucasus that was already widely embraced by the public. Obshchepit's leaders sought to make the grilled meat available everywhere. Affordable dining establishments specializing in *shashlyk*, known as *shashlychnye*, were opened across the Soviet Union, believed to be a good source of nutrition for hungry workers and a convenient way to feed the public through mass-produced foods. While there had been *shashlychnye* within Obshchepit's network since the 1930s, their number was expanded greatly under Khrushchev thanks to explicit directives adopted at the Twentieth Party Congress in 1956. Thus at the same event where Khrushchev denounced the ills of Stalinism in his "secret speech," the food of Stalin's native Georgia was given a considerable boost, with the party supporting "measures to improve the work of public food service enterprises" and calling for the number of specialized eateries like *shashlychnye* to be increased.[96] It is possible that this was not seen as a contradictory decision, since Georgian cuisine was equated with fine dining and its political meanings were malleable. Soon almost every neighborhood in Moscow had its own *shashlychnaia na uglu* (*shashlyk* stand on the corner). Some of these, like the one profiled in a 1963 issue of *Obshchestvennoe pitanie*, Obshchepit's journal, also offered a range of Georgian dishes to accompany the grilled meat, including *lobio*, an increasingly popular Georgian bean dish that was easy to mass produce, and the spicy soup *kharcho*.[97]

The Aragvi's renowned chicken *tabaka* similarly went from the halls of the elite dining establishment to the neighborhood cafe, worker's cafeteria, and home dining table. Kiknadze himself revealed the secrets of the Aragvi's most famous dish in the pages of Obshchepit's journal in early 1961.[98] The technology necessary for mass production soon followed. A few issues later, a device was unveiled in the journal that would allow this dish, "one of the favorites of restaurant customers," to be prepared at more modest dining establishments—cooked not individually, as at the Aragvi, but in batches, and seasoned more quickly with a specially designed "aromatizer."[99] Two years later, a Moscow factory began making simple pans with presses that could produce one to four portions of chicken *tabaka* in the average cafeteria or at home.[100]

Popularizing a fine dining experience based in part on rare ingredients was sometimes an expensive proposition. Obshchepit's management eventually found a practical solution: the mass production of Georgian sauces that evoked the taste of the southern republic but could easily be shipped and stored. The most popular was *tqemali*, the tart Georgian plum sauce used to accompany *shashlyk* and chicken *tabaka*. The sauce was first discussed at length during a 1950 meeting of the Obshchepit leadership. In response to the Deputy Minister of Trade's suggestion that "shortages of herbs and spices could be overcome by more widely producing a variety of sauces," Nikolai Kiknadze, attending the meeting as a representative of the Aragvi restaurant, suggested the Georgian plum sauce. The following year, fifty tons of *tqemali* were produced in Tbilisi for Union-wide consumption.[101] By the early 1960s *tqemali* was widely available at *shashlychnye* and at stores for home use; by the latter part of that decade, it was joined by the spicy tomato-based *satsibeli* and the fragrant Georgian walnut sauce used for *satsivi*.[102] These sauces, with foreign-sounding Georgian names, entered common use throughout the Soviet Union. Georgian producers in turn carved out an enviable niche for themselves, producing new condiments for the Soviet table.

The construction of a multiethnic dining culture on the mass level was based on the idea of integrating diverse culinary traditions drawn from across the Soviet Union. While ethnic culinary specialists were seen as bearers of special knowledge, the new emphasis on democratization meant that they were expected to render their national culture in an accessible form, turning it into a commodity suitable for public consumption. As one author profiling Kiknadze's role in promoting Georgian cuisine wrote in the *Obshchestvennoe pitanie* journal:

> Soviet culinary workers affirm the rule that cuisine in our country never was and never will be a secretive, isolated part of national culture. We can only welcome mutual cultural penetration and mutual sharing, and the leading experts of national cuisine certainly should not keep their recipes a "mystery," passing them along like secrets only to the select few.[103]

If a refusal to share was evidence of suspicious secrecy, then the state's endorsement of multiethnic dining might be said to have had an undercurrent of imperial coercion. Although ethnic guests became hosts at national restaurants in the Soviet capital, they were required to impart their knowledge and transmit their cultural heritage to a predominantly Russian audience, which threatened to make the inversion of roles a temporary one.

Despite this fact, the opportunities for imperial prominence that the state's dining infrastructure opened up were rather alluring and many Georgian culinary specialists eagerly participated. Nikolai Kiknadze, for example, dutifully instructed his non-Georgian employees in the ways of Georgian cuisine. He had been an active participant at Obshchepit meetings and had showcased Georgian cooking abroad at international expositions.[104] And it was by widely publishing his recipes that he reached a mass audience and ultimately made his most profound impact on Soviet cooking.

Kiknadze's contributions to major Soviet cookbooks brought his recipes into the ordinary Soviet kitchen and infused Soviet home cooking with Georgian flavors. Georgian recipes submitted by Kiknadze figured prominently in the 1956 edition of the Soviet *Kulinariia*, perhaps the most ambitious effort to capture the ethnic diversity of the new Soviet diet and often referred to as *Stalinskaia Kulinariia* because it was prepared in the late Stalinist period, though published shortly after.[105] The encyclopedic cookbook was divided into several sections: the main section, representing the bulk of the book, listed the volume's core recipes, while a separate section, much smaller, showcased recipes for "national dishes," organized by country. In terms of national dishes, there were more recipes for Georgian dishes than for any other republic.[106] Revealing the growing centrality of Georgian cuisine was the fact that many of these dishes were also listed in the main section, most under their original Georgian name.[107]

The cookbook's illustrations showed that Georgian cuisine continued to be synonymous with material abundance and culinary sophistication. A depiction of a Georgian table had five bottles of wine for six place settings, bountiful *shashlyki* with skewers stretching off the plate, two bottles of Borjomi, long loaves of Georgian bread, and a gigantic centerpiece with fresh vegetables spilling over in cornucopia-like fashion.[108] Despite the cookbook's plea for moderation in the consumption of alcohol, each setting was assigned four separate glasses for various wines and spirits (as well as mineral water) to be consumed throughout the course of the meal. The cookbook became a fixture in Soviet dining establishments and private kitchens, promoting Georgian cuisine to the masses and widely disseminating Kiknadze's recipes.

Kiknadze also supplied recipes to the most popular Soviet cookbook, the *Book about Delicious and Healthy Food*. First published in 1939, this book did not reach most Soviet kitchens until the postwar period. In 1952 it was dramatically expanded, with the addition of thirty-two sumptuous color illustrations, and printed on a large scale, ultimately reaching millions of Soviet kitchens.[109] Although it underwent minor revisions in 1955, 1961, 1965, 1974, 1978, 1981, 1989, and 1990, it remained—in its structure, presentation, and logic—a high Stalinist document that informed popular attitudes toward eating in enduring ways. While

*Kulinariia* was geared more toward professional chefs, the *Book about Delicious and Healthy Food* was expressly written for the "female home-maker" as an instructional manual on how to prepare "tasty and healthy food for the family" using a "diverse and rich assortment" of ingredients.[110] The cookbook was a gendered project of bringing the "expertise" of pre-dominantly male culinary specialists into the female-run kitchen, but it also encouraged female homemakers to take the lead in cultivating a taste for nationally diverse Soviet culinary trends among their families. Like the diners at the Aragvi restaurant, these idealized homemakers were tacitly understood to be upwardly mobile urban residents, with access to a range of ingredients and time to prepare elaborate recipes.[111] Alongside traditional Russian dishes like cabbage soup, beef cutlets, and mushrooms in sour cream, the modern Soviet housewife might introduce her family to *chanakhi*, the fragrant Georgian lamb stew, the Georgian bean dish, *lobio*, served with crushed walnuts, or, for the less adventurous, a Georgian version of the Russian stew *solianka*, called *solianka po-gruzinskii* and marked as ethnically distinct by the inclusion of red wine and garlic.[112] Perhaps reflecting the growing demand for fine ethnic dining in the home, the number of Georgian recipes included in the collection nearly doubled between the 1952 and 1965 publications of the *Book about Delicious and Healthy Food.*[113]

Kiknadze was far from the only Georgian in Obshchepit's institu-tional networks touting the virtues of Georgian cooking. Many others besides him continued to hold high positions in the organization in the post-Stalinist period, and knowledge of cooking remained an easily transportable skill for new waves of Georgian migrants as demand for Georgian cuisine increased. In 1956 Georgians could be found heading the Tashkent restaurant trust and a number of Moscow's most promi-nent dining establishments, including the newly opened Kafe Druzhba (Cafe Friendship) on Kuznetskii Most.[114] The following year an ethnic Armenian from Tbilisi directed Mosrestorantrest, and the Ministry of Trade's food production laboratory, which spearheaded the develop-ment of prepared foods, was led by a Georgian from Kutaisi.[115] A num-ber of Georgian chefs continued the prerevolutionary pattern of work among the network of restaurants along Russia's railways and in some cases progressed from work at regional train depots to jobs in Moscow's restaurants.[116] In the Soviet capital itself, the head of the trust of railway restaurants and buffets was Georgian.[117] In addition, in the 1960s Obshchepit began sponsoring exchanges that brought Georgian chefs to cities in the other Soviet republics to train their counterparts in the ways of Georgian cooking. One such exchange brought a team of Georgian chefs to Kiev's cafeterias to help the Ukrainian capital's eateries prepare for their celebratory "days of Georgian cooking." As a result of the exchange, Georgian-style *shashlyk*, the stew *chakhokhbili*, and cheese-filled *khachapuri* were introduced to Kiev's cafeteria menus.[118]

The results of the post-Stalinist culinary revolution within Obshchepit were mixed. Flavor, style, and national color were injected into the cafeteria menu, though chronic shortages remained and cafeteria renditions of Georgian dishes were often a far cry from the images of Georgian cuisine that appeared in Soviet cookbooks. However, even though restaurants, *shashlychnye*, and cafeterias experienced shortages and often produced goods below the standards promised at Obshchepit meetings and on the pages of its journal, Soviet society had been exposed to and had developed a taste for Georgian food.[119] Soviets sought out new ways to fulfill their appetite for Georgian cooking beyond the cafeteria and welcomed the national traditions of the Georgian table into their homes.

## Georgian Recipes and Rituals in the Soviet Home

Restaurants like the Aragvi were expensive and inaccessible to many. Moscow's *shashlychnye* were often overcrowded, and the worker's cafeteria afforded little opportunity to relax, as employees sometimes had as little as fifteen minutes to eat.[120] For most Soviets, the best way to enjoy the exotic flavors of Georgian cooking and the intimate rituals of the Georgian table was to bring them inside their own homes. Georgian food took on an even more personal meaning for Soviets who prepared it for themselves with the help of Kiknadze's recipes, serving home-cooked Georgian fare with mass-produced Georgian wines and sauces. Georgian cuisine retained its ethnic markers as an exotic food of celebration, one best enjoyed when paired with toasts made by a *tamada*. In the Thaw years and afterward, Georgia's culture of hosting, which held the guest to be a near-sacred figure, and its custom of heartfelt speechmaking around the table, proved well-suited for domestic life in the Soviet Union, a place where the most intimate moments were those shared by friends who gathered in one another's apartments and sat cramped around a kitchen table, telling stories, making toasts, and marking important occasions with food and drink.[121]

The mechanisms of Georgian cuisine's diffusion from household to household are difficult for historians to trace. However, it is clear that some Soviets learned of the traditions of the Georgian table through direct contact with the Soviet Union's Georgian diaspora. Georgian students studying in Moscow brought recipes and food from Georgia, which they shared with their Russian classmates. The culinary reputation of Georgia often preceded them; one Georgian who studied at a prestigious medical institute in the Soviet capital recalled that her Russian classmates would routinely ask her to prepare Georgian food for group events and noted that if there was a male Georgian student at a social gathering, he would almost always serve as *tamada*.[122] As the concept of the *tamada* spread beyond Georgia, best friends and army buddies might be chosen to serve as toastmasters for private wedding receptions and birthdays.[123] However, Georgians were known as the most expert masters of ceremony and the Georgian toastmaster remained the ideal for all who aspired to be *tamada*. In his memoirs, the Soviet poet Evgenii Dolmatovskii praised a non-Georgian companion by stating that he conducted himself around the table like a real "Georgian *tamada*."[124] Dolmatovskii and others in Moscow's literary and artistic community would likely have experienced Georgian-style toasting firsthand at the numerous cultural events and conferences that brought Georgian intellectuals and artists to Moscow, fetes which often culminated in long, celebratory banquets.[125]

Through the medium of popular culture, artists and entertainers—most of them Georgian—also helped spread the rituals of the Georgian table as Georgian food was accepted into the Soviet home in the 1960s. Such themes were subsequently taken up by non-Georgian Soviet artists, many of whom were drawn in by the increasingly bohemian atmosphere at the Aragvi restaurant.[126] Representations ranged from the quasi-ethnographic portrayals of Georgian village feasts in Otar Ioseliani's 1966 film *Falling Leaves* (*georgobis tve*) to Leonid Gaidai's wildly popular *Prisoner of the Caucasus, or Shurik's New Adventures* (*Kavkazskaia plennitsa, ili Novye prikliucheniia Shurika*), released in 1967, with its humorous rendition of Georgian toasting as a regional obsession. While Ioseliani's black-and-white film was warmly praised by the Soviet intelligentsia as a work of cinematic artistry, Gaidai's film, with its whimsical take on Georgian dining rituals, reached a wider audience. Scenes of the Georgian table also appeared in the films of Moscow-based Georgian director Giorgi Danelia, whose 1969 film *Don't Grieve!* (*Ne goriui!*) concluded with a huge banquet thrown for a dying man. Danelia developed the banquet scene as an inversion of the Georgian ritual of toasting the deceased; in the film, the dying man asks for these toasts to be made while he is still alive so that he can hear them. The Georgian director filled his film with images of tables laden with the food of his homeland, lengthy toasts made with wine drunk from horns, and even longer dinners punctuated by song and dance.

Danelia's film helped make Vakhtang Kikabidze, the actor and musician who served as *tamada* in the pivotal banquet scene, into a Soviet star. Kikabidze in turn helped popularize the institution of *tamadoba* with his song "Pei do dna" ("Bottoms up"), which was as much a drinking song as it was a set of instructions for Soviet listeners on the Georgian way of toasting. According to the song, the role of the *tamada* was dictated by the "ancient code" of the Caucasus. At the table, one needed to do as he said and drink "bottoms up." In his song, Kikabidze followed the sequence of toasts at the Georgian table: for meeting, for the embrace of friends, for the host, his home and his family, for beautiful women, for the departed and for the health of the living, and for the motherland (*rodina*). Here, Kikabidze notably shied away from ethnic exclusivity; although he was intimately associated with Georgia in the Soviet imagination, the notion of *rodina* he employed in the song was open-ended and could be understood as pan-Soviet as well as national. As a matter of fact, he did not mention his native republic by name at any point in the song. Kikabidze thus recast the Georgian toasting tradition as one that did not need to be specific to Georgia, making it a suitable practice for all. Even those Soviets who had never met a Georgian gained familiarity with the traditions of the Georgian table as interpreted by the performances and productions of Kikabidze and other Georgian cultural entrepreneurs.

The spread of Georgian cuisine derived not only from what Georgians promoted beyond the borders of their native republic, but also what Soviet tourists took back from visits there. The development of Georgia's tourist infrastructure in the post-Stalinist period made it possible for ordinary Soviets to get their own taste of the Georgian "good life."[127] In Soviet travel guides Georgia was advertised as a place for restorative relaxation and adventure, an abundant land of plenty available to all socialist citizens.[128] For the same reasons, Georgia was also a culinary destination. Arriving in Tbilisi, one of the first things Soviet tourists would see was the massive aluminum statue of "Mother Georgia" looming over the city.[129] The statue held a goblet of wine in one hand to welcome friends and a sword in the other to stave off foes. The statue simultaneously evoked Georgia's warrior culture and its tradition of hospitality, a tendency celebrated in Soviet tourist magazines, which claimed that "since time immemorial the Georgian's greatest pleasure" had been "to welcome people into his home." Hospitality meant food, served at large banquets for tourists who were entertained by Georgian singers and dancers.

A vast system of restaurants welcomed Soviet tourists to Georgia. These dining establishments operated under the Union-wide system of Obshchepit, but enjoyed a great deal of local autonomy. At Obshchepit meetings in Moscow, Georgian representatives regularly asked for special dispensations to serve the tourists who came to Georgia "from all corners of the Soviet Union" and pushed against restrictions that limited where wine could be sold.[130] The number of enterprises in Georgia's system of Obshchepit exceeded that of other republics of its size, and plans for expansion in the late 1950s and early 1960s put the quantity of new establishments behind only Russia and Ukraine.[131] In addition, Georgia's finest dining establishments evinced a sense of quality and luxury that could rarely be found outside Moscow or Leningrad. In 1965 the journal *Obshchestvennoe pitanie* ran a special issue devoted exclusively to Georgia, featuring profiles of its seaside resorts, tourist restaurants, and the elegant cafes that dotted Rustaveli Avenue, Tbilisi's main street.[132] The journal's writers claimed that the city's finest restaurants could compete "with the best in Europe."[133]

Luring visitors away from the cold climate and quotidian realities that characterized life for most Soviet citizens, Georgia was portrayed as a land of readily consumable marvels. An article in *Obshchestvennoe pitanie* profiled Margo Aptsiauri and Omar Lebanidze, employees of a cafeteria by day and traditional Georgian folk dancers at Tbilisi's House of Culture by night.[134] In addition to dancing cafeteria workers, Georgia also was home to a singing group of centenarians in Abkhazia, audible promoters of the renowned health benefits of a Georgian diet. It was little wonder that Soviet tourists wanted to bring Georgia's culinary culture home with them. One of Tbilisi's largest restaurants provided visiting diners with a brochure detailing the recipes of three of the restaurant's most popular dishes, including its chicken *tabaka*.[135] Other Soviet visitors might pick up recipes from personal contact with Georgians that later became standard household dishes when they returned home. Growing up in a Russian Jewish family, Ol'ga Grinkrug noted that her mother's two "signature dishes" were her Georgian *khachapuri* and her *chakhokhbili*, both brought back to Moscow following a trip to Tbilisi.[136]

Beyond the tourist itinerary, Georgia's domestic dining culture was not always seen in a uniformly positive light when experienced firsthand. Visitors who lingered in Georgia sometimes encountered things around the Georgian table that seemed strange or even offensive to Soviet sensibilities. The range of emotion expressed by a Georgian *tamada* might be attractive to some, off-putting to others. In the words of a Bulgarian visitor, "the kind of little speeches he [the Georgian *tamada*] gave before these grown men with moustaches were of the type which we save for children and pretty girls."[137] Visitors used to the more relaxed style of Russian toasting might have been confused by the more rigid rules that governed behavior at the Georgian table: only the *tamada* could make toasts, wine was never to be sipped, only drunk with toasts, and toasts had to be made—and glasses clinked—in a set order. Just as the *tamada*'s role in Georgia was fixed, so too were gender roles around the table: men often feasted while women served, and it was unheard of for women to make a toast.[138] While the republic's dining traditions provided a rich repertoire for the diaspora of Georgian culinary specialists working in Soviet cities, they could sometimes appear jarring when experienced in their local context.

Because of the multiple and shifting meanings of material culture, eating and drinking in a Georgian way could be taken as an endorsement of the state's multiethnic policies, but in other cases might be interpreted as a rejection of Soviet values.[139] Although the state celebrated abundance and promoted Georgia as a culinary destination, there was a fine line between celebration and ideologically suspect gluttony when it came to large, semipublic gatherings in the southern republic. Soviet authorities frequently criticized the vast amount of money spent on Georgian weddings and wakes as a "harmful tradition," and lampooned the conspicuous and competitive consumption of copious amounts of food and drink at the Georgian *supra* as an undesirable cultural trait.[140] The state, however interventionist, could never fully control the varied uses of Georgian cuisine or the themes to which Georgian diners raised their glasses.

From Nikolai Kiknadze's native western Georgian countryside to the center of Moscow, and from Stalin's dinner table to the private Soviet kitchen, Georgian food changed in transit. Chicken *tabaka* lost some of its spice, and foods like turkey *satsivi*, traditionally served at Georgian New Year's celebrations, were taken out of cultural context and became dishes for year-round consumption.[141] Georgian dining rituals also changed. While having a *tamada* lead celebrations became a Soviet-wide practice, the rules of the table were different outside Georgia. The order and nature of the toasts became a matter of personal interpretation. The tendency of a Russian *tamada* hosting a wedding celebration to introduce games and events into the festivities would have upset a Georgian's sense of decorum. Although the dissemination of Georgian cuisine was linked to a diaspora of Georgians within the Soviet Union, the connection between the two was never fixed. Once it was promoted by the state and spread by members of the diaspora, the diffusion of Georgia's culinary culture took on a life of its own, reaching beyond a limited group of people with specialized knowledge and into the homes of Soviet citizens. Georgian food became a part of Soviet imperial culture rather than the exclusive domain of one nationality, and yet in so doing, its consumption moved even further beyond the control of the state. From the outset, the state had been forced to rely on preexisting national ingredients in its effort to construct a multiethnic diet. Once these national products were popularly available, the state had difficulty limiting the way they were utilized and in some cases unexpectedly combined by Soviet consumers.

Yet the dominance of identifiably Georgian dining practices around the dinner table secured a permanent niche for ethnic Georgian culinary specialists, who continued to serve as experts and interpreters of Georgian cuisine for the Soviet public. For a distant republic represented by a small diaspora beyond its internal borders, Georgia made a remarkable contribution to the creation of a diverse Soviet cuisine that met the needs of Soviet ideology, the desires of the Soviet public, and reflected the nature of the Soviet Union as a profoundly multiethnic empire. The connotations of Georgian cuisine may have shifted over time, but its significance never faltered as it was welcomed into the Kremlin under Stalin, developed as an elite form of fine dining amidst a return to luxury in the late 1930s, and popularized for the masses in the post-Stalinist period.

As it spread, the culture of the Georgian table proved remarkably malleable, but even as it became Soviet, its "national form" remained distinctly recognizable and continued to shape consumption practices on the mass level. The song of Soviet entertainer Vakhtang Kikabidze seemed a far cry from the toast given by Stalin, yet both employed a spirit of candor that arose from the same tradition of Georgian *tamadoba*. Through the form of the toast, the provision of ingredients from the Georgian republic, and the efforts of Georgian culinary specialists, the everyday habits of millions of Soviet citizens were indelibly altered.

# 4

# Dances of Difference

The Georgian dancers entered from both sides of the stage of Moscow's Tchaikovsky Concert Hall to the sound of a rapid drumbeat. Each male dancer, dressed in a black *chokha* (Caucasian warrior's cloak) and armed with a *khanzhali* (dagger), was paired with a female dancer in a sparkling white dress, her head crowned by a silk veil and her face framed by two long braids of dark hair. The men and women formed lines across the stage in black and white, first parallel, then spiraling, the men marching forward with one arm held close, the other outstretched, the women spinning, angling their wrists, and seemingly floating across the stage, their feet concealed by their long dresses.

Suddenly, the lines of male and female dancers formed a ring. As one of the male dancers entered the circle, the accompanying music, previously jubilant, became hypnotic, with the musicians repeating a melancholy and focused refrain of drum and *duduki*, a Caucasian woodwind instrument. Dancing on the tips of his toes, the man advanced across the stage, shuffling his feet in coordination with the drum, while keeping his upper body motionless and his face perfectly composed. Finally drawing near to one of the female dancers, the man gave a bow, inviting her to dance. She gracefully set herself into motion, floating in circles around the stage, with upright posture but downcast eyes, her hand gestures evocative of Persian courtliness. They drew closer together, the man following her as she floated by him, and then moved forward in complete synchrony, though without once touching one another.[1]

This performance of Georgia's national dance ensemble, held on March 21, 1958, marked the opening day of the grandiose *Dekada* (Festival) of Georgian Art and Literature in the Soviet capital.[2] Soviet ideologists held national costume and national dance to be emblematic of national character, and in few performances was nationality performed so vividly as in this paired partner dance, whose name, *kartuli*, simply meant "Georgian."[3] In the words of Georgian choreographer Davit Javrishvili, the *kartuli* was a "dancing novel," an evocative display of the Georgian virtues of "beauty, ingenuity, and agility."[4] Soviet critics characterized the repertoire of these Georgian dancers as "sunny," "bright," and "heartfelt," a performance that evoked the warmth of the Georgian homeland and "brought joy" to the hearts of Muscovites. Referring to acclaimed features of the Georgian national character, the authors stated that the dancers "captivated viewers with their heated, unrestrained temperament and sunny brilliance."[5]

The warm displays on the stage and the heartfelt reaction among Soviet audiences reflected the accompanying "Thaw" in Soviet politics,

*Figure 4.1* Leila Dumbadze and Tengiz Utmelidze of Georgia's national dance ensemble perform the *kartuli*, 1960. National Archives of Georgia.

which had stimulated the development of a vibrant post-Stalinist Soviet popular culture.[6] On stage and screen, the Thaw entailed a new style of Soviet performance. Whereas late Stalinist artistic life had been carefully scripted to adhere to rigid ideological formulas, the Thaw years celebrated improvisation and openness. While labor productivity was still accorded the highest official honors, independent artistic creativity garnered increased prestige and state support; it also opened up new opportunities for international travel and transnational cultural exchange, since Soviet authorities came to rely on artists, musicians, and dancers for popular diplomacy in the Cold War. Soviet literature was reinvigorated by younger voices and daring explorations of the Stalinist past; Soviet musicians borrowed and adapted the sounds of Western jazz and rock; and expanded radio broadcasts and the emergence of television created new audiences and new popular expectations, much as they did in Western Europe and the United States at this time.[7]

In the context of the Thaw, Georgian culture proved to be a highly marketable commodity. A diaspora of Georgian musicians, singers, and dancers gave the southern republic a disproportionate role in the production of Soviet culture at home and the representation of Soviet multiethnicity abroad. In 1959–1960, Georgians touring the Soviet Union held by far the largest number of concerts in proportion to their native republic's small population, and the third largest total number of concerts among all Soviet republics, behind only Russia and Ukraine.[8] Drawing on new international influences, Georgian performers transformed Soviet *estrada* ("small stage," or popular music) into an innovative artistic medium that combined folk motifs with electric guitars and rock and roll beats.[9] By the end of the 1960s, Georgian *estrada* performers played more concerts in Russia than any other national group and twice as many concerts as groups from Ukraine and Belarus combined.[10]

Recalling the successes of the Georgian diaspora in political life and around the dinner table, these performances on stage succeeded because they balanced strangeness with familiarity. Just as Georgian restaurateurs were able to render their ethnicity in an edible form that remained palatable to broader Soviet tastes, so too did Georgian performers succeed in choreographing their national character as an intelligible array of movements set to appreciably distinctive music.[11]

Possessing an elaborate repertoire that surpassed that of other national ensembles, Georgian performance was open to a variety of interpretations; Georgian dance, for example, could be read as a form of national protest or as an affirmation of Soviet power.[12] Georgia's artists benefitted from Tbilisi's well-developed cultural institutions, which skillfully synthesized aspects of Russian and Georgian culture. Unlike most other republic-level centers of cultural production, these institutions predated the Soviet state, received special patronage in the Stalinist era, and enjoyed greater autonomy in the Thaw years. Soviet audiences appreciated and sometimes even imitated the choreography and musicality of Georgian performance, perceiving it as springing from a longstanding cultural tradition and not an artificial product created solely to support state policies. Though they were often limited to expressing a positive image of their native republic for domestic and international audiences, Georgian performers were also skilled auto-ethnographers, striving to manage the terms of the representation of their native culture and using the Soviet stage to acquire economic and cultural capital.[13]

While it built on established patterns, the cultural prominence of the Georgian diaspora during the Thaw was also somewhat surprising, at least from a political perspective. De-Stalinization, a defining feature of the period, had particularly profound ramifications for Georgians and the Georgian SSR. In Khrushchev's secret speech at the Twentieth Party Congress on February 25, 1956, the Soviet leader concluded his description of Stalinist crimes by sarcastically referring to Stalin as "the great son of the Georgian people," noting that "Georgians loved to refer to their countryman" in such terms.[14] The speech quickly reached Georgia in the form of exaggerated rumors. In the southern republic, many feared that their entire nation would be scapegoated for Stalinist excesses and that upwardly mobile Georgians would lose coveted opportunities for advancement beyond the Georgian SSR. Members of the Georgian elite believed that their children would no longer be admitted to the top universities in Moscow, Georgian officers worried about being forced out of military service in favor of ethnic Russians, and some even predicted deportation from their homeland, a vengeful application of the Stalinist logic of collective ethnic responsibility to the Great Leader's own people.[15] Stoked by such fears, the third anniversary of Stalin's death on March 5, 1956 became an occasion for mass demonstrations in Tbilisi and other Georgian cities. The protests were violently suppressed by Soviet troops, leading to at least twenty-one deaths in Tbilisi alone.[16] However, the Soviet state's decision to expand its funding of Georgian culture in the aftermath of the protests can be interpreted as a concession to the Georgian public and a sign of its continued support for multiethnicity more generally.[17] In some ways, increased cultural clout helped compensate for the loss of political power once held by Georgian networks.

An examination of Georgian cultural prominence during the Thaw suggests some new ways of thinking about the period's relationship to the decades that preceded and followed it. First, from a Georgian perspective, many of the cultural products of the Thaw were firmly rooted in the Stalinist past and even the late imperial era, lending support to scholarship that portrays the era as one of creative reinterpretation rather than complete innovation.[18] Second, the style and content of Georgian performances reveal that the Thaw was not just about the adoption of foreign influences, but the accompanying evolution and transformation of Soviet domestic internationalism as its performers selectively drew upon artistic trends beyond Soviet borders. Finally, the Georgian diaspora's experience on the Soviet stage points to a rather long period of artistic experimentation, one that lasted, at least in Soviet popular music, well into the 1970s.[19] Accounting for the flexibility and endurance of the repertoire of Georgian performance, this chapter explores its historical foundations in Georgia, its cultivation by cultural entrepreneurs skilled at seeking state support under Stalin, and its reinvigoration by a new generation of artists in Soviet popular culture during the Thaw years and after.

## Imperial Foundations and Stalinist Patronage

Inspired by the performance of a group of Georgian actors from Tbilisi's Rustaveli State Theater on their first tour of Moscow in 1930, a Russian theater critic summarized the multiethnic cultural ideal of the new socialist state when he wrote: "The representatives of the national republics are no longer our 'guests,' but instead stand together with us as masters of our country, where old words like 'center' and 'periphery' have become obsolete."[20] The revolution promised to collapse the distance between center and periphery, discard the old ethnic hierarchies, and create a new society of equals. The radical promotion of the cultures of the periphery by Soviet authorities was meant to mark a significant departure from the Russian Empire and differed from the practices of other imperial states. While European colonial administrators in Africa and Asia tended to view indigenous singing and dancing as politically and morally sub-versive, often banning or relegating them to the realm of Orientalist exotica, Soviets celebrated the centrality of non-Russian song and dance as characteristic of the new order.[21] Non-Russian cultural elites from the republics were enlisted by the Stalinist state to introduce national themes into popular literature, music, film, and painting. Eroding the distinctions between folk and classical culture that too often cordoned off non-Russian cultural contributions, folkloric operas, symphonies, and ballets became the standards of the new Soviet artistic canon.

Because they were so vigorously promoted by the state, these non-Russian forms of musicality have been viewed as inauthentic Soviet-era creations built from the top-down. Musicologist Marina Frolova-Walker emphasizes the role of the center in the establishment of national con-servatories and musical practices, particularly in the Central Asian republics where "architects, instrumental and vocal teachers, compos-ers, liberettists, and so on, were sent out, their activities closely coordi-nated by Moscow, in much the same way that teams of Russian experts and workers would be sent out to construct a hydro-electric power sta-tion in a Central Asian republic."[22] Yet this experience did not hold true for all national republics. While the Kyrgyz SSR did not have an opera company until 1942, Georgia's first theater and opera house had been built long before the revolution, in 1851. Prior to the establishment of the Soviet Union, Georgians and Armenians had operas in their national languages, hybrid creations that blended national and European classical styles.[23] Furthermore, though they may have been coordinated and endorsed by the Soviet state, national musical forms were enthusiasti-cally embraced and employed in various ways by national intelligentsias, including in Central Asia.[24] While they were influenced by prevailing trends in the center, national artistic forms were culturally embedded artifacts that reflected the cultural and historical logic of their local language and context; despite the admonition that Soviet culture was supposed to be "national in form, socialist in content," when it came to artistic production, form and content were inseparable and mutually constitutive.

The repertoire of Georgian entertainers evoked distinctive practices of Georgian everyday life, which was imbued with a lyrical style of expansive performance. The anthropologists Mars and Altman claim that Georgian men in particular were "perpetually 'on show,'" competing with one another for status in lavish displays of consumption and hospitality.[25] Such theatricality readily lent itself to institutionalization as Georgian theater, and the singing that accompanied the consumption of food and drink at the *supra* could be fashioned into a standardized repertoire. However, the field of arts and entertainment also accorded a prominent place to Georgian women. In part this trend reflected overall Soviet patterns of gender distribution, which saw more women involved in cultural production than in political life.[26] Yet it also drew on a long-standing Georgian culture of female entertainment on the theatrical stage and in the music hall.[27] The script generally followed by Georgian female performers, passionate but restrained, could serve to balance the displays of their male counterparts or could stand alone, with Georgian women singing songs and wearing clothing that played on established patterns of exotic entertainment in Russia or suggested the ancient pedigree of Georgian culture.

This distinctive repertoire, with its masculine and feminine forms, had been cultivated by the artistic community of late imperial Georgia, part of the same revolution in local culture that had influenced the national sensibilities of the early Georgian Bolsheviks. The late nineteenth century saw a flowering of interest in all things Georgian among intellectuals in Tbilisi and Kutaisi, including the polyphonic singing common in Georgian folk songs and the wide variety of dances found in Georgia's regions. The rediscovery and reinvention of native culture was linked to a broader trend of growing national self-consciousness throughout the Russian Empire. More than most other nationally minded intellectuals, however, the Georgian nobility had privileged access not only to native inspiration, but also to the Russian court and, by extension, Russian imperial high culture. This particular feature stood in contrast to Ukrainians, whose nobility was Russian, or those from the Baltic region, where the nobility was largely German, to say nothing of the Muslim populations of the Caucasus and Central Asia, who scarcely participated in the cultural life of the Russian court. Where Georgian nobles first went in the middle of the nineteenth century, upwardly mobile professionals followed in the late imperial period, studying at Russian conservatories, performing on the Russian stage, and partaking in the cultural life of Moscow and St. Petersburg.

Modern Georgia's folk songs and dances were symbolically and sometimes actually developed between the centers of Russian imperial cultural production and the mountains and villages of Georgia. The professional biography of the late imperial Georgian composer Zakaria Paliashvili illustrates this tendency. After studying at the Moscow Conservatory, Paliashvili developed a keen interest in the folk songs of his native land. In 1903, he toured the mountains of the remote Georgian region of Svaneti, collecting rare folk songs. Combining ethnographic authority with knowledge of the musical forms of Russian imperial high culture, Paliashvili composed choral and orchestral works based on Georgian folk melodies.[28] The culmination of his efforts was the Georgian opera, *Absalom and Eteri* (*abesalom da eteri*), a story of tragic love performed in traditional Georgian costume and incorporating many of the Georgian folk dances that would later find their way to the Soviet stage, including the *kartuli*.

In Soviet song and dance ensembles, the Georgian repertoire developed in the imperial period was honed for pan-Soviet audiences. Their performances fit an established cultural mythology, which held dance to be the most spontaneous and intimate expression of national spirit. In the words of Igor Moiseev, the founder and director of the State Ensemble of Folk Dancing of the USSR:

> The soul of a people is revealed in dance, as well as in song . . . In dance one can see a people's character and temperament, their relationship to the surrounding world, their spiritual and material culture. Every people creates their own distinctive art of

the dance. Among every people there is an intrinsic language of dance, an original form of expression, mannerism, movement, coordination.

To demonstrate his claim Moiseev turned to Georgian dance as a well-known counterpoint to Russian dance, stating that "the way that Russian dances differ from Georgian ones . . . is understandable to all people regardless of their nationality or racial background."[29] Further emphasizing these differences to make their work understandable to new audiences, Georgian ensembles explicitly appealed to the deep reservoir of popular ethnographic knowledge about Georgia drawn from imperial Russian literature.[30] In fictional accounts, Georgian men were celebrated as warriors and skilled horsemen. Georgia's national dance ensemble played on this theme accordingly, with dances showing men engaged in spirited battle as masters of acrobatic display, and another dance, "Dzhigity," dedicated to their famed skill in Caucasian horse-riding.[31] Drawing on a literary trope that extended back to Mikhail Lermontov but was further popularized in prerevolutionary Russian kopeck novels, Georgian women were often represented as ethereal princesses, reinforced by their costumes and their graceful way of floating across the stage.[32]

Established on the basis of imperial theaters, amateur ethnographic song and dance companies, and a musical conservatory in Tbilisi that was closely linked to the artistic life of Moscow, Georgian performance took center stage as the most successful non-Slavic form of song and dance in the 1930s and 1940s. While the Ukrainians celebrated the first major *Dekada* of national culture in Moscow in early 1936, the Georgians followed closely in 1937, preceding Azerbaijan (1938), Armenia (1939), Kyrgzstan (1939), and Belarus (1940).[33] Although Kazakhstan had celebrated a *Dekada* slightly earlier, in late 1936, its national opera had only been established in 1933 and did not receive the prestigious Order of Lenin until 1958, while the Georgian Opera was given the award around the time of its first *Dekada*. Given the state's close supervision of cultural production, the symbolism of the order of the *dekady* and the prestige of official awards were seen as highly significant by Soviet performers and audiences alike.

In this period Georgian culture also benefitted from high-ranking institutional patrons. Stalin and other leading Georgian political figures played a particularly hands-on role in directing cultural production in their homeland. Stalin repeatedly expressed praise for Georgian folk ensembles and operas and was known as an amateur singer of Georgian songs himself. Keenly aware of Stalin's tastes, Lavrenti Beria took the lead in monitoring preparations for the first *Dekada* of Georgian culture in 1937.[34] Other Georgian political figures served as patrons to specific groups of artists. Abel Enukidze, the Secretary of the Presidium of the Central Executive Committee, had personally helped organize the performance by Tbilisi's Rustaveli State Theater in Moscow in 1930. Enukidze's patronage was expressed demonstrably; in official press photographs the party leader could be seen walking arm-in-arm with the Georgian theater's director, Sandro Akhmeteli.[35] Thanks in part to such patrons, Georgian artists played a central role in the state-funded construction of a multiethnic Soviet culture. Yet it is unlikely that Georgian song and dance ensembles would have received such conspicuous patronage if their repertoire had not been as polished as it was at the beginning of the Soviet period.

The interplay between cultural practices established in the imperial period and Stalinist political patronage can been seen in the biographies of Iliko Sukhishvili and Nino Ramishvili, the founders of the Soviet Georgian dance ensemble that astonished Moscow audiences during the 1958 *Dekada*. The husband and wife duo utilized patronage to build on the imperial legacy of Georgian song and choreography. Like the generation of artists who preceded him, Sukhishvili was fully fluent in both Georgian and Russian culture.[36] Born in 1907, he trained as a dancer and choreographer with Moscow's Bolshoi Theater from 1931 to 1936 before returning to his native Georgia to serve as a stage director for the Tbilisi Opera's production of *Keto and Kote* (*keto da kote*). Composed by Viktor Dolidze and based on Avksenti Tsagareli's nineteenth-century novel *khanuma*, the opera offered light social satire, depicting a prerevolutionary Tbilisi populated by bankrupt but proud nobles, wealthy merchants, mischievous matchmakers, and merry *kintoebi*, the traders and tricksters of the Georgian marketplace. The opera, which skillfully matched Georgian folk culture with the cosmopolitan sensibilities of the Georgian intelligentsia, was celebrated for its renditions of the songs and dances of the Georgian table, bazaar, and matrimonial fete. It was choreographed by Sukhishvili, with sets designed by Lado Gudiashvili, a painter who had resided in Paris amidst leading members of the artistic avant-garde.[37] The production was directed by Evgeni Mikeladze, who had trained at the Leningrad State Conservatory before becoming a leading figure in the Georgian artistic world.[38]

Sukhishvili and his wife, a famed dancer from a prominent Georgian family, were not only sophisticated interpreters of a distinctive national culture, but also effective cultural entrepreneurs skilled at operating in a Soviet political context. On June 12, 1945, following a decree by the Central Committee of the Georgian Communist Party, a directive of the Artistic Committee of the Georgian Council of Ministers established what would become a leading Soviet folk ensemble. According to the directive, a group of forty dancers was to be created under the auspices of the Georgian State Philharmonic, with Sukhishvili appointed as the ensemble's leader.[39] This group was among the largest folk ensembles in the Soviet Union and one of the first permanent folk collectives to be established and granted institutional affiliation. By contrast, Berezka, the famous Russian folk dance troupe, was not established until 1948.[40] Thus even in the late Stalinist period, when the state endorsed some expressions of Russian nationalism, Georgian culture continued to receive political support, thanks in no small part to the efforts of cultural entrepreneurs and party leaders based in Georgia.

Operating under the auspices of the Georgian State Philharmonic, Sukhishvili and Ramishvili benefitted greatly from state sponsorship, especially at the republic level. In addition to being a well-known dancer who had trained at the Bolshoi, Sukhishvili was a party member, and as early as 1946 he wrote directly to Kandid Charkviani, Georgia's Communist Party chief, to request additional tour dates for his ensemble, a private train car for their tour, and permission to have two of his top dancers excused from service in the Red Army.[41] Only one year after its establishment, the ensemble received invitations to perform in Moscow, Leningrad, Riga, Tallinn, and elsewhere. In asking permission from the Georgian Communist Party to accept these invitations, Sukhishvili did not hesitate to appeal to the national pride of party members, writing that it was "absolutely necessary ... to more widely show Georgian dance to our country's population." Yet cultivating such close ties with the authorities was not without risk. Ramishvili had to downplay the fact that she had relatives among the exiled Georgian Mensheviks, a fact that Beria had once darkly alluded to during a meeting with her in the 1930s.[42] In contrast to her husband, she did not seek admission to the party, perhaps hoping to avoid further scrutiny.

Successfully navigating the political landscape of the Stalinist Soviet Union, Sukhishvili and Ramishvili elaborated on an artistic idiom created by an earlier generation of Georgian artists. The ensemble's performances drew on both the late nineteenth-century revival of Georgian folk music and Sukhishvili's tenure with the Bolshoi Theater, evident in his emphasis on balletic coordination.[43] Costumes for the Georgian ensemble were designed by another Georgian with a deep understanding of the sensibilities of Russian high culture, Simon "Soliko" Virsaladze, who simultaneously worked as the lead designer for Leningrad's Kirov Opera and Ballet. A hybrid product of national and imperial culture, Georgia's dance ensemble conveyed an elaborate and exoticized Caucasian ethnography through movement and costume.

Reflecting its exceptional level of development, the Sukhishvili and Ramishvili ensemble depicted intricate subnational and regional variations in its repertoire, each with its own distinctive colorings. In addition to the paired *kartuli* dance, the group's repertoire also included the *khevsuruli*, a dance of Georgian highlanders, part of the choreographed "Khevsuretian suite," in which a fight among men in a mountainous village was broken up by a woman throwing her headdress among the warriors, which suddenly concluded the acrobatic clashing of daggers by the group's male dancers. Other dances conveyed the urbanity of prerevolutionary Tbilisi, with the *karachokheli* dance depicting the black-clothed *kintoebi* engaged in spirited displays of cunning and jest, punctuated by toasting and carousing. Each dance featured different costumes designed by Virsaladze, capturing Georgia's regional diversity, from the colorful clothing of the inhabitants of Ajara, on Georgia's Black Sea coast, to the long cloaks and furry hats of Georgia's highland shepherds in the north.

The adaptation and codification of a national choreography in service to the Soviet empire meant tailoring performances for predominantly Russian audiences. Yet artists like Sukhishvili and Ramishvili were genuinely committed to the elevation of Georgian folk traditions to high culture and eagerly sought out new audiences and further state support to achieve this goal. In staking their claim to the Soviet stage, Georgian song and dance ensembles ensured a prominent place for their nation's culture and prestige and material benefits for their members.

## Redeploying the Georgian Repertoire After Stalin

Georgian song and dance ensembles created room for themselves on the Soviet stage by building on existing traditions. However, because of the special patronage they received from the Stalinist state, their prominence was also seen as a reflection of the political leadership of Stalin and Beria and Georgia's special status within the Soviet imperial hierarchy. Accordingly, the popular protests that greeted de-Stalinization in Georgia in 1956 evinced a great deal of concern about the place of Georgian culture in the post-Stalinist state.

As tens of thousands of Georgians took to the streets of Tbilisi, they joined a commemoration of Stalin's death with a spirited defense of Georgia's national culture. The gathered crowds sang Georgian songs, some of them reputed to be Stalin's favorites, others more explicitly nationalist, like "dideba," the national anthem of Menshevik Georgia.[44] Vasili Mzhavanadze, the recently appointed First Secretary of the Georgian SSR who had built his career in Ukraine under Nikita Khrushchev, made an attempt to pacify the crowd with a conciliatory speech. According to one eyewitness, however, this attempt floundered when Mzhavanadze began his speech by addressing the crowd as "comrades" in Russian, briefly switched into faltering Georgian, and then returned to Russian after a few words. Eduard Shevardnadze, then the head of the Komsomol (Young Communist League) in Kutaisi, recalled hearing that Mzhavanadze's poor grasp of his native language had led to derisive laughter among the assembled crowd.[45] Support for Georgia's distinctive language and culture was a common theme uniting a rather chaotic coalition of protestors with a diverse set of political views.

A report assembled by the party's Central Committee in Moscow following the popular demonstrations detailed instances of more aggressive nationalist sentiment in Georgia, including calls for ethnic Russian "occupiers" to leave Georgia and violent threats against Russian and Armenian residents in the Georgian SSR.[46] According to the report, in a number of cases local party officials tolerated and even tacitly supported such nationalist demands. In the wake of the violent suppression of the protests, the Central Committee considered a range of potential responses to the crisis in Georgia, but ultimately made concessions that assuaged nationalist sentiment by reaffirming state support for Georgian culture. Most local party officials in Georgia kept their posts, though their activities faced greater central surveillance; in 1962, for instance, a number of party members in Georgia's Ajara region were expelled from the regional party branch for fining one another for using Russian words instead of Georgian ones in everyday conversation.[47] At the same time, ideologically acceptable forms of Georgian culture that were intelligible to a pan-Soviet audience were vigorously promoted. The Sukhishvili and Ramishvili ensemble took center stage at the 1958 *Dekada* in Moscow and was even invited back to perform at the Twenty-Second Party Congress of the Soviet Communist Party in 1961.[48] Although some in the party may have resented the continued prominence of non-Russians, the state actually expanded its promotion of multiethnic culture in this period.[49] The decision to do so was strategic as well as ideological; in addition to unrest in Georgia, the party had to deal with the aftermath of the popular revolt in Hungary in 1956, and it faced the threat of nationalist mobilization spreading to the Baltic republics.[50]

Accordingly, the emphasis on domestic diversity in Soviet culture outlasted Stalinism and in fact became even more widespread. In the years after Stalin's death, there was a further proliferation of national festivals, *druzhba* (friendship) holidays, and performances by artists from the national republics in outdoor parks and on factory floors.[51] While Moscow was still considered the "city of the leading masters of the stage" in the words of one Georgian artist, similar festivals were now held throughout the Soviet Union, part of a process of reinvigorated artistic exchange that promoted cultural circulation beyond the capital.[52] Efforts were also made to spread resources more evenly among the republics and to elevate other national ensembles to the level achieved by Georgians. Taking advantage of this renewed state promotion, dancers from Azerbaijan toured the Russian Far East, choirs from Belarus played in Tashkent, and symphonies based on Armenian folk melodies were broadcast over the airwaves.

Domestic internationalism was also more closely intertwined with the state's efforts at public diplomacy. Although the Thaw is justly associated with the growing popularity of Western jazz and rock in the Soviet Union, culture also flowed in the other direction through Soviet song and dance ensembles. In the 1950s, Soviet productions of folk dances proved to be genuinely popular abroad; not only did folk ensembles based on the Soviet model predictably crop up in the socialist states of Eastern Europe, but similar folk groups also arose in Greece, the Philippines, Mexico, Turkey, and Iran.[53] Even in the United States, the 1958 tour of the Moiseev Dance Company was a success, and the group appeared on the Ed Sullivan show.[54]

Although the Soviet state sought to rebalance multiethnic culture by giving increased support to other nationalities, the repertoire of Georgian performance was better developed and proved readily adaptable to changing Soviet needs. Of the Moiseev ensemble's non-Slavic dances, only the Georgian "Khorumi" evoked ethnographic authority; unlike the Uzbek "Cotton Dance" or the Azeri-inspired "Three Shepherds," it was referred to by a national name and seemed authentic, even if it was performed by a mainly Russian ensemble.[55] With its established artistic pedigree and wide range of forms, Georgian culture could be presented as timeless yet unmistakably modern in its relevance. Igor Stravinsky wrote in 1966 that Georgian polyphonic singing was a "tradition of musical performance with its roots in ancient times," which could nevertheless contribute more to the musical world than "any achievement in contemporary music." Georgian ensembles eagerly seized on this praise from one of the Soviet Union's leading composers and cited Stravinsky's claims in their promotional literature.[56]

During the Thaw, the Sukhishvili and Ramishvili ensemble became a mainstay of official Soviet ceremonies at home and the promotion of

Soviet multiethnic harmony abroad. Along with memorable performances at the Bolshoi in Moscow and La Scala in Milan, the troupe took
part in ideologically appropriate Soviet celebrations, and by 1971 performed between twenty to thirty concerts each year at collective farms,
between ten to twenty concerts at construction sites, and twenty to thirty
concerts in Soviet "industrial regions."[57] However, while a prominent
Soviet institution, the ensemble was effectively maintained as a private
dynasty of the Sukhishvili-Ramishvili family, and in Georgia it was popularly referred to as the "Sukhishvilebi" (the Sukhishvilis). Sukhishvili
and Ramishvili's twelve-year old son, Tengiz Sukhishvili, joined the
ensemble in 1953; he would go on to lead the dancers after his parents'
retirement, joined by his wife and, eventually, his own children.[58]

The success of Sukhishvili and Ramishvili's dance troupe inspired the
establishment of new groups. Singing and dancing ensembles arose at the
regional level in Georgia, with smaller ensembles gaining Soviet-wide
prominence. In 1968 Anzor Erkomaishvili, a Georgian composer, collaborated with Revaz Morchiladze, a local cultural official, to establish a song
and dance ensemble in the industrial city of Rustavi, outside of Tbilisi.[59]
Like Sukhishvili and Ramishvili's ensemble, the Rustavi troupe drew on
prerevolutionary musical traditions. Erkomaishvili came from a long line
of musicians and prerevolutionary intellectuals who had collected and performed the folk songs of rural Georgia.[60] He had close ties to Tbilisi's classical music community, since in 1961 he had established another Georgian
singing group, Gordela, under the auspices of the Georgian Philharmonic.
In addition to being a composer, he was a professor who specialized in ethnomusicology, lending his renditions of Georgian folk songs a certifiable
authenticity. Beginning with performances in Georgia, Erkomaishvili's
group found success touring the Soviet Union. In 1976, less than ten years
after their founding, the group performed at the Kremlin Palace. Their lead
soloist, Hamlet Gonashvili, eventually became the most famous singer of
traditional Georgian songs in the Soviet Union.[61]

By the late 1960s and early 1970s, Georgian ensembles played almost
annually in every Soviet republic, while the Georgian SSR welcomed
national song and dance troupes from across the Soviet Union to its
stages and concert halls.[62] Around the same time, Soviet citizens readily commented on the choreography of national character in another

pursuit, one that drew bigger audiences with the advent of television: soccer.[63] On the pitch, Georgian soccer players came to epitomize a distinctly ethnic style of play, one that built on the same qualities of "beauty, ingenuity, and agility" in movement that were celebrated in Georgian dance. Georgian soccer and Georgian dance shared a common mythology, one that both athletic promoters and choreographers capitalized on. An official fan guide to the Dinamo Tbilisi soccer team contained sketches of star Georgian players singing while engaged in acrobatic leaps toward the ball, and depicted Avtandil Ghoghoberidze, the team's striker, performing the *kartuli* dance with his hands while balancing on the ball.[64] Ghoghoberidze himself endorsed such depictions, describing the Georgian style of play as passionate and balletic, an athletic form of art. "Inspiration," wrote Ghoghoberidze, was needed "not only by poets and artists, but by everyone," and the success of Dinamo Tbilisi could be attributed to the players' "love of improvisation."[65] The association of Georgian soccer with Georgian dance worked both ways; for the 1958 *Dekada* of Georgian culture in Moscow, Sukhishvili and Ramishvili's dance ensemble introduced a new number whose playful choreography included passes made between dancers of a ball, evoking the "beautiful game."[66] Georgian soccer seemed like another manifestation of an innate Georgian artistry and helped further popularize the repertoire of Georgian performance.

Increasingly, Georgia's national choreography was directed toward international audiences as well, with "friendship" festivals held in the Soviet bloc countries of Eastern Europe and the achievements of Soviet culture promoted as part of the Soviet model for national development in Asia, Africa, and Latin America.[67] With these international audiences in mind, Soviet musical directors gathered in November 1960 to discuss the reorganization and strengthening of Goskontsert, the state's central concert agency. In their words, they sought to "enhance and expand cultural cooperation between the USSR and foreign countries . . . and show the peoples of these countries the achievements of Soviet culture, multiethnic in form, socialist in content."[68] Party officials were enlisted to help promote the works of Soviet artists and musicians, and Goskontsert was instructed to cooperate closely with the Ministry of Culture to improve the quality of concert promotion outside the Soviet Union.[69]

In Eastern Europe, Georgian performers were used to propagate Soviet claims that the culture of national minorities flourished under centralized socialist rule, and in the developing world they were deployed to dampen criticism that Soviet influence was simply another form of European imperialism. As identifiable ethnics who represented the diverse cultural crossroads of the Caucasus, Georgians could represent generic non-Russian ethnic diversity at international events and festivals, or engage in more targeted cultural diplomacy. Soviet cultural policymakers sent Armenian song and dance ensembles to perform in Lebanon, where there was a sizable Armenian diaspora, and Azeri groups to Iran, where Azeris were the largest national minority group.[70] Georgian groups not only appealed to closely related ethnic populations like the Laz along Turkey's Black Sea coast, but also excelled at offering an ethnographic performance spanning the Caucasus. In Turkey, Georgian folk ensembles sang songs in Laz (a language closely related to Georgian), but also in Abkhaz and Circassian, engaging two other groups from the Caucasus with sizable populations in Turkey.[71] While Soviet officials were wary of Soviet diasporas that did not have homelands within the Soviet Union, they did not hesitate to employee their own ethnic entertainers to appeal to the sympathies of diasporas abroad.

By virtue of their high level of professionalism, Georgian ensembles were also encouraged to tour in Western Europe and the United States, a privilege enjoyed by Moscow-based groups like the Moiseev ensemble but less frequently granted to ensembles based in the republics. In the 1970s, the Sukhishvili and Ramishvili ensemble performed in West Germany, Austria, Belgium, the Netherlands, and Switzerland.[72] The Georgian ensemble Gordela toured the United States in 1974, playing a series of concerts at Carnegie Hall that all received standing ovations from the audiences.[73] A follow-up report on the tour written by one of the Georgian directors for Goskontsert optimistically noted: "Despite the language barrier the American public did their best to express their warm feelings for the artists and the Soviet Union."[74] The ensemble was even invited to a dinner hosted by George Balanchine, a prominent Georgian emigre who had graduated from the Imperial Ballet in St. Petersburg and went on to cofound the New York City Ballet. As during the group's tour of Turkey, the contradictions of the Soviet Union's policy toward its diasporas lurked below the surface of the report; the fact that the Georgian ensemble traveled freely while many Jews were denied the right to emigrate from the Soviet Union led the US-based Jewish Defense League to set up pickets outside several of the concert venues.[75]

In a nod to the high profile Georgian culture achieved abroad in the context of the Cold War, in 1977 the Georgian folk song "Chakrulo" was among the pieces of music selected to be included in the 1977 Voyager space probe, the purpose of which was to broadcast information about human civilization to other intelligent life forms in the universe.[76] While they could be seen throughout the world and even heard in space, Georgian singers and dancers continued to maintain a solid institutional basis in their native republic throughout this period. In Tbilisi, members of state ensembles were given centrally located apartments and furnished with impressive rehearsal space. The Georgian republic provided an enviable base for Georgia's diaspora of cultural entrepreneurs and would nurture further innovations in the Georgian repertoire.

## Electrifying Folkloric Performance

Beginning in the late 1950s, Georgian popular music more directly engaged foreign culture in the realm of Soviet *estrada*. Although folkloric song and dance ensembles received the blessing of the state as solidly Soviet producers of culture, party ideologists were less sure of how to treat jazz, rock, and the popular Gypsy songs of prerevolutionary Russia. In the context of the Thaw, which increased exposure to new forms of popular music, the Soviet Union's ethnic entertainers borrowed the Western sounds of jazz and rock and blended them with national themes. In so doing, they helped create an enduring yet innovative form of multiethnic musical entertainment that proved both ideologically palatable and popular with Soviet audiences.

The state's complicated position toward rock and roll was a frequent subject of discussion among Soviet concert agencies. The genre was initially eschewed before Soviet ideologists finally conceded that it had already "entered the everyday lives" of Soviet citizens in the Thaw years.[77] Since banning the musical style was impossible, rock needed to be made Soviet, which meant it had to be infused with Soviet folkloric sensibilities. Reflecting the logic of domestic internationalism, the head of Goskontsert proclaimed at a meeting of concert organizers in 1966: "Our *estrada* must have its own identity, one that might counter the influence of Western artistic tendencies in the arts of *estrada* in our [socialist] countries."[78] The readiest means of lending popular musical forms like rock a Soviet identity was to ethnicize them and link them to national cultures within Soviet borders. Doing so built on preexisting institutions dedicated to the production of national culture and was met with great interest by artists from the national republics.

Historians of Soviet culture have until recently drawn a sharp distinction between a vibrant, creative, and internationalist artistic culture during the Thaw period and a stifled, repetitive, and insular cultural life during the Brezhnev era of *zastoi*.[79] However, such a neat dichotomy ignores a latter period characterized by a thriving culture of popular music, to say nothing of the burgeoning second economy and the production of witty and ironic films.[80] Rather than growing stagnant after Khrushchev's ouster in 1964, the world of Soviet *estrada* benefitted from the logistical decentralization and benign neglect of the Brezhnev era. While the Thaw saw increased exposure to foreign musical styles, it was also an era of assertive cultural policy. Khrushchev made pronouncements on which forms of art and music he did and did not approve of, publicly complaining in 1963, "When I hear jazz, it's as if I had gas on the stomach."[81] Even in the early years of the Thaw, efforts were made to extend state control over the haphazard Soviet concert circuit, theoretically centralizing the production of *estrada* under the auspices of Gosestrada, a state-run agency, and increasing the state's capacity to influence musical output. Brezhnev, by contrast, was less likely to weigh in with his own musical preferences, and a relative laxity in exercising central controls allowed for the emergence of new institutional patrons for musical ensembles, including factories and higher education institutions.

In the Brezhnev era, Soviet concertgoers flocked to performances by Azeri jazz musicians like Vagif Mustafazadeh and Rafik Babaev, often accompanied by Azeri crooners such as Rashid Beibutov and Muslim

Magomaev, who combined the modal scales of the Azeri musical style of *mugham* with the rhythm and instrumentation of jazz. Others, particularly the younger generation who came of age in the late 1960s and 1970s, closely followed the Belarusian folk rock group Pesniary, who performed in colorful polyester outfits that evoked the national costume of Belarus. Official and unofficial progressive rock bands from Estonia gained cult followings performing in Estonian and Russian.[82] Not only were many popular musical entertainers not Russian, but some of the most artistically innovative rock and jazz concert festivals were also held in cities on the periphery, like Baku, Riga, Tallinn, Yerevan, and Tbilisi. The capitals of Soviet national republics sometimes offered more creative freedom, and artists only had to contend with republic-level concert agencies (in contrast to Moscow, where artists had to deal with the competing agendas of Roskontsert and Moskontsert, the concert agencies of the RSFSR and the city of Moscow).[83] National republics also had their own distinct schools of music, some more developed than those in Russia. For example, in the 1920s and 1930s, independent Estonia was home to one of the first homegrown jazz bands in Europe; after the Soviet incorporation of the Baltic states, Estonian musicians gained fame in the world of Soviet jazz.[84] The same was true of socialist Central European countries like Hungary, where artists drew on the traditions of Budapest's interwar nightclubs and theaters to become leading *estrada* performers in the Soviet Union.[85] The emphasis of Goskontsert, however, remained on the promotion of the music of domestic Soviet nationalities.

Georgia had a host of artists fully fluent in both the folk culture of their republic and the imperial culture of the Soviet capital. Thanks to this cultural bilingualism Georgians dominated the world of *estrada* in all its forms, from ballads and prerevolutionary romances (*romansy*), to jazz, Georgian folk rock, and psychedelic rock operas. Not only did Georgians draw creatively on the existing idiom of ethnic entertainment, but they proved adept at walking what cultural officials described as the "very fine, but nevertheless quite clear line" of ideological acceptability, ensuring themselves a prominent place on the Soviet stage.[86] In exchange for their acceptance of the rules of Soviet cultural politics, their albums were widely released and they were given access to a large audience through state-sponsored radio and television broadcasts.

By the late 1960s the resources of the Georgian Philharmonic supported a large number of Vocal-Instrumental Ensembles (VIAs), a Soviet response to the rock band format. While they represented the state's effort to co-opt the more threatening aspects of rock music, Vocal-Instrumental Ensembles were genuinely popular and were equally influenced by Western music, folk traditions, and the work of established Soviet composers.[87] Their members became officially sanctioned stars, visible in movies and Soviet television specials. They helped fabricate a culture of entertainment that was at once artistically progressive and nostalgically indebted to Soviet folk culture.

Orera, Georgia's best-known *estrada* group, was also the first Vocal-Instrumental Ensemble registered in the Soviet Union. The group was informally organized in 1958, the same year that Georgia's song and dance ensemble took the stage as part of the *Dekada* of Georgian culture in Moscow. Its founders were a group of young students from Tbilisi's Institute of Foreign Languages: Robert Bardzimashvili, the ensemble's leader, who studied French at the Institute; Teimuraz Davitaia, a language student who had earlier considered a career in Georgian dance; and another classmate, Zurab Iashvili. Shortly after, Vakhtang Kikabidze, yet another student from the Institute of Foreign Languages, joined the ensemble, as did Nani Bregvadze, who had received more formal training as a pianist and vocalist at the Tbilisi Conservatory. Bardzimashvili came up with the group's name, a nonsensical expression of joy that formed the chorus to many Georgian folk songs. In its first years Bardzimashvili led the group, singing and playing keyboard and guitar. Davitaia accompanied him on guitar, while Iashvili played keyboard and harmonica. Kikabidze began as a drummer, but eventually became one of the group's lead singers. Nani Bregvadze, the group's only female member, performed with the group on slower numbers, singing jazz and folk songs, as well as classic Russian *romansy*.[88]

Orera began as an effort to entertain fellow students with renditions of the songs of Western performers like Louis Armstrong, whose records were impossible to find in the Soviet Union.[89] Soon, they expanded their repertoire to include classic Georgian folk songs infused with jazz sensibilities, as well as songs in the languages they studied at the Institute, including French, Italian, and English. What started as an informal group was officially registered as a Vocal-Instrumental Ensemble under the auspices of the Georgian State Philharmonic in 1961. From these modest beginnings, the ensemble became one of the most popular groups on the Soviet concert circuit; their success helped launch Kikabidze and Bregvadze as Soviet cultural celebrities.

Orera's repertoire reflected the diverse musical influences of its members, the distinctive musical heritage of Tbilisi, and the new demands of Soviet audiences. Kikabidze grew up in a cramped apartment in Tbilisi's historic and close-knit Mtatsminda neighborhood, located on the slopes of a hill overlooking the city. Although his mother was a scion of the Bagrationi dynasty that had ruled Georgia until the nineteenth century, she lived modestly. Indeed, Kikabidze was raised in relative poverty after his father died in the Second World War. Like many other Georgians of his generation, Kikabidze regularly gathered with his friends in the entryway of their building, where they took turns playing a guitar and imitating the rock and jazz songs that one of them picked up with a receiver that could capture broadcasts of the Voice of America.[90] In addition to rock and jazz, Kikabidze grew up singing the traditional songs of the Georgian table, the urban folk songs of Tbilisi, and the popular wartime ballads of Soviet singers like Mark Bernes, Leonid Utesov, and Klavdiia Shulzhenko.

Nani Bregvadze, a childhood friend of Kikabidze who grew up in the same neighborhood, was also exposed to diverse musical influences. Her mother, Olga Mikeladze, was an amateur pianist descended from a Georgian noble family, and her maternal grandmother and aunt were both professional singers. While Kikabidze drank deeply of Tbilisi's musical street culture of guitars, organ grinders, and drinking songs, Bregvadze was trained at the piano from an early age, performing Gypsy songs and Russian *romansy* for guests at her family's home, which, with its ornate prerevolutionary furniture, had the air of an aristocratic salon. Coached by her grandmother and her aunt, the young Bregvadze would studiously wrap herself in a shawl and perform songs for visitors.[91] All members of Orera grew up singing in Russian as well as Georgian, many coming from prominent Georgian families in which the high culture of late imperial Russia was still cherished. Their fluency in multiple languages and diverse musical styles accorded with the state's continued push for domestic internationalism.

*Figure 4.2* Orera, the Soviet Union's first Vocal-Instrumental Ensemble, performing in Moscow in 1972. Vakhtang Kikabidze sings in the foreground. Russian State Archive of Film and Photo Documents.

Drawing on elements of pan-Soviet *estrada* and the repertoire of Soviet Georgian folk performance, Orera's concerts were a combination of polyglot musical virtuosity and flamboyant showmanship. The group's male members, though dressed in colorful and modish Soviet jackets, occasionally broke into traditional Georgian dances on stage. The performance might then shift to a more modern key, often with the help of backup singers, dancers, a piano player, and a saxophonist.[92] The group alternated between jazz and rock songs and Georgian polyphonic *a capella* singing, occasionally slowing the pace with ballads sung by Nani Bregvadze, who dressed in sequin gowns evocative of the jazz age.[93]

Orera's concert programs from the late 1960s reveal a good deal about this hybrid form of musical entertainment that retained elements of national distinctiveness. As one of their first songs, they often performed the upbeat "U devushek nashikh" ("Our Girls"). The composition was written by Giorgi Tsabadze, a Georgian songwriter affiliated with the Georgian Philharmonic, whose light, lyrical style was beloved by Georgian audiences and who later reached a wider Soviet public with songs written for films, including a popular musical, *Melodies of the Vera Quarter* (*veris ubnis melodiebi*), set in old Tbilisi. "U devushek nashikh" was a predictable song about women whose hearts were true and whose beauty was unsurpassed. More original was the song's arrangement; set to a cheerful, swinging beat, most of the song's verses were in Georgian, while the song's title and final verse were in Russian. Such musical arrangements made Georgian music accessible to a wider audience.[94] Other songs in the group's repertoire drew more heavily on Georgian folk traditions. The Georgian-language "Adandali," described in the program as a set of musical "pictures of old Tbilisi," was a composition based on the urban folk songs of Tbilisi's streets.[95] In the ensemble's rendition traditional Georgian drumming was matched with the more contemporary sound of a trumpet, and a jazz organ imitated the hand-turned organs popular in prerevolutionary Tbilisi. Performing the number, each male member of Orera took turns singing, clapping his hands, and performing brief dances that recalled the mischievous market traders and street entertainers of old Tbilisi. After these energetic dances, which often had the audience clapping along, the piece concluded with intricate *a capella* harmonizing.[96] Other songs drew on a similar sense of folkish nostalgia, but not always a Georgian one. The group's rendering of Grigorii Ponamarenko and Gennadii Kolesnikov's whistful "Topolia" ("Poplars") summoned an overtly Slavic sentimentality for a village love symbolized by a lone poplar tree. Orera's musicians played the song on two guitars, while all of the group's members harmonized the tune's plaintive refrain.[97]

Often, the group's finale would be Revaz Laghidze's "Tbiliso," listed in Russian on the program as "A Song about Tbilisi."[98] A love ballad addressed to the Georgian capital, it was probably the second most well-known Georgian tune in the Soviet Union after "Suliko," a song popularized in the 1930s with Stalin's endorsement. Its lyrics spoke to the enduring place of Georgia in the Soviet imagination, describing the capital as the "land of sun and roses." Drawing on imagery familiar to Soviet citizens, the sun stood for warmth and brightness, the rose for romance, passion, and possibly seduction. The lyrics described a Georgian's love for his native capital, exclaiming: "Tbiliso . . . without you I live without my heart." Most Soviets found the lyrics of the song convincing, especially when sung by Bregvadze, who took the lead as the group's male members harmonized and offered light instrumental accompaniment.[99]

By the late 1960s, Orera toured the Soviet Union continuously, performing frequently in Moscow and playing thirty concerts in Leningrad in less than a month.[100] In 1967, the group received the honor of representing the Soviet Union at an international musical contest held in connection with the Expo 67 World's Fair in Montreal.[101] Their strength lay in the depth of their repertoire. When performing in eastern bloc countries like Bulgaria, they represented a more Westward-leaning face of the Soviet Union with songs of international friendship sung in French; when they performed in Turkey in 1968 they sang folk songs in the languages of Turkey's Abkhaz and Circassian minorities, as well as popular songs in Turkish.[102] Such specialized set lists were reminiscent of the targeted cultural appeals made by Georgia's song and dance ensembles while performing abroad.

Orera's success spawned a number of imitators and spin-off projects, including the ensemble Iveria, which tended more toward rock than jazz, but followed its predecessor in finding inspiration in Georgia's folk traditions.[103] For her part, singer Nani Bregvadze translated her success with the ensemble into enduring fame by emphasizing the high culture aspects of Orera's performance. Since she was the ensemble's only female member and typically performed solo works with the group's backing, it was a relatively simple transition for her to launch a separate career in the 1970s. Although unmistakably Georgian, she became best known as a singer of Russian *romansy*, a genre that earlier had been dominated by Romani performers.[104] Together with Georgian pianist Medea Gongliashvili, Bregvadze toured the Soviet Union and became a favorite of Soviet audiences. Her performances were attended by Brezhnev himself, who reportedly loved this highly emotive musical genre.[105] In addition to her captivating voice, part of Bregvadze's appeal lay in her air of aristocratic elegance, which conveyed the sophistication of late imperial Russian high culture. This appeal was evinced by official programs for her concerts, such as the one printed for a 1970 performance in Moscow, which emphasized the noble bearing of Gongliashvili and Bregvadze. In a sepia-toned photograph Gongliashvili was shown seated at an ornate Baroque style piano, an oriental carpet and parquet floor in the background, while Bregvadze struck an even more luxurious pose, resting her elbow on the top of the piano, her head on her hand, and casting an alluring gaze as her long dress reached down to the floor. The photographs suggested a certain forbidden intimacy, as if the two were playing a private concert for the listener alone. The back cover featured a close-up shot of Nani Bregvadze, shown from the waist up wearing a necklace and pearl earrings, with a worldly look of enchantment on her face.[106]

Bregvadze never forgot that her audience was predominantly Russian when she planned her concerts. In an interview, she noted: "In Russia, you could not just sing in Georgian. As a Georgian, you could sing three or four songs in Georgian, which people found pleasant to hear, but they wanted something to listen to." She recalled how at first the musical authorities were not interested in her *romansy*, seeing them as vestiges of aristocratic life, but there was such a demand for them that they eventually became a bigger part of her repertoire.[107] By the late 1970s and early 1980s, she played dozens of concerts in Moscow each year and took up periodic residence at the Hotel Moskva near the Kremlin.[108] Although she often socialized with the Georgian musicians and singers in residence at Moscow's Bolshoi Theater, she was startled by the celebrity status she was accorded in Russia. According to her, even the most well-known female artists in Georgia would never be approached by strangers on the street, but in Russia "men and women greeted you and came up to you when they recognized you," and in Moscow devoted fans began waiting for her at her hotel after her concerts. Yet Bregvadze welcomed the respect she garnered among the Russian intelligentsia, which saw her as an authentically original performer whose work was officially sanctioned, yet remained artistically innovative and evocative of the bygone Russian Empire.

While Bregvadze's career trajectory reflected her classical training and the more restrained culture of Georgian female entertainment, Orera's Vakhtang Kikabidze placed more emphasis on the exuberant culture of the Georgian feast, while still maintaining the cosmopolitan sensibilities appropriate for an heir to a Georgian aristocratic line. His songs combined both and presented them with a trademark gap-toothed smile and charismatic style of crooning that made him a recognizable

*Figure 4.3* Nani Bregvadze performs for a gathering of influential Georgian cultural figures at sculptor and painter Zurab Tsereteli's house in Tbilisi, 1970. Film director Eldar Shengelaia is seated at the far left, while Tsereteli looks on from the far right. National Archives of Georgia.

star of Soviet film and television. One television special, from the late 1960s, showed Kikabidze and the other members of Orera performing a jazzed-up version of a musically complex Gurian folk song near the banks of the Moscow river atop Lenin Hills.[109] The Georgian-produced televised film, *Orera, Full Speed Ahead* (*orera, sruli svlit*), widely broadcast in 1970, showed Kikabidze and the rest of the group touring the world, performing songs in Georgian, Russian, French, Italian, Spanish, and English.

Granted a lead role in the 1969 production of *Don't Grieve*, directed by the Moscow-based Georgian director, Giorgi Danelia, Kikabidze sang, danced, and toasted, all the while proving himself as a convincing actor. In 1977, Kikabidze again joined Danelia for the tragicomic *Mimino*. In the film, Kikabidze played the hapless but honorable Georgian pilot Valentin Mizandari, who leaves his native Georgia to seek success in Moscow, only to fall into a series of misadventures. Mizandari was an example of an archetypal Caucasian naif.[110] Danelia, who was born in

Georgia but grew up and was educated in Moscow, added a twist, placing his naif in the Soviet capital and using him to wryly comment on
Russian as well as Georgian life. Danelia wrote the part of Mizandari
with Kikabidze in mind, and together the two drew on their knowledge
of Georgia and their experiences in Moscow to convincingly depict a
character caught between his native village in the mountains of eastern Georgia and the frenetic life of the Soviet capital.[111] As the film was
developed, it was altered to better reflect the realities of life in Georgia as
both of them knew it. Initially, the film was to be a musical comedy that
would showcase Kikabidze's singing skills.[112] However, at a recording
session, Kikabidze noted the unrealistic nature of a scene in which the
hero, Mizandari, was supposed to sing aloud as he walked through the
forest: a Georgian highlander like Mizandari would be more reserved.
Based upon Kikabidze's ethnographic observation, the character was
made more restrained, though he sang and danced with appropriate ethnic spirit when called upon to do so, including during a banquet scene at
a Moscow hotel.[113]

The movie was eventually transformed from a musical to a comedy
whose lyricism lay in its accented and witty dialogue. Nevertheless, the
expressive song that accompanied the film's opening credits, "Chito
gvrito," ("Little Turtle Dove"), added to the film's popularity. The song's
lyrics were written by Petre Gruzinskii, a respected Georgian poet, and it
was set to folkish, orchestrated music composed by the Soviet Georgian
musician Gia Kancheli. Kikabidze would go on to perform the song at
events such as the televised Soviet New Year's special in 1981.[114] Before
performing, he explained the song's connection to his homeland for the
Soviet studio audience, who could not understand its Georgian lyrics. It
was a song of personal nostalgia for a Georgian childhood presented to
and shared with the Soviet public. The song's structure made it especially
well-suited to Russian audiences; after Kikabidze sang each Georgian-
language verse, Russian speakers could easily sing along to a repetitive
refrain based on the words "chito gvrito, chito margalito" ("little turtle
dove, little pearl").

A film that was made for a pan-Soviet audience but meant to be culturally credible among the Georgian public, *Mimino* provided the well-
known commodity of Georgian performance while offering a unique

perspective on Soviet life as it was experienced by members of the Georgian diaspora. Mizandari's naivete was paired with a rigid code of honor that was noble in comparison with the behavior of many of those around him, yet misunderstood and reflective of the strict patriarchal life of his native mountain village in Georgia. The modernity and internationalism of Moscow was shown as colorful and alluring, yet also hectic and lonely when compared with the provincial backwardness and human charm of the Georgian regional capital of Telavi. According to the notes of the film's editor, *Mimino* showed that "every person needs to have his own place on this earth."[115] Eventually, Mizandari realizes that his home is in Georgia, despite the occasional attentions of an attractive Russian flight attendant and the temptation of piloting Soviet jets to Berlin. In the end, the film was a loving portrayal of a charming but haphazard Georgia that creatively played with existing representations.

## Representing an Internal Diaspora

Although celebrated as identifiably ethnic, Georgian cultural production in the Soviet Union was always a hybrid mixture created out of Georgian cultural trends from the late imperial period, Soviet institutions, and the expectations of a predominantly Russian audience. After all, succeeding within the framework of domestic internationalism was about successfully performing otherness in ways that met the needs of the Soviet state and society. While Soviet cultural officials made use of Georgian culture for political ends, Georgian cultural entrepreneurs leveraged state support to gain prominence for themselves and the Georgian cultural repertoire in which they specialized. Even as they showed sensitivity and flexibility in anticipating the expectations of Soviet and international audiences, a substantial part of their repertoire remained in the Georgian language. This made them different from most Soviet Jewish artists of the Thaw, who performed exclusively in Russian and often positioned themselves as heirs of the Russian intelligentsia.[116] It also distinguished them from groups like the Estonians, who excelled as jazz musicians but whose own ethnic expression was more muted. Instead,

Georgian entertainers performed audible and vibrantly colorful songs and dances of ethnic expressiveness, using otherness to achieve professional success and national representation beyond the borders of their southern republic.

Indeed, outside of Georgia there was only one official institution that could claim to represent the Soviet Union's Georgian diaspora: a Moscow-based Georgian song and dance ensemble and school founded during the Thaw. The ensemble's origins dated back to 1955, when Revaz Janiashvili, a Georgian graduate of the Moscow Electro-Technical Institute, was asked by the Komsomol to help a number of soldiers prepare for an anniversary concert. Among the soldiers were many men from the Caucasus, who, like Janiashvili, had been raised on Georgian song and dance. Two years later Janiashvili helped establish Kolkhida, a permanent Georgian dance ensemble, and Iveria, a Georgian children's dance collective, in the Soviet capital.[117]

Janiashvili's dance troupe gave members of the Georgian diaspora a framework in which to pass Georgian practices of music and dance on to their children. The group's costumes were made in Tbilisi, and their dance studio in Moscow featured a library dedicated to the history and culture of Georgia.[118] Group members traveled to Georgia frequently to train with Georgian dancers and to perform before Georgian audiences.[119] The dance group became a fixture in Moscow's cultural landscape and by 1982 had performed over 1,200 concerts, made thirty-three televised appearances, and received more than two hundred awards.[120] When a visiting delegation of Georgian artists visited Moscow that same year they were delighted by the performance of the children's Iveria dance collective, whose members were apparently so convincing in their renditions of Georgian dances that they could have been mistaken for children from the Georgian cities of "Chiatura or Gori, Telavi or Zugdidi."[121] Although institutional representation for an internal diaspora like the Georgians was permitted only when it was strictly cultural in nature, having an officially sanctioned national ensemble and a children's collective in Moscow gave the Georgian community a gathering place where a range of personal and professional relationships could be forged.

With unique access to the Soviet stage, members of the Georgian diaspora projected an influence far beyond their native republic. They claimed privilege as interpreters of a vibrant national culture that was embraced by a broader Soviet audience and received state support even as it pushed the limits of ideological acceptability. However, the repertoire of Georgian performance that came to the fore in this period soon spilled beyond the realm of officially sanctioned popular entertainment and into the Soviet marketplace.

# 5

# Strangeness for Sale

On October 22, 1968, the body of a young man was discovered along the banks of the Tskhenistsqali River near the town of Abasha, in western Georgia's Tskhakaia region. Dressed in a dark suit and white silk shirt, his legs and arms bound together and weighed down with a heavy metal tractor part, the victim could not be readily identified. The local authorities were notified and the corpse was taken to the morgue for a forensic examination. Investigators soon found further evidence detailing the victim's violent end: two of his teeth were missing, and bruising on his neck attested to likely strangulation. No form of identification could be located on the victim, and because his face was swollen and disfigured, the forensic examiners could only state that he was "an unknown man, approximately 30–35 years of age."[1] After an exhaustive search, investigators from the Tskhakaia region's Prosecutor's Office managed to recover only one scrap of potential evidence from the top pocket of the victim's jacket: a small receipt for gasoline which, according to the stamp on it, had been issued in Volgograd, a Russian city almost five hundred miles away.

A few weeks later, Shota Jvebenava was recovering from the November holidays at the lavish Sandunovsky Baths in central Moscow. Originally from western Georgia, Jvebenava lived a charmed life in the Soviet capital as a currency speculator and dealer in illicit goods. Operating in dollars and gold coins, he frequented the finest restaurants, taking friends from Georgia and his female companion, a dancer from the Berezka Russian folk dance ensemble, to dine at Seventh Heaven, the revolving restaurant located atop Moscow's Ostankino tower. Although far from his homeland, Jvebenava stayed in close contact with friends and family from western Georgia, playing host when they visited Moscow, helping them obtain scarce luxury goods in the capital, and regularly exchanging personal and professional information of mutual interest and benefit. Jvebenava also enjoyed ties with Moscow's Georgian community. Though the Georgian diaspora was varied and composed of different social circles, its members shared information about other Georgians as well as strategies of survival in the Soviet metropolis. In particular, Mingrelians from western Georgia like Jvebenava had a reputation for remaining in close contact with one another, bound by a distinctive regional culture and a unique dialect of Georgian.[2]

On that day at the Sandunovsky Baths, Jvebenava met a fellow native of western Georgia who worked in Moscow as an engineer.[3] Sitting down with Jvebenava in the ornate steam room, the engineer passed along the latest rumors picked up during his recent visit home to Georgia. He reported that a corpse had been discovered on the shores of a river near Jvebenava's hometown. He told his friend that after an exhaustive investigation the authorities had finally identified the body as that of Roman Churgulia, another native of western Georgia, who had left to study in Volgograd and since his graduation worked as a driver for a consumer goods factory in Russia. The engineer indicated that the likely suspect was Aleksandre Bedia, the head of the Georgian Ministry of Internal Affairs' police force in the Tskhakaia region. Bedia apparently blamed the young Churgulia for the death of his own son in a fight in Volgograd a few months earlier, and many in the Tskhakaia region remembered how Bedia's bereaved wife had called for vengeance at her son's funeral. Rumors of the circumstances of Churgulia's murder soon circulated widely among Moscow's Georgian community, including gruesome claims that the victim's hair had been pulled out by Bedia's wife prior to his death.[4]

As these detailed accounts of the homicide spread through informal Georgian circles in Moscow, Soviet law enforcement authorities operating in both Russia and Georgia were closing in on the perpetrators. They established that the suspect, Bedia, had come to Volgograd with his associates, asked Churgulia to take a ride with him, and then brought the young man back to western Georgia, where Bedia and the others strangled him and dumped his body in the river. The Volgograd branch of the Ministry of Internal Affairs tried a number of different approaches to discover the identity of Bedia's accomplices, including the ethnic profiling of potential Georgian suspects, combing passenger manifests and hotel guest lists "with the goal of identifying all persons of Georgian nationality" who were present in their city around the time of Churgulia's murder.[5] Law enforcement officials questioned a number of Georgians living in Volgograd, including many who had come to study in the city's institutes in the early to middle 1960s and one of Churgulia's classmates from an evening course at the Institute of Soviet Trade.[6]

The interrogation transcripts recorded by law enforcement officials shed light on everyday life among the Georgian diaspora in a Russian city in the late 1960s, revealing a community bound together by common origins and family acquaintances in western Georgia, joint celebrations, and expectations of mutual assistance. The group included stellar medical students, but the well-liked, less scholarly Churgulia was also among them. Before his death, he apparently supplemented his income by illicitly selling wine from Georgia and goods from the factory where he worked at the city's market.[7] Like Jvebenava and his associates in Moscow, Georgians in Volgograd maintained close ties with their homeland and regularly shared news about events there.

The investigation had hardly begun before it was compromised. In Moscow, Jvebenava maintained contact with Bedia and other Georgian members of the Ministry of Internal Affairs of the Tskhakaia region, who often visited him there. These regional notables seldom hesitated to use the resources available to them as law enforcement agents to assist friends and associates. Once they had tipped off Jvebenava that the Moscow police were on his trail for currency speculation, and another time they allegedly forged a special passport that allowed a Georgian acquaintance involved in informal trading to live in any Russian city he chose.[8] In fact, Bedia's abuse of his official post went much further. It later was discovered that he dealt in illegal firearms and unregistered vehicles, paid a hefty bribe to have his son admitted to medical school in Volgograd, and received assistance from his friends in the Georgian Ministry of Internal Affairs in abducting and killing Roman Churgulia,

whom he blamed for his son's death. It is little wonder that Bedia's col-
league in the local Georgian branch of the KGB immediately suspected
Bedia's involvement when Churgulia's body was identified and raised
the issue with his superiors in the KGB.[9] Bedia responded by directing
an associate to steal and destroy classified materials relating to his investigation from the safe of the regional Georgian KGB office.[10]

When the theft of the classified documents was discovered, the KGB
brought its full resources to bear on the investigation. KGB officials from
the agency's headquarters in Moscow became involved, as did republic-
level KGB agents in Tbilisi, serving to counterbalance the sway that
Bedia had over local law enforcement in western Georgia. By stealing
these highly secret documents, Bedia had violated the Soviet state's sac-
rosanct information regime. Bedia and his associates were arrested, one
by one, and charged with an array of crimes, including the murder of
Churgulia. Jvebenava, who had been notified that the authorities were
looking for him, fled Moscow for his native town of Gegechkori, in western Georgia, but was called in for questioning soon after his return to
Moscow in mid-1969.[11] It is unclear whether Jvebenava was charged with
a crime; his questioners seemed more interested in his knowledge of
Bedia's activities and may have been willing to overlook his involvement
in illicit trade in exchange for information on the murder and the leaking
of state secrets by Bedia and his associates.

KGB agents painstakingly compiled a twenty-volume classified report
on the events, collecting evidence, detailing interrogations, and laying
out their case against those implicated. The pages of the report reveal
that in the era of late socialism, informal Georgian networks were sometimes more effective than the state when it came to sharing information
and gaining access to scarce resources. Economic entrepreneurs among
the Georgian diaspora maintained close links to their native Georgia,
where personal ties with local officials and a general atmosphere of tolerance of unofficial economic activity created unique opportunities for
mutual profit. Their networks were flexibly organized along regional,
social, and familial lines, and they shared information and resources for
mutual benefit. It was not entirely by coincidence that Jvebenava learned
of the details of Churgulia's murder at a bathhouse in Moscow before
this information became available to state investigators.

The Georgian diaspora was well positioned to capitalize on the new economic opportunities of the Brezhnev era. As participants in a closely networked community, Georgian entrepreneurs enjoyed access to the rare goods in which their homeland specialized; as skilled performers of ethnic difference in the marketplace, they elaborated on an established Georgian brand of exoticism, crossing national boundaries when necessary to make mutually beneficial deals and sell their products to Soviet consumers of all ethnic backgrounds. Although they had some of the same skills and inherited a familiar repertoire of national difference, they differed from past iterations of the Georgian diaspora in some important ways. Unlike Georgian artists, they were more likely to come from outside Tbilisi and were more interested in personal profit and local control than participation in the cultural life of the center. In part, their background and attitudes reflected important changes in Georgia and Moscow after Stalin. The rapid political advancement that Bolshevik revolutionaries had experienced as they were propelled from the Georgian countryside to the heights of power in the early Soviet state seemed an increasingly faint possibility. Faced with political limitations, the Georgian diaspora that came to the fore in the Brezhnev era piggybacked on the official Soviet economy instead. Their activities were less directed by Moscow and thus never fully aligned with the goals of the center. The fruits of Georgian economic success were also more bittersweet. While their understanding of the Soviet economy and ability to operate in a predominantly Russian host society helped Georgians benefit from a period of limited economic liberalization, their methods and noticeable economic gains exposed them to potential prosecution and revealed growing tensions in the Soviet empire of diasporas.

## The Georgian Diaspora and Brezhnev's Little Deal

On the surface, the rule of Leonid Brezhnev was a time of stagnant economic growth rates. However, official economic figures concealed the growth of a flourishing "second economy" that sprang out of and in some cases supported the official one.[12] The state viewed the second economy with distrust, but eventually came to see it as a necessity.

Literary scholar Vera Dunham suggested the concept of a "Big Deal" to account for the state's accommodation of the material tastes of a new Soviet middle class under Stalin.[13] Economist James R. Millar has argued that the burgeoning second economy under Brezhnev was made possible by a "Little Deal" struck between the leadership and the Soviet Union's urban population.[14] The Little Deal implied a greater tolerance of petty private economic activities, both legal and illegal, as a means of providing consumer goods for an expanding and increasingly skilled Soviet population without enacting any major institutional reform.[15] While the Big Deal meant large-scale structural adjustments and value shifts that reflected the aspirations of the nascent Soviet bourgeoisie, the Little Deal entailed the acceptance of economic exchange at the micro-level.[16] "Developed socialism," as Brezhnev often called it, could also be described as "acquisitive socialism," and what one could acquire depended not only on access to growing urban markets, but also to kinship and "friendship reciprocity networks" through which scarce goods were distributed.[17] The opportunities created by the Little Deal were by no means evenly distributed.

The Little Deal had important consequences for the multiethnic Soviet empire. It led to greater local control over economic activity in the republics and brought a range of diasporas to the fore in new ways. In an economy of shortages and in the absence of legal regulation, diaspora communities proved most effective in obtaining goods and enforcing informal agreements. Azeri entrepreneurs gained a foothold in fruit and vegetable markets, Jews and Armenians came to occupy key economic positions as middlemen minorities, and Chechens gained a reputation for violent contract enforcement. The ethnic nature of the Soviet second economy was often lampooned in Soviet-era jokes (*anekdoty*) that played on stereotypes and exaggerations of real cultural differences.[18] In the Soviet second economy, however, a reputation for being able to obtain rare goods or for having a propensity to violence could be a form of capital. Economic activity, therefore, was as much about performance as it was about profit.

Among Soviet diasporas, few groups were so enviably positioned to take advantage of the economic opening of the Little Deal as the Georgians. At a time when social networks mattered more than ever, the networks of the Georgian diaspora proved easily adaptable to economic exchange in the shadowy world of the second economy. Georgians were an exclusive community bound by a distinct language that was unintelligible to outsiders; at the same time, most spoke Russian and a large number, including Bedia's son and the victim, Churgulia, studied at Russian universities.[19] They were, like Jvebenava, comfortable operating in a Russian environment, yet tied to networks that linked them to the Georgian homeland. These networks were strengthened by shared and enforceable norms of reciprocity, acceptable behavior, and codes of honor.

The Georgian diaspora's skill in employing otherness for both internal and external purposes proved effective in the Soviet second economy. Georgian culture celebrated the importance of risk-taking, but the Georgian entrepreneurial ethic was far from the spirit of sociologist Max Weber's vision of capitalism: money was made to be spent in lavish displays that improved one's standing in a Georgian social network.[20] The need to overtly demonstrate one's value to a network made these informal social groupings highly dynamic, with all members vying to outdo one another and build up their own prestige as potential patrons. For example, the Moscow entrepreneur Jvebenava's capacity to wine and dine his visitors from Georgia and regale them with scarce goods allowed him to extend his influence in his network. In these circles, the prosaic details of economic exchange were ritualized as an affirmation of friendship and social obligation. This performative aspect of Georgian economic activity also proved well suited for operating in the broader Soviet context as a more demonstrative and stylized version of *blat*, the Russian practice of exchanging favors with friends and associates.[21] It was arguably more readily received outside of Georgia because it was complemented by a widespread familiarity with the expansive repertoire of Georgian performance around the dinner table and on stage.

As an internal diaspora, Georgian entrepreneurs also benefited from links with regional officials and managers in Georgia. For someone like Aleksandre Bedia, personal obligations to his social and familial network were of greater importance than official responsibilities. He used his position in law enforcement to assist Jvebenava in his illicit economic activity and marshaled state resources to avenge the death of his son. In his case, as with other Georgians active in the second economy, personal interests and professional capacity were fused.[22] During the Little Deal the use of official positions for private benefit took place in Georgia on an unprecedented scale, particularly under the rule of First Secretary Vasili Mzhavanadze. While Mzhavanadze had come to power as Khrushchev's client in the southern republic, he survived the ouster of his patron and built his own power base at the expense of the center. It was not until 1972 that he was ultimately ousted for his inner circle's corrupt practices and ostentatious displays of wealth. Yet the unique political economy of the Soviet Union, where the state emphasized domestic self-sufficiency and refused to significantly adjust prices, kept the supply of certain valuable agricultural goods scarce and ensured near monopolies for Georgians involved in the production of these goods within Soviet borders.

Because most activity in the second economy was illegal, and largely tolerated in the Brezhnev era, the archival record of the involvement of Georgian entrepreneurs in the second economy is admittedly

*Figure 5.1* The notoriously corrupt Georgian First Secretary Vasili Mzhavanadze (right foreground) hosting Leonid Brezhnev in Tbilisi, 1971. National Archives of Georgia.

incomplete. Economic activity was investigated only when the operation of Georgian networks transgressed the limits of the unspoken terms
of the Little Deal. Thus, archival documents reveal as much about the
limits of the Little Deal as they do about the networks of Georgian entrepreneurs. The most obvious constraint on economic activity was that of
scale: petty trade was "winked at by the regime" while larger operations
were targeted.[23] But there were also social constraints. Participants in
the second economy were expected to abide by notions of fairness and
a rough Soviet egalitarianism; economic success was to be modestly
enjoyed and the privileges of the few concealed. The ethnically distinctive Georgian entrepreneurs of late socialism, for whom the execution of
elaborate and risky schemes and conspicuous displays of wealth brought
prestige, saw things differently.

## Cultivating the Georgian Brand

The prominence of informal Georgian traders is difficult to divorce
from the particular role played by Georgia within the official economy
of the Soviet Union. Just as it gave preferential treatment to the cultural
products of internal diasporas, Soviet domestic internationalism favored
internally produced commodities. Within the relatively autarkic Soviet
economy, Georgia dominated the production of tea, tobacco, and citrus
fruits, as well as earning widespread fame for its wine and mineral water.
These goods were inextricably linked in the minds of Soviet citizens to
state-sanctioned depictions of Georgia as a subtropical paradise. As a
result, Georgian goods were synonymous with luxurious abundance and
held a central place in socialist dreams of the "good life." Long before the
Little Deal, Georgian territory and the agricultural goods it yielded had
been effectively "branded" by Georgian experts, artists, and designers
working in close collaboration with the Soviet state, meaning that the
resources later available to Georgian entrepreneurs had symbolic as well
as material value.

From the beginning, the agricultural development of Georgia benefitted from special treatment by the Soviet state. Since building socialism in
one country meant cultivating all the goods Soviet citizens could desire

within sovereign borders, the region south of the Caucasus Mountains, of which Georgia formed the heartland, with its warm, inland territories and subtropical coastline, was viewed as an ideal location for the development of particular agricultural products. In absorbing the southern republic the Soviet empire inherited networks of local scientific and technical expertise, hundreds of vineyards and wineries, and established botanical gardens and research institutes in Batumi and Sukhumi. While tropicality brings to mind the extraction of valuable commodities in a manner structured by colonial or postcolonial power inequalities, Georgia was not strictly tropical but "subtropical," a liminal category between tropical and temperate that was first heralded by Russian imperial agricultural societies before it was endorsed by the Soviet state in its drive for domestic development and internal economic equality.[24] Far from being a straightforward discourse of Russian colonial domination, the term was used from the outset by Georgian scientists as a way of laying claim to a privileged place in the Russian and Soviet empires and as a means of attracting state investment.

Seeking ready access to needed goods, Soviet planners worked closely with local Georgian specialists and managers almost immediately after the Red Army's arrival in Tbilisi. One early concern was finding a replacement for the 72,000 tons of tea that prerevolutionary Russia imported for the widely embraced ritual of *chaepitie* (tea-drinking).[25] Tellingly, the state-planning commission, Gosplan, was forced to give leeway to Georgian tea producers to do what was necessary to produce these goods. Gosplan even suggested that in order to obtain the raw materials they needed, Georgian tea producers be allowed to enter into agreements with tea producers in China and India and to trade on the London Market.[26]

During the tumultuous years of the First Five-Year Plan (1928–1932), officials in Moscow mandated the rapid expansion of the production of tea, citrus fruits, and bay leaves in Georgia. They turned to local experts to oversee the development of the coastal areas of western Georgia, and, when specialists were unavailable, they trained more. The botanical garden in coastal Batumi was expanded in 1925 to become a center for research on subtropical agriculture.[27] In 1930 the All-Union Institute of Tea and Subtropical Agriculture was established in the western

Georgian city of Makharadze, with affiliates along Georgia's Black Sea coast. Georgian experts participated in the professional lives of these new institutions from the very beginning and in time came to dominate them, as the heads of the local affiliates were often nominated by local Georgian party committees.[28] Meanwhile, the Soviet Union's overall Committee on Subtropical Agriculture (Subtropkom) was generally headed by Georgians and employed teams of predominantly Georgian scientists. Political patronage was also a factor, since Georgia's subtropical development received special attention from leading Georgian political figures, particularly Lavrenti Beria.[29]

In an important sense, Georgia was never viewed as a blank slate by central planners but instead as a land imbued with a particular culture that "naturalized" a certain path of economic development. There was a belief among those who set economic policy in the center that certain local agrarian traditions gave Georgians an advantage when it came to cultivating its specialized agricultural goods. In 1924, representatives from Gosplan traveling to the region noted that nearly every household made wine and that for inhabitants of the Caucasus "the culture of the grape, not to mention its existence in this region for thousands of years" meant that wine production had a "special meaning" for the local population.[30] Such findings point to the fact that various Soviet commodities had their own distinctive "social lives."[31] The development of Uzbekistan's cotton plantations required only unskilled labor for harvesting before the cotton could be taken elsewhere for processing. Siberia had its oil and gas concerns, but these were seen as the domain of technical rather than national expertise; moreover, once operational, fossil fuels could be extracted with little local involvement. Most Georgian goods, by contrast, had to be carefully cultivated, and local processing added value and a sense of authenticity to Georgian wine. The socialist paradise of subtropical agriculture may have been envisioned by planners in Moscow, but it was largely operated by Georgians.

The importance of Georgian goods only increased in the postwar period. While the latter half of the 1930s had seen the expansion of consumer opportunities for the new Soviet middle class, the millions of Soviet citizens who had made wartime sacrifices felt entitled to compensation as well.[32] Many expected the Soviet state to offer opportunities

for consumption similar to those available in Western Europe and the
United States. The regime's ability to provide a greater and more diverse
array of commodities thus became essential for its legitimacy at home
and its international prestige abroad. As a result, Georgia's specialization
in the production of desirable goods became ever more vital. It would
eventually produce 95 percent of the tea and 90 percent of the citrus
fruits grown in the Soviet Union, along with the socialist state's most
popular wines.[33]

Economic figures attest to Georgia's rapid postwar development.
Government purchases of Georgian grapes increased from a prewar
level of thirty-six tons in 1940 to 245 tons by 1965.[34] Similarly, purchases of citrus fruits nearly doubled from their 1940 level of 23.3 tons
to an average of 41.7 tons per year by the late 1960s.[35] During the same
period, purchases of sorted tea leaves from Georgia increased more than
fourfold, from 51.3 tons in 1940 to an average of 231 tons per year by
the late 1960s.[36] The production of goods processed in Georgia also
increased, with wine production more than doubling, from 1.7 million
deciliters in 1940 to 4.2 million deciliters in 1965, and the production
of mineral water rising fivefold, from around 12 million liters in 1940
to nearly 63 million liters in 1965. The land devoted to the production
of Georgia's specialized agricultural products drastically expanded and
these goods in turn came to define the larger Georgian economy.[37] By
the early 1960s, 28 percent of Georgia's overall agricultural production
was devoted to tea, 22 percent to grapes, 19 percent to tea, and a small
but significant 3 percent to tobacco.[38]

Goods produced in Georgia were effectively promoted by the Soviet
state far beyond the borders of the Georgian SSR, perhaps most prominently in the Georgian Pavilion of VDNKh in Moscow. The pavilion,
a miniature version of Soviet Georgia's subtropical paradise, was distinguished by a palatial, 18-meter-tall façade decorated with Georgian
motifs, held up by a row of columns, and flanked by palm trees. Following
Khrushchev's de-Stalinization campaign, signs celebrating Georgia as
the homeland of Stalin were removed, but exhibits on Georgia's exotic
goods further expanded.[39] Entering the pavilion's "orangery," located
behind large stained glass panels, visitors could see tea plants, orange
and lemon trees, grapes growing on the vine, palm trees, and bamboo

stands.[40] In three expansive exhibition halls, displays educated visitors about the delights of Georgian wines with foreign-sounding names like Rkatsiteli, Mtsvane, and Tsolikauri, not to mention the Khvanchkara and Kindzmarauli known to have been favored by Stalin and still counted among the most sought after wines by Soviet consumers. An exhibit developed by the Georgians who headed Glavvino, the Soviet organization in charge of wine production, described the process of making red table wine from Kakheti, identified as "the most popular wine in the Soviet Union."[41] Although the pavilions of the other republics highlighted agricultural abundance (even when there was less natural abundance to be found), there was something mythical about Georgia's natural wealth, a sentiment reinforced by a mural near the entrance depicting "Fiery Colchis," a reminder to visitors that Soviet Georgia had once been the land of the Golden Fleece sought by Jason and his Argonauts in Greek myth.[42]

The exhibit was peopled with real-live Georgians, who frequently appeared at special events and at the ceremonial "Days of the Georgian SSR" organized at VDNKh nearly every year.[43] At the Sixth World Festival of Youth and Students in 1957, representatives of Georgia served wine to guests outside their pavilion and distributed cigarettes marked with the date and location of the event and made with Georgian tobacco from the most recent harvest.[44] VDNKh was a centerpiece in the efforts of organizers to "transform Moscow into a city of celebration," and Georgian dancers took a prominent part in the celebration, dancing their traditional "national dances" and performing newer dances devoted to economic production, such as the horticulturally inspired "Dance of the Flower Children."[45] Elsewhere, visitors could enjoy the "Dance of Silk" and "Dance of Cotton," or the "Dance of Taxi Drivers"; everywhere, economic activity became a performance of economic abundance.[46]

Georgians were just as involved in marketing their goods as they were in producing them. The Georgian pavilion was designed by architects from the southern republic, and Georgian artists devised labels appropriate for imperial tastes. Boxes of Georgian tea, for example, offered an approachable exoticism geared toward pan-Soviet consumption; marked *Gruzinskii chai*, they stressed the national origin of the tea over its flavor. Although tea labels were generally written only in Russian, they featured a stylized Cyrillic script that called to mind the Georgian alphabet and were decorated with images of Georgia's mountainous terrain, a landscape romanticized in the writings of nineteenth-century Russian authors widely read by Soviet citizens. Others were embellished with images emphasizing Georgia's subtropical coastline and its celebrated products, especially flowers. Of course, there was an inevitable interplay between the Georgian artists who designed such packaging, which emphasized a certain type of national exoticism, and the expectations of consumers outside of Georgia. But the stress on otherness was not merely imposed from the outside.

Georgians also played a leading role when it came to distribution and trade. While Georgian entrepreneurs in the 1960s and 1970s would find innovative and sometimes illegal ways to bring their goods to consumers, officially sanctioned distribution networks connected production in Georgia with markets in Russian cities long before the Brezhnev era. Stalin's table was supplied by Georgian specialists, and Moscow's famous Georgian restaurant, Aragvi, had operated under the auspices of the Georgian Ministry of Trade until the late 1950s. Seeking to make their republic's goods more widely available to Russian consumers, Georgians opened production facilities in Russia, including wine factories in Moscow and Leningrad run by Samtrest, a Georgian union of wine producers, which produced tens of thousands of bottles of wine and cognac from grapes purchased from Georgia's state farms.

The temptation to seek personal profit through these official trade networks was always present, although excesses were for a time kept in check by strict Stalinist discipline. Nevertheless, even under Stalin, the management of Samtrest came under fire for theft and embezzlement. At a 1949 meeting of the management of Glavvino, the head legal advisor of the Ministry of Food Production detailed the large-scale disappearance of grapes and alcohol products, seemingly lost in transit on their way to Samtrest's factories in Moscow and Leningrad, with more still lost when the finished products were shipped out from these factories.[47] More criticism of Samtrest's Georgian directors arose in the years immediately following Stalin's death; in 1955, the entire leadership of Samtrest was dismissed, accused of enriching themselves through the theft of state property.[48] With the advent of the Little Deal, however, open discussions of wrongdoing practically disappear from the archival record. Georgian private traders could now more freely capitalize on the existing economic infrastructure, which linked Georgian state and collective farms with facilities and distribution channels in Russian cities.

Despite Georgia's increase in postwar production, however, demand still outstripped supply. In particular, flowers proved hard to come by, especially in the winter months.[49] A report delivered at an all-Union meeting of the Soviet Ministry of Agriculture in 1966 noted with shame that due to shortfalls in Soviet production of flowers, Moscow was forced in the preceding year to import cut flowers and flower bulbs from abroad in exchange for hard currency.[50] Another report to the Ministry, submitted on behalf of collective and state farms in Georgia nearly a decade later, observed that the production of citrus fruits "was still far from meeting the demands of the population for this valued product."[51]

As opportunities for informal trade on the margins of official distribution networks increased during the Little Deal, a wider variety of Georgians cropped up at markets throughout the Soviet Union. Some had well-developed connections with formal Georgian enterprises; others opportunistically filled their suitcases with goods that were more readily available in Georgia and drove their cars to Russian cities or caught the flight from Tbilisi to Moscow. The period was characterized by the growth of private car ownership, and, thanks to the development of air travel networks in the 1960s, the trip from Georgia to Russia by plane was under three hours long and affordable to most Soviet citizens.[52]

The appearance of Georgians in Russian urban markets led to interactions that were less scripted and more unsettling than those experienced by visitors to VDNKh. While recording his memoirs in the late 1960s, Khrushchev noted that his guards complained that there were now Georgians "everywhere . . . And they're profiteering and speculating everywhere they go."[53] Actual encounters did not always live up to Russian expectations of Georgia and Georgians; they referenced but did not fully adhere to the established repertoire of Georgian performance and involved goods that did not always match the appeal of the Georgian brand. Russian writer Viktor Astaf'ev described in a travelogue his meeting with a trader, who despite his nationality he did not consider "a true Georgian" on the grounds of the trader's bad behavior. The trader,

*Figure 5.2* A Caucasian trader selling grapes and pomegranates engages customers at a Moscow market, 1965. Central State Archive of the City of Moscow, Division for the Preservation of Audio-Visual Documents of Moscow.

Astaf'ev wrote, was like so many Georgians one now encountered, sticking out "like a sore thumb, turning up in all the Russian town markets, up to Murmansk and Norilsk, scornfully robbing trusting Northerners blind." While urban residents may have earlier encountered Georgians—real or imaginary, they had never met any like these emboldened entrepreneurs from the Soviet Union's rural periphery, who were, in Astaf'ev's words, "greedy, illiterate" and "without restraint."[54] Astaf'ev's disparaging remarks arguably betrayed a degree of Russian chauvinism, but there were also important changes underway in Georgia that influenced the increasingly assertive practices of economic networks rooted in the southern republic.

## Economic Life in a Soviet "Paradise"

The differences separating Georgia from the rest of the Soviet Union and Georgians from other Soviet citizens were most frequently expressed in terms of climate and culture. Nikita Khrushchev certainly had the former in mind when recording his memoirs in the late 1960s. Trying to account for the preponderance of Georgians "profiteering and speculating everywhere they go," Khrushchev explained: "This part of the Soviet Union is a paradise, with citrus trees growing year round." He warned that Georgia's mythical abundance could also be a curse, noting that "there are many temptations in Georgia for speculators: the climate is warm, there are many vineyards and many other human delights." His explanation for the prominence of Georgian traders was climatic rather than cultural; in fact, he even admitted: "If people of some other nationality lived there, the same weaknesses would have been true of that nationality . . . if Russians lived in Georgia, they would do the same thing."[55]

Yet Georgia was also seen as a culturally distinctive territory marked off by internal borders; particularly in the post-Stalinist era, these borders were reinforced by political and economic practices aimed at exerting greater local control. A joke likely dating to the Brezhnev era told that the loudspeaker at the Tbilisi rail station announced trains "leaving Tbilisi for the USSR."[56] For Soviet tourists visiting the tropical paradise, Georgia's appeal was that it somehow seemed to exist outside of Soviet everyday life. They encountered signs and documents in Georgian, abundant agricultural goods that could only be obtained with great difficulty in the north, higher living standards, and a colorful urban life in Tbilisi. Even those Russians residing permanently in Georgia sometimes felt as if they were guests in a foreign country, rather than citizens in a Soviet republic. Different rules seemed to govern social interactions, professional habits, and republic-level politics.

While bribes and *blat* networks were becoming commonplace in Brezhnev's Soviet Union, jokes about corruption in Georgia emphasized that it was practiced openly and in accordance with formalized yet unwritten rules. One joke featured a hapless Russian visitor, who was traveling along the Georgian Military Highway when his car was stopped by a Georgian traffic policeman. The Russian was asked to write a statement explaining why he was driving so fast in the "Georgian language," which was of course foreign to him. After a moment, he handed the policeman several rubles, to which the policeman responded: "And you were saying that you don't know Georgian. You have already written half of your explanatory note!"[57] While such jokes showed Georgian corruption to have a friendly face, they also implied that it could be used to extort Russians and invert the assumed imperial hierarchies.

In everyday life, the foreignness of Georgia could sometimes be troubling. Some Russians living in Tbilisi expressed shock that they were not treated with the proper deference—or worse, that they were second class citizens—in a Soviet country they held to be their own. The Soviet literature on the "friendship of the peoples" cast Russians as Georgia's historical protectors and their leading role received greater official emphasis after victory in the Great Patriotic War.[58] Yet in the postwar and post-Stalinist period Georgia became ethnically more Georgian, stemming in part from the migration of Russians out of Georgia.[59] While the Politburo in Moscow grew ever more Slavic in composition, the leadership of the southern republic remained overwhelmingly Georgian, reflecting Moscow's continued reliance on ruling through local elites.[60] By 1970 Georgians made up 76 percent of their republic's Communist Party, higher even than the percentage of ethnic Georgians in the republic.[61] These features became grounds for complaint, especially given widespread perceptions that the Georgian state itself was highly personalized and its resources controlled by Georgians through informal networks.

Other ethnic minority groups in the republic, particularly Armenians, joined Russians in complaining of Georgian dominance. In a letter sent to the Central Committee of the Communist Party in the wake of the 1956 protests, G. V. Sukhiasov, an ethnic Armenian military officer living in Tbilisi, complained of Georgian discrimination. What bothered him most of all was that Georgians seemed to occupy all leadership and management positions in the republic, while Armenians and Russians could only aspire to work for their Georgian superiors. In contrast to the expected imperial hierarchies, the "majority of workers" were Russians and Armenians, while the "directors, Party Secretaries, Regional Secretaries, and all the other authorities" were "all Georgian."[62] He noted that it was impossible to find an "enterprise, industry, or educational institution where the director or boss was not Georgian." What was worse, Georgians were able to skirt regulations by appealing to a leadership that was "their own" and, gravest of all, held themselves to be inherently better than representatives of other ethnic groups:

Many of these leading Georgian comrades truly believe that they are better, smarter, and more talented than comrades of other nationalities, and that this gives them alone the right to lead, especially in Georgia, where their people are of a superior type and everyone else nothing better than second-class.[63]

Similar letters protested anti-Russian discrimination and the "lack of respect" with which Georgian men treated Russian women.[64] It was not only Russians living in Tbilisi who found their sense of hierarchy upset; tourists who left their cramped apartments in Russia to vacation at resorts along the Black Sea coast of Abkhazia saw seaside cliffs dotted with massive two and three-story private homes built—legally and illegally—on the proceeds of the sale of citrus, tea, tobacco, and wine to Russian markets.[65]

While state supervision of collective farms—especially of the private plots developed by farmers—was problematic everywhere, Georgian collective farms operated beyond the pale of what was acceptable even during the period of the Little Deal.[66] Well aware that they could obtain better prices on the open market than from the state, Georgian crops were increasingly grown on private plots and sold by individual Georgian traders. According to reports submitted to the Soviet Union's Ministry of Agriculture, by the mid-1970s, 40 percent of Georgia's grapes were cultivated on private plots. The same reports noted that the quality of tea and tobacco purchased by the state was in marked decline, perhaps because the choicest tea and tobacco were now sold by individual traders.[67]

Anomalous statistical reports received from Georgia alarmed Moscow's central planners. In 1965, a report noted that in the preceding year 25.7 percent of Georgia's able-bodied population was not involved in industrial and agricultural production for state enterprises, but instead in what the state considered "domestic and private ancillary economic activity," a level much higher than the Soviet average of 17.2 percent.[68] Tellingly, from 1960 to 1971 Georgia's national income grew at the third lowest rate in the USSR, while in 1970 the size of the average Georgian savings account was almost twice that of the Soviet average.[69]

Traveling to Georgia's collective farms, authorities found greater cause for concern. Speculators lurked around collective farms, buying goods from farmers to sell in Russian markets. A 1962 report on the situation in Abkhazia submitted to the Central Committee of the Communist Party noted that there were over two thousand people on collective farms in the region who did not take part in "socially useful labor."[70] While authorities warned of "harmful elements" on and around collective farms, they grew worried that the farmers themselves were behaving badly. A 1976 report submitted to Georgia's Communist Party called attention to the use of unauthorized laborers on collective farms in Abkhazia; while those who were supposed to farm pursued private profit, others were paid to farm in their place.[71] To avoid the intrusion of the central authorities, Caucasian practices of wining and dining guests were employed to turn leaders visiting Georgia's Black Sea coast into political patrons. A report submitted to the Central Committee of the Communist Party in 1959 raised this issue in regard to Abkhazia:

> The organization of various banquets and the regaling of leading workers is widespread in the republic, so much that it promotes conditions of complacency and unscrupulousness in work. Furthermore, every effort is made to explain such generosity in terms of Abkhaz customs, though all of the banquets and regaling is paid for through the funds of the state collective farms, or collected from others by the organizers of these banquets.[72]

In a Soviet economy characterized by shortages, food and drink had real economic value, and their utilization in Caucasian rites of hospitality sent a powerful signal about the wealth to be earned through mutually beneficial deals between center and periphery.[73] According to one Georgian with ties to the Soviet construction industry, some of the lavish homes constructed along Abkhazia's Black Sea coast belonged to top Soviet officials and enterprise directors. The properties were secured and their new inhabitants feted by local officials and entrepreneurs seeking patronage and protection from the politically connected in Moscow.[74]

The same conditions of lax oversight that made Georgia a base for unauthorized trade in agricultural goods also made it fertile soil for underground entrepreneurs of all varieties. Public tolerance of illicit entrepreneurship in Georgia was particularly high. According to those who lived through the late Soviet period, by the 1960s many Georgians did not view the theft of state resources as a serious crime, as long as one conformed to informal cultural norms of obligation and respectability.[75] This was part of a larger trend; contemporaries in Russia and elsewhere noted that tolerance of stealing from the state was on the rise throughout the Soviet Union.[76] Yet nowhere else in the Soviet Union were elaborate schemes of stealing and diverting state resources tolerated and indeed celebrated as they were among Soviet Georgians. Although entrepreneurs were motivated primarily by profit, many Georgians condoned the appropriation of wealth from a state whose center was geographically distant and increasingly Russified. Rumors of audacious economic schemes and displays of wealth often brought prestige rather than censure in Georgian circles, attracting adherents among friends, relatives, and acquaintances and allowing entrepreneurs to build their networks beyond the confines of the Georgian SSR. In expanding their reach, however, these entrepreneurs were also likely to attract the scrutiny of the central authorities.

## Georgian Economic Networks and Their Limits

In a manuscript written in Moscow but later published abroad, Konstantin Simis, a senior member of the Institute of Soviet Legislation in the 1970s, wrote of the Soviet Union as a state in which the "rights and duties of its citizens . . . are defined not by a constitution or any other written laws but by a whole body of unwritten laws, which, although not published anywhere, are perfectly well known to all Soviet citizens."[77] The terms of the Little Deal were struck in this spirit, as an unspoken agreement among the state, private traders, and the Soviet Union's urban population. As long as informal trade occurred within acceptable limits the state was silent, and the archival record, as a consequence, mute. State concern was aroused and governmental documents generated only when the boundaries of what officials deemed to be acceptable behavior were overstepped. These boundaries were sometimes disputed, but could ultimately be defined and patrolled by selective enforcement of existing Soviet legislation. The Soviet state sought thus to tame informal networks of exchange when they grew too large in scale and scope, when they undermined central control or crossed international borders, or when entrepreneurs behaved in ways that overtly flouted Soviet ideology.

The case of Aleksandre Bedia is a representative illustration. The KGB only got involved when the case spread beyond the confines of one republic, especially when Bedia's theft of sensitive documents undermined its centralized system of control and disrupted the surveillance functions of the panoptic agency.[78] It took the appearance of a body on the banks of a river to bring a Georgian network engaged in illicit activity to light and a violation of the KGB's information regime by a corrupt law enforcement agent to draw the state's vast capacity for observation and prosecution into the investigation. Investigators recorded details of illegal residencies, false passports, and the private lives of Georgian speculators in Moscow almost as an afterthought in their drive to punish Aleksandre Bedia. Additional charges may have been a way of encouraging the confessions of Bedia's accomplices, perhaps a method used in tandem with the KGB's technique of gathering testimony from a variety of individuals and then using inconsistencies among the various testimonies to charge suspects with providing false information to the authorities.[79] Accordingly, Jvebenava does not appear to have been prosecuted for his economic crimes; he was only threatened with the charge of providing false or incomplete testimony to prompt him to divulge information about Bedia's violent crime and his role in the theft of materials from a KGB safe.[80]

The KGB intervened with even greater urgency when traders in the Soviet second economy crossed international borders. A series of reports compiled by the Georgian branch of the KGB after a series of raids in 1972 and 1974 shed light on efforts to crack down on the international smuggling rings operated by Georgian sailors, which brought contraband goods into the country for sale in Soviet markets. Such goods included gold coins and other foreign currency, tea sets, women's scarves "of a foreign make," Japanese handkerchiefs, and Wrigley's chewing gum.[81] It was typical for Georgian sailors to bring back a few items of clothing purchased abroad as favors for friends, relatives, and associates.[82] However, the KGB was concerned with the existence of more organized smuggling rings that operated on a larger scale. Having received inside information, they intercepted several major shipments of contraband goods arriving in the Georgian port of Poti, on the Black Sea. The goods had been purchased by Georgian sailors visiting foreign ports, in one case in collusion with the Bulgarian crew of another ship. After arresting and interrogating those sailors involved in secreting the goods across Soviet borders, the KGB interrogated them for details on the smuggling ring's reach within Georgia.

In the most elaborate case, the KGB identified a circle of people with little or no permanent employment but a mysteriously steady supply of gold coins. Among them was Abram Elishakashvili, a Georgian Jew whose last official job had been as chief of "ice cream production" at a restaurant located at a train station in western Georgia.[83] In more recent years, Elishakashvili, in the words of one witness, "could always be seen at the Poti bazaar," where he was a buyer and seller of contraband goods. "Abrashka," as he was known in the market, paid thousands of rubles to Georgian sailors, requesting that they bring back gold coins and consumer goods. He then kept the coins and traded the goods through his associates, who sold them to tourists at a resort in Yalta or had them distributed by "local Gypsy women" in Kutaisi. He was assisted by several other people from his native village in western Georgia, all Georgian Jews, though their network included non-Jewish Georgians as well.[84] One had worked with Elishakashvili in the railways' official trade network in the 1950s, where they began their involvement in contraband trade. Some of Elishakashvili's associates involved in the operation had since left for Israel, and there were indications that Elishakashvili planned to emigrate in the near future. Perhaps he wanted the gold coins so that he could have a readily convertible form of currency upon leaving the country.[85]

The case files give no indication of the nature or source of the tip that alerted the authorities to the arrival of contraband goods. Elishakashvili may have been scrutinized because of his ties to members of the Georgian Jewish community who had recently emigrated. Alternately, the case may have been part of a larger crackdown on illicit economic activity that accompanied the ouster of Georgian First Secretary Mzhavanadze that year. Whatever the reason, this case and others like it show that the KGB's resources were rapidly mobilized when traders crossed international borders, bringing contraband goods into the Soviet Union, or, as Elishakashvili may have hoped to do with his gold coins, smuggling them out again. The state's borders were to be as inviolable as its information regime. As part of a series of reprisals against the smugglers, the head of the investigative unit of the Georgian KGB suggested that all sailors needed to be more carefully screened by the state prior to foreign travel and that those abroad be restricted to limited daylight hours off the ship.[86]

Negative press attention and the protests of Soviet Russian agencies and enterprises also spurred Georgian authorities to take action against traders in the second economy. On May 16, 1967, the Council of Ministers of the Georgian republic discussed the illicit sale of flowers by Georgians in Moscow's markets. The report of Georgia's Council of Ministers was prepared upon the special request of First Secretary Mzhavanadze and came in response to numerous complaints of the Moscow City Soviet, letters published in central and local Russian newspapers, and protests of the Moscow-based state flower company, Tsvety.[87] According to the report, since the Moscow City Soviet started allowing flower cultivators to sell directly on the streets of Moscow, Georgians had begun to dominate the flower market, selling flowers at high prices. These Georgians were not themselves flower cultivators, but were people "without a specific occupation" who transported "large batches of flowers" on numerous back and forth flights between Tbilisi and Moscow. In order to avoid growing public discontent with the sale of flowers at three to four times the price set by the government, the Georgian entrepreneurs were reportedly "employing local citizens" to sell their goods for them in Moscow. In addition, the Moscow flower company lodged a complaint indicating that the illegal sale of so many flowers from Georgia meant that their enterprise had not received the 800,000 flowers it had ordered from Georgia in November and December 1966. The issue continued into the following year: in the first four months of 1967, Georgia neglected to ship 1,000,000 flowers agreed on in the Moscow flower company's official contract with the Central Union of Consumer Cooperatives of Georgia.[88]

When considering the true extent of the informal flower trade, the archival record can be supplemented by observations of everyday life in contemporary Soviet literature. In a novel published in West Germany in 1977, Russian Jewish emigre author Efraim Sevela discussed the business of Georgian flower selling when describing the activity of Vakhtang, a Georgian character:

> In the Caucasus, where it is summery even in the winter, the price of one flower is at most a kopeck, in Moscow the price is at least a ruble. The profit is one hundredfold. The flight from Tbilisi to Moscow and back is 60 rubles. Vakhtang could pack and press 40,000 flowers into two suitcases. That's 40,000 rubles. Firm. Expenses: tickets on each end, a hundred or so on girls and restaurants. Well, maybe a couple hundred more for the police and inspectors so that they mind their own business. Everything else: profit.[89]

It was unimaginable for Soviet citizens to attend parties, celebrations, and dinners with friends without bearing flowers, and there were very few places in the Soviet Union with the right climate to produce enough flowers to meet Soviet demand. The archival record confirms that flower selling was a large-scale enterprise in the second economy and drew the scrutiny of republic-level authorities in Georgia, although Georgian leaders ultimately refrained from harsh reprisals to combat unauthorized trading. Instead, the Georgian Council of Ministers directed the Central Union of Consumer Cooperatives of Georgia to look into the possibility of opening an official store in Moscow to sell Georgian flowers directly to consumers.[90]

Flower selling was not the only example of how local officials were frequently more tolerant of informal economic activity. Under the supervision of First Secretary Mzhavanadze, underground entrepreneurs became especially prominent in Georgian society, building new homes, throwing extravagant parties, and engaging in neighborhood philanthropy.[91] Some entrepreneurs ran unofficial workshops where they used state resources to produce cheap consumer goods.[92] These "businessmen" or *del'tsy* (*sakmosanebi* in Georgian) enriched themselves not only through the sale of key Georgian products, but by identifying and producing less glamorous "niche goods" of the kind that "middlemen minorities" typically specialize in.[93] The *del'tsy* were often officially employed as mid-level managers in factories, but in reality they directed the factories' unauthorized production in consumer goods, which they then distributed for sale throughout the Soviet Union.

The most famous *delets* of the period was Otar Lazishvili, who was involved in the illicit production of a host of everyday consumer goods, from beach slippers and bags to turtleneck sweaters and raincoats. By the late 1960s Lazishvili presided over a vast production and distribution network, reportedly earning millions of rubles by selling his wares for affordable prices throughout the Soviet Union. In Georgia, he ran facilities that produced these unauthorized goods from state-supplied materials, while in Russia his associates distributed his products and made sure bribes were paid to the relevant law enforcement officials.[94] According to the newspaper *Trud*, Lazishvili frequently traveled to Moscow, where he would "lay tables for a thousand rubles" whenever his beloved Dinamo Tbilisi soccer team won a game.[95] Lazishvili's operation was so vast that it could not easily be concealed. He had little to worry about in Tbilisi, where officials looked the other way. Lazishvili reportedly gave several gifts to First Secretary Mzhavanadze's Ukrainian wife, Viktoria, who was so well-known for the lavish parties she threw for friends and the "salons" she held that some in Tbilisi jokingly referred to the period of flourishing illicit wealth and official corruption as a Georgian "Victorian Era."[96]

Lazishvili's downfall coincided with the dismissal of Mzhavanadze from his post in 1972 and the rise of Eduard Shevardnadze, who as head of the Ministry of Internal Affairs of Georgia led an anti-corruption drive against many Georgian "ruble millionaires" with ties to Mzhavanadze.[97] In a confidential report from 1971, Shevardnadze noted the progress he was making in uncovering Lazishvili's underground workshops.[98] Written in a tone guaranteed to please his superiors in Moscow who wanted to rein in Georgia's second economy, Shevardnadze stressed the harmful effect of underground production not just on Georgia, but on the "economic basis of the Soviet government" as a whole.

Shevardnadze's report targeted perhaps the most prosaic niche good in Lazishvili's line, easily transportable nylon net bags of various colors.

The banality of this particular item speaks to the peculiarities of the Soviet second economy. These bags were so highly desired because the scarcity of official goods required Soviet citizens to always have a bag on hand in case goods suddenly became available. Shevardnadze's investigation discovered that Lazishvili in at least one instance had used 460 kilograms of state-owned nylon material to produce 30,000 bags worth 57,000 rubles.[99] Because the bags were produced with diverted state resources and sold at affordable prices through Lazishvili's trade network, they surely earned the underground entrepreneur a handsome profit. As Shevardnadze noted in his report, there were theoretically at least twelve workshops in Georgia capable of producing this item. Yet the same command economy that caused shortages and long lines could not produce the consumer solution identified by Lazishvili.

As an underground entrepreneur with extensive political connections, Lazishvili lived a comfortable life between Tbilisi and Moscow. He was a party member and, although he had not finished university, he was officially registered as the associate laboratory director of a major synthetic materials factory.[100] As Shevardnadze's investigation broadened, Lazishvili decided to flee to Moscow, where he reportedly hoped to seek out the protection of Roman Rudenko, the Prosecutor General of the Soviet Union. The KGB, then led by Yuri Andropov, allegedly arrested Lazishvili in Rudenko's outer office; as in the Bedia case, the KGB intervened and prevailed in a potential contest with another Soviet law enforcement institution.[101] Ultimately, though, the Georgian entrepreneur may have benefited from his contacts in the upper echelons of Soviet power.[102] While he was tried and his case made an example in the Soviet press, he escaped the recommended capital punishment and was instead sentenced to fifteen years, part of it spent in a medical clinic. The larger implications of the affair were hushed up. Mzhavanadze was quietly removed from the post of Georgian First Secretary and retired as a member of the Politburo. According to the minutes of a meeting of the Central Committee, the ousted Georgian leader was "relieved of his duties" in the Politburo and placed on a pension due to his "advanced age"; the decision on this "organizational question" was reached unanimously and without mention of his abuses of power, though Brezhnev's silence at the meeting on Mzhavanadze's long period of service to the party might have been a way of condemning him with faint praise.[103] None of Lazishvili's associates in Moscow were touched, and other *del'tsy* operating out of Georgia escaped prosecution, even after Shevardnadze became First Secretary at the end of 1972. Still, Georgia's underground entrepreneurs restrained their activities, and especially their displays of wealth, at least for the next several years.

Over time Shevardnadze's anti-corruption campaign waned, while popular demand for Georgian goods endured and many in the republic remained favorably disposed toward the *del'tsy*. By the late 1970s crackdowns seemed to occur only when periodic resolutions on the "fight against speculation and the theft of socialist property" were adopted by Georgia's Communist Party and Council of Ministers, or passed down from the center.[104] In response to such resolutions there were occasional bursts of law enforcement activity, a way of demonstrating that targets were being met and goals fulfilled. Incentives for informal trading and unauthorized production persisted, and despite Shevardnadze's effort to shape public opinion through newspaper articles and television specials on the cost of corruption, classified reports of the Ministry of Internal Affairs noted that Georgian society remained tolerant of economic crime, a troubling trend that suggested a deviation from supposedly shared Soviet values.[105] Even the mighty Soviet state could not police all of Georgian society, nor was there necessarily the political will to do so.

It is most likely that the second economy continued to grow. Reports on periodic law enforcement operations give some sense of the massive scale of Georgia's informal trade networks in this period, though historians can only guess at the range of second economic activity that escaped the attention of the authorities or was tacitly tolerated by them. A 1980 report detailed large, seemingly well-organized groups of illicit traders and producers involved in transporting counterfeit Georgian fruit wine to Perm Oblast in central Russia.[106] At least five groups of eleven to nineteen members were allegedly involved in producing, shipping, and selling the counterfeit wine. Regrettably, the report gives few biographical details on those involved, but they presumably had connections to managers in the official economy in order to get the materials to produce the wine. They reportedly accumulated a "serious amount" of money by producing the wine from goods stolen "on an especially large scale." The authorities apparently only became aware of the operation when several Russian consumers got sick and died after drinking the falsified product. Despite an official crackdown, the report noted that while several people involved in the operation were in custody, others had not yet been brought to justice, and one of those in custody somehow managed to escape temporarily.

Another operation against unauthorized trading in Georgian agricultural goods was launched in 1982.[107] The reports generated by this operation indicate continued growth in the scale of informal Georgian trade networks. The broad scope of the law enforcement operation may have reflected the rise of Yuri Andropov, who succeeded Brezhnev as General Secretary in late 1982. Acting at the direction of the Central Committee, which expressed deepening concern with the theft of agricultural and consumer goods, the Ministry of Internal Affairs of the Soviet Union and Georgia's republic-level branch cooperated in an effort to target wrongdoing at "all stages of agricultural production." A series of raids, this time launched by authorities throughout the Soviet Union, arrested Georgian "speculators" operating at collective farm markets in Moscow, Dnepropetrovsk, Riga, Lviv, and other major Soviet cities. An anti-smuggling operation led to the arrest of fifty Georgian speculators in Leningrad alone, where they were attempting to sell 35 tons of agricultural goods worth 44,000 rubles. In total, the anti-smuggling operation led to the seizure of more than 10,000 tons of agricultural goods worth more than 400,000 rubles, all of them intended for sale in the second economy. As a result of the operation, the number of cases of smuggling brought before the courts in the first eight months of 1982 was up 10 percent from the previous year. Following Brezhnev's death in November 1982, Andropov launched a broad effort to prosecute corruption at all levels, severely restricting if not entirely revoking the terms of the Little Deal.

According to a companion report prepared by the Georgian Central Committee and marked "secret," Georgia still had much distance to cover in eradicating trading in the second economy.[108] The report estimated

that in the past year those whom it called "lovers of easy profit" attempted
to trade 300 tons of fruits and vegetables from Georgia, including 120
tons at various markets throughout the Soviet Union. The report called
for renewed vigilance against "parasites" who fed off the "healthy body
of society." It also warned of new tendencies that did not bode well for
the anti-corruption drive, including the increasingly open manner in
which underground entrepreneurs operated, a factor the report's author
attributed to dangerous levels of public tolerance of unauthorized economic activity in Georgia.

The report's Georgian author indicated that the struggle against speculation was imperative to protect his nation's reputation. He noted that
"an uncompromising struggle against speculators involved in transporting agricultural goods beyond the borders of Georgia will boost the reputation of our republic in the country at large and will restore her good
name." He went on to describe the fight against speculators as "a matter
of honor for all citizens of Soviet Georgia."

Such language may have echoed the voice of the center, but it also
evoked an ongoing debate within Georgian society regarding the
socially acceptable boundaries of economic behavior. Yet another
glimpse beyond the archival record is necessary to understand the terms
of this debate and the author's preoccupation with restoring Georgia's
"good name." Georgian success in the second economy and the tendency of Georgian entrepreneurs to engage in showy displays of wealth
had won them a representational prominence that matched and sometimes exceeded their actual economic clout. In many Soviet *anekdoty,*
Georgians came to stand in for all ethnically distinct traders from the
Caucasus in Soviet markets, whether they were Georgians, Armenians,
or Azeris. Given the prominence of the Georgian diaspora in Soviet politics and culture, the script of presumed Georgian behavior in such jokes
was more fully developed than it was for other ethnic groups.[109] For a
joke to be effective, it had to be told in a believable Georgian accent, a
speech pattern familiar to all Soviets from Stalin's publicly broadcast
speeches. It might be argued that ethnic jokes say as much about those
who tell them as they do about the ethnic group at the butt of the joke.[110]
Nevertheless, jokes told about Georgians also reflected, however distortedly, significant cultural differences between Russians and Georgians.

The anecdotal preoccupation of Georgians with honor and conspicuous consumption in jokes was, in a sense, an exaggeration of attri-
butes essential to the functioning of Georgian networks. In one joke,
a Georgian residing in Russia buys a subcompact Zaporozhets car, the
cheapest automobile then made in the Soviet Union, only to find it stolen
the next morning. The next day, he buys the same car again (incidentally
avoiding the waiting lists that most Soviets would have to contend with),
leaving a note on the dashboard addressed to prospective thieves asking
that he be allowed to "drive about a bit." The next day, he awakes to find
a far more luxurious Volga sedan outside his home, with a note reading: "Drive about, friend, but don't bring shame to our nation."[111] In a
related joke, a Georgian student writes home to Georgia, telling his parents that studies are going well but he feels "awkward" because "All [his]
Russian friends come to school by bus, and [he] is the only one coming in his own car." To which his parents answer: "Sonny, why should
you stand out from the others? Be like everyone else. Go ahead and buy
yourself a bus."[112] The wealth of Georgian entrepreneurs, it was held,
was displayed in expansive performances of consumption and spending
that were unthinkable—if not impossible—for those outside a Georgian
network.

In some cases, the actual behavior of Georgians prominent in the
second economy matched—or perhaps imitated—such anecdotal
extravagance. Writing about the late Soviet period, the Georgian writer
Irakli Iosebashvili recalled that his father-in-law and his friends, a
group of men involved in smuggling and speculation, attended weddings "with their suit pockets stuffed with rubles." In the words of
Iosebashvili: "They danced with the bride and sent showers of bills cas-
cading over her head. They tossed handfuls at the band and the band
played like madmen. And deep in the night, when half the guests had
already passed out, they sat around a table and, with smiles of pure
enjoyment on their faces, set fistfuls of money on fire."[113] Such a story
referred to the established trope of Georgian flamboyance, but also
suggested that the seemingly irrational destruction of Soviet currency
could send a powerful message about the extent of one's wealth and
status, albeit in a manner that might strike Soviet citizens, and some
Soviet Georgians, as wasteful and offensive.

Other jokes linked flagrant displays of Georgian wealth with the widespread practice of bribery in Georgia. Universities in Georgia, it was alleged, were notoriously corrupt; one joke has a young Georgian buying his way into the musical conservatory, though he is unable to identify a single note in his entrance exam.[114] In another joke, the exam "tickets" used to indicate question assignments for oral examinations are reportedly "sold out."[115] In fact, in some quarters of Georgian society, where economic exchange was ritualized and affluence an asset, making payments in exchange for access to higher education might not have been seen as such a flagrant violation of law and morality. Bedia himself paid a bribe to have his son admitted to an institution of higher education in Volgograd, and the Georgian sailors caught smuggling goods into the Soviet Union pleaded with their captors that they did so only to finance their children's education.[116] In other cases, however, Georgian students strove for admittance into Russian universities through formal channels and no doubt resented jokes that undermined their academic reputation.

Jokes supplement the official record by showing how Georgian success was perceived and debated in the Soviet Union. Admittedly, Georgian economic clout was often exaggerated, the full context of Georgian culture misunderstood, and the diversity of views within Georgia overlooked. But perceptions were not entirely uninformed, nor simply the product of an imperial imagination. Indeed, the jokes' silences reveal almost as much as their embellished accounts of Georgian wealth. Georgian women, for example, were almost entirely missing from Soviet jokes. Their absence reflected real patterns of migration; although there were certainly women in the diaspora and they sometimes performed essential functions in a Georgian economic network, it was far more common for Georgian men to travel far from their homeland to work, study, and bring Georgian agricultural goods to market.

Jokes that poked fun at the Georgian preoccupation with honor and the ostentatious wealth of Georgian entrepreneurs were seen as disgraceful by officials in Georgia concerned with corruption as well as by segments of Georgian society that did not wish to be associated with such practices. Among Georgians, attitudes regarding their nation's prominence in the Soviet second economy ranged from pride to disdain, sometimes comingled, with many shades in between. For his part,

Eduard Shevardnadze reportedly lamented at a closed party meeting in the 1970s: "Once the Georgians were known throughout the world as a nation of warriors and poets; now they are known as swindlers."[117] Some members of Tbilisi's intelligentsia tolerated informal economic activity but limited their contact with underground entrepreneurs. Neighborhood loyalties meant that university professors might continue to greet entrepreneurs who lived on their street, but would be embarrassed to have shadowy traders appear at their house for dinner in "polite company."[118] Georgian culture celebrated risk-taking and the ability to provide for those in one's network, but not necessarily the everyday details of trading. Accordingly, well-established Georgian entrepreneurs sometimes employed other ethnic groups to sell their goods in Soviet markets, distancing themselves from the less-privileged rural Georgian traders who traveled north with suitcases and carloads of agricultural produce.[119]

In Georgian culture, wealth was only supposed to be a means for gaining prestige; economic success itself did not automatically denote honor. Accordingly, moral character was still accorded primary importance in Georgia, even among those labeled by the state as criminals. One could be honest, it was believed, while breaking the law, since Soviet justice was seen as arbitrary. The alleged Georgian organized crime figure Jaba Ioseliani was supposedly the inspiration for Georgian novelist Nodar Dumbadze's character Limona Devdariani in the prison novel *White Flags*. In the novel, Devdariani is described as a morally honest thief.[120] Dumbadze's ambivalent attitude toward the law may have reflected his childhood experiences as the son of parents officially classified as "enemies of the people"; his father, a local party official, and his mother were arrested in the purges in 1937 and not rehabilitated until 1956.[121] Yet the novel might also be read as a commentary on the actual overrepresentation of Georgians among Soviet "thieves-in-law" (*vory v zakone*), an elite class of criminals bound by a distinctive code of behavior.[122]

While they disavowed cooperation with official authorities, Georgian "thieves" were believed to specialize in providing informal arbitration— *garcheva*, as it was known in Georgian—among rival groups of criminals and entrepreneurs.[123] In effect, they were yet another facet of the Georgian diaspora's involvement in the informal economy. Their networks reached throughout the Soviet Union and their speech was a hybrid mixture of Russian, Yiddish, and Georgian-derived jargon; they partook of, yet remained distinctive within, a pan-Soviet criminal subculture. According to law enforcement estimates, by the late Soviet period Georgians made up 30 to 50 percent of all thieves-in-law in the Soviet Union and could even be subdivided into three regionally-based groups: Tbilisskaia, from the Georgian capital, Sukhumskaia, from the Black Sea port of Sukhumi, and Kutaisskaia, from Georgia's second largest city, whose reputation among criminals was so vaunted that a popular saying held that among thieves Odessa was the "mother city," Rostov "the father," and Kutaisi "the son."[124]

Ioseliani, the likely model for the character in Dumbadze's novel, was perhaps the most famous Georgian thief-in-law. A native of Tbilisi, he gained respect for his refusal to cooperate with authorities, his wild risk-taking, his loyalty to friends, and his lively wit. First arrested for robbery in 1942 at the age of sixteen, he made a daring escape from a Georgian prison camp and fled to Leningrad, where he enrolled in the Oriental Languages Department at Leningrad State University on the basis of forged documents.[125] Praised by his instructors as a promising student, he continued to pursue a life of crime. In 1956, he and a group of Georgian associates dressed as a television repair crew in order to gain entry to the home of a Leningrad jeweler who had amassed a sizable collection of gold watches, diamond rings, and hard currency. This time, however, the robbery went astray and two of his conspirators stood accused of killing the jeweler's wife after she tried to stop them. Although he was never charged with taking part in the murder itself, Ioseliani was given a twenty-five-year prison sentence for participating in an "armed gang," a severe punishment that reflected his refusal to incriminate the others on trial.[126] After a series of legal reviews, in 1965 he was allowed to return to Georgia, thanks in part to an appeal submitted by that country's leading cultural figures.[127] Ioseliani's subsequent career is a wonderful, if literal, example of how some Georgian criminals were as thoroughly invested in performance as they were in the economic details of exchange. Leaving his Russian prison for Tbilisi, the former convict went on to become a professor at the Georgian

Institute of Theater Arts, writing a doctoral dissertation entitled "The Comic Masks of Georgian Theater." At the same time, after witnessing the gains made by *del'tsy* in his native Georgia, Ioseliani reportedly persuaded the Soviet Union's thieves-in-law to play a more active role in the official Soviet economy.[128]

## Ethnic Entrepreneurship and the Tensions of Soviet Empire

Hedrick Smith, a *New York Times* reporter traveling in the Soviet Union in the mid-1970s, told of the following joke, popular among Russians during the time of his visit:

> A little Georgian . . . was on an Aeroflot airliner bound for Moscow when a hijacker broke into the cockpit, brandished a pistol and demanded that the plane go to London. The pilot changed course and soon a second hijacker, with two guns, burst in and ordered the pilot to head for Paris. Another change of course. Finally, the wiry little olive-skinned Georgian entered with a bomb and declared, "Take this plane to Moscow or I'll blow it up." The pilot agreed, and changed course a third time. When they landed in Moscow, the first two hijackers were carted off to jail and the little Georgian was congratulated by a high-level delegation.
>
> "Tell us, Comrade," said one slightly incredulous dignitary, "Why did you divert the plane from Paris back to Moscow?"
>
> "What was I going to do with 5,000 carnations in Paris?" the Georgian replied.[129]

The joke alluded to several important dimensions of informal Georgian trading in the Soviet period. First, the trading occurred in a relatively closed society, one which citizens may have wanted to leave but could not, and one whose command economy created strange incentives for moneymaking based on the sale of prosaic goods like carnations. Second, because of Georgian involvement in informal trading, Moscow was for such entrepreneurs a city of opportunity, not simply the capital of a repressive state. Third, high-ranking officials often turned a blind eye to illicit Georgian economic activity. Despite his intent to illegally sell flowers, the Georgian ends up being congratulated by the authorities, while the other two hijackers are sent to prison.

Because of Georgia's unique position in the political economy of the Soviet Union, an established national brand, and a preexisting cultural repertoire, numerous opportunities were created for entrepreneurs to trade Georgian goods throughout the Soviet Union. Unlike other so-called middlemen minorities, such as Jews and Armenians, Georgian entrepreneurs often retained a connection to the land where many of their goods were grown, and this link was vital for their ability to bring these desired products to Soviet markets.[130] The connection was also integral to the way these goods were marketed: Georgian traders commodified and sold a subtropical abundance rooted in Georgian territory, offering the charms of their distinctive climate and culture in markets throughout the Soviet Union. The borders that divided the official and unofficial Georgian economy—much like the distinctions that separated entrepreneurs and state officials in the Georgian SSR—were often blurred. Flowers grown on a state farm might be illegally sold in Moscow, wine produced in a Georgian factory might be illicitly traded in Siberia, and citrus fruits grown for a collective farm might unexpectedly brighten a winter market in Leningrad.

The Little Deal opened up new opportunities for Georgia's economic entrepreneurs. But the deal itself was a constant process of negotiation, and the fact that its terms were unspoken served to lessen but not eliminate inherent ideological and imperial tensions. Entrepreneurs whose operations grew too large, too flashy, or too threatening to central control were prosecuted, but exactly where the limits of acceptability lay was always subject to question. As might be expected, central control was generally weaker the further one moved from Moscow, especially so in Georgia under the rule of Party Secretary Vasili Mzhavanadze, where ethnic and linguistic difference, an entrepreneurial propensity for risk-taking, and economic exchange through social networks for a time combined to create a corner of the Soviet Union that seemed vaguely foreign. It was not, as contemporaries joked, the Georgian Soviet Socialist Republic, but instead the "FRG," the "Federal Republic of Georgia," where living standards and liberties not only surpassed Moscow but were allegedly comparable to those in West Germany.[131]

The goods and services provided by Georgian networks were highly desirable to Soviet citizens. Their provision opened up a space for greater economic autonomy, if not self-sufficiency, in Georgia itself. But in a Soviet empire based upon the centralized rule of Moscow, the independent streak of the Georgian SSR and the economic successes of its diaspora also strained the imperial order, especially since the empire accorded a leading role to the Russian people. While Soviet central planners envisioned Georgia as a reliable supplier of subtropical goods, their policies resulted in creeping local control over these products, driving what was perceived to be the virtual colonization of Russian markets by Georgian traders. The Georgians, it was charged, lived like kings in Georgia and princes in Moscow, and their economic success was particularly striking since it came at the heels of several decades during which the Soviet Union had been led by Stalin, the most famous representative of the Georgian diaspora.

Georgians were certainly not alone in taking part in the burgeoning second economy. During the Little Deal, millions of Soviet citizens relied on personal connections to obtain scarce goods and services, bartered, and bribed to get what they needed or desired. Using public property for personal gain and relying on personal relationships rather than official ones—in other words, corruption—was part and parcel of the Soviet system under Brezhnev, from the lowest-level bureaucrat or plant manager to the leader's own son-in-law.[132] It seemed to many at the time, though, that smaller, ethnically distinct diasporas with the ability to construct effective social and economic networks were better at operating in this system than were the Russians who made up the majority. In the economic sphere, the success of the Georgians was conspicuous, even if the state sought to reign in excesses through surveillance and prosecution. Despite the growing preponderance of Slavs in the Politburo, some Russians worried that they were becoming second-class citizens when it came to economic clout, even in the RSFSR. In half-jest, a Russian joke rhetorically asked: "Can a Georgian purchase a Volga?" (a Soviet luxury automobile, and also the main river running through the Russian heartland). And then answered: "He can. But what does he need so much water for?"[133] "Mother Russia" herself, it was implied, was being bought up by outsiders.

In a way, Georgians became the victims of their own successes in the Soviet second economy. Such a fate was not uncommon for an economically prominent diaspora, though the rooted nature of Georgian networks meant that the Georgian land and the goods associated with it were also implicated. By the end of the Brezhnev era, there was certainly evidence of a tarnishing of the Georgian brand thanks to its association with underground entrepreneurs. An article published in *Izvestiia* in February 1982 even proclaimed the need to "restore the former glory of Georgian tea."[134] Because of corruption on Georgian tea plantations the once celebrated Georgian tea had become known as an inferior product. According to another article published around the same time in *Pravda*, consumers went to great lengths to avoid *Gruzinskii chai*, seeking out the Indian tea that was shipped across external Soviet borders to make up for shortages in Georgian production.[135] Writing shortly after the collapse of the Soviet Union, the Russian food historian Vil'iam Pokhlebkin went so far as to suggest that Georgians deliberately sabotaged tea production because they found it increasingly unprofitable; according to Pokhlebkin, Georgia was the "spoiled daughter" of the Soviet Union, unwilling to contribute its tea for the sake of the common good, all the while seeking a "comfortable living off the hard work and resources of the other republics, especially the RSFSR."[136] The failure of Georgians to adhere to the desired repertoire and live up to the promise of the Georgian brand was thus cast as a form of imperial betrayal.

It was the Soviet state that had enabled Georgian success with its peculiar features: a northerly geographic position, an economy dependent on domestic goods, an ideology that emphasized national distinctiveness, and an infrastructure that granted a high degree of mobility to an internal diaspora held together by ties of family, friendship, and homeland. Yet many Georgian entrepreneurs had come to see the state as not quite their own, an institution to be taken advantage of, or an entity that limited, rather than facilitated, their economic potential. These sentiments reflected a growing sense of frustration among non-Russians in the late Soviet Union. Critical views of the Soviet empire found particular resonance among Georgia's intelligentsia, who sought to break out of an assigned role that brought imperial prominence but threatened national authenticity.

# Beyond the Ethnic Repertoire

The wedding party was made up of painters, actors, artists, and doctors, the children of Soviet Georgia's leading intellectual families. After a long night of celebration in a Tbilisi restaurant, the group made its way to the airport on the morning of November 18, 1983. They boarded Aeroflot Flight 6833, one of the many flights operating daily between Georgia and Russia. The bride, Tinatin Petriashvili, an undergraduate student at Tbilisi's Fine Arts Academy, and the groom, Germane "Gega" Kobakhidze, a successful young film actor, had informed family members that they would spend their honeymoon among the canals and theaters of Leningrad, accompanied by their close friends, painters Davit Mikaberidze and Gia Tabidze, as well as the young art student Soso Tsereteli, Tinatin's classmate at the Fine Arts Academy. The brothers Kakha and Paata Iverieli, both doctors educated in Moscow, boarded the plane with the group to see them off.

What appeared to be an innocent escapade was in fact a desperate and ultimately tragic attempt to hijack and divert the plane abroad, an effort that was doomed almost from the start.[1] The members of the wedding party were not seasoned dissidents, but a group of artists and intellectuals who represented the relatively privileged bohemian subculture of the Georgian intellectual elite. Their plot to escape the Soviet Union had been hatched at gatherings in apartments whose walls were decorated with painted images of the American flag, while they listened to the Rolling Stones and Led Zeppelin. Photos taken of the group in the weeks and months before show them walking the streets of downtown Tbilisi dressed in American blue jeans, smoking foreign cigarettes given to them by friends and relatives with official connections abroad.[2] Looking back on the hijacking incident, many members of the Georgian intelligentsia would see the group's ill-fated effort to flee the Soviet Union as evocative of Eldar Shengelaia and Rezo Gabriadze's 1973 film *The Eccentrics* (*sherekilebi*), a fantastical tale of an idealistic young man and an elderly mathematician who dream of freedom while locked in an underground cell, plotting an improbable escape in a whimsical flying machine.

Their plan was to wait until the plane took off, then demand that the flight change course and land in Turkey, where they hoped to find sanctuary at an American military base. Although they had smuggled small pistols and a couple of hand-grenades onto the plane, they were unprepared when they encountered armed resistance upon entering the pilot's cabin. Gia Tabidze was killed almost immediately, while Kakha and Paata Iverieli were wounded. An ensuing firefight resulted in the deaths of several crew members and passengers caught in the crossfire. Instead of acceding to the hijackers' demands, the pilot launched into a tight spiral above Tbilisi, eventually bringing the plane back to the runway. Davit Mikaberidze committed suicide as it became clear that the group's desperate attempt had failed. A Soviet special forces unit sent specially from Moscow stormed the aircraft, riddled the cabin with bullets, and seized the surviving members of the errant wedding party.

The event, and the resulting death sentences handed down for most of the hijackers, shocked the Soviet Georgian intelligentsia. Following a brief investigation, Gega Kobakhidze, the Iverieli brothers, and Teimuraz Chikhladze, a former film actor who called himself "Father Tevdore" and was accused of being the group's spiritual mentor, were executed in a field outside Tbilisi. Although the executions were carried out in secret, news spread quickly among Georgia's intellectual and artistic community. An effort by Vazha Iverieli, a prominent physicist, to intervene on behalf of his sons came to nothing, despite the fact that he personally knew Georgian First Secretary Eduard Shevardnadze.[3] Gega Kobakhidze's close friendship with Irakli Charkviani, the grandson of Kandid Charkviani, the longtime Communist Party chief of Georgia, similarly failed to prevent execution. In the aftermath of the hijacking attempt, the production of Tengiz Abuladze's new film, *Repentance*, was temporarily halted; the ideologically risqué film was further scrutinized for its association with Kobakhidze, the young groom and lead hijacker, who had been slated to play the grandson of the tyrannical dictator Varlam Aravidze in the movie.

Like their Russian counterparts, the Soviet Union's Georgian intelligentsia consisted of a loose coalition of intellectuals who espoused an eclectic collection of ideological beliefs.[4] Seeking to maximize their autonomy, they engaged in a diverse set of tactics in their relationship with the Soviet state, which both funded and restricted their artistic and intellectual pursuits. In most cases, members of the Georgian intelligentsia were not outspoken in their criticism of the state and the shortcomings of society; instead, the majority sought sheltered "oases" where they could pursue their intellectual interests, or expressed their criticism obliquely as "semidissidents" frustrated with the system but unwilling to lose their professional positions.[5] Even the hijackers had not publicly spoken of their political discontent prior to the incident and only settled on leaving the Soviet Union by force after ruling out other options for emigration as unrealistic.[6] Their seizure of a Soviet aircraft was a rare instance of a risky public protest staged by a group of Georgian intellectuals and artists.

It is tempting to compare the incident to the Dymshits-Kuznetsov affair of June 1970, in which a group of predominantly Jewish Soviet citizens who had been denied exit visas plotted to hijack a plane outside Leningrad to seek emigration, or the case of the Brazinskases in October 1970, when a Lithuanian father and son forcefully seized a Soviet aircraft in Georgia and crossed the border into Turkey.[7] Yet unlike Soviet Jews, Georgians did not pursue emigration to a national homeland abroad but instead fled to a loosely imagined West. Furthermore, the "captive nation" label widely used among Lithuanian diaspora communities outside the Soviet Union did not quite seem to fit when applied to Georgians.[8] Georgia, unlike Lithuania, had been a foundational Soviet republic and Georgians as a diaspora had been at the forefront of the Bolshevik Revolution.

Given the Georgian diaspora's relative success under Soviet rule, the fact that frustration among the Georgian intelligentsia could run so high as to provoke a hijacking attempt might seem unusual. Georgians had taken active part in constructing the Soviet state; around the table and on stage they had produced the multiethnic culture that defined Soviet life; and in the marketplace they had profited by providing desirable goods and services. If Georgians were so skilled at deploying their networks to capitalize on the culture, reputation, and unique geographic position of their homeland, why would the children of privileged Georgians seek to escape the Soviet Union?

The hijacking episode hinted at broader discontent among Georgian intellectuals emboldened by their success but frustrated by its limitations in the Soviet empire. The late Soviet period was not only a time of economic and social change below the surface of a sluggish official economy, but also an era of restive intellectual life set against a backdrop of repetitive political slogans and a bureaucratic political culture.[9] The Soviet Union had transformed a rural, largely illiterate society into one of the world's most educated populations, but the gains of the Soviet intelligentsia seemed to heighten their frustration with the party officials who ruled the Soviet Union and made the final decisions when it came to intellectual matters. As artists achieved new levels of high culture virtuosity and technical specialists sought to expand the frontiers of Soviet science, they found their success soured by restrictions on creative expression, research, and international travel. The party's claim to a monopoly on truth had eroded with the end of Stalinism; after the Thaw, the gap between party officials and intellectuals widened even further. Emboldened scientists drew newfound authority from their expertise, and alienated intellectuals turned away from political life to seek more authentic forms of expression through art, film, and literature.

Concerns about authenticity found particular resonance among the Soviet Union's internal diasporas, which grew at once more self-confident and self-conscious in this period. By training highly educated national cadres to meet the needs of state-sponsored domestic internationalism, the Soviet empire eventually produced its intellectual opponents. The Soviet state had endowed each republic with its own opera house and printing press, endorsed a pantheon of national literary figures, and sponsored national film studios. The artists who staffed these institutions of national culture were invited to study in Moscow and circulated throughout the Soviet Union thanks to a state-sponsored infrastructure of intellectual exchange. These efforts aimed to place national culture in service to the revolutionary aims of Soviet socialism. While the system offered the possibility of pan-Soviet prominence, it also demanded that national culture be rendered intelligible for imperial use, which meant adhering to established ethnic repertoires that translated well into Russian. Even as accessible repertoires of otherness continued to be employed by national entertainers in Soviet *estrada* and ethnic entrepreneurs in the Soviet marketplace, they began to strike many national intellectuals as clichéd and restrictive, a compromised and domesticated form of their native culture.

While Russian intellectuals also harbored concerns about cultural authenticity under Soviet rule, Georgian intellectuals more readily appealed to the national to express their discontent. As uneasy representatives of the Soviet empire's ambiguous national core, members of the Russian intelligentsia could be divided into "left-liberals" espousing universal values and "Russian patriots" who sought to rekindle a connection to the Russian land, turning for inspiration to the Russian village and Russian Orthodoxy.[10] By contrast, Georgian intellectuals across the political spectrum tended to engage national themes. Even if they traveled throughout the Soviet Union, most remained connected to cultural institutions based in the Georgian republic that were representative of national traditions and invested in projecting national distinctiveness. As a visible diaspora their nationality could not escape comment, and as a small, non-Russian minority, many felt that their national culture needed greater protection. Yet in expressing the national, the Georgian intelligentsia also gave voice to the broader intellectual demands of a multiethnic empire in flux.

This chapter focuses on the two areas of late Soviet life in which the Georgian intelligentsia was most prominent, classical music and film, and uses these fields to illuminate larger intellectual trends. The first, a realm of high culture performance, offered a way to move beyond the typical Georgian cultural repertoire without sacrificing national authenticity; the second, a nationally distinctive artistic medium, employed Georgian culture to assert creative authorship and engage in subtle social criticism. During this period a diaspora of Georgian musicians rose to the highest positions in Moscow's Bolshoi Theater and the

Moscow Conservatory, while Moscow-trained Georgian filmmakers like Eldar and Giorgi Shengelaia, Otar Ioseliani, and Tengiz Abuladze grounded poignant intellectual critique in a national setting to express the concerns of the Soviet intelligentsia at large. Following the course of Georgian intellectual life from the late 1960s to the final years of Soviet power, this chapter reveals how the high culture worship and ironic commentary of *zastoi* presaged the direct political engagement and nationalist demands of perestroika.

## The Pursuit of High Culture Virtuosity

During *zastoi*, Soviet artists and intellectuals achieved new levels of high culture virtuosity in officially sanctioned forms of art and knowledge. Although the state restricted overtly political expression, it continued to nurture cultural and intellectual achievement, especially in classical music and applied science, and tolerated oases of intellectual creativity in areas not directly related to political life. While wary of dissident intellectuals, the state upheld cultural development and scientific progress as ideals for all Soviet citizens. The state's ideological stance in this regard was actually shared by many members of the Soviet intelligentsia, who claimed a leading role as bearers of knowledge and culture. High culture expertise had its limits, in that its canon was largely classical and fixed in scope to specific artistic works and established fields of knowledge. Within these limits Soviet intellectuals attained new heights of sophistication in existing forms and found private spaces of creativity, the logical endpoints of a system whose outward surface was unchanging.

For Georgians, high culture performance led beyond the explicitly Georgian cultural repertoire. While folkloric displays of national culture were promoted in the Soviet Union, high culture was cherished as the pinnacle of human achievement. Moreover, although Russian contributions were particularly celebrated in the Soviet context, high culture was seen as a more transnational phenomenon that in some ways transcended the boundaries of domestic internationalism and hinted at a broader cosmopolitanism. It was linked to an established pan-European tradition and gave Soviet intellectuals access to true "classics," not merely the cultural substitutes found within Soviet borders. Largely inherited from the Russian imperial period, the Soviet high culture canon included Bach and Mozart as well as Tchaikovsky, Shakespeare and Goethe as well as Pushkin. It celebrated the concept of genius across state borders in all its manifestations, from art to science.

Though the state saw rather mixed success in its efforts to forge a unified Soviet people, it did effectively nurture a shared notion of high culture that the intelligentsias of all Soviet republics held sacred. Soviet high culture production flourished most of all in multiethnic Moscow and Leningrad, but also in institutes, universities, and conservatories outside the center, such as the Siberian intellectual city of Akademgorodok, built outside Novosibirsk in 1957, the University of Tartu in Estonia, and the Tbilisi Conservatory in Georgia.[11] The first was a Soviet-era creation, the latter two built on prerevolutionary intellectual and artistic foundations.

Even as Soviet political life came to be dominated by ethnic Russians in the post-Stalinist era, the upwardly mobile children of non-Russian Soviet professionals found a sense of imperial belonging through participation in high culture. Fluency in Russian was required for entry into this vaunted realm, although minority ethnic groups like Jews, Armenians, and Georgians, who earlier had succeeded in politics, were overrepresented in Soviet high culture.[12] While Jews and Armenians built on a diasporic history of performing in the Russian-language culture of the host society while downplaying their national origins, Georgians blended cosmopolitan yearning with a sense of belonging within the European cultural tradition on their own terms.

Although it reached beyond the confines of explicitly national performance, Georgian prominence in Soviet high culture had a long historical trajectory and deep roots in the Georgian republic. The Georgian intelligentsia was comfortable participating in European artistic and intellectual life through the medium of Russian culture, a process begun in the nineteenth century and one that remained well-suited to the Soviet context, where world literature was discussed in Russian translation and much higher-education instruction carried out in the Russian language. At the same time, educated Georgians were expected to remain fluent in their native language and often referred to their nation's unique cultural pedigree. Unlike other national groups

seeking entry to the temples of Soviet high culture—most notably
Soviet Jews—Georgian intellectuals could claim symbolic, and sometimes actual, descent from the Georgian aristocratic poets and musicians who participated actively in nineteenth-century Russian imperial
intellectual life. They could also claim status as representatives of an
ancient cultural lineage that was famed not for an oral folk tale, such
as the Armenian *Daredevils of Sassoun* (*Sasna Dzrer*), but for Shota
Rustaveli's *Knight in the Panther's Skin*, an authored twelfth-century
Georgian epic, which, according to Soviet scholars, prefigured Dante.[13]
While Georgian high culture had been nurtured by the Soviet state
along with other Soviet national cultures, it was not seen as a Soviet-era
fabrication, but a vital tradition with a justifiable claim to its place in the
European high culture canon.

The growing prominence of Georgians in Soviet artistic and intellectual life—most apparent in the sphere of classical music, but also
noticeable in science and medicine—was further propelled by prior
Georgian successes in Soviet politics, economics, and officially sanctioned displays of Soviet multiethnicity. The children of party officials
and entrepreneurs were raised in an atmosphere that emphasized the
attainment of cultural sophistication to match their parents' political
and economic success. Accordingly, they were sent to musical conservatories, art institutes, and leading Soviet universities. Stalin's daughter
took up work as a literary translator, while Beria's son pursued a career
as a physicist; both would later write memoirs that portrayed the Soviet
political world their parents inhabited as grim and oppressive. The son of
the Georgian Bolshevik Vano Sturua became a painter and his grandson,
Robert Sturua, gained fame as a theater director known for his productions of Shakespeare. Bulat Okujava, the son of a Georgian father and
an Armenian mother, both fervent communists, traded the triumphant
choruses of his parents' generation for reflective poems set to music,
played solo on an acoustic guitar. Party bosses and enterprise managers in Tbilisi considered it the "highest prestige" to have their daughters
teach piano classes at the Tbilisi Conservatory and used every connection to get them a job there.[14] Elsewhere in the Georgian capital, the
funding provided by Moscow to develop Georgian theaters and film studios as models of national cultural achievement fostered sophisticated

centers of cultural production, whose directors sought out diverse artistic influences and produced works for a broader Soviet audience.

While their political prominence waned after the Second World War and the subsequent demise of Stalin, Georgians sought out new ways to ascend through the Soviet Union's educational and cultural infrastructure. By 1961, residents of the Georgian SSR had the highest per capita levels of higher education degrees of any Soviet republic and the highest republic-level rates of advanced education among both men and women in the USSR, at almost twice the national Soviet average.[15] In actual numbers, Georgians only came in behind the much more numerous Russian and Ukrainian populations when it came to the highest number of Soviets representing a titular republic with doctoral (both *doktor nauk* and *kandidat nauk*) degrees as well the greatest number of practicing medical doctors with higher education degrees.[16] Remarkably, the number of physicians in Georgia tripled in the period between 1941 and 1959.[17] Soviet Komsomol records show that Georgians enjoyed success in pan-Soviet competitions for the opportunity to study in Russia and noted the tendency of some students from the Caucasus to apply for study in Siberian institutes, where the competition was less fierce, before transferring to a more prestigious higher education institution in Moscow or Leningrad.[18] Many who studied in Moscow sought to remain there upon graduation, forging a life in the Soviet capital defined by specialized expertise in medicine, mathematics, architecture, philosophy, and music.

By the 1960s and 1970s, Georgians were not only overrepresented among Soviet white-collar professionals in general, but had moved to the forefront of a number of visible fields requiring a high level of training. Georgian surgeons occupied some of the leading positions in Moscow's hospitals, among them the cardiologist Leo Bokeria, who arrived in Moscow in 1965 to study at the Moscow State Medical University and by 1977 was a leading member of the Academy of Medical Sciences of the USSR and the Deputy Director of the Soviet Union's leading cardiovascular research center.[19] Other specialists, like Shota Tavartkiladze, who entered the Moscow Architecture Institute in 1949, oversaw the development and construction of the Soviet capital's new avenues and apartment buildings in the 1960s.[20] In the realm of applied mathematics,

Viktor Gelovani, who received his doctorate in 1971 from the Moscow Physics-Technical Institute, headed a cutting-edge research center devoted to complex systems analysis under the Soviet Academy of Sciences from 1976 onward.[21] In philosophy Merab Mamardashvili, who graduated from Moscow State University in 1954, developed a unique and internationally recognized approach to neo-Kantian thought.

The social origins of Georgian professionals in Moscow differed, though they were far less likely than their Russian counterparts to be the children of workers. According to Komsomol records, among Georgians accepted into Russian institutes of higher education in 1969, a greater proportion of them were the children of public servants—including state and party officials—than those of any other republic, and Georgian students were half as likely as Russian students to hail from strictly pro-letarian families of workers.[22] Many Georgian students translated their parents' success in party work, wartime service, and politics into professional opportunity. The parents of the architect Shota Tavartkiladze were revolutionaries, and his father had headed one of Tbilisi's leading publishing houses until he was arrested during the purges of 1937.[23] The father of the mathematician Viktor Gelovani had supervised construction of wartime defenses along the Black Sea, eventually attaining the high-ranking post of Chief Marshal of Engineering Troops of the USSR for his efforts in overseeing the construction of numerous Soviet military installations.[24] The philosopher Merab Mamardashvili spent part of his childhood in central Ukraine, where his father was stationed for military service at the start of the Second World War.

These members of the Georgian intelligentsia were well versed in dealing with colleagues from a variety of ethnic backgrounds, having spent a good deal of their childhoods outside of Georgia. Privileging universally applicable knowledge over national origin, they took active part in the multiethnic student friendship circles that arose in leading Soviet educational institutions during the Thaw. It was in a dorm room discussion among friends in the mid-1950s, for instance, that the philosophy major Merab Mamardashvili encountered a young student couple, Mikhail and Raisa Gorbachev.[25] Most were more concerned with professional discussions than political affairs, although some would eventually find fault with state practices and seek a return to the moral mission at the heart of the Soviet intelligentsia's worldview. In 1970, Georgian Valeri Chalidze joined fellow physicist Andrei Sakharov as one of the founding members of the Moscow Human Rights Committee. During perestroika, the philosopher Mamardashvili would also emerge as a leading critic of the Soviet regime.

## Georgian Mastery of the Classical Canon

Although Georgians achieved success in a variety of fields requiring technical mastery and engagement with a cosmopolitan intellectual culture, their particular prominence in the realm of classical music perhaps best illustrates the national and imperial dimensions of their achievements. While taking advantage of a Soviet-wide system of artistic exchange, the Georgian artists who sang Puccini's opera *Tosca* at the Bolshoi Theater and performed the orchestral works of Beethoven at the Moscow Conservatory traveled cultural pathways between Georgia and Russia that had been established in the late nineteenth and early twentieth century and were only reinforced by Soviet institutional infrastructure. Their achievements may have been touted by the Soviet state, but Georgian musicians could claim to represent a pre-Soviet tradition of high culture with a distinctive history in their native republic.

The Tbilisi Conservatory traced its origins to 1902, when the Tiflis Division of the Imperial Russian Musical Society was established and staffed by Georgian musicians educated in Russia—many of them of noble origin—as well as by notable Russian musicians who took up periodic residence in Georgia. The Conservatory was officially opened in May 1917 and incorporated into the Soviet system following the Red Army's arrival in Tbilisi. Manana Andriadze, a musicologist and graduate of Tbilisi's Central Musical School and the Tbilisi Conservatory, recalled that the centralization of the Soviet system served to further link Tbilisi to musical institutions in central Russia. The Tbilisi Conservatory's lesson plan was based on a "common program" coordinated in Moscow, for which they received schoolbooks, course guidelines, and instructions.[26]

To students at the Tbilisi Conservatory in the Soviet period, Moscow was the leading destination for Soviet-wide concerts, festivals, and musical competitions as well as the main point of entry onto the world stage. According to Andriadze, "everyone had high hopes of reaching Moscow."[27] For Georgians who traveled to study with famous instructors affiliated with the Moscow Conservatory or to take up more permanent artistic residence, the Soviet capital offered both professional excitement and occasional frustration. There, musicians found themselves in the middle of a "tumult of creative activity," and while some secured a place for themselves, others returned to Tbilisi exhausted and disillusioned. Andriadze contrasted the frenetic pace of life in Moscow, a metropolis that "ran like a machine," where one rushed about afraid to "lose a second," with Tbilisi, "an eastern place with a more relaxed atmosphere." However, she noted that the relatively "strict Russian regime" of practice and performance in Moscow produced "good results."

It is important to note that this "Russian regime" was by no means ethnically Russian. When the Georgian virtuoso pianist Eliso Virsaladze trained at the Moscow Conservatory in the 1950s, her teachers were Genrikh Neigauz, the son of a German musical teacher who had moved to Russia in the nineteenth century to teach classical music to the children of Russian noble families, and Iakov Zak, an accomplished Soviet Jewish pianist born in Odessa and educated in Moscow.[28] In the Soviet capital, Georgians took part in a particular Russian-Soviet brand of imperial universalism at a musical conservatory whose origins lay in the multiethnic court culture of the nineteenth century. The Moscow Conservatory, after all, had been founded in 1866 by Nikolai Rubinshtein, the son of a Jewish industrialist, with support from an organization run by Anton Rubinshtein, Nikolai's brother, and sponsored by the Grand Duchess Elena Pavlovna, the German-born aunt of Tsar Alexander II.[29]

Although the Soviet state promoted a standardized system of musical education, instruction was highly personalized, built around the particular school represented by an instructor and his or her own educational lineage in musical genealogies that stretched back generations. At Soviet conservatories, personal relationships overlapped with institutional affiliations, and both generated dense networks of artistic exchange between musical communities in Russia and Georgia. The wave of accomplished Georgian vocalists and pianists who arrived in Moscow in the 1950s, for instance, built on personal connections established with Russian musicians during the Second World War. Evacuated from Leningrad and Moscow in the war years, composers like Sergei Prokofiev and Dmitrii Shostakovich found refuge at the Tbilisi Conservatory, where they built lasting relationships with Georgian pedagogues and their students.[30]

Just as Moscow held the promise of a larger stage for Georgian performers, so, too, did Tbilisi possess its own unique appeal for Russian musicians. Restive members of the Russian intelligentsia sometimes wanted to live there rather than in Moscow or Leningrad as a form of "internal emigration."[31] Lev Markiz, the former concertmaster of the Moscow Chamber Orchestra, recalled:

> For a large number of Russian intellectuals (including musicians), living in Georgia, having contact with its local cultural elite, and having exposure to the more specific aspects of local life, with its festive atmosphere, the unbelievable hospitality of Georgians, the country's magnificent natural beauty, the traditions of the table, all of this was a genuine respite from the stresses of Soviet life.[32]

Traveling to Tbilisi in the Soviet period, Markiz encountered a large number of talented Georgian musicians, particularly vocalists and pianists. He attributed Georgian vocal success to the country's native musical culture, in which "an ear for music was honed from early childhood." In this sense, it represented a certain degree of national distinctiveness. He also noted, however, that Georgian pianists greatly benefited from links to the "Russian system" of musical education. Most either studied in Russian musical schools or with Georgian instructors who had spent time in Russia, making them in effect the "'children' or 'grandchildren' of Russian professors" at conservatories in Moscow and Leningrad. According to Markiz, ties between Russian and Georgian musical communities ran so deep as to make them inseparable; instead, he claimed that Georgian classical musicians represented a hybrid "Russian-Georgian school."[33]

Georgian musicians learned to perform the standard Soviet repertoire of European classical music flawlessly, and those who successfully launched careers in Moscow became leading members of Russian ensembles and represented the RSFSR on Soviet-wide tours. Georgian pianist Eliso Virsaladze took third prize at the 1962 Tchaikovsky Competition in Moscow and eventually became a professor at the Moscow Conservatory, her alma mater. In 1968, Virsaladze was highlighted as a "winner of international competitions" among the artists representing Soviet Russia. Similarly, the violinist Marine Iashvili, the daughter of a professor at the Tbilisi Conservatory, left to study at the Moscow Conservatory in 1957. Eventually joining the ranks of Moskontsert, she regularly performed as part of the "Moscow Stars" festival in the Soviet capital.[34] By 1979 there were two Georgian pianists playing for the Moscow State Philharmonic, along with two Georgian violinists.[35] If they stood out because of their names and appearance, their repertoire was seen as universal rather than strictly national.

Georgian vocalists became especially prominent at Moscow's storied Bolshoi Theater. In 1973 and 1974, four out of fifteen guest artists performing with the Bolshoi's opera company were Georgians. They took leading roles in the Bolshoi's productions of Russian operas and international classics.[36] Makvala Kasrashvili, a Georgian soprano, became a regular member of the opera troupe and was cast as Tatiana, the epitome of Russian feminine virtue, in the Bolshoi's international production of Tchaikovsky's *Evgenii Onegin* at New York's Metropolitan Opera in 1979. Sponsored by the Georgian Ministry of Culture, Georgian performers took up residence not only in Moscow, but also in cities throughout the Soviet Union for periods of time ranging from days to months. In 1973 and 1974, Georgian guest performers starred in operas produced by Leningrad's Kirov Theater and joined opera houses in the Russian cities of Novosibirsk, Sverdlovsk, Perm, and Chelyabinsk, as well as the national operas of Belarus, Estonia, Latvia, Lithuania, Moldova, Tajikistan, and Armenia.[37] The travels of Georgian artists were part of a larger system of Soviet artistic circulation, within which special, bidirectional ties existed between Georgian and Russian ensembles. Some even traveled abroad, like the soprano Medea Amiranishvili, who was accepted for a one-year residence at Milan's La Scala in 1963.[38]

Georgians sought participation in a more universal imperial culture and were assisted in doing so by the strength of Georgian institutions like the Tbilisi Conservatory, the multicultural fluency of the Georgian

*Figure 6.1* Georgian virtuoso pianist Eliso Virsaladze, 1975. National Archives of Georgia.

diaspora, and their ability to take advantage of an established Soviet system of artistic and intellectual exchange. While their success had local roots and could be linked to a verifiable national pedigree, Georgian musicians transcended the confines of specifically Georgian performance, pursuing creative expression within the more cosmopolitan world of classical music. As long as they adhered to the established canon, Georgian virtuosos enjoyed relative artistic freedom and were sometimes even permitted to travel outside the Soviet Union.

# From the Classical Canon to Cinematic Critique

High culture virtuosity and achievement in the specialized fields of Soviet science provided an escape from some of the restrictions of late Soviet intellectual life and allowed non-Russians to move beyond the limitations of a specifically national repertoire. However, Soviet artists and scientists were not simply intellectuals, but members of the intelligentsia, a category that entailed a moral mission to uplift society as well as the pursuit of excellence in high culture. Imperial belonging through high culture achievement entailed the ability to speak to pan-imperial concerns; the celebration of the idea of genius exalted artistic authorship over the temporal authority of the state. Seeking to assert themselves creatively, members of the late Soviet intelligentsia sought artistic independence by mastering oblique forms of criticism, some couched in irony and ethnographic specificity, others composed of semiconcealed references. The intellectual culture of *zastoi* was defined not by high culture virtuosity alone, but also by artists who expertly skirted the limits of allowable expression.

With the exception of music, cinema was perhaps the freest and most internationally-oriented of the arts in the post-Stalinist period. It was also in the process of undergoing a rapid expansion in terms of production; while only nine Soviet films were made over the course of 1951, by 1969 the annual number of films produced reached one hundred and fifty.[39] In contrast to classical music, Soviet cinema was a more recent artistic medium created by revolutionaries like Sergei Eisenstein. As such, its geniuses were twentieth-century personages and its canon was potentially more destabilizing, offering a rich language for social critique and an inspiration for ongoing innovation.[40] During the Thaw, Soviet directors established contact with an international community of artists at European film festivals and developed their craft in dialogue with Italian Neorealism, the French New Wave, and the Polish Film School.[41] Reflecting the concerns of the post-Stalinist intelligentsia, their films expressed a profound interest in authenticity; they earnestly tackled morally complex issues, challenged conventional gender roles, and did not always offer the viewer complete dramatic resolution.

It is difficult to pinpoint a precise end to the cinema of the Thaw, but by the late 1960s filmmakers attracted greater official scrutiny even as the mood of their films grew more pessimistic.[42] Yet if the filmmakers of *zastoi* faced greater restrictions and were less hopeful of achieving social change, the Thaw-era concern with authenticity persisted, though it was now expressed through sly mockery and ironic commentary on the shortcomings of public life in the Soviet Union. Internationally as well as in the Soviet Union, authenticity was linked to the idea of cinematic authorship; film critics and directors alike expounded on the idea of a *cinéma d'auteur* (translated in Russian as *avtorskoe kino*), summoning the idea of artistic genius to claim that a film ought to express the personal creative vision of its director.[43] With central institutions so intimately involved in funding and controlling cinematic production, however, the focus on authenticity and authorship drew attention to the imperial dilemmas of the multiethnic Soviet Union.

As it did in other areas of cultural production, the Soviet state gave special attention to the development of cinema in the national republics while sponsoring a pan-Soviet system of artistic exchange and education based in Moscow. "National cinema" was very much a Soviet imperial genre, typically created by non-Russian directors who had been educated at the All-Union State Institute of Cinematography (VGIK) in Moscow and then placed in a republic-level film studio to produce work expressive of national character but attractive to a pan-Soviet audience. In some ways national cinema affirmed well-trodden repertoires of national otherness, often positing non-Russian nations as rural and backward. However, national cinema also had its own artistic traditions, and republic-level studios sometimes offered a greater degree of artistic freedom than the film studios in Moscow and Leningrad. Soviet national cinema had first been developed in the 1920s and early 1930s by directors like Oleksandr Dovzhenko, who worked in Ukraine, and Nikoloz Shengelaia and Mikhail Kalatozov (Kalatozishvili), who worked in Georgia; their movies, often produced by multiethnic film crews, combined ethnographically spe-cific depictions of national life with innovative cinematography and were widely praised and imitated for their richly expressive qualities. By the lat-ter half of the 1930s the established language of national cinema was effec-tively canonized and employed for more blatantly propagandistic pieces, but in the post-Stalinist period national cinema once again became a vital arena for artistic creativity, one that benefitted from continued central support and the rising autonomy of local film officials. By the 1960s film studios in the Central Asian republics had expanded and were producing artistically original films, while directors in Ukraine and Georgia aimed to revitalize the work of their early Soviet predecessors.[44]

The leading figures of national cinema during *zastoi* were never purely national. Instead, their artistic output represented another blend of cosmopolitan universalism, one that looked beyond Soviet borders to Europe for themes and techniques and back to their native republics for a lyrical sense of place, language, and culture. If they drew on national folklore and ethnography, they did so self-consciously to create a cinematic language whose meaning was subject to multiple interpretations.[45] Many were, in some sense, national outsiders. One of the leading figures of Ukrainian cinema in the 1960s was Sergei Parajanov, an ethnic Armenian born in Tbilisi and trained in Moscow. His fluid visual compositions employed an array of national symbols and motifs. His 1964 film *Shadows of Forgotten Ancestors* (*Tini zabutykh predkiv*) was informed by the folkloric imagery of the Ukrainian Hutsul culture of the Carpathians; he comfortably shifted to express his ethnic Armenian roots in *The Color of Pomegranates* (*Tsvet granata*), released in 1968; and he returned to cinema in the 1980s with the Georgian-language *Legend of Suram Fortress* (*ambavi suramis tsikhisa*) and the Azeri-flavored *Ashik Kerib*.[46] The other critically acclaimed Ukrainian directors of this period, Yuri Ilienko and Leonid Osyka, were ethnic Ukrainians who produced works expressive of their native culture, but both were trained in Moscow and sought out broader audiences. The same could be said about the major Georgian directors of *zastoi*, representatives of an artistic community that was thoroughly bilingual and bicultural, lived in multiethnic urban centers, and made films with pan-Soviet audiences in mind. Yet just as the international auteurs of the period were claimed as representatives of distinct national film schools—Federico Fellini for Italian cinema, Ingmar Bergman for Swedish cinema, and Akira Kurosawa for Japanese cinema—Ukrainian and Georgian directors were seen as speaking for their respective nations, even as they expressed universal artistic concerns.[47]

However, the pursuit of national authorship in an imperial state was often difficult. Signaling a shift from the relatively permissive atmosphere of film production in the 1960s, Mikhail Bleiman, a leading film critic and a major reviewer of film scripts for Goskino, the central state film committee, took aim at certain trends in national cinema in a lengthy article published in *Ikusstvo kino* in 1970.[48] Singling out a group of Ukrainian directors as well as the Georgian director Tengiz Abuladze, he argued that while they claimed to be "innovators" and were technically skilled, their work was based on "archaic thinking" and had "archaic roots." While Bleiman did not say so explicitly, the need for empire-wide intelligibility was at the core of his critique. He defended the authorial independence of directors, calling it a "truism" that all artists "have the right to choose their own approach," but claimed that some national directors left true meaning unknowable, hidden in "allegories" and ethnographically specific "codes," "the key to which was possessed by the artist alone."[49] These words may have been indicative of a generational conflict between a longstanding critic and a group of young Soviet artists, but they also had an imperial cast, coming from a major Russian film figure and addressed to non-Russian directors. The message was clear: national culture would be allowed its specific features, but needed to remain legible to the state and the general public. This requirement was ideologically important but also economically driven; films that could not be understood would not draw a pan-Soviet—and predominantly Russian-speaking—audience, nor would they generate revenue.[50]

Despite the limits imposed on national expression, many Georgian directors embraced the task of producing pan-Soviet works of Georgian culture and occasionally offered veiled critiques of Russian domination, even as they operated within the system and maintained their connections with the center. In some ways, Georgian directors benefitted from the fact that the terms of their national difference were well established. In contrast to the work of Ukrainians, there was no expectation of pan-Slavic similarity in Georgian cinema. Instead, Georgian films were celebrated for their distinctiveness. Typically dubbed into Russian for wide release, the Georgian origin of these films was unmistakable in their use of recognizably Georgian actors and Georgian settings.

Yet Georgian cinema went beyond the routine performance of Georgian nationality, instead appealing to universal themes and pan-Soviet intellectual concerns, from the amoral irony of *zastoi* to the high moralism of perestroika. Like Georgia's classical musicians, Georgian actors and directors in the Soviet period drew on a hybrid culture of imperial artistic exchange with its origins in tsarist Russia. Links with Russia were carried into the Soviet period, as early Georgian film was strongly influenced by the Moscow Art Theater, where the first generation of Georgian directors studied.[51] Their cinematic productions met the needs of Soviet domestic internationalism but also aspired beyond its confines and chafed against its presumed hierarchies; Georgian directors looked to Russia but sought out equal footing with their Russian counterparts. The leading directors of the Georgian Film Studio expertly pushed against the limits of the Soviet film industry, and for this reason their works were eagerly consumed by intellectuals in Moscow and Leningrad and considered the finest expressions of a Soviet school of *avtorskoe kino*.

Although it became a form of intellectual critique, Georgian cinema built on decades of Soviet patronage. The Georgian Film Studio was well established, tracing its origins to the early 1920s, whereas film studios in the Kyrgyz SSR, by contrast, were not established until 1942 and did not begin making films for wide release until the late 1950s. The Georgian studio also had high-level connections, since the prior successes of Georgian directors who began their careers in Georgia, like Mikhail Kalatozov, had placed them in influential posts in central cinematic production. While he continued to make innovative films, including *The Cranes are Flying (Letiat zhuravli)*, one of the most important works of Thaw cinema, Kalatozov occupied a leading position at Mosfil'm, the Soviet Union's largest film studio, and for a time served as Deputy Minister of Cinematography of the Soviet Union, making him a valuable protector for aspiring filmmakers from Georgia.[52]

The styles of the filmmakers who worked in the Georgian Film Studio were unmistakably Georgian, but also diverse. Pursuing their respective artistic visions, they sought to reach a wide audience while engaging in a variety of tactics to reduce the influence that Goskino had over film production. An examination of the personal and professional histories of Eldar and Giorgi Shengelaia, Otar Ioseliani, and Tengiz Abuladze, some of the best-known figures of Georgian cinema, reveals how these directors sought out authorial independence and worked to preserve some sense of national authenticity while producing films that met the demands of a state-led industry.

## National Authorship and Authenticity in the Soviet Film Industry

Like many other Georgian filmmakers, the brothers Eldar and Giorgi Shengelaia grew up in a prominent intelligentsia family with long-established ties to the stage and screen.[53] Their father was Nikoloz Shengelaia, the iconoclastic Georgian poet who had played a leading role in the development of Georgian national cinema. Their mother, Nato Vachnadze, had been born in Warsaw in 1904 to a Georgian nobleman and a Polish mother and became a famous Soviet film actress in the 1930s. Nikoloz Shengelaia and Nato Vachnadze lived in Georgia, but traveled frequently to Moscow to attend film festivals and collaborate with their Russian colleagues. Their first son, Eldar, was born in Tbilisi in 1933; their second son, Giorgi, was born in Moscow in 1937, while his parents were attending a film event.[54] Their home in Tbilisi was a gathering place for artists and intellectuals from across the Soviet Union. Enthusiastic participants in the multiethnic creative networks that arose in the early years of Soviet power, they regularly hosted luminaries like the playwright Sergei Tret'iakov and the critic Viktor Shklovskii.[55] In an interview, Eldar Shengelaia spoke of a childhood spent amidst endless "artistic evenings, events, museum openings, and musical concerts."[56] Their father died fairly young, suffering a heart attack in 1943, and in 1953 their mother perished in a plane crash while flying from Moscow to Tbilisi. According to Giorgi Shengelaia, both sons felt a desire to carry on the work of their parents, although Eldar Shengelaia noted that their mother discouraged her older son's interest in film, believing that it had become a professionally risky career path due to Stalin's imposition of strict cultural controls in the postwar period.[57]

Undaunted, Eldar Shengelaia arrived in Moscow in 1952 to study at VGIK. After Stalin's death the following year, he found himself in the heart of emerging debates about artistic expression that were central to the Thaw. At the institute, students were freed from the rigid constraints of the late Stalinist era; in Eldar Shengelaia's words, the curriculum shifted from an "ideological program" to a "system of instruction that emphasized artistic achievement." The artistic vision of Shengelaia's generation was informed by a sense of return to the revolutionary spirit of early Soviet national cinema as well as an opening to new international influences. Among the instructors at VGIK were the Ukrainian director Oleksandr Dovzhenko and the Georgian director Mikheil Chiaureli, two pioneers of national cinema who had produced propagandistic historical epics in the Stalinist era but had their roots in the avant-garde experimentalism of the 1920s. The institute's film library granted students access to the classics of international cinema and the latest films from France, Germany, and Italy.[58] As a cohort, Thaw-era students at VGIK were nationally aware but internationalist in their outlook and habits. According to Giorgi Shengelaia, who arrived in 1959 to study at VGIK, the Georgian students at the relatively small institute all knew each other, but their peer group was not bound by nationality; it also included future Russian directors like Andrei Tarkovskii and Andrei Konchalovskii.[59]

After graduating from VGIK both Shengelaia brothers returned to Tbilisi, where they took up work as directors for the Georgian Film Studio. Even given their internationalist aspirations, this career move made sense. In addition to well-financed studios, Georgia offered filmmakers access to the actors and designers of Tbilisi's famed Rustaveli Theater. The Shengelaia brothers had grown up in an atmosphere that stressed the cosmopolitan contributions of Georgian culture and their education emphasized the merits of artistic excellence over commercial compromise, so they believed that they could address themes of universal importance in a Georgian setting. In a way, such an approach echoed the old Stalinist prescription that Soviet culture be "national in form, socialist in content"; in the case of the Shengelaia brothers, however, their interests did not concern explicitly socialist issues, but appealed to the ideals of authenticity and creative independence now celebrated by the Soviet intelligentsia.[60]

As the relative freedom of the Thaw years gave way to greater official scrutiny, both Shengelaia brothers learned to operate within the confines of a more closed system, each in his own way. Eldar Shengelaia developed a close partnership with Rezo Gabriadze, the Tbilisi writer, theater director, sculptor, and artist. The two worked together on the 1968 film *An Unusual Exhibition* (*arachveulebrivi gamopena*), which revealed Gabriadze's penchant for tragicomedy, or what the Moscow-based Georgian filmmaker Giorgi Danelia termed "tearful comedy," paired with Eldar Shengelaia's interest in the ironies and absurdities of everyday life. In his interview Shengelaia stressed that the use of humor was not simply a convention with its own traditions in Georgian theater, but it also offered "the possibility to speak about one thing, and comment on another, as in a parable."[61] *An Unusual Exhibition* depicted a talented young sculptor in a small Georgian village who is forced to resort to carving grotesque tombstones for money in order to support his family after his wife gives birth to twins. Although full of humorous situations, the film was an attack on artistic compromise that was all the more pointed because it was set in contemporary Georgia. Early viewings of the completed film drew the scrutiny of the Georgian Ministry of Culture, which supervised the film studios, and eventually of Goskino in Moscow. According to Eldar Shengelaia, "the form of the film saved me ... humor made it ultimately seem unserious to the editors."[62] Shengelaia avoided official rebuke, but Goskino still demanded that cuts be made to the film to remove ideologically troublesome scenes. Taking advantage of chronically poor coordination between the center and the national film studios, Shengelaia returned to Moscow with an edited copy of his original film, submitted for wide release. Unbeknownst to Goskino, he preserved the uncut film's negative in Tbilisi, where it was screened on a limited basis at film clubs.[63]

Giorgi Shengelaia's first film to garner widespread attention, *Pirosmani*, was completed in 1969. In contrast to his brother, Giorgi Shengelaia used the genre of tragedy to touch upon the same theme of artistic integrity. The artist Niko Pirosmani, who had helped establish the visual language of modern Georgian culture, was depicted in the film as a genius who endured poverty, the hypocrisy of his high-society patrons, and public ridicule in heroic, if naive, pursuit of his artistic vision. The film was both a defense and an expression of Georgian creative authorship. Although Giorgi Shengelaia's social criticism was cushioned by the fact that it was set in prerevolutionary Tbilisi, his decision to open the film with a moralistic passage from the New Testament all but ensured that his movie would not see wide release. Ultimately Goskino decided not to cut the film, but to limit its viewership by making only a handful of copies available for screening in the Soviet Union. However, *Pirosmani* garnered critical acclaim at several international film festivals and at the Kinoteatr Povtornogo Fil'ma (the Cinema of Second-Run Film) in central Moscow, a small movie theater with a cult-like following among Moscow's intelligentsia. Clamoring to attend these limited screenings, Russian intellectuals gathered to view and discuss Shengelaia's portrayal of an artist with an unflappable sense of personal dignity and aesthetic vision.[64] The film self-consciously engaged the familiar Georgian repertoire; Pirosmani was a historical personage, but he fit the well-established role of a Caucasian naif. At the same time, the dilemmas that Pirosmani faced as an artist were immediately recognizable to the broader Brezhnev-era intelligentsia, whose members had to constantly negotiate between artistic integrity and professional success.

Both Shengelaia brothers made concessions to secure the release of their films without entirely forsaking creative authorship. In 1973 Giorgi Shengelaia released the popular *Melodies of the Vera Quarter*, a lively musical comedy starring the Georgian singer and actor Vakhtang Kikabidze and the actress Sopiko Chiaureli, then Shengelaia's wife. The film was a loving ode to the culture of Tbilisi's old neighborhoods, but also evoked the established repertoire of Georgian song and dance performance, helping it gain success among a broader audience. Shengelaia saw the film as a "genre piece" that allowed him to pursue his limited distribution "auteur films." In his interview, he regarded the musical as a "compromise," but one of "artistic quality that was done according to [his] own tastes."[65] As someone working in the Soviet film industry, he realized it was sometimes necessary to comply with the demands of the state and the expectations of an imperial audience.

His brother, Eldar Shengelaia, managed to evade the censors by retreating further into folkloric Georgian settings and whimsical comedies. Again teaming up with writer Rezo Gabriadze, Shengelaia's 1973 film *The Eccentrics* made it into wide release and was lauded by the Soviet intelligentsia in general and the Georgian intelligentsia in particular for the forceful statements it made, veiled in humor, on the plight of late Soviet intellectuals. In contrast to their 1968 film, *An Unusual Exhibition*, Shengelaia and Gabriadze decided to set *The Eccentrics* in prerevolutionary Georgia. Thus the plight of the story's main characters, who are unfairly locked in prison, could be blamed on the tsarist authorities. Yet the petty cruelty, incompetence, and officiousness of the military officers who run the prison clearly evoked intellectuals' frustration with the Soviet bureaucracy. The film was filled with joyful Georgian singing and moments of comedy bordering on slapstick humor, but buried beneath the surface were poignant phrases that became rote expressions among the Georgian intelligentsia. The film's two heroes, the young man and the mathematician, plot their escape from the underground cell by devising an elaborate flying contraption through sketches and equations on the cell walls. However, a guard intervenes and wipes the walls clean with a rag. In response to the temporary destruction of his carefully laid plans, the mathematician taps himself on the head and shouts, "you cannot erase them from here!" The phrase evoked Mikhail Bulgakov's aphorism that "manuscripts do not burn" and suggested that intellectuals might somehow triumph in their struggle with the state. Rather than ending on a tragic note, the film concluded with a brief glimpse of freedom. The pair's fantastical flying machine actually works, and as the two prisoners rise far above their captors, a Georgian landscape of hills, rivers, and ancient churches can be seen stretching out in all directions on the horizon. While the 1983 hijacking attempt that was later associated with the film ended in failure, on screen the dreams of the "eccentrics" were ultimately realized.

The film's production notes show that *The Eccentrics* was sufficiently couched in folklore, history, and comedic situations to avoid serious scrutiny at the time of its release. The notes also reveal that Eldar Shengelaia and Rezo Gabriadze had grown skilled at framing their projects in terms that resonated with Soviet officials. Adopting the same language used in official discourse to describe the triumph of the Bolshevik Revolution and the recent achievements of Soviet cosmonauts, the film's description, first presented to Goskino on May 19, 1971, described it as a "fable" of "man's first attempt to reach for the skies, to overcome the 'gravitational pull' of popular consciousness, to break free from the old rules of life held for centuries."[66] Shengelaia and Gabriadze were required to meet regularly during production with the leadership of the Georgian Film Studio and occasionally with Goskino. The meeting minutes of the Georgian Film Studio reveal little discussion and a series of rubber-stamp approvals of the film's development; those of Goskino show greater skepticism as the movie's production went on. One Goskino official expressed the view that a "social emphasis" ought to be placed on conflicts between the "'positive' and 'negative' characters." While the official praised the actions of the film's heroes as "a popular protest against the world of shopkeepers and oppressors," the scenes involving a doctor, a supposed man of science, and the strange cast of characters kept in his insane asylum offered a more ambiguous social message. Some of these scenes were presumably cut, but the scheming doctor remained, along with the film's basic structure. The film was approved for production and received full state support, with assistance even rendered by aircraft of the Transcaucasian Military Division for filming the flying scenes.[67] As with other *zastoi* intellectuals, Shengelaia was critical of the Soviet state but also dependent upon it. Looking back on the situation, he commented: "Bureaucrats controlled the number of prints made, where the film would be shown, and whether it would be sent abroad. But . . . they gave us money."[68]

In addition to mastering bureaucratic strategies to pursue their creative visions, Georgian filmmakers like the Shengelaia brothers boosted their influence by integrating into powerful creative networks. Building on his family connections and his own reputation in Georgia's artistic community, Eldar Shengelaia became chair of the Georgian Filmmakers Union in 1976. He even participated in political life, joining the Communist Party and serving in the Georgian SSR's Supreme Soviet from 1980 to 1985. His political service may have allowed Eldar Shengelaia to continue making the movies he wanted to make, including his 1983 film *Blue Mountains, or An Unbelievable Story* (*tsisperi mtebi anu daujerebeli ambavi*), a humorous critique of professional mediocrity and bureaucratic ineptitude at a Soviet publishing house.[69]

Giorgi Shengelaia, the director of *Pirosmani*, remained more wary of Soviet politics, but his family's connections and his marriage to Sopiko Chiaureli gave him a high standing in Tbilisi society. Both Shengelaia and Chiaureli were the children of prominent Georgian cultural figures: her father was Mikheil Chiaureli, an influential filmmaker and VGIK professor; her mother was a famous Georgian actress, Veriko Anjaparidze; and her cousin was director Giorgi Danelia. Party membership helped, but, on the basis of their prominent positions in networks of influence, celebrated members of the Georgian intelligentsia were sometimes begrudgingly accommodated by the state. Their power outside the artistic realm was limited, but in the tight-knit world of Georgian cinema, friendships and personal relationships could sometimes be counted on for assistance. Indeed, the personal intervention of the celebrated Georgian actor Dodo Abashidze allowed Sergei Parajanov, who had been attacked for artistic subversion in his films and arrested on charges of homosexuality, to take up work with the Georgian Film Studio in the early 1980s.[70]

Like the Shengelaia brothers, the Georgian director Otar Ioseliani also came from a fairly prominent Tbilisi family with its own cosmopolitan connections. His father had been an officer in the tsarist army and worked as a railway engineer until he was swept up in the purges of the 1930s. His mother, who raised Otar on her own after his father's arrest, came from an aristocratic family and had studied at a tsarist-era institute for noble girls, where she gained fluency in French as well as Russian. Otar Ioseliani first gravitated toward classical music, studying violin at the prestigious musical school in the Georgian capital. Instead of going on to the Tbilisi Conservatory, he left for Moscow in 1953, where he began to study mathematics and astronomy at Moscow State University. Finding himself in the Soviet capital during the Thaw, he then drifted toward film as the most innovative medium of intellectual expression in the Soviet Union. In 1955, he enrolled at VGIK.

Ioseliani's professors at VGIK found his early work to be evocative of the Georgian cinematic tradition in its twin commitment to ethnographic particularism in setting and artistic universalism in theme.[71] His influences were certainly diverse; an early artistic manifesto that the young director wrote for himself, but never published, cited Shakespeare, Cervantes, Moliere, and Tolstoy, as well as the French director Jacques Tati, also of Russian aristocratic background.[72] Elsewhere, he stated that the "heights of cinema" were exemplified by Vittorio De Sica's neorealist *Miracle in Milan* (*Miracolo a Milano*), released in 1951, and Georgian director Nikoloz Shengelaia's quasi-ethnographic 1928 film *Eliso*.[73] From the beginning, Ioseliani was less inclined than the Shengelaia brothers to make artistic compromises or otherwise alter his films; one of his student projects showed a series of flowers and meadows crushed by Soviet bulldozers, while another depicted with gritty detail daily life in a Soviet Georgian foundry. Both were declared unsuitable for academic credit as Ioseliani sought to graduate from VGIK in the early 1960s. Ioseliani was, however, willing to exploit his personal connections. Finding the first in a long succession of patrons in the Soviet filmmaker Grigorii Chukhrai, who had won the Lenin Prize for his 1959 film *Ballad of a Soldier* (*Ballada o soldate*), Ioseliani was finally able to graduate from the film institute based on a letter of recommendation written and signed by Chukhrai.[74]

Like the Shengelaia brothers, Ioseliani returned to Georgia to pursue his film career. In Tbilisi he was partially shielded from the scrutiny of Goskino by a series of powerful national studio chiefs. The first studio director Ioseliani worked under, Misha Kveselava, gave repeated assurances to the young director, telling him, "as long as I am alive, you should pursue your work." The second, Tengiz Gordeladze, was remembered by Ioseliani as "a principled Bolshevik," who told Ioseliani: "It is your job to make films, so I will not impede."[75] Both studio chiefs sought to maximize the autonomy of the Georgian Film Studio, the first because of a commitment to artistic excellence, the second because he took seriously the Soviet effort to foster the development of national culture.

Ioseliani's first major film, *Falling Leaves*, caused a sensation far beyond the Georgian republic on its release in 1966. The film's protagonist, Niko, is an awkward and naive young man who works at a Georgian wine factory. Niko's hapless pursuit of a female coworker leads only to failure and disillusionment, and his brief rebellion against the low standards of production at the winery is erratic and unexpected. In contrast to the humorous, Aesopian critique of Eldar Shengelaia or the dramatized morality of Giorgi Shengelaia, *Falling Leaves* offered no unambiguously positive heroes and no clear moral. With his slouching posture and hopeless efforts at romance, young Niko diverged from the typical Soviet masculine hero and also contrasted with the bellicose masculinity of Georgian folk dancers and widespread conceptions of male Georgian braggadocio.

Despite his departure from the established Georgian repertoire, Ioseliani was able to claim authorial privilege in representing his own nation. In their discussions, Goskino's reviewers were initially divided over the film's merits, but were seemingly swayed by the argument of one critic, Arnshtan, that Georgian directors had license to accurately convey the complexities of "their own environment."[76] Meanwhile, Ioseliani commanded the full support of the Georgian Film Studio, whose reviewers stated that his film marked a new level of "high professionalism," and, after all, depicted the winemaking "for which Georgia is world-famous, but never before has been made the subject of a movie."[77] Ioseliani not only received permission to proceed with the film, but also was granted several extensions and enjoyed control over choosing actors and filming locations.[78]

It is likely that Goskino also tolerated the film because it was seen as artistically suitable for international release at a time when *cinéma d'auteur* was favored by foreign critics; indeed, the film was entered by the Soviets in the 1968 Cannes Film Festival, where it won a top prize.[79] Abroad, Ioseliani was hailed as the creator of a characteristic cinematic style that was suggestive of Italian Neorealism in its preference for black and white and the use of nonprofessional actors, yet unmistakably Georgian in its detailed depictions of wine harvests in the Georgian countryside. In Moscow, Ioseliani became something of a celebrity; when he visited the city, he hosted rambunctious gatherings of leading Russian and visiting French artists and intellectuals at an acquaintance's apartment across from the Bolshoi Theater.[80]

Ioseliani's distinctive style was further developed in his next film, *Once Lived a Song-Thrush* (*iqo shashvi mgalobeli*), released in 1971. The film's protagonist is a young Georgian musician who lives with his mother in Tbilisi. He has a spontaneous approach to life, wandering about town, meeting women, spending time with friends, and enjoying a carefree existence. Despite his musical talent, he never manages to write the first notes of the song he means to compose. Once again,

*Figure 6.2*  Georgian director Otar Ioseliani on the set of *Once Lived a Song-Thrush* in Tbilisi, 1970. National Archives of Georgia.

Goskino's editors strove in vain to understand the film's message and its social significance. Although his dashing appearance more readily accorded with expectations of Georgian masculinity, the film's hero was deemed too attractive to serve as a warning to viewers about the moral hazards of wasting time and energy. Goskino's editors also worried that the hero's seemingly random death in a car accident would leave the audience further confused. Although the editors explicitly praised Ioseliani as an original auteur for his cinematic style, they informed him in January 1970 that "an author's attitude toward his protagonist ought to be expressed precisely and unequivocally."[81]

In a note to Goskino's Moscow editors in March 1970, Ioseliani reasserted his authorial privilege, using language that echoed official Soviet rhetoric. He claimed that his was "a film about creative work in our society," reassuring Goskino that he wanted "to demonstrate the necessity for every Soviet person to focus all his energy and talent on making a contribution to the common cause."[82] The film went back and forth repeatedly between Tbilisi and Moscow, and Ioseliani eventually agreed to cut several scenes out of concern for the film's growing length, though these edits did little to address the underlying criticisms of Goskino officials. Apparently the gestures made by Ioseliani to appease his critics worked in his favor, as did the international acclaim the Georgian director received for his previous film, a factor cited in letters of support written by the leadership of Georgia's film studio.[83] Ioseliani's new movie was dubbed in Russian and widely released, quickly gaining the status of a cult film among the Soviet intelligentsia. The Russian film historian Andrei Plakhov recalled a contemporary review that praised Ioseliani for creating a film in which "the flow of life foamed like Borjomi in a glass," in which there was "the aftertaste of bitterness, the wisdom of genius, and an unmistakable 'French taste.'"[84] Like the mineral water Borjomi, Ioseliani's films were produced in the Caucasus and shipped to Moscow, seen as authentic works of Georgian culture but celebrated for evoking more sophisticated sensibilities.

Whether it was indicative of increasingly strict state censorship or the director's growing frustration with the limitations of working within the system, Ioseliani's final Soviet film, *Pastorale* (*pastorali*), was completed in 1975 but never saw wide release. The film depicted the brief stay of a group of musicians from Tbilisi in a western Georgian village. Admittedly, it went further than his first two films; *Pastorale* not only lacked a positive hero and moral, it also had no main character, no clear plot, and large portions of the dialogue were spoken in Mingrelian, a regional dialect barely intelligible to most Georgian speakers. The film's production notes show confusion over how to classify the film; it was alternately referred to as an "artistic film" or a "comedy."[85] Again, Ioseliani received support from the Georgian Film Studio, whose editorial chief described it as "a study of the moral, social problems of the contemporary Georgian countryside."[86] Yet Goskino's editors immediately found problems with Ioseliani's quasi-ethnographic depiction of everyday struggles, corruption, and drunkenness in rural Georgia. If post-Stalinist national cinema had returned to folklore for an aesthetic language that could be employed with authorial independence, this film went one step further, suggesting that true folk culture was ultimately inscrutable to outsiders, perhaps even to Georgians from Tbilisi. Ioseliani's unwillingness to alter the film raised the ire of Goskino, which dispatched M. G. Maruchkova, one of its editors, to Tbilisi. Upon her return to Moscow, she leveled charges of "lengthy procrastination" at Ioseliani and implied that that the new Georgian studio director, Rezo Chkheidze, was partially to blame since she had sent him a letter outlining her concerns several months before, but to no effect.[87] Ultimately only three copies of the film were made, and few saw it outside Georgia. The Soviet photographer Yuri Rost, a close friend of Ioseliani, recalled the despair of the Georgian director after the Tbilisi screening of *Pastorale*. Though he was reluctant to accept artistic compromise and insistent on maintaining control over his depictions of Georgian culture, Ioseliani felt that continuing to make films was pointless if his cinematic work could not be shown outside his native republic. As an exceptionally high-profile intellectual with supporters abroad, he eventually was allowed to emigrate to France to pursue his career.[88]

Aspiring to be cinematic auteurs, late Soviet Georgian directors struggled to maintain authorship of their art and to present creatively vital productions of Georgian culture, difficult tasks in an imperial state where public discourse was tightly scripted and non-Russian cultural repertoires seemed to be growing stale. Some, like Eldar Shengelaia, shrouded their authorial statements in humor and absurdist parables. Others, like Giorgi Shengelaia, alternated between serious *avtorskie fil'my* and ideologically palatable genre pieces of national cinema. Otar Ioseliani, by contrast, expressed his aversion to the intellectual compromises of *zastoi* by trading sanctimonious moralizing for morally uncertain irony. All of them employed canny tactics to cope with the state institutions that funded their work, yet could potentially limit their viewership.

Reflecting the social complexity of *zastoi*, the institutions that these directors navigated were hardly monolithic: Goskino's critics often presented opposing views, and the Georgian Film Studio typically lobbied on behalf of its directors. Relatively frank discussion took place in the closed meetings of Goskino, and Ioseliani and other directors found that some bureaucrats were more "enlightened" than others.[89] Although Georgian directors frequently came up against restrictions, they arguably had greater latitude than their Russian counterparts;

Giorgi Shengelaia, for one, felt that he had an easier time getting around the censor than the Russian director Andrei Tarkovskii.[90] Yet the limitations that Georgian directors did encounter echoed the broader concerns of the Georgian intelligentsia in the late Soviet period. Georgian success was based on an increasingly unsteady combination of state promotion and Georgian participation in the fabrication of a multiethnic culture. By the late Soviet period Georgian intellectuals sought to move beyond the official niches that enabled, but ultimately limited, their achievements. Georgian high culture virtuosos had found oases of artistic freedom where they could transcend their established national repertoire, and Georgian directors had found ways to maintain a sense of artistic integrity through concealment and clever bureaucratic tactics. With the release of Tengiz Abuladze's *Repentance* the failings of the Soviet system would be addressed directly, and the Georgian intelligentsia would grow more critical, both of the Soviet empire and their own role in perpetuating it.

## *Repentance* for an Empire

When the film *Repentance* opened for unrestricted screenings in Moscow in early 1987, Soviet critic Tatiana Khlopliankina triumphantly declared: "The release of *Repentance* is one of those big events that certify that the order of our life is happily and inevitably changing." Describing the film's significance, she wrote: "It is indeed a work of art. But first of all it is a fact of our current social life."[91] Indeed, the film's bold denunciation of the Stalinist legacy and its call for frank discussion—and repentance—of past Soviet sins captured the sentiment of an era defined by Gorbachev's program of glasnost, or openness. However, the film was launched and developed in the final years of *zastoi*, and its roots stretched back several decades, firmly planted in the terrain of post-Stalinist Georgian intellectual culture. *Repentance* was conveniently ready for release at a time when Gorbachev called for open debate. It was no coincidence, however, that it was a Georgian film that pushed the limits of cinematic expression the furthest, offering a critique of Soviet empire that resonated as much in Stalin's homeland as it did in the Soviet capital.

According to director Tengiz Abuladze, *Repentance* was the third part of a film trilogy begun in 1967 with his black-and-white film *The Prayer* (*vedreba*) and continued with his 1977 film *The Tree of Dreams* (*natvris khe*).[92] Like *Repentance*, these first two films were set in Georgia but concerned with larger issues of moral obligation. *The Prayer* drew on the work of Georgian poet Vazha Pshavela to examine the struggle of a Georgian highlander trapped between his personal faith in God and village customs requiring him to take vengeance against his enemies; *The Tree of Dreams*, based on the work of Georgian writer Giorgi Leonidze, explored the upheaval caused by revolutionary movements in a traditional Georgian village. In these films Abluadze created a lush picture of Georgia's past, meditating on the fact that his nation's history was, in his own words, full of "blood, vengeance, and sacrifice."[93]

Like the Shengelaia brothers and Otar Ioseliani, Tengiz Abuladze was a graduate of Moscow's VGIK and skilled at operating within the confines of the Soviet cinematic world. He was a close friend of Rezo Chkheidze, the head of the Georgian Film Studio in the latter half of the 1970s and the 1980s; the two had known each other since collaborating on Abuladze's first major film, *Magdana's Donkey* (*magdanas lurja*), in 1955. Although *The Prayer* had been criticized by film critic Mikhail Bleiman a few years after its release, the second film of Abuladze's trilogy encountered little resistance from Goskino when its script was reviewed in 1975. Instead, it was praised as a "social commentary" on the superstitions and social ills of Georgia's prerevolutionary past.[94] Although it was artistically daring, there was little in the film to indicate Abuladze's views on the Soviet system. After the film's release he was treated as an ideologically acceptable filmmaker, welcomed into the ranks of the Communist Party in 1978, and hailed as a People's Artist of the USSR in 1980.

It might have seemed unlikely that a few years later Abuladze would produce the film that led many to ultimately condemn Soviet power. However, like many intellectuals who first came of age during the Thaw, he believed a frank discussion of the past was essential for overcoming the excesses of Stalinism. While other Georgian directors turned to irony during *zastoi*, Abuladze, who made his first films at the height of the Thaw, remained optimistic that the system might still be changed by laying bare its flaws. Combined with this idealism, he dreamed of revitalizing Georgian culture, though his "cultural nationalism" was not initially wedded to a program of political independence.[95]

By the early 1980s Eduard Shevardnadze, Georgia's Communist Party chief, had become a powerful patron and protector of Abuladze. Although an unlikely pair, the two were close in age and both were outsiders in the Georgian capital. Shevardnadze, the son of a poor teacher from western Georgia's Guria region, viewed Tbilisi's native intelligentsia with suspicion; Abuladze was accepted as a member of the intelligentsia, but having come to Tbilisi from modest beginnings in the provincial city of Kutaisi, was thought to lack the sophistication of Tbilisi's more prominent families.[96] Both were beneficiaries of Soviet upward mobility, though each had reasons to be critical of the Stalinist past. Abuladze had witnessed the suppression of leading Soviet actors and directors while studying at VGIK in the final years of Stalin's rule; Shevardnadze had a personal encounter with Stalinist terror when his father was arrested and his father-in-law was executed during the Great Purges. While Shevardnadze had ambitiously pursued a political career at a time when many intellectuals were turning away from politics, he also had been affected by the Thaw. Shocked by the violent suppression of Georgian protests in 1956, he later claimed to have a "1956 complex," which led him to "reject force as both a method and a principle of politics."[97] Although he could be ruthless when necessary, there was clearly something to this assertion. In 1978, he resisted the impulse to use Soviet troops to end popular demonstrations in Tbilisi over a law that would have downgraded the status of the Georgian language in the republic's constitution; instead, he addressed the demonstrators in person and worked out a deal to preserve the language's status. Shevardnadze was also a shrewd politician who realized that he needed a degree of support from Georgia's powerful intelligentsia, both before the hijacking incident of 1983 and, especially, in its aftermath. Understanding that there were potential political benefits, he cast himself as Georgia's artistic patron, giving Abuladze the political cover he needed to make his next movie.[98]

Abuladze started working on the script for *Repentance* in 1981 and fin-ished writing in 1982, the year of Brezhnev's death. With the support of Rezo Chkheidze, then at the helm of the Georgian Film Studio, Abuladze began filming the first scenes in 1983, although production was quickly halted after the arrest of actor Gega Kobakhidze for his role in the hijack-ing plot. Renewing support for the film became a way for Shevardnadze to demonstrate to the Georgian intelligentsia that he continued to pro-tect the relative intellectual freedom they cherished, even if he would not tolerate acts of outright resistance like the hijacking attempt. Seizing upon a bureaucratic loophole, Shevardnadze suggested to Abuladze that he develop *Repentance* as a television special, since Georgian television had a three-hour daily slot reserved for local broadcasting that was gen-erally free from the scrutiny of Gosteleradio, the central television and radio agency in Moscow.[99] Thus, with little supervision from the cen-ter, Abuladze completed work on the film in December 1984, just a few months before Gorbachev was elected General Secretary.

The following year, Gorbachev surprised many observers, includ-ing members of his own government, by appointing Shevardnadze as his Minister of Foreign Affairs.[100] It was the most significant migration of a Georgian official to the imperial center since the deaths of Stalin and Beria and occurred at a time when, according to Gorbachev, "many thought that only a Russian should hold such an important state func-tion." Granted, Shevardnadze was not, in Gorbachev's words, a "typical Georgian": neither a "live wire" nor an "outstanding orator," but instead a "self-disciplined" and "reserved" party member.[101] Nevertheless, he remained just as connected to his native republic as the political fig-ures from the Georgian diaspora who had preceded him. Frustrated that *Repentance* was complete but still shelved, Abuladze telephoned Shevardnadze in his Moscow office to request that his patron inter-vene with Gorbachev to secure its release. After Shevardnadze person-ally arranged a viewing of the film for Gorbachev, the Soviet General Secretary subsequently encouraged the Congress of Cinematographers to allow its screening, and in 1986 the film first appeared in limited engagements packed by intellectuals at the Moscow's Writers' Union, the House of Cinema, and the Artists' Union.[102] When it was widely released the following year, the dissident historian Roy Medvedev called it "the most important event in Soviet cultural life in at least a decade."[103] In Moscow alone, 1.8 million viewers saw the film in the first four months of its public release.[104]

In his 1991 memoir, Shevardnadze claimed that the film's release was meant to "break the conspiracy of silence about the tyranny, lawlessness, and persecution to which millions of people in our country had been subjected," noting that his "intuition" told him that "the time was approaching when we would have to go much further than Khrushchev himself had gone" during the Thaw.[105] Indeed, *Repentance* successfully anticipated the searching moral tone of glasnost, though the way it shrouded some of its most profound political statements in dream sequences and symbols was more reminiscent of the Georgian cinematic art of *zastoi*. The film, as critics have pointed out, was essentially a "story within a story within a story," complete with long flashbacks and dream sequences.[106] The plot centered on the tyranny of a fictional dictator, Varlam Aravidze, the crimes committed during his reign, and his repeated burial and disinterment by one of the victims of his terror. Stalin was not mentioned by name—Aravidze literally meant "son of no one" in Georgian—but Aravidze's mannerisms and mood swings were evocative of Stalin and his appearance reminiscent of Beria. Beneath its layer of fantasy, the film offered the Soviet public a vivid rendering of Stalinist terror and of intellectual soul-searching that had earlier been confined to private conversations.

The film confronted the *zastoi*-era dilemmas of the Soviet intelligentsia directly. While they spoke mainly in Georgian and inhabited a Georgian setting, the film's characters carried on frank conversations of pan-Soviet significance about the role of the artist, the significance of religion, and the dangers of compromise. The film celebrated the high culture aspirations of the Soviet intelligentsia, while hinting at a deeper cultural philistinism within their ranks. *Repentance* juxtaposed the cultural polish of the dictator, Varlam Aravidze, with the true cultural commitment of the suffering artist, Sandro Barateli. Implicating the Soviet intelligentsia in its historically close relationship to the state, the film alluded to the two characters as relatives tracing their descent to a common forefather. Aravidze and Barateli come into conflict over the fate of an ancient Georgian church that has been turned into a

"Temple of Einstein" devoted to the worship of modern science. Aravidze, who shows off by singing Italian arias and reciting Shakespeare, champions culture in the name of progress and truth so long as it is "useful." Barateli instead seeks to protect the deeper, "life-giving roots" of culture, as embodied by the church, a cultural monument he considers on par with the works of "Rustaveli, Dante, and Bach." The conflict between the two is carried on by their children. Abel Aravidze is content to remain silent about his father's crimes, comfortably playing a Beethoven sonata in his large house, surrounded by French posters and other trappings of high culture. By contrast, Keti Barateli, the artist's daughter, is depicted as the idealized Georgian intellectual, effortlessly sophisticated but committed to the pursuit of artistic and spiritual truth.

*Repentance* was a Georgian film that achieved broader resonance because it was not only about Georgia. A product of the Georgian intelligentsia's simultaneous pursuit of national distinctiveness and Soviet prominence, it was exotic in its setting, but recognizable in its characters and themes. Despite their Georgian origins, Stalin and Beria were tyrants who belonged to the entire Soviet Union. The film's generational and Christian metaphors could be recognized by Russians as their own, whether or not Russian intellectuals agreed with them. Importantly, as a Georgian asserting national cultural autonomy and universalism at the same time, Abuladze was more comfortable exhorting intellectuals to return to Christianity than a large and influential elite in Russia, the "left-liberals," who worried that liberalism and Orthodoxy were incompatible.

While it succeeded as a pan-Soviet film, *Repentance* also betrayed a deep ambivalence about Georgian participation in the Soviet empire. For Georgian viewers *Repentance* criticized not only Stalin, but also Georgian intellectuals for whom culture was only a polish, the arts an avenue for professional achievement, and who spoke, like Varlam Aravidze, interspersing their native Georgian with Russian words and phrases. The film presaged a sense among the Georgian intelligentsia that Soviet prominence and socialist ideology had compromised national culture. Some saw it as a call to repent for their complicity in the Stalinist past and to affirm Georgia's authentic cultural heritage, as represented by its ancient Christian Orthodox traditions. In the film's poignant final scene, the character played by the legendary Georgian actress Veriko Anjaparidze, when told that the street named after Varlam Aravidze does not lead to a church, asks: "What good is a road if it does not lead you to a church?" The line could be interpreted as a personal apology by Anjaparidze, who first gained fame for her role in Nikoloz Shengelaia's pro-Soviet film *Twenty-Six Commissars* (*Dvadtsat' shest' komissarov*), released in 1933, and whose husband, Mikheil Chiaureli, had been the director of the 1931 anti-religious film *Out of the Way! (khabarda!)*[107] In this sense, *Repentance* questioned the foundational canon of Georgian national cinema.

As an artistic medium, post-Stalinist Georgian cinema had displayed a renewed interest in national authenticity while remaining committed to pan-Soviet intelligibility. However, *Repentance* was not the first Georgian film to suggest that something could be lost in the translation of national culture for an imperial audience. In an important scene in Ioseliani's *Falling Leaves*, spoiled wine from the factory, which the Georgian employees refuse to drink, is offered to visiting Russian tourists. The Russians enthusiastically down the wine and then launch into the Georgian song "Suliko" (known among Georgians to be one of Stalin's favorites), while the Georgian employees look away in embarrassment. The implication of the scene, at least among sympathetic Georgian viewers, was that the demanding pace of Soviet planning and the undistinguishing tastes of the Russian palate were ruining the integrity of one of Georgia's most famous national products, and that Georgians were knowingly complicit in the process.

In a similar vein, Irakli Kvirikadze's 1981 film *The Swimmer* (*motsurave*), which was never widely released, chronicled the progressive degradation of three generations in a Georgian family under Soviet rule, from the proud and traditional grandfather of the prerevolutionary period to the energetic but compliant son of the Stalinist era, to Anton, the obese and morose grandson of the early 1980s, who spends his days cheerlessly leading groups of drunken Russian tourists around Georgia as an employee of the Tbilisi Excursions Bureau. In addition to his Russian name, Anton speaks mainly Russian and passes off translated and staged renderings of Georgian culture as the genuine article. In one scene he leads a group of Russian-speaking tourists through the motions of "Tbiliso," the sentimental song dedicated to the national capital. The tourists have no sense of harmony and no grasp of the sounds of the Georgian language, and they struggle to read the Georgian lyrics that Anton has dutifully transliterated into Cyrillic on large white boards. In the next scene Anton hosts a group of Russian tourists at a picnic, where a drunken and inauthentic Georgian dance is performed. Animal sounds are played in the background, until the camera pulls back to reveal a Georgian church on the hill above and the soundtrack is reduced to the tolling of a single church bell. The film implied that familiar forms of Georgian culture had lost their meaning, having become the property of a socialist state and a commodity consumed by an imperial society. It also suggested that the translation of Georgian culture might ultimately be a futile exercise, with Russian audiences unable or unwilling to understand.

At the start of the Bolshevik Revolution, many Georgian intellectuals embraced the idea that their culture would be widely understood and appreciated and that they would be treated as equals in the multiethnic Soviet state. Yet over the course of *zastoi*, even as they continued to benefit from the patronage of the center, the artists and intellectuals who staffed Georgian cultural institutions began to perceive Soviet rule as culturally degrading. The forms that Soviet domestic internationalism offered for expressing ethnic distinctiveness came to be seen as tainted by their association with the state. Georgian intellectuals grew increasingly self-conscious, aware that their cultural achievements were valued inasmuch as they were politically useful or readily consumable at the mass level. They grew tired of the condescension of being treated as a "younger brother" in the "fraternal union of the Soviet peoples"; they lamented the need to dilute Georgian culture to cater to a predominantly Russian audience; and they rallied around their ancient language and religious traditions in staking claim to a deeper cultural legacy.

Outside the cinema, the intelligentsia's interest in revitalizing Georgian culture began to take on explicitly political connotations. In the early 1970s Zviad Gamsakhurdia, a professor of literature at Tbilisi State University, formed a group to protect Georgian architectural monuments, especially churches. Gamsakhurdia's family history and personal biography fit the narrative of national and intellectual degradation at the hands of the Soviet state rather neatly. His father was the famous Georgian writer Konstantine Gamsakhurdia, who began his career as an artistically daring author but, after persecution by the Soviet regime, was pressured to write a hagiographic novel about Stalin's childhood in 1939 as a demonstration of political loyalty. As for Zviad Gamsakhurdia, he had been arrested for taking part in the 1956 protests in Tbilisi and once again in 1958 for distributing nationalist literature; for the latter crime he was confined to a mental hospital in Tbilisi for six months. Arrested again in 1977, he was released two years later, but only after a humiliating televised confession in which he admitted his supposed ideological failings.[108] While Gamsakhurdia's early intellectual and political activities had broad humanist dimensions—he was the cofounder of Georgia's Helsinki Group and a renowned translator of world literature into Georgian—he came to see the Soviet state as an instrument of imperial oppression and increasingly focused on the idea of complete national liberation. If authenticity was a notion that Otar Ioseliani had engaged through irony and Tengiz Abuladze had explored through an examination of the Stalinist past, Gamsakhurdia turned it into a political platform that demanded radical national purification. Although his influence was limited in the early years of glasnost, Gamsakhurdia was at the forefront of a dissident Georgian intellectual movement that held that Soviet power and Georgian culture could not coexist.[109]

Most Georgian intellectuals still believed that a national revival might be achieved within the framework of a more democratic Soviet Union. *Repentance* may have been anti-Stalinist and even anti-imperialist, but it was not necessarily anti-Soviet. When the film and television section of the committee to award the Lenin Prize met in January 1988, there was broad consensus that *Repentance* deserved the award. It was a box office success, a politically relevant film, and an artistic achievement that had garnered critical praise. According to one committee member: "Even judged by the old standards, even if *Repentance* were not such sensation of our time and had not risen up into some kind of general wave of social repentance, it would still be a beautiful film."[110] Changes at the top had altered the context of Georgian intellectual dissent, and Abuladze's risky engagement with the Stalinist period was now squarely in line with Gorbachev's policies.

As a result, the film became politically useful. After it was awarded the prestigious Lenin Prize, Eduard Shevardnadze wrote to congratulate Abuladze in April 1988. Shevardnadze skillfully framed the movie as an intrinsic part of the political program of perestroika: "Your film *Repentance* was the one of the earliest examples of the beginning of perestroika, when many people were afraid to believe that our course might not be reversed . . . We should remember now that the path to *Repentance* from *The Prayer* and *The Tree of Dreams* was not simple or easy. It did not necessarily hold the promise of prizes and was not guaranteed a favorable outcome." In a remarkable turn of phrase, Shevardnadze closed the letter by adopting the rhetoric of an increasingly assertive Georgian intelligentsia:

> Today, when the bravery of honest talent is recognized according to its merits, I think about what a wonderful thing it is . . . to express the people's yearning for truth and justice, to answer the expectations of society, and to give people hope in the victory of good over evil. Of course, this would be impossible without a sense of spiritual continuity with our great ancestors and the living root of our connection with our native soil.[111]

Shevardnadze's approving allusion to religion—"a sense of spiritual continuity with our great ancestors"—and to nearly nationalistic pride in the Georgian homeland—"the living root of our connection with our native soil"—was a striking reminder of how much the political landscape had shifted. Although he offered a moderated version linked to universal notions of artistic merit, truth, and justice, Shevardnadze joined Gamsakhurdia, whose arrest he had once overseen as Georgia's Communist Party chief, in making national authenticity an important part of his politics.

By early 1989, it appeared that the Georgian intelligentsia was on the cusp of a cultural renaissance that promised to revitalize their nation and remake the Soviet Union. Soviet leaders like Shevardnadze seemed to support their vision of a more autonomous Georgian republic. Meanwhile, in Moscow, the Georgian diaspora had finally been granted a semiofficial status with the opening of the Georgian cultural center,

Mziuri, in December 1987. The center offered a sanctioned gathering place for members of the diaspora and even provided instruction in the Georgian language for their children, something that the state had not allowed outside the Georgian SSR since the late 1920s.[112] Once again, the Georgian diaspora was at the forefront of multiethnic expression, as the pathbreaking Mziuri was praised as a potential model for other internal Soviet diasporas.[113] Another Georgian cultural organization, the Rustaveli Society, was established around the same time, based in Georgia but with regional branches in Russia that connected the diaspora to its homeland. Soon the Rustaveli Society began to engage in more expressly political activity, assisting the director Tengiz Abuladze in early 1989 as he sought election to the forthcoming Congress of People's Deputies by organizing meetings with potential voters in Russia.[114]

Throughout the Soviet Union, Georgians were allowed forms of intellectual and creative expression that had been forbidden for decades. Many artists began to give voice to explicitly political themes and some, like Abuladze, even entered politics directly. While less than six years earlier a desperate group of Georgian artists and intellectuals, alienated from Soviet power, had made a desperate attempt to seek freedom outside the Soviet Union, the Georgian intelligentsia now stood at the very helm of the Soviet state. On March 26, 1989, the Soviet Union held a competitive election to choose delegates for the Congress of People's Deputies. Among the representatives selected from Georgia were Tengiz Abuladze, fellow film director Eldar Shengelaia, and the Georgian violin virtuoso Liana Isakadze; not coincidentally, they represented the Georgian intelligentsia in the fields where it had gained the greatest prominence: music and film. In May 1989 they were scheduled to convene in Moscow to help determine the future course of the Soviet Union and the place of Georgia within it.

Before they met, however, a series of violent confrontations irrevocably changed the tenor of the debate. The advent of electoral politics in the Soviet empire had elevated the standing of the intelligentsia but also created new possibilities for nationalist mobilization, producing numerous local challenges to the state's multiethnic regime.[115] In the Abkhaz Autonomous Soviet Socialist Republic, Abkhaz activists called for secession from Georgia, while in Tbilisi tens of thousands of people gathered to denounce the secessionists and advocate for Georgia's territorial integrity and national sovereignty. The Georgian protestors in Tbilisi were nonviolent, though they ignored several calls to disperse, including an impassioned plea from the Patriarch of the Georgian Orthodox Church, Ilia II.[116] On April 9, 1989, Soviet troops violently broke up the peaceful demonstration, using sharpened shovels and toxic gas to force a crowd off the Georgian capital's main thoroughfare. Nineteen people, most of them women, were killed. While the Soviet state had exercised its repressive capacity in responding to the hijacking incident six years earlier, and while the number of deaths was fewer than during the suppression of popular protests in March 1956, glasnost and perestroika gave this particular outbreak of violence a new context.

In the aftermath of the protests, the contradictions of the period—and of the Soviet state—were laid bare on the pages of the official newspaper of the Georgian republic, *Zaria vostoka*. On April 11, 1989, instead of offering their typical summary of state accomplishments, the editors of the daily column "Yesterday in the Republic" questioned the initial estimate of sixteen deaths and noted reports suggesting that more had died, some of them perhaps "killed by tanks," others possibly wounded when "the military opened fire on unarmed people." In a striking juxtaposition, published just below these alarming reports was the official statement to the "population and workers of the city of Tbilisi" from Colonel General I. N. Rodionov, which lambasted the protests as "anti-Soviet," blamed the violence on "provocateurs," and announced mandatory curfews and the enforcement of temporary martial law in the Georgian capital.[117] The following day, the sense that Georgians were living under a Russian-led military occupation was reinforced by the newspaper's publication of a photograph showing a Georgian mother leading her child past Russian soldiers and a Soviet tank on one of Tbilisi's major bridges.[118] Finally, on April 13, the newspaper published an appeal "to the communists and all the workers of Georgia" from Gorbachev, who offered conciliatory words about the unfortunate "shedding of innocent blood," but still criticized the demands of Georgian protestors who sought to leave the "brotherly family of Soviet peoples." Gorbachev expressed his faith that the Georgian working class would "defend perestroika, our common socialist values, our brotherhood, and our unity."[119]

However, April 9 dealt a lasting rebuke to Georgians who believed that the Soviet system could be reformed through participation. Its coverage in the press suggested that perestroika merely meant the repetition of official lies alongside occasional expressions of doubt that hinted at the truth. Behind Gorbachev's rhetoric of brotherhood and "common socialist values," Georgians saw the brutality of a Russian-led army. The public debates that followed empowered the Georgian intelligentsia's most radical wing, a previously small fringe who called for outright independence. The political climate in Georgia changed radically, alienating the diaspora of Georgian intellectuals who remained committed to a broader Soviet universalism from the national institutions that supported them and the national constituency they claimed to represent.

# Conclusion

Georgian success had always depended on a state invested in multiethnicity and a diaspora interested in cultivating intelligible difference; as familiar strangers, their pursuit of imperial prominence required an understanding audience and willing performers. Their rootedness in a Soviet republic ensured a steady supply of reliable clients for political patrons, fresh staples for the Soviet diet, ethnically distinctive entertainers for the Soviet stage, and virtual monopolies on the domestic production and provision of coveted goods. For a time, the Soviet empire seemed to offer the ideal forum for this rooted diaspora with cosmopolitan aspirations. Moscow, the imperial capital, offered Georgian Bolsheviks the opportunity to join—and lead—an international movement and provided a vast stage for entertainers, an attractive market for entrepreneurs, and a receptive public for the intellectual contributions of the Georgian intelligentsia.

More than any empire before it, the Soviet Union sanctioned and supported a diverse array of national repertoires while harnessing them to a unified state. However, tensions between the state's vigorous promotion of nationalities and its insistence on centralized rule were present from the beginning. The state sought to root titular ethnic groups in their national republics, where national languages and cultures were promoted and national cadres given preferential treatment; at the same time, the republics and their respective nationalities were subsumed—sometimes forcefully—within a larger political, economic, and cultural framework with its center in the Soviet capital. One outcome of these twin policies, which upheld national difference but oriented nation-alities toward Moscow, was the gathering of internal diasporas like the Georgians in the heart of Soviet empire.

The multiethnic empire was dependent on its internal diasporas, but regarded them with unease. It sought to contain their activities, limit their mobility, and obscure their presence by preventing their official categorization as diasporas. As a result, third-generation Muscovites of Georgian ancestry were marked as Georgians in their passports, but were generally barred from establishing any formal group based on their ethnic distinctiveness. Georgians were the most visible internal diaspora because they appeared at each stage of Soviet history and did so explic-itly as Georgians, but they were not alone. In Soviet politics national cadres were promoted from the republics to the center, and ethnic net-works colored Soviet political life and informed enduring systems of patronage. In Soviet culture, the state nurtured a domestic internation-alism that promoted national repertoires and stimulated the circulation of cultural entrepreneurs. When it came to the economy, the Soviets established a relatively closed system that, like the Soviet diet, made do with domestically available ingredients drawn from the national repub-lics. Because the Soviets relied on domestic production they stressed internal economic diversification, which overlapped in interesting ways with internal diversity in culture.

The Georgian case demonstrates that the cultures of national minorities sometimes flourished in a Soviet imperial context and that there were even advantages to be found in articulating accept-able forms of national difference instead of Russianness. Because the empire never truly had a nation at its core, internal diasporas could claim a place for themselves in the imperial center. However, while all Soviet nationalities were supposed to meet in Moscow on equal terms, internationalism, particularly in its domestically defined form, lent itself to imperial hierarchies and generated imperial grievances. Soviet nations differed in terms of size and culture; some translated better for a predominantly Russian audience than others. In addition, because Soviet internationalism was directed by the state, some nationalities were better integrated into its ruling structures and thus gained preferential status.

Nationality, reinforced by republic-level institutions, also created powerful constituencies for national sovereignty. The production of national culture created a sense of exclusive ownership among its authors, and state efforts to direct national expression toward imperially useful ends led some intellectuals to associate Soviet rule with a centrally imposed regime of obligatory sharing and national self-denial. Because the Soviet empire never really had a nation at its center, it could be cast as a foreign imposition by a whole range of groups, including Russians. Not all forms of imperial grievance were national, however. Just as the promotion of nationality eventually produced critics of Soviet empire, the promotion of multiethnicity led to unexpected and unpredictable forms of cosmopolitan universalism that sometimes stood in opposition to the state. Yet these forms of multiethnicity all but vanished with the collapse of the Soviet state that enabled them, while national categories lived on. Unlike Soviet multiethnicity, nationality claimed an ancient heritage and, amidst the collapse of the Soviet empire, proved a valuable currency in a world of nation-states.

For Georgians, charting a course between imperial prominence and national assertion grew more complicated as the empire evolved and members of the diaspora confronted its limitations. Particularly after the Second World War, Georgian political success was a potential source of tension and had to be handled delicately, even by Stalin. Following Stalin's death, mass demonstrations shook Tbilisi in 1956 after Khrushchev's denunciation of Stalinism in his secret speech; Soviet authorities in Moscow responded by offering cultural concessions while forcefully suppressing political dissent. The subsequent loosening of restrictions on small-scale economic activity under Brezhnev presented the opportunity for greater local control, though Georgian entrepreneurial networks were tamed by the state and viewed with envy by Russians, as evident in Soviet *anekdoty* that pointed to the higher living standards enjoyed by many Georgians. Georgian cultural and intellectual success meant developing national culture under Moscow's direction for consumption by outsiders, leading to growing concerns about authenticity. At the end of the Soviet period Georgian intellectuals shared many of the frustrations held by their Russian counterparts, but they were more likely to cast them in national terms.

The dissolution of the Soviet Union once again accorded a prominent position to Georgians and other internal diasporas, this time as proponents of independence and, ultimately, casualties of imperial collapse.[1] Nationalism, which meant the open articulation of ethnic grievances and the explicit politicization of ethnic difference, helped split the national republics from the center. It also threatened to tear apart the complicated fabric of national peoples, cultures, and products that defined life throughout the empire. The Georgian skill in performing otherness, seen in a dramatically different political context where sovereignty rested on national difference, placed a vocal segment of the Georgian intelligentsia at the forefront of efforts to secede from the Soviet Union. However, the end of the Soviet empire, which transformed the Georgians from an internal Soviet diaspora into a transnational population living across state boundaries, ultimately undermined the very basis of Georgian success.

## The Shattering of a Shared Past

The violent suppression of popular protests in Tbilisi on April 9, 1989 and the enforced curfews that followed paradoxically occurred at a time when Soviet citizens were freer than ever before, especially when it came to public expression. Shocked by the Soviet military's virtual seizure of their capital but emboldened by glasnost, Georgian intellectuals reexamined the Soviet past and interpreted the central authorities' crackdown on the demonstration as the latest in a long series of Russian imperialist crimes that stretched back to the beginning of the Soviet period. Historical figures such as Sergo Orjonikidze, who had helped establish Soviet rule in Georgia, were denigrated as national traitors; as a result, the statue of Orjonikidze in Tbilisi's Saburtalo district was defaced and eventually toppled. Even Georgia's Writers' Union, originally organized as a forum for developing ideologically sound national intellectual cadres to serve the Soviet empire, became a haven for nationalist sentiment. In June 1989, the Writers' Union issued a demand to the republic's Supreme Soviet, calling upon delegates to officially recognize the fact that Georgia had been invaded and illegally annexed by the Red Army on February 25, 1921.[2] The implication was that Georgian independence meant the restoration of the "natural" order of things—above all, a reassertion of the most naturalized form of government, the nation-state.

Georgia's nationalist intellectuals called themselves the *meotkhe dasi* (fourth generation), claiming symbolic descent from Georgia's nineteenth-century intelligentsia and dismissing the intervening generations that had lived under the Soviet empire as irredeemably compromised. At the helm of the movement for Georgian independence were Zviad Gamaskhurdia, a former dissident and literary scholar, and Merab Kostava, a graduate of the Tbilisi Conservatory. Although both were trained by the Soviet system in the universal arts of high culture, they rejected cosmopolitanism in favor of a supposedly untainted Georgian cultural heritage located in the pre-Soviet past. Despite the fact that the Soviet empire promoted national difference at least as much as it curtailed it, Gamsakhurdia charged that Soviet power meant nothing less than the complete "mixing together all peoples in order to make a conglomerate, destroying nations altogether."[3]

*Figure C.1* The statue of Georgian Bolshevik Sergo Orjonikidze in Tbilisi, defaced with paint in the aftermath of the Soviet military's suppression of protests on April 9, 1989. National Archives of Georgia.

As nationalists garnered popular support in Georgia by selectively interpreting the past to emphasize national grievances, the seeming triumph of the more cosmopolitan members of the Soviet intelligentsia in Moscow, which came with the election of such delegates as Andrei Sakharov to the Congress of People's Deputies, was marred by infighting and a growing sense of irrelevance. At the first meeting of the Congress, one delegate disrupted the proceedings by calling for a moment of silence for the victims of April 9.[4] Even Tengiz Abuladze, who initially hoped to transform the Soviet Union into a multiethnic democracy, began using nationalist language. In one speech he decried the "annexation of independent Georgia" in 1921, though he importantly noted that this "crime" was in fact perpetrated by two Georgians, Stalin and Orjonikidze.[5]

More extreme Georgian nationalists insisted that threats to Georgian sovereignty came primarily from Russia. In Gamsakhurdia's words, relations between Georgia and Russia were akin to those "between servant and lord" or "between slave and master."[6] Movements for greater autonomy in Abkhazia and South Ossetia were regarded by Gamsakhurdia as nothing more than "provocations" engineered by Moscow to undermine Georgia's territorial integrity.[7] The Georgian leader's prophecies were in part self-fulfilling; faced with Gasmakhurdia's fiery rhetoric and his ominous description of non-Georgians as "guests" in the Georgian republic, local elites in Abkhazia and South Ossetia saw a grim future in an independent Georgia and redoubled their efforts to secure political and military support from Moscow. However, despite the Soviet state's experience managing multiethnic diversity, its efforts to adjudicate among competing nationalities were faltering and inconsistent as central control weakened. The military's suppression of Georgian protests in April 1989 backfired, and the Red Army intervened too late to stop the violent expulsion of most of Baku's ethnic Armenian population in January 1990. In the wake of the state's collapse, wars in Abkhazia and South Ossetia would displace over two hundred thousand ethnic Georgians from territories that were once integrated into their titular republic (and still internationally recognized as part of Georgia).[8] Throughout the region, the multiethnic regime established by the Bolsheviks was torn apart as local groups seized power and the boundaries dividing national republics hardened into sovereign, though sometimes contested, borders.

While Russian nationalists and Georgian nationalists had long been opponents, unrest in Abkhazia and South Ossetia provoked new a rift between the cosmopolitan branch of the Soviet Russian intelligentsia, which had typically viewed Georgian complaints against "Russian chauvinism" with sympathy, and many Georgian intellectuals, who seemed to be advancing their own brand of national exclusivity.[9] In an article published in *Ogonek* in late 1989, Andrei Sakharov infuriated Georgians by calling the Georgian republic, with its Abkhaz and Ossetian autonomous regions, a "miniature empire." Sakharov's article led many in the Georgian intelligentsia to feel that Russian intellectuals were no longer their allies. In a published response to Sakharov, D. L. Muskhelishvili, a member of the Georgian Academy of Sciences, wrote that he considered it "unfortunate" that such a "respected academic" as Sakharov would criticize Georgia for "ethnic problems he knows only poorly." Blaming Russia for fomenting ethnic discord in Georgia, Muskhelishvili invoked the victims of the April 9 demonstrations, stating: "We ourselves did not kill our women and children with shovels and suffocate them with gases . . . it was not we who attacked, but we who were attacked."[10]

Mutual understanding between Georgian and Russian intellectuals was replaced with incomprehension. Sergei Badurin, the Russian writer and editor of the expressly multiethnic Soviet journal *Druzhba narodov*, took aim at Georgian "extremism" in an article published in *Pravda* on February 25, 1990, the anniversary of the Soviet annexation of Georgia. In Tbilisi the date, once the occasion for state-directed festivities, was marked by solemn commemorations and speeches condemning Soviet imperialism. Dismissing Georgian concerns, Badurin affirmed a common Soviet identity by appealing to a shared history forged in the Second World War. He wrote: "Who among us asked in those years, 'am I Russian or Georgian, Kazakh or Ukrainian, Moldovan or Estonian, Belarusian, Jewish, or Yakut?' We fought together and worked together . . . Shoulder to shoulder we faced and surmounted a terrible fate." He ridiculed Georgian criticism of "Russian occupiers" and "the imperial ambitions of Moscow," stating that such language could only be the result of the "clouding of reason" or "the hardening of hearts at the mass level"; both, he noted, were "neglectful of historical memory."[11] Badurin's article immediately provoked a fierce reaction in the increasingly assertive

Georgian press. One respondent, Liudmila Esvanjia, criticized Badurin for a reading of the Soviet past that omitted the Gulag and ignored the tragic significance of the Red Army's invasion of Georgia.[12] Another respondent, a Georgian party official, remarked bitterly that centuries of Georgian contributions to Russian political, cultural, and intellectual life, "dating back to the time of Peter the Great," went little noticed among contemporary Russian writers.[13] The charge was that Russians had ultimately failed to reciprocate in their centuries-long relationship with Georgia.

As a shared understanding of the past fragmented and new visions for the future were articulated, rifts widened within the Georgian intelligentsia as well. The philosopher Merab Mamardashvili, who had spent most of his career at Moscow State University but returned to Georgia in the 1980s, criticized Gamsakhurdia and his cohort for considering Georgian cultural and political independence as an end in itself rather than a means for advancing universal values. In an article, Mamardashvili criticized those he called "Georgian chauvinists" and staked out his own vision for an independent Georgia, writing: "My struggle is not for the Georgian language, since [that struggle] is already won, my struggle is for what will be said in the Georgian language."[14] Gamsakhurdia, however, believed that the triumph of the particular was more vital than the pursuit of the universal. The Georgian leader was convinced that his nation was endowed with a special historical role, one that far exceeded the bounds of Georgian prominence in the Soviet Union. In a lecture entitled "The Spiritual Mission of Georgia," delivered to a large crowd in the Tbilisi Philharmonic on May 2, 1990, Gamsakhurdia ignored the numerous contributions made by Georgians to Russian and Soviet culture. Instead, he linked the Georgian people to the most important developments in Western civilization more broadly, from the achievements of the ancient Greeks to the spread of Christianity, for which, in his view, Georgians had been and were destined to remain the "chief bearers of spirituality."[15] Gamsakhurdia claimed that it was time for Georgians to recover their illustrious past and meet the glorious future that awaited them as an independent nation.

As the Soviet Union unraveled, Georgians faced a choice between a fading vision of Soviet cosmopolitanism and a promise of national greatness; unsurprisingly, many chose the latter. In March 1990, the local Supreme Soviet unilaterally declared Georgia to be a sovereign republic; in November 1990, Gamsakhurdia was chosen as its leader. Sensing an enormous shift in local attitudes, even the head of the Georgian Communist Party, Givi Gumbaridze, proclaimed that the main goal of the party was to "restore" Georgian independence.[16]

Changes in Georgia reverberated deeply among an internal diaspora intimately linked to its homeland. Georgians living in Moscow, though a largely integrated group at the center of Soviet life, sought new ways of asserting their national identity. By the end of 1989, Georgians in the Soviet capital formed a new society based around a historically Georgian church near the city's center. As in the film *Repentance*, the rekindling of an "authentic," non-Soviet Georgian culture meant the revival of Georgian Orthodox Christianity. Through the church-based society Georgians in Moscow gained access to a special library, concerts, exhibits, and clubs, as well as a formal network of assistance catering to recent migrants.[17] As still more Georgian diaspora organizations were established, what was previously an informal diaspora based upon personal ties and cultural affinity became an officially recognized group with numerous, and sometimes competing, representative institutions.

Yet the collapse of the Soviet Union also led to a profound sense of isolation among the Georgian diaspora. Georgian author Aleksandr Ebanoidze, a longtime resident of Moscow, felt alienated from events in independent Georgia even as he was compelled to defend his homeland from critics. On the one hand, he argued that describing Georgia as a "miniature empire" and carving it up into multiple independent states was as absurd as separating the streets named for historic Georgian settlements in Moscow, Malaia and Bol'shaia Gruzinskaia, from the rest of the Soviet capital.[18] On the other hand, Ebanoidze, who eventually took up the reins of the journal *Druzhba narodov* after the collapse of the multiethnic empire it was meant to serve, was deeply disturbed by Georgian nationalist attacks on the Soviet-era intelligentsia.[19] Ebanoidze lamented the departure from Georgia of the theater director Robert Sturua, who staged many of his productions outside the former Soviet Union, as well as the violinist Liana Isakadze, who left to play in Germany. He noted with concern the fact that some of Georgia's most prominent intellectuals, among them Soviet Georgian filmmakers Tengiz Abuladze, Eldar Shengelaia, and Giorgi Shengelaia, faced constant pressure from Gamsakhurdia's government.

Ebanoidze was particularly distressed by the language that Gamsakhurdia and his companions used to describe members of the Soviet Georgian intelligentsia whose lives and careers spanned Georgia and Russia. He feared that as the situation in Georgia worsened, they were at risk of being labeled "betrayers of the motherland" and "agents of the Kremlin." Comparing Gamsakhurdia's actual behavior to that of the fictional tyrant in Tengiz Abuladze's *Repentance*, he wrote: "Georgia has twice gone through a catharsis: first in art, now in life." As Ebanoidze wrote from Moscow, it was unclear what would remain of the Georgian diaspora's Soviet-era achievements when the catharsis of independence was over.

The demise of the Soviet Union seemed to signal an end to longer-term processes as well. Imperial Russia had offered Georgians the promise of integration into a larger political and cultural community connected to modern Europe. The Soviet state that succeeded the Russian empire inherited a great deal from its predecessor, including a diverse array of nationalities, some with established cultural repertoires that were repurposed to meet the needs of the new state. It was unclear, however, if there would be a role for familiar strangers in post-Soviet Russia. The collapse of the Soviet Union meant not only the abandonment of socialism, but also the end of the empire of diasporas. Diasporas that had long resided in Russia and Eurasia began departing in great numbers, while formerly internal groups became external ones as their homelands fell away. The Georgian blend of familiarity and strangeness that had been forged in the Russian Empire and elaborated under Soviet rule was at risk of becoming a politically undesirable artifact of the past.

## Strangers Without Empire

Georgians were just one of many diasporas transformed by the collapse of the Soviet Union from fellow citizens into potentially foreign nationals.[20] Groups with homelands beyond Soviet borders, whose loyalty had long been called into question, could now freely emigrate. Many Soviet Jews departed for Israel; the descendants of ethnic Germans who had settled in Russia hundreds of years earlier were welcomed as German citizens.[21] Smaller ethnic groups deported by Stalin, including Meskhetian Turks, remained scattered throughout Central Asia and faced a more uncertain future.[22] Chechens, who had been deported but organized their own return following Stalin's death, seized control of their autonomous republic and eventually sought independence from Russia.[23] Violent ethnic cleansing reordered the complex terrain of the Caucasus, as a predominantly Armenian population claimed independence in Nagorno-Karabagh, even as thousands of Armenians were violently forced out of other regions of Azerbaijan.[24] Internal diasporas who once migrated with ease throughout the Soviet Union became transnational populations divided by international borders. Of the many transnational diaspora populations created by Soviet collapse, the largest was composed of ethnic Russians, residing at the end of empire in Central Asia and the Baltic states, and comprising a substantial portion of the population of independent Ukraine.[25]

While Moscow was no longer the capital of a multiethnic empire, in demographic terms it actually grew more diverse as a major destination for postimperial and global migration. While many Jews and Germans left, the number of Georgians residing in Moscow more than doubled from 1989 to 2002; in the same span the number of Armenians nearly tripled, and the number of Azeris increased more than four times over.[26] In an even shorter period of time, the number of Central Asians living in Moscow grew more than tenfold.[27] Some migrants fled ethnic conflicts in the former imperial periphery; many more sought to escape the economic devastation that accompanied Soviet collapse. The concentration of capital in Moscow and the opening of the former Soviet Union's external borders also attracted migration from other countries, including Turkey, China, Vietnam, Afghanistan, Pakistan, India, Iran, and Nigeria.[28]

Moscow became more global than ever before, and also more like other postimperial capitals in its patterns of migration and settlement.[29] As in many European cities, the place of guest workers in the host society was fiercely contested, even though most were drawn from the former imperial domains.[30] In contrast to the Soviet period, migrants were more likely to live apart in territorial clusters, relying on their own schools and mutual aid societies.[31] Unlike the national specialists that the Soviet empire drew to its center, many were unskilled laborers with a poor grasp of Russian. Seen as culturally alien, they were associated with crime and disease, and their differences were more frequently drawn in racial terms.[32]

The Georgian diaspora's post-Soviet experience raised particularly troubling questions for a community once defined by its imperial prominence. Although their numbers were larger than ever and they were no longer bound by Soviet borders, Soviet-era specializations were no longer available to the same extent and did not offer the same level of prestige they once had. Certainly, Georgian political prominence, which waned after the death of Stalin, was all but impossible following the separation of Russia and Georgia into two independent states with a strained relationship. As a population divided by state borders, the Georgian diaspora became a politically charged community of contention. Like Baltic Germans in the ruling structures of the late Russian Empire or Jews in the Soviet elite after the establishment of Israel, their allegiances were now seen as suspect. The development of mass politics following the collapse of the Soviet Union amplified demands that the leadership of the Russian state reflect the ethnic composition of the population. The Georgian diaspora, which had excelled at state-sanctioned performances of difference, was cast as an unwanted group of outsiders, most notably in 2006, when amid heightened tensions between the two countries, hundreds of ethnic Georgians were systematically deported from the Russian capital.[33] For its part, the Georgian government claimed to speak on behalf of Georgians living beyond the nation's borders and in 2008 established a State Ministry of Diaspora Issues to coordinate ties with Georgians living abroad.[34] In Georgia members of the diaspora were seen as potential allies, though those who grew too close to the Russian government risked being denounced as traitors.[35]

The political boundaries separating Georgia and Russia were reinforced by conflicting views of the Soviet past cultivated by the governments of the two independent states. Following the example of Estonia, Latvia, and Lithuania, in 2006 the Georgian state opened a Museum of

Soviet Occupation in Tbilisi.[36] The institution was dedicated to telling the story of the Soviet Union as one of ethnically exclusive suffering on the part of the Georgians. Its exhibits characterized the entire Soviet period as a Russian-dominated occupation and carefully documented cases of national victimhood, counting the number of Georgians who were executed and deported in political purges. Controversially, the museum even classified the 400,000 Georgians who had died fighting against Nazi Germany in the Second World War as "victims of the Soviet occupation in Georgia."[37] Meanwhile, a large number of Russians remained proud of Soviet accomplishments, particularly the victory in World War II, and viewed the demise of the Soviet Union as a negative development.[38] In important ways the Russian state sought to cast itself as the successor to the Soviet Union, converting central Soviet institutions into national ones, assuming the international debts of the Soviet state, and adopting a number of Soviet political rituals in slightly modified form, including a national anthem set to the music of the Soviet anthem and an annual Victory Day parade in Moscow that resurrected the choreography of the Soviet period, complete with Soviet-era symbols and uniforms.

However, both Georgia and Russia remained unsure about how to treat the legacy of Stalin, the Georgian who led the Soviet Union at the height of its power. Following years of debate, Stalin's statue was removed from the main square of his hometown of Gori by the Georgian authorities in a secretive overnight operation in 2010. Just three years later, the city council voted to reinstate it.[39] Once again, the film *Repentance* seemed evocative not only of Georgia's Stalinist past, but of its present circumstances; much like the corpse of the fictional dictator Varlam Aravidze, the Stalin statue was hidden, moved about, and ultimately not so easily disposed of. Stalin haunted Russia as well, conspicuous for his absence in official celebrations of the Great Patriotic War but openly praised in popular history books that described him as a "genius" who had successfully defended Russia from its enemies.[40]

The multiethnic material culture forged in the Soviet period proved less controversial and more enduring, preserving a niche for Georgian culinary specialists in Russia. Much as curry remained a staple of the British diet long after the demise of the British Raj, *khachapuri* and *lobio* were still available at most Russian supermarkets. Even when they had many more culinary options, Muscovites continued to flock to the capital's Georgian restaurants, a number of them opened by more recent Georgian migrants. Many of these establishments employed the symbols of Georgian abundance and hospitality first promoted in the Soviet period, recalling the old Aragvi in their menus and decor. However, while Georgian dishes could be readily enjoyed at Russian restaurants or prepared in the home thanks to spice packets and sauces made in Russia, goods originating from Georgia were sometimes more difficult to obtain. In what was widely seen as a punitive political action, from 2006 to 2013 Russia banned the import of Georgian wine and mineral water, depriving Georgian entrepreneurs of their ability to deliver two of Georgia's best-known products to Russian markets.[41]

Limited opportunities remained for Georgian cultural entrepreneurs, although the common popular culture created and shared by Georgian and Russian entertainers during the Thaw was largely the domain of nostalgic older generations in both countries. Against the backdrop of political conflict, many Georgian artists who resided in Moscow returned home or chose to perform for eager emigre audiences in the United States and Israel instead. It seemed unlikely, however, that forms of Georgian ethnic entertainment developed within the Soviet context would ever garner the same level of success on the world stage. While Georgia was one of the first republics to pull out of the Soviet Football Federation in 1990, Georgian soccer failed to replicate its Soviet-era successes, deprived of Soviet levels of funding and faced with increased international competition. Similar patterns held true for Georgian cultural institutions, which faced budget cuts and, though enjoying limited success abroad, failed to find the same cachet they had enjoyed in the Soviet Union. The cultural capital of Georgian national difference, once prized in the context of Soviet domestic internationalism, was simply not as valuable beyond former Soviet borders.

Responding to domestic and international trends, some Georgian ensembles pursued the path of purification, purging their repertoires of supposed Soviet influences and seeking to return to more authentic forms of national performance. Others embraced hybridity. Iliko Sukhishvili Junior, the grandson of the founders of Georgia's most famous song and dance ensemble, set Georgian melodies to new instrumentation and explored national motifs in novel rhythmic settings, like reggae. He dubbed his style "folkotheque," and it joined Serbian "turbofolk" and Ukrainian "Hutsul punk" as a form of self-consciously global folk performance.[42] However, it was only one of many options available to international audiences, who had access to a panoply of "world music" and ethnic entertainment, not simply those forms sanctioned and promoted within the borders of a single state.

When it came to the economy, the demise of the Soviet empire severed economic linkages among the republics and ended the monopolies Georgia enjoyed on the provision of valuable goods. All the same, the revenue generated by the Georgian diaspora in Russia remained an important part of the Georgian economy. Among Georgians working in Moscow in the post-Soviet period, a handful emerged as successful "Russian" oligarchs and some were important figures in the criminal world; the former stood out because of their non-Russian names and appearances but tended to keep low profiles, while the latter continued to appeal to established tropes of Georgian difference, often bearing nicknames that referred to their national origins.[43] However, the vast majority of migrants were skilled and unskilled laborers engaged in prosaic occupations who supported their families in Georgia through remittances.[44] In the absence of visible and prominent specializations, the terms of their national distinctiveness collapsed, and they were often grouped together with other non-Russian nationalities. Stereotypes of Georgian profiteers, for example, were infused with more general Russian anxiety surrounding "peoples of Caucasian nationality." Inflation and economic suffering were sometimes blamed on Caucasian "mafias" that allegedly controlled Russian markets. As economically engaged outsiders in the wake of imperial collapse, the precarious position of Caucasian entrepreneurs in some ways brought to mind the fate of Lebanese and South Asian traders in east Africa or the overseas Chinese in Indonesia following decolonization.

There were still a few oases of high culture that remained for cosmopolitan Georgian artists and intellectuals within the former Soviet Union. While Georgian film struggled in the absence of state support and the disappearance of a broad viewership, international partnerships, sometimes involving Georgian artists residing in Europe, produced the occasional movie evocative of Georgia's cosmopolitan cultural heritage.[45] One of the most popular authors to emerge in the post-Soviet period was the unmistakably cosmopolitan Grigori Chkhartishvili, a translator of Japanese literature who was born to a Georgian Jewish family, grew up in Moscow, and published in Russian under the pseudonym Boris Akunin. Meanwhile, Georgian classical musicians and singers continued to be prominent figures in Moscow's Bolshoi Theater.[46] The Tbilisi Conservatory, which struggled financially for several years following Georgian independence, managed to preserve itself as a vital cultural institution that maintained ties with Russian and European musical schools. Yet these oases of cosmopolitanism were noticeable precisely because they contrasted with the broader contours of the postimperial landscape. As a transnational population split between Russia and Georgia, it was difficult for Georgians to remain rooted in their native republic while participating in a shared cosmopolitan culture. Political divisions often forced the choice between rooted Georgianness in Tbilisi and rootless cosmopolitanism in Moscow.

Moscow was no longer the political and cultural capital of an international socialist movement, but simply the largest city in Russia. The paradigm of domestic internationalism, which created such vital opportunities for internal diasporas, collapsed along with the Soviet Union. Few Russian citizens desired locally produced imitations when they could consume the real thing. Concert halls, restaurants, and stores offered American rock bands, French cuisine, and Italian luxury goods. Those formerly internal, now transnational diasporas that remained in Moscow could capitalize on imperial nostalgia and the remnants of a shared Soviet material culture. Yet at best, groups like the Georgians could only hope to be a diaspora of moderately successful people in a more precarious global environment.

The waning prominence of the Georgian diaspora has only served to highlight the dynamics of their vibrant success in Soviet times. Although their Soviet advances built upon longer-term factors, including political, social, and cultural upheaval that began well before 1917, they rose and fell as familiar strangers with the promise and abandonment of a multiethnic socialist revolution. While their longer-term fate is far from decided, their twentieth-century history reveals the unique opportunities empire can sometimes offer minority populations as well as the chronological limitations of any typology of diaspora.

Empires seek to establish the terms of difference among their populations and rule through them, whether defined by race, language, ideology, or class. Unlike nation-states pursuing ethnic homogeneity, empires permit and even require diversity, though rarely on equal terms. However, imperial categories of difference can be inhabited in unpredictable ways by diasporas that are able to adapt successfully to the imperial order. Indeed, many empires come to depend on their diasporas and even allow ethnically distinctive groups to achieve prominence at the center of imperial life rather than at its periphery. In some cases these groups embrace the cosmopolitan aspects of the host society's culture, even as they specialize in key areas of imperial life and actively maintain the boundaries that preserve them as distinctive communities. Such a strategy was pursued by Phanariot Greeks in the Ottoman Empire, Parsis in the British Raj, and some Jews and Armenians in the Russian and Soviet empires.[47] In other cases, diasporic difference is visibly performed; sometimes it is employed in an exaggerated way and limited to a circumscribed facet of imperial life, like that occupied by Romani entertainers in imperial Russia, and other times it is carefully calibrated and prominent in a range of fields. This book has described diasporas that pursue the latter strategy as familiar strangers, and Georgians in the Soviet Union exemplified the opportunities as well as the constraints of this approach.

The strategies of groups dispersed beyond their homeland are far from static; they can shift as populations move, empires evolve, imperial borders change, and new states arise. Diasporas whose cultural repertoire involves performing the culture of the host society might in time come to emphasize otherness and alienation, disenchanted with the terms of their participation in the host society or emboldened by the establishment of a homeland. The sizable Jewish emigration from the late Soviet Union is an illustrative example of this phenomenon. Likewise, familiar strangers, who specialize in the performance of otherness, might grow less interested in expressing difference. Italians were among the most familiar strangers of the multiethnic United States, but by the end of the twentieth century, many saw Italians (and some Italians saw themselves) as just another group of "white folks."[48] As a result of the dialectical interplay between the strange and the familiar, the terms of diasporic difference can come to be seen as clichéd and inauthentic over time, both to erstwhile familiar strangers and members of the host society.

While all diasporas are potentially transitory, familiar strangers are arguably more dependent on an expressly multiethnic setting, most likely an empire. There is little place for familiar strangeness in a homogenous nation-state; in such a context the chances are perhaps better, though by no means secure, for diasporas specializing in the culture of the host society. In time the otherness of familiar strangers might fade away, be concealed, or result in their being cast as marginal outsiders. As a result, Georgians in post-Soviet Russia may eventually become a diaspora of the more commonly understood type, one that performs similarity rather than difference. Such a development might mean that they endure for longer as an identifiable—if less visible and less successful—community. However, as political landscapes shift, new forms of mobility arise, and difference is articulated in new ways, familiar strangeness might appear once again as a viable strategy, arising to meet the demands of state and society and informed by the logic of a distinctive cultural repertoire.

# NOTES

## Introduction

1. The choice of the two soldiers to represent Soviet victory was no accident. Though Egorov and Kantaria were officially recognized as being the first to raise the Soviet flag they were likely not the first to do so, but were credited afterward as a result of high-level political directives. See Valerii Iaremenko, "Kto podnial znamia nad Reikhstagom? Geroicheskaia istoriia i propagandistskii mif," *Polit.ru*, May 6, 2005, accessed August 26, 2010, www.polit.ru/analytics/2005/05/06/banner.html. The significance of the photograph is discussed in David Shneer, *Through Soviet Jewish Eyes: Photography, War, and the Holocaust* (New Brunswick, NJ: Rutgers University Press, 2011), 226–27.

2. These statistics are from the 1989 census, which counted ethnic Georgians throughout the Soviet Union. CIS Committee for Statistics, *The Statistical Handbook of Social and Economic Indicators for the Former Soviet Union* (New York: Norman Ross Publishing, 1996), 39.

3. For an introduction to the various definitions of diaspora, see Stephane Dufoix, *Diasporas* (Berkeley: University of California Press, 2008).

4. Russian and Soviet historiography has most often employed the term diaspora in reference to the emigres who fled Russia and the Soviet Union in several waves over the course of the twentieth century. See Robert Chadwell Williams, *Culture in Exile: Russian Emigres in Germany, 1881–1941* (Ithaca, NY: Cornell University Press, 1972); Marc Raeff, *Russia Abroad: A Cultural History of the Russian Emigration, 1919–1939* (New York: Oxford University Press, 1990); Larissa Remennick, *Russian Jews on Three Continents* (New Brunswick, NJ: Transaction, 2007).

5. William Safran argues for a stricter definition of diaspora in "Diasporas in Modern Societies: Myths of Homeland and Return," *Diaspora* 1, no. 1 (1991): 83–99. Rogers Brubaker critiques the term's proliferation in "The 'Diaspora' Diaspora," *Ethnic and Racial Studies* 28, no. 1 (2005): 1–19.

6. Unless otherwise noted, this book uses "transnational" to refer to phenomena existing across state borders, since the crossing of such borders has distinct consequences and is best described by a single term with a designated meaning.

## Chapter 1

1. For a discussion of the term, see Paul Manning, *Strangers in a Strange Land: Occidentalist Publics and Orientalist Geographies in Nineteenth-Century Georgian Imaginaries* (Brighton: Academic Studies Press, 2012), 29–31.

2. Throughout the book, I use the more familiar English-language term "multiethnic," rather than the potentially confusing "multinational," as a translation for *mnogonatsional'naia*.

3. Rabochii arkhiv Goskostata Rossii, Tablitsa 9s, "Raspredelenie naseleniia po natsional'nosti i rodnomu iazyku," cited online in *Demoskop*, accessed March 11, 2011, http://demoscope.ru/weekly/ssp/rus_nac_89.php?reg=18.

4. Official registration in Moscow in the Soviet period was often hard to come by, so the census data did not include nationalities unofficially residing in the Soviet capital.

5. The case of Georgia is illustrative. When Ronald Grigor Suny first published *The Making of the Georgian Nation* in 1988, there had been no comprehensive monograph in the English language on Georgia since the publication of David Marshall Lang's *A Modern History of Soviet Georgia* in 1962. See Suny, *The Making of the Georgian Nation* (Bloomington: Indiana University Press, 1988); Lang, *A Modern History of Soviet Georgia* (London: Weidenfeld and Nicolson, 1962). Reflecting the rapidly evolving field of nationalities studies, Suny's work on Georgia was republished in a significantly revised second edition in 1994; the latter edition emphasized a new understanding of the nation as a discourse articulated by national intellectuals. See Suny, *The Making of the Georgian Nation*, 2nd ed. (Bloomington: Indiana University Press, 1994), ix–xii. All subsequent citations refer to the latter edition.

6. Two of the most influential works in this regard were Benedict Anderson, *Imagined Communities: Reflections on the Origin and Spread of Nationalism* (London: Verso, 1983) and Ernest Gellner, *Nations and Nationalism* (Ithaca, NY: Cornell University Press, 1983). Both were both published in the same year and stimulated much scholarly debate in the 1990s.

7. Yuri Slezkine, "The USSR as a Communal Apartment, or How a Socialist State Promoted Ethnic Particularism," *Slavic Review* 53, no. 2 (1994): 414–52. The sentence refers to Robert Conquest's *Stalin: Breaker of Nations* (New York: Viking, 1991).

8. Terry Martin, *The Affirmative Action Empire: Nations and Nationalism in the Soviet Union, 1923–1939* (Ithaca, NY: Cornell University Press, 2001).

9. Francine Hirsch, *Empire of Nations: Ethnographic Knowledge and the Making of the Soviet Union* (Ithaca, NY: Cornell University Press, 2005).

10. See, for example, Daniel R. Brower and Edward J. Lazzerini, eds., *Russia's Orient: Imperial Borderlands and Peoples, 1700–1917* (Bloomington: Indiana University Press, 1997).

11. Benjamin Nathans, *Beyond the Pale: The Jewish Encounter with Late Imperial Russia* (Berkeley: University of California Press, 2002), 15.

12. Of these groups historians have looked most extensively at Jews, while not always engaging theories of diaspora. For a theoretically rich study that points to their critical role, see Yuri Slezkine, *The Jewish Century* (Princeton, NJ: Princeton University Press, 2004).

13. On Roma, see Alaina Lemon, *Between Two Fires: Gypsy Performance and Romani Memory from Pushkin to Post-Socialism* (Durham, NC: Duke

University Press, 2000); Brigid O'Keeffe, *New Soviet Gypsies: Nationality, Performance, and Selfhood in the Early Soviet Union* (Toronto: University of Toronto Press, 2013).

14. While the concept of internal diaspora has not been applied to the Soviet Union, it has been discussed in the context of the Byzantine Empire. For an intriguing but preliminary investigation, see Hélène Ahrweiler and Angeliki E. Laiou, eds., *Studies on the Internal Diaspora of the Byzantine Empire* (Washington, DC: Dumbarton Oaks Research Library and Collection, 1998).

15. Soviet nationality policy rejected extraterritorial autonomy for national groups. Even before the revolution, Stalin denounced the idea in *Marksizm i natsional'nyi vopros*, first published in 1913. See I. V. Stalin, *Marksizm i natsional'nyi vopros* (Moscow: Gospolitizdat, 1946).

16. Aleksandr Etkind, *Internal Colonization: Russia's Imperial Experience* (Cambridge: Polity Press, 2011), 255.

17. The literature on empire and whether or not the Soviet Union was one is voluminous. For a cautious approach, see Mark R. Beissinger, "Soviet Empire as 'Family Resemblance,'" *Slavic Review* 65, no. 2 (2006): 294–303. The Soviet Union was arguably not alone in being a self-consciously anti-imperialist empire; one might also place the United States in the same category. For a comparative view, see Paul A. Kramer, "Power and Connection: Imperial Histories of the United States in the World," *American Historical Review* 116, no. 5 (2011): 1348–92.

18. Jane Burbank and Frederick Cooper, *Empires in World History: Power and the Politics of Difference* (Princeton, NJ: Princeton University Press, 2010), 11–13.

19. This definition is in part drawn from Frederick Cooper, *Colonialism in Question: Theory, Knowledge, History* (Berkeley: University of California Press, 2005), 27.

20. Living standards were higher in the Baltic states and Georgia than they were in most of Russia. See Michael Bradshaw, Phil Hanson, and Denis Shaw, "Economic Restructuring," in *The Baltic States: The National Self-Determination of Estonia, Latvia and Lithuania*, ed. Graham Smith (New York: St. Martin's, 1994), 158–80. In addition, education levels were generally higher for Jews, Georgians, and Armenians than they were for ethnic Russians, according to statistics in Tsentral'noe statisticheskoe upravlenie SSSR, *Vysshee obrazovanie v SSSR: statisticheskii sbornik* (Moscow: Gosstatizdat TsSU SSSR, 1961).

21. CIS Committee for Statistics, *The Statistical Handbook of Social and Economic Indicators for the Former Soviet Union*, 39.

22. While the former was linked to a centuries-old Georgian settlement in Moscow, the latter was renamed in the Soviet period. On the history of Georgians in Moscow, see V. Tatishvili, *Gruziny v Moskve: istoricheskii ocherk (1653–1722)* (Tbilisi: Zaria vostoka, 1959).

23. For a comparative study of ethnically distinct soldiers, see Cynthia H. Enloe, *Ethnic Soldiers: State Security in Divided Societies* (Athens: University of Georgia Press, 1980).

24. On Hapsburg Spain and its contemporaries, see J. H. Elliott, "A Europe of Composite Monarchies," *Past & Present*, no. 137 (1992): 48–71; on Maltese merchants, see Carmel Vassallo, "Maltese Entrepreneurial Networks," in *Diaspora Entrepreneurial Networks: Four Centuries of History*, ed. Ina Baghdiantz McCabe, Gelina Harlaftis, and Ioanna Pepelasis Minoglou (Oxford: Berg, 2005), 125–44.

25. On Welsh prominence within the British Empire, see Aled Jones and Bill Jones, "The Welsh World and the British Empire, c. 1851–1939: An Exploration," in *The British World: Diaspora, Culture and Identity*, ed. Carl Bridge and Kent Fedorowich (London: Frank Cass, 2003), 57–81.

26. Caroline Plüss, "Globalizing Ethnicity with Multi-local Identifications: The Parsee, Indian Muslim and Sephardic Trade Diasporas in Hong Kong," in *Diaspora Entrepreneurial Networks*, 245–68; Ioanna Pepelasis Minoglou, "Toward a Typology of Greek-Diaspora Entrepreneurship," in *Diaspora Entrepreneurial Networks*, 173–89.

27. On the Irish experience as internal colonialism, see Michael Hechter, *Internal Colonialism: The Celtic Fringe in British National Development, 1536–1966* (Berkeley: University of California Press, 1975); on the migration of the Irish and other populations within the British Empire, see Marjory Harper and Stephen Constantine, *Migration and Empire* (Oxford: Oxford University Press, 2010); on the Irish diaspora, see Kevin Kenny, "Diaspora and Comparison: The Global Irish as a Case Study," *Journal of American History* 90, no. 1 (2003): 134–62.

28. Robert Johnson, *British Imperialism* (New York: Palgrave Macmillan, 2003), 76; Robin Cohen, *Global Diasporas: An Introduction* (Seattle: University of Washington Press, 1997), 57–81.

29. Alice Conklin, "Colonialism and Human Rights, A Contradiction in Terms? The Case of France and West Africa, 1895–1914," *American Historical Review* 103, no. 2 (1998): 419–42.

30. Pieter M. Judson, *Exclusive Revolutionaries: Liberal Politics, Social Experience, and National Identity in the Austrian Empire, 1848–1914* (Ann Arbor: University of Michigan Press, 1996).

31. On Eurasia as a concept, see Mark Von Hagen, "Empires, Borderlands, and Diasporas: Eurasia as Anti-Paradigm for the Post-Soviet Era," *American Historical Review* 109, no. 2 (2004): 445–68.

32. Kliuchevskii as translated in Willard Sunderland, *Taming the Wild Field: Colonization and Empire on the Russian Steppe* (Ithaca, NY: Cornell University Press, 2004), 209.

33. On the history of the idea of Russia as the "Third Rome," see Judith E. Kalb, *Russia's Rome: Imperial Visions, Messianic Dreams, 1890–1940* (Madison: University of Wisconsin Press, 2008), 3–33; on the complexities of Russification, see Theodore R. Weeks, *Nation and State in Late Imperial Russia: Nationalism and Russification on the Western Frontier, 1863–1914* (DeKalb: Northern Illinois University Press, 1996); on the empire's accommodation of Islam and confessional diversity, see Robert D. Crews, *For Prophet and Tsar: Islam and Empire in Russia and Central Asia* (Cambridge, MA: Harvard University Press, 2006) and Paul W. Werth, *The Tsar's Foreign Faiths: Toleration and the Fate of Religious Freedom in Imperial Russia* (Oxford: Oxford University Press, 2014).

34. Heath W. Lowry, *The Nature of the Early Ottoman State* (Albany: State University of New York Press, 2003); Karen Barkey, *Bandits and Bureaucrats: The Ottoman Route to State Centralization* (Ithaca, NY: Cornell University Press, 1994); Selim Deringil, *The Well-Protected Domains: Ideology and the Legitimation of Power in the Ottoman Empire, 1876–1909* (New York: I. B. Tauris, 1998).

35. Ronald Grigor Suny, *Looking Toward Ararat: Armenia in Modern History* (Bloomington: Indiana University Press, 1993), 94–115; Traian Stoianovich, "The Conquering Balkan Orthodox Merchant," *Journal of Economic History* 20, no. 2 (1960): 234–313; Metin Ibrahim Kunt, "Ethnic-Regional (*Cins*) Solidarity in the Seventeenth-Century Ottoman Establishment," *International Journal of Middle East Studies* 5, no. 3 (1974): 233–39.

36. Andreas Kappeler, *The Russian Empire: A Multiethnic History*, trans. Alfred Clayton (Harlow: Longman, 2001); John A. Armstrong, "Mobilized Diaspora in Tsarist Russia: The Case of the Baltic Germans," in *Soviet Nationality Policies and Practices*, ed. Jeremy R. Azrael (New York: Prager, 1978), 63–104.

37. Among the founders of the Ottoman Union Society, Ibrahim Temo was Albanian, Abdullah Cevdet and İshak Sükûti were Kurds, and Mehmed Reşid was Circassian. On the history of the organization, see M. Şukrü Hanioğlu, *The Young Turks in Opposition* (New York: Oxford University Press, 1995), 71–74; on the founders, see Joost Jongerden, "Elite Encounters of the Violent Kind: Milli İbrahim Paşa, Ziya Gökalp and the Political Struggle in Diyarbekir at the Turn of the 20th Century," in *Social Relations in Ottoman Diyarbekir, 1870–1915*, ed. Joost Jongerden and Jelle Verheij (Boston: Brill, 2012), 55–84.

38. On the formation of the Soviet Union, see Jeremy Smith, *The Bolsheviks and the National Question, 1917–23* (New York: St. Martin's, 1999).

39. On the Kazakh SSR, see Martha Brill Olcott, *The Kazakhs* (Stanford, CA: Hoover Institution Press, 1987).

40. Jeremy Smith, "The Georgian Affair of 1922: Policy Failure, Personality Clash or Power Struggle?" *Europe-Asia Studies* 50, no. 3 (1998): 519–44.

41. Stalin, *Marksizm i natsional'nyi vopros*, 9.

42. Drawing on a series of interviews conducted from 2004 to 2009, Jeff Sahadeo suggests that by the late Soviet period national categories sometimes intersected with racialized understandings of difference. All the same, national labels remained prevalent, and it is difficult to imagine Georgians (or any other Soviet nationality) representing themselves as "blacks." See Jeff Sahadeo, "Soviet 'Blacks' and Place Making in Leningrad and Moscow," *Slavic Review* 71, no. 2 (2012): 331–58.

43. In 1932, the Abkhaz republic was downgraded from a Soviet socialist republic to an autonomous republic within Georgia. Suny, *Making of the Georgian Nation*, 321.

44. Lewis H. Siegelbaum and Leslie Page Moch, *Broad is My Native Land: Repertoires and Regimes of Migration in Russia's Twentieth Century* (Ithaca, NY: Cornell University Press, 2014), 303–07.

45. Moshe Gammer, *The Lone Wolf and the Bear: Three Centuries of Chechen Defiance of Russian Rule* (Pittsburgh: University of Pittsburgh Press, 2006); Brian Glyn Williams, *The Crimean Tatars: The Diaspora Experience and the Forging of a Nation* (Leiden: Brill, 2001).

46. Khachig Tölölyan, "The Contemporary Discourse of Diaspora Studies," *Comparative Studies of South Asia, Africa and the Middle East* 27, no. 3 (2007): 649–50.

47. This book is not the first to use the term "familiar strangers," but it does use it in a new way, positing it as a particular type of diaspora. The term is also used in Jonathan N. Lipman, *Familiar Strangers: A History of Muslims in*

*Northwest China* (Seattle: University of Washington Press, 1997). Lipman, however, describes a group at the periphery of Chinese society and does not offer a broader typology. At the root of most discussions of the stranger lies Georg Simmel's influential essay, "The Stranger," first published in 1908 and translated in Donald N. Levine, ed., *Georg Simmel on Individuality and Social Forms: Selected Writings* (Chicago: University of Chicago Press, 1971), 143–49.

48. Cohen, *Global Diasporas*, 1–56.

49. Among more recent scholarship, see Jeffrey Veidlinger, *The Moscow State Yiddish Theater: Jewish Culture on the Soviet Stage* (Bloomington: Indiana University Press, 2000); Kenneth B. Moss, *Jewish Renaissance in the Russian Revolution* (Cambridge, MA: Harvard University Press, 2009); Jarrod Tanny, *City of Rogues and Schnorrers: Russia's Jews and the Myth of Old Odessa* (Bloomington: Indiana University Press, 2011).

50. James Clifford suggests "a homology between defining aspects" of the Jewish and African diasporas. See Clifford, "Diasporas," *Cultural Anthropology* 9, no. 3 (1994): 302–38, esp. 321–25.

51. For an overview, see Edna Bonacich, "A Theory of Middleman Minorities," *American Sociological Review* 38, no. 5 (1973): 583–94.

52. The term "professional boundary crossers" is from Philip D. Curtin, *Cross-Cultural Trade in World History* (Cambridge: Cambridge University Press, 1984).

53. Erik R. Scott, "The Nineteenth-Century Gypsy Choir and the Performance of Otherness" (working paper, Berkeley Program in Eurasian and East European Studies, University of California, Berkeley, Fall 2008).

54. On Romani integration, see Lemon, *Between Two Fires*; O'Keeffe, *New Soviet Gypsies*.

55. Levine, ed., *Georg Simmel on Individuality and Social Forms*, 143.

56. Albert Hourani and Nadim Shehadi, eds., *The Lebanese in the World: A Century of Emigration* (London: Center for Lebanese Studies and I. B. Tauris, 1992); Akram Fouad Khater, *Inventing Home: Emigration, Gender, and the Middle Class in Lebanon* (Berkeley: University of California Press, 2001); Salvatore Primeggia and Joseph A. Varacalli, "Community and Identity in Italian American Life," in *The Review of Italian American Studies*, ed. Frank M. Sorrentino and Jerome Krase (Lanham: Lexington Books, 2000), 245–80.

57. George J. Sanchez, "Race, Nation, and Culture in Recent Immigration Studies," *Journal of American Ethnic History* 18, no. 4 (1999): 66–84; Dalia Abdelhady, *The Lebanese Diaspora: The Arab Immigrant Experience in Montreal, New York, and Paris* (New York: New York University Press, 2011); Martin, *The Affirmative Action Empire*, 127.

58. Donna R. Gabaccia, "Is Everywhere Nowhere? Nomads, Nations, and the Immigrant Paradigm of United States History," *Journal of American History* 86, no. 3 (1999): 1115–34.

59. On the importance of village-based networks among Italian migrants, see Samuel L. Baily, *Immigrants in the Lands of Promise: Italians in Buenos Aires and New York City, 1870–1914* (Ithaca, NY: Cornell University Press, 1999).

60. The linkage between exoticized representation and imperialism was argued by Edward W. Said in *Orientalism* (New York: Random House, 1979) and elaborated by him in *Culture and Imperialism* (New York: Random House, 1993).

61. Paul Gilroy, *The Black Atlantic: Modernity and Double Consciousness* (Cambridge, MA: Harvard University Press, 1993).

62. Erik R. Scott, "Ottoman Imperial Identities Between Istanbul and the Caucasus," *Journal of Associated Graduates in Near Eastern Studies* 12, no. 2 (2007): 3-29.

63. David Marshall Lang, *The Last Years of the Georgian Monarchy, 1658-1832* (New York: Columbia University Press, 1957).

64. Stephen Jones, *Socialism in Georgian Colors: The European Road to Social-Democracy, 1883-1917* (Cambridge, MA: Harvard University Press, 2005), 260-62.

65. Translated in Donald Rayfield, *The Literature of Georgia: A History* (Surrey: Curzon Press, 2000), 19-20.

66. Gerald Mars and Yochanan Altman, "The Cultural Bases of Soviet Georgia's Second Economy," *Soviet Studies* 35, no. 4 (1983): 546-60.

67. Mediterranean societies have been characterized as publicly emphasizing common concepts of honor and shame. For an introduction to the literature on the subject, see Jean G. Péristiany, *Honour and Shame: The Values of Mediterranean Society* (Chicago: University of Chicago Press, 1966). Similar tendencies in the Caucasus are discussed in Ronald Grigor Suny, "Beyond Psychohistory: The Young Stalin in Georgia," *Slavic Review* 50, no. 1 (1991): 48-58.

68. Sanchez, "Race, Nation, and Culture in Recent Immigration Studies"; Aristide R. Zolberg, *A Nation by Design: Immigration Policy in the Fashioning of America* (Cambridge, MA: Harvard University Press, 2006).

69. Humbert S. Nelli, *From Immigrants to Ethnics: The Italian Americans* (Oxford: Oxford University Press, 1983).

70. The "contributionalist" approach to US immigration history was dominant at least until the middle of the twentieth century. Oscar Handlin offered an important critique in *The Uprooted: The Epic Story of the Great Migrations That Made the American People* (Boston: Little, Brown, 1951).

71. John E. Bodnar, *The Transplanted: A History of Immigrants in Urban America* (Bloomington: Indiana University Press, 1985), 204.

72. Rudolph J. Vecoli, "The *Contadini* in Chicago: A Critique of *The Uprooted*," *Journal of American History* 51, no. 3 (1964): 404-17; Vecoli, "The Formation of Chicago's 'Little Italies,'" *Journal of American Ethnic History* 2, no. 2 (1983): 5-20.

73. Among the most famous Italian American crooners were Frank Sinatra, Dean Martin, and Tony Bennett.

74. Among Italian American directors, Martin Scorcese and Francis Ford Coppola are best known for films focusing on both Italian American and universal themes and for referencing (and reshaping) established cinematic traditions.

75. Humbert S. Nelli, *The Business of Crime: Italians and Syndicate Crime in the United States* (New York: Oxford University Press, 1976).

76. For a long-term study of migration in a range of state environments, see Leslie Page Moch, *Moving Europeans: Migration in Western Europe since 1650* (Bloomington: Indiana University Press, 1992).

77. Martin, *The Affirmative Action Empire*, 404. Martin argues that this development was the result of state pressure and Russification policies; however, because of cultural similarity, Ukrainians and Belarusians were more easily Russified than Germans, Koreans, or Chechens.

78. For a somewhat dated but comprehensive history of Georgia before Russian conquest, see W.E.D. Allen, *A History of the Georgian People from the Beginning Down to the Russian Conquest in the Nineteenth Century* (London: K. Paul, Trench, Trubner and Co., 1932).

79. Anatoly M. Khazanov, *Nomads and the Outside World*, trans. Julia Crookenden (Cambridge: Cambridge University Press, 1984).

80. The example of Mir Ali Shir Nava'i, whom the Soviets referred to as the "father of Uzbek literature," is a case in point. Nava'i was born in present-day Afghanistan in 1441 and wrote in Chaghatay, not Uzbek. See Edward A. Allworth, *The Modern Uzbeks: From the Fourteenth Century to the Present; A Cultural History* (Stanford, CA: Hoover Institution Press, 1990), 37, 228–31.

81. Mervyn Matthews, *The Passport Society: Controlling Movement in Russia and the USSR* (Boulder, CO: Westview Press, 1993), 50; Sahadeo, "Soviet 'Blacks' and Place Making in Leningrad and Moscow."

82. Orthodox Christianity was made the official religion of the eastern Georgian kingdom of Kartli in 337 and the Georgian church became autocephalous in the fifth century. The Russian Orthodox Church traces its origin to the conversion of Prince Vladimir I of Kiev several centuries later, in 988. For background, see John Binns, *An Introduction to the Christian Orthodox Churches* (Cambridge: Cambridge University Press, 2002).

83. Austin Jersild, *Orientalism and Empire: North Caucasus Mountain Peoples and the Georgian Frontier, 1845–1917* (Montreal: McGill-Queen's University Press, 2002).

84. Austin Jersild and Neli Melkadze, "The Dilemmas of Enlightenment in the Eastern Borderlands: The Theater and Library in Tbilisi," *Kritika: Explorations in Russian and Eurasian History* 3, no. 1 (2002): 27–49.

85. One contributor to the mythology of the Armenian SSR was the Soviet poet Osip Mandel'shtam, who published an account of his travels there. Mandel'shtam, "Puteshestvie v Armeniiu," *Zvezda*, no. 5 (1933): 103–25.

86. I. V. Shirokii, *Tamara Khanum* (Leningrad: Iskusstvo, 1941).

87. According to the census, only 1.3 percent of Georgians in the Soviet Union (including those within and outside the Georgian republic) considered Russian their native language, compared with 8.3 percent of Armenians, 12.2 percent of Ukrainians, 15.3 percent of Belarussians, and 76.4 percent of Jews. A. A. Isupov, *Natsional'nyi sostav naseleniia SSSR (po itogam perepisi 1959 g.)* (Moscow: Statistika, 1961), 34.

88. Iu. V. Arutiunian, "Armiane-moskvichi. Sotsial'nyi portret po materialam etnosotsiologicheskogo isledovaniia," *Sovetskaia etnografiia*, no. 2 (1991): 3–16.

89. Vilius Ivanauskas, "Soviet 'Exotic' and Soviet 'West': Embodying Ethnic Particularism among Georgian and Lithuanian Writers" (unpublished article, 2013).

90. For a discussion of Baltic intellectual culture, see David Ilmar Beecher, "Ivory Tower of Babel: Tartu University and the Languages of Two Empires, A Nation-State, and the Soviet Union" (PhD diss., University of California, Berkeley, 2014).

91. See, for example, Lowell Tillett, *The Great Friendship: Soviet Historians on the Non-Russian Nationalities* (Chapel Hill: University of North Carolina Press, 1969).

92. As Serguei Alex. Oushakine has written, even in the Russian core, Russian ethnicity was something of a "blank spot . . . an indeterminate source of power, framed by ethnic differences of other Soviet nationalities." See Oushakine, *The Patriotism of Despair: Nation, War, and Loss in Russia* (Ithaca, NY: Cornell University Press, 2009), 10.

93. Mayhill C. Fowler describes the fate of internal transnational trends in Soviet theater in "Mikhail Bulgakov, Mykola Kulish, and Soviet Theater: How Internal Transnationalism Remade Center and Periphery," *Kritika: Explorations in Russian and Eurasian History* 16, no. 2 (2015): 263–90.

94. On the production, exchange, and circulation of commodities across regimes of value, see Arjun Appadurai, *The Social Life of Things: Commodities in Cultural Perspective* (Cambridge: Cambridge University Press, 1986).

95. Gijs Kessler, "The Origins of Soviet Internal-Migration Policy: Industrialization and the 1930s Rural Exodus," in *Russia in Motion: Cultures of Human Mobility since 1850*, ed. John Randolph and Eugene M. Avrutin (Urbana: University of Illinois Press, 2012), 65.

96. Matthews, *The Passport Society: Controlling Movement in Russia and the USSR*; Matthew Light, "Migration Controls in Soviet and Post-Soviet Moscow: From 'Closed City' to 'Illegal City,'" in *Russia in Motion*, 80–98. Siegelbaum and Moch offer a long-term perspective on these migration trends in *Broad is My Native Land*.

97. Alexander Gerschenkron, "Economic Backwardness in Historical Perspective," in *Economic Backwardness in Historical Perspective*, ed. Alexander Gerschenkron (Cambridge, MA: Harvard University Press, 1966), 5–31; Ken Jowitt, "Soviet Neotraditionalism: The Political Corruption of a Leninist Regime," *Europe-Asia Studies* 35, no. 3 (1983): 275–97.

98. Stalin, *Marksizm i natsional'nyi vopros*, 9.

99. On the production of domestically produced Soviet luxury goods, see Jukka Gronow, *Caviar with Champagne: Common Luxury and the Ideals of the Good Life in Stalin's Russia* (Oxford: Berg, 2003).

100. Catriona Kelly, "Learning about the Nation: Ethnographic Representations of Children, Representations of Ethnography for Children," in *An Empire of Others: Creating Ethnographic Knowledge in Imperial Russia and the USSR*, ed. Roland Cvetkovski and Alexis Hofmeister (Budapest: Central European University Press, 2014), 253–78; Diane P. Koenker, "Pleasure Travel in the Passport State," in *Russia in Motion*, 235–52.

101. Katherine Verdery examines the function of ethnic identity in the socialist economy of shortages in *What Was Socialism, and What Comes Next?* (Princeton, NJ: Princeton University Press, 1996).

102. On transnational linkages with Europe, see Michael David-Fox, *Showcasing the Great Experiment: Cultural Diplomacy and Western Visitors to the Soviet Union, 1921–1941* (Oxford: Oxford University Press, 2012); Katerina Clark, *Moscow, the Fourth Rome: Stalinism, Cosmopolitanism, and the Evolution of Soviet Culture, 1931–1941* (Cambridge, MA: Harvard University Press, 2011).

103. For a discussion of the possibilities and limitations of cosmopolitanism, see Pheng Cheah and Bruce Robbins, eds., *Cosmopolitics: Thinking and Feeling Beyond the Nation* (Minneapolis: University of Minnesota Press, 1998); Kwame Anthony Appiah, *Ethics of Identity* (Princeton, NJ: Princeton

University Press, 2005); Kwame Anthony Appiah, *Cosmopolitanism: Ethics in a World of Strangers* (New York: Norton, 2006); Edwin Jurriens and Jeroen de Kloet, eds., *Cosmopatriots: On Distant Belongings and Close Encounters* (Amsterdam: Rodopi, 2007).

104. On the anti-cosmopolitan campaign and the state's targeting of Soviet Jews, see Benjamin Pinkus and Jonathan Frankel, *The Soviet Government and the Jews, 1948-1967: A Documented Study* (Cambridge: Cambridge University Press, 1984); Yaacov Ro'i, *Soviet Decision Making in Practice: The USSR and Israel, 1947-1954* (New Brunswick, NJ: Transaction Books, 1980).

105. The idea of an emergent "Soviet people" gained traction under Khrushchev and became a prominent—if not dominant—feature of official rhetoric in the 1970s. See Şener Aktürk, *Regimes of Ethnicity and Nationhood in Germany, Russia, and Turkey* (New York: Cambridge University Press, 2012), 213-19.

106. The study of Russian became mandatory in non-Russian schools by the late 1930s, reinforced by a 1938 decree passed by the Party's Central Committee. Martin, *The Affirmative Action Empire*, 457-58.

### Chapter 2

1. RGASPI, f. 85, op. 3, d. 68, ll. 1-4.

2. RGASPI, f. 124, op. 1, d. 1426, ll. 5-6.

3. V. I. Lenin, *Polnoe sobranie sochinenii* (Moscow: Gos. izd-vo politicheskoi literatury, 1961), 21: 134-35.

4. The risk of betrayal was especially present in this case. In prison, Orjonikidze also appealed for help from Roman Malinovskii, a high-ranking Bolshevik who would soon be exposed as a tsarist double agent. See Robert Service, *Stalin: A Biography* (London: Pan Books, 2005), 108.

5. In *The Literature of Georgia: A History* (Surrey: Curzon Press, 2000), 77, Donald Rayfield writes that the poetry of Georgia's Rustaveli "puts male friendship and courtly love on the same plane." For a comparative study of fictive and adoptive kinship, see Peter Parkes, "Milk Kinship in Southeast Europe: Alternative Social Structures and Foster Relations in the Caucasus and the Balkans," *Social Anthropology* 12, no. 3 (2004): 341-58.

6. RGASPI, f. 85, op. 3, d. 68, ll. 1-4.

7. On the relationship between class and national revolution in the Caucasus, see Ronald Grigor Suny, *The Baku Commune, 1917-1918: Class and Nationality in the Russian Revolution* (Princeton, NJ: Princeton University Press, 1972). Suny offers a comparative view of the subject in *The Revenge of the Past: Nationalism, Revolution, and the Collapse of the Soviet Union* (Stanford, CA: Stanford University Press, 1993).

8. Henry Jack Tobias, *The Jewish Bund in Russia from its Origins to 1905* (Stanford, CA: Stanford University Press, 1972); Joshua D. Zimmerman, *Poles, Jews, and the Politics of Nationality: The Bund and the Polish Socialist Party in Late Tsarist Russia, 1892-1914* (Madison: University of Wisconsin Press, 2004); Andrew Ezergailis, *The 1917 Revolution in Latvia* (New York: Columbia University Press, 1974).

9. The results of the 1927 Party Census were revealing. Contrary to population figures, there were more Jews than Belarusians, and, among the top ten most represented nationalities, Armenians, Georgians, Latvians, and Poles figured prominently. Statisticheskii otdel TsK VKP(b), *Vsesoiuznaia partiinaia perepis' 1927 goda* (Moscow, 1927), 7: 6-7.

10. On Jews, see O. V. Budnitskii, *Evrei i russkaia revoliutsiia: materialy i isledo-vaniia* (Moscow: Gesharim, 1999); Yuri Slezkine, *The Jewish Century*. On the Latvian Riflemen, see Geoffrey Swain, "The Disillusioning of the Revolution's Praetorian Guard: The Latvian Riflemen, Summer—Autumn 1918," *Europe-Asia Studies* 51, no. 4 (1999): 667–86.

11. On the personalization of politics in the Soviet Union, see J. Arch Getty and Oleg V. Naumov, *Yezhov: The Rise of Stalin's 'Iron Fist'* (New Haven, CT: Yale University Press, 2008).

12. To cite several representative examples in a vast body of popular and scholarly literature, see Robert Conquest, *Stalin: Breaker of Nations*, on Stalin as a despotic tyrant; Robert Service, *Stalin: A Biography*, on Stalin as a committed Marxist; Robert C. Tucker, *Stalin as Revolutionary, 1879–1929: A Study in History and Personality* (New York: Norton, 1973), on the Soviet ruler's psychological tendencies; Isaac Deutscher, *Stalin: A Political Biography* (New York: Oxford University Press, 1966), on Stalin as a representative and master of the new Soviet bureaucracy; Iurii Mukhin, *Stalin: khoziain Sovetskogo Soiuza* (Moscow: Algoritm, 2008), on Stalin as a modernizer and economic manager; Jörg Baberowski, *Der Feind ist überall: Stalinismus im Kaukasus* (Munich: Deutsche Verlags-Anstalt, 2003), on how the violence of Stalinism emerged from a Caucasian context; Alfred J. Rieber, "Stalin: Man of the Borderlands," *American Historical Review* 106, no. 5 (2001): 1651–91, on the significance of Stalin's Georgian origins and his efforts to transcend them; and Stephen Kotkin, *Stalin. Volume I, Paradoxes of Power, 1878–1928* (New York: Penguin, 2014), on the geopolitical dilemmas faced by the Soviet leader.

13. Gerald Easter's *Reconstructing the State: Personal Networks and Elite Identity in Soviet Russia* (Cambridge: Cambridge University Press, 2000) is insightful but does not thoroughly examine ethnic networks. John P. Willerton's *Patronage and Politics in the USSR* (Cambridge: Cambridge University Press, 1992) considers ethnic networks but focuses on the Brezhnev period. Though limited to regional developments, a valuable exception is Charles H. Fairbanks Jr. "Clientelism and Higher Politics in Georgia, 1949–1953," in *Transcaucasia: Nationalism and Social Change*, ed. Ronald Grigor Suny (Ann Arbor: Michigan Slavic Publications, 1983), 339–68.

14. For a study of Stalin that shows the leader's involvement in cultivating his public image, see Robert Hatch McNeal, *Stalin: Man and Ruler* (New York: New York University Press, 1988).

15. For details, see Jersild, *Orientalism and Empire*.

16. Iakov Mansvetashvili, *Vospominaniia* (Tbilisi: Literatura da khelovneba, 1967), 26.

17. Georgii Dzhavakhishvili, ed., *Iz perepiski N. A. Nikoladze s russkimi i zarubezh-nymi literaturno-obshchestvennymi deiatel'iami* (Tbilisi: Izd-vo Tbilisskogo universiteta, 1980), 29.

18. Kappeler, *The Russian Empire*, 374. Kappeler also notes that among Christian Orthodox ethnic groups, the literacy gap between men and women was not as great among Georgians as it was among Russians and Ukrainians (311–12).

19. Jonathan Frankel, *Prophecy and Politics: Socialism, Nationalism, and the Russian Jews* (Cambridge: Cambridge University Press, 1981); Moss, *Jewish Renaissance in the Russian Revolution*.

20. Daniel R. Brower, *Training the Nihilists: Education and Radicalism in Tsarist Russia* (Ithaca, NY: Cornell University Press, 1975).

21. The economic and social transformation of rural Georgia is discussed in Suny, *The Making of the Georgian Nation*, 96–112, 144–64.
22. RGASPI, f. 124, op. 1, d. 661, ll. 4–9.
23. Suny, *The Making of the Georgian Nation*, 91–93.
24. SShSSA, II, f. 8, op. 2, d. 66, ll. 1–5.
25. SShSSA, II, f. 8, op. 3, d. 748, ll. 1–5.
26. Laurie Manchester, *Holy Fathers, Secular Sons: Clergy, Intelligentsia, and the Modern Self in Revolutionary Russia* (DeKalb: Northern Illinois University Press, 2008).
27. RGASPI, f. 124, op. 1, d. 1234, ll. 4–24.
28. Service, *Stalin: A Biography*, 36.
29. The poems of the teenage Stalin were celebrated by Tbilisi's intelligentsia and published in the Georgian-language *Iveria*, no. 23 (1895). Translated in Service, *Stalin: A Biography*, 39.
30. RGASPI, f. 124, op. 1, d. 639, ll. 3–6.
31. The same was true of future Bolshevik Malakia Toroshelidze. RGASPI, f. 124, op. 1, d. 1941, ll. 4–8.
32. For a discussion of the "leveling" tendency within the Russian Revolution, see Richard Stites, *Revolutionary Dreams: Utopian Vision and Experimental Life in the Russian Revolution* (Oxford: Oxford University Press, 1989), 126–30.
33. SShSSA, II, f. 8, op. 2, d. 66, ll. 3–4.
34. For an account of Eliava's childhood by a relative, see SShSSA, II, f. 8, op. 2, d. 66, ll. 3–4; on Orjonikidze, see his autobiography, RGASPI, f. 124, op. 1, d. 1426. Stalin's mother kept a Georgian-language diary, which was recently published. See Ekaterine Jughashvili, *stalinis dedis mogonebebi* (Tbilisi: Bakur Sulakauri, 2012).
35. SShSSA, II, f. 8, op. 2, d. 66, l. 1.
36. According to their party autobiographies. RGASPI, f. 124, op. 1, d. 639, 640, 641, 1098.
37. RGASPI, f. 124, op. 1, d. 1874, ll. 5–16.
38. For a more contemporary work with fascinating implications for historical study, see Tamara Dragadze, *Rural Families in Soviet Georgia: A Case Study in Ratcha Province* (New York: Routledge, 1988).
39. Suny, *The Making of the Georgian Nation*, 67–78.
40. Stephen F. Jones, "Marxism and Peasant Revolution in the Russian Empire: the Case of the Gurian Republic," *Slavonic and East European Review* 67, no. 3 (1989): 403–34.
41. Akakii Mgeladze, *Stalin kakim ia ego znal* (Tbilisi, 2001), 22–23.
42. See Daina Bleiere, *History of Latvia: The Twentieth Century* (Riga: Jumava, 2006).
43. As Stephen Jones succinctly refers to it in his book of the same title, "socialism in Georgian colors." The preponderance of western Georgians in general and Gurians in particular is evident from a perusal of the autobiographical files of the All-Union Society of Old Bolsheviks, RGASPI, f. 124, op. 1.
44. On Poles and Jews, see Zimmerman, *Poles, Jews, and the Politics of Nationality*; on Armenians, see Suny, *Looking Toward Ararat*.
45. RGASPI, f. 124, op. 1, d. 1234, ll. 4–24.
46. Tadeusz Swietochowski, *Russian Azerbaijan, 1905–1920: The Shaping of a National Identity in a Muslim Community* (Cambridge: Cambridge University

Press, 2004), 38–46. The city's Muslim population was dominated by Azeri speakers, but also included Lezgins, Persians, and Volga Tatars.

47. Swietochowski, *Russian Azerbaijan, 1905–1920*, 39.

48. On Shaumian and other Armenians in the Bolshevik party, see Razmik Panossian, *The Armenians: From Kings And Priests to Merchants And Commissars* (New York: Columbia University Press, 2006).

49. RGASPI, f. 124, op. 1, d. 639, ll. 3–4.

50. A. Enukidze, *Bol'shevistskie nelegal'nye tipografii* (Moscow: Molodaia gvardiia, 1930).

51. RGASPI, f. 124, op. 1, d. 641, l. 4.

52. RGASPI, f. 124, op. 1, d. 1874, ll. 5–16.

53. RGASPI, f. 124, op. 1, d. 1941, ll. 4–8.

54. His Georgian wife succumbed to tuberculosis shortly after the move, making Jughashvili a widower until his marriage to the young Nadezhda Allilueva in 1919.

55. Service, *Stalin*, 78.

56. I. V. Stalin, *Sochineniia* 2: 46–77, cited in Deutscher, *Stalin*, 91.

57. RGASPI, f. 124, op. 1, d. 639, ll. 5–6.

58. RGASPI, f. 124, op. 1, d. 641, ll. 4–5.

59. RGASPI, f. 124, op. 1, d. 328, ll. 15–27.

60. Service, *Stalin*, 110–12.

61. RGASPI, f. 124, op. 1, d. 2074, ll. 3–4.

62. V. I. Lenin, *Sochineniia* 19: 30–31.

63. I. G. Tsereteli, *Vospominaniia o fevral'skoi revoliutsii* (Paris: Mouton, 1963), 15.

64. *Rabochaia gazeta* 50 (May 7, 1917), preserved in the Hoover Institution Archives, "Boris I. Nicolaevsky Collection," Box 37: 3.

65. Jones, *Socialism in Georgian Colors*, 286.

66. Zhordania, *Moia zhizn'*, trans. Inna Zhordania (Stanford, CA: Hoover Institution Press, 1968), 49.

67. RGASPI, f. 124, op. 1, d. 2074, ll. 1–2.

68. RGASPI, f. 124, op. 1, d. 328, l. 25.

69. RGASPI, f. 124, op. 1, d. 639, ll. 3–6; RGASPI, f. 124, op. 1, d. 641, ll. 4–5.

70. RGASPI, f. 124, op. 1, d. 1426, ll. 5–6.

71. "Eliava, Shalva Zurabovich," *Bol'shaia sovetskaia entsiklopediia*, ed. A. M. Prokhorov et al. (Moscow: Sovetskaia entsiklopediia, 1970–1981).

72. Karl Kautsky, *Georgia: A Social Democratic Peasant Republic*, trans. H. J. Stenning (London: International Bookshops, 1921).

73. L. Trotskii, *Mezhdu imperializmom i revoliutsiei: osnovnye voprosy revoliutsii na chastnom primere Gruzii* (Moscow: Gos. izd-vo, 1922), 83.

74. Mikheil Javakhishvili, *tkhzulebani rva tomad* (Tbilisi: sabchota sakartvelo, 1970), 2: 17, 24.

75. See Stephen Blank, *The Sorcerer as Apprentice: Stalin as Commissar of Nationalities, 1917–1924* (Westport, CT: Greenwood, 1994).

76. For the contrasting account of a contemporary, see Uratadze, *Vospominaniia*.

77. The letter is dated January 23 and is written on the stationary of the Workers' and Peasants' Inspectorate, which Stalin headed starting on February 7, 1920. While the exact year is not indicated in the letter, its contents point to events taking place in late January 1921. RGASPI, f. 558, op. 11, d. 777, l. 25.

78. SShSSA, II, f. 14, op. 1, d. 36, l. 3.
79. RGASPI, f. 298, op. 1, d. 137, ll. 7–8.
80. Suny, *The Making of the Georgian Nation*, 217.
81. Stephen Jones, "The Establishment of Soviet Power in Transcaucasia: The Case of Georgia, 1921–1928," *Soviet Studies* 40, no. 4 (1988): 616–39.
82. SShSSA, II, f. 14, op. 2, d. 439, l. 14.
83. SShSSA, II, f. 14, op. 2, d. 439, l. 16.
84. Svetlana Allilueva, *Dvadtsat' pisem k drugu* (New York: Harper and Row, 1967), 63.
85. RGASPI, f. 558, op. 11, d. 132, ll. 90–99, cited in J. Arch Getty, *Practicing Stalinism: Bolsheviks, Boyars, and the Persistence of Tradition* (New Haven, CT: Yale University Press, 2013), 168.
86. In his memoirs, Khrushchev stated that "among the party activists it was often said that there was a 'Caucasian group' [*kavkazskaia gruppa*] in power." N. S. Khrushchev, *Vospominaniia: vremia, liudi, vlast'* (Moscow: Moskovskie novosti, 1999), 1: 72.
87. Contemporaries, including Anastas Mikoian, recalled that Kirov understood and respected Caucasian patterns of friendship, kinship, and feasting. A. I. Mikoian, *Tak bylo: razmyshleniia o minuvshem*, ed. S. A. Mikoian (Moscow: Vagrius, 1999), 510.
88. Institutions may have come to matter more in late Stalinism. See Yoram Gorlizki, "Ordinary Stalinism: The Council of Ministers and the Soviet Neopatrimonial State, 1946–1953," *Journal of Modern History* 74, no. 4 (2002): 699–736.
89. Slezkine, *Jewish Century*, 247.
90. Oleg V. Khlevniuk, *In Stalin's Shadow: The Career of "Sergo" Ordzhonikidze*, ed. Donald J. Raleigh, trans. David J. Nordlander (Armonk, NY: M. E. Sharpe, 1995), 25.
91. E. A. Rees, *State Control in Soviet Russia: The Rise and the Fall of the Workers' and Peasants' Inspectorate, 1920–1934* (New York: St. Martin's, 1987).
92. Allilueva, *Dvadtsat' pisem*, 132.
93. In particular, he supported Beso Lominadze against charges of deviation from the party line during the "Syrtsov-Lominadze Affair." See R. W. Davies, "The Syrtsov-Lominadze Affair," *Soviet Studies* 33, no. 1 (1981): 29–50.
94. RGAE, f. 6884, op. 1, d. 1, ll. 1–43.
95. Orjonikidze helped orchestrate press coverage of major industrial efforts in collaboration with his own personnel and officials in Moscow. See his correspondence on media coverage in RGAE, f. 6884, op. 1, d. 6, ll. 1–161.
96. A concept introduced by Stephen Kotkin in *Magnetic Mountain: Stalinism as Civilization* (Berkeley: University of California Press, 1997), 198–237.
97. For a discussion of the phenomenon, see Barbara E. Bullock and Almeida Jacqueline Toribio, eds., *The Cambridge Handbook of Linguistic Code Switching* (Cambridge: Cambridge University Press, 2009).
98. RGASPI, f. 85, op. 28, d. 55, ll. 1–3.
99. A point compellingly made by Jeffrey Veidlinger in his study of the Moscow State Yiddish Theater. See Veidlinger, *Moscow State Yiddish Theater*, 3.
100. Despite the Jewish cultural revival described by Moss in *Jewish Renaissance*, most Jewish Bolsheviks saw Russian as the ideal medium for literary and spoken expression. Slezkine writes of the "eager conversion to the Pushkin faith" in *Jewish Century*, 127.

101. RGASPI, f. 85, op. 29, d. 759, ll. 1–2.

102. RGAE, f. 631, op. 1, d. 14, ll. 12–13.

103. Amy Knight, *Beria: Stalin's First Lieutenant* (Princeton, NJ: Princeton University Press, 1993), 49–50.

104. RGASPI, f. 85, op. 28, d. 70.

105. A thoroughly Soviet city, Magnitogorsk is the subject of Kotkin's *Magnetic Mountain*.

106. RGAE, f. 332, op. 4, d. 56, ll. 59–64.

107. For a discussion of Georgian hospitality, see Mary Ellen Chatwin, *Socio-Cultural Transformation and Foodways in the Republic of Georgia* (Commack, NY: Nova Science Publishers, 1997).

108. RGASPI, f. 85, op. 1/s, d. 136, cited and translated in Khlevniuk, *In Stalin's Shadow*, 93.

109. Khlevniuk, *In Stalin's Shadow*, 34.

110. RGASPI, f. 85, op. 1/s, d. 162, l. 33.

111. Khlevniuk, *In Stalin's Shadow*, 74–75.

112. As he is described in Yoram Gorlizki and Oleg Khlevniuk, *Cold Peace: Stalin and the Soviet Ruling Circle, 1945–1953* (Oxford: Oxford University Press, 2004).

113. Based on a careful reading of Orjonikidze's correspondence with Stalin. RGASPI, f. 558, op. 1, d. 777–79.

114. RGASPI, f. 558, op. 11, d. 728.

115. RGASPI, f. 558, op. 11, d. 758, ll. 157–58.

116. Letters from Georgians made up only a fraction of the many messages Stalin and other top officials received from Soviet citizens. For more on these letters, see Sheila Fitzpatrick, *Everyday Stalinism: Ordinary Life in Extraordinary Times: Soviet Russia in the 1930s* (New York: Oxford University Press, 1999), 175–78.

117. RGASPI, f. 558, op. 1, d. 5978, 5080, cited in Simon Sebag Montefiore, *Young Stalin* (New York: Knopf, 2007), 316.

118. An official note appended to the letter revealed that Stalin earlier held a personal meeting with the same childhood friend who requested to be flown to Moscow. He was a former classmate from the Gori seminary. RGASPI, f. 558, op. 11, d. 722, ll. 128–30.

119. RGASPI, f. 558, op. 11, d. 722, l. 105.

120. RGASPI, f. 558, op. 11, d. 1549, l. 7.

121. RGASPI, f. 558, op. 11, d. 1549. In Tbilisi, Beria personally attended to Stalin's mother. Stalin himself was notably absent from her funeral in 1937. Simon Sebag Montefiore, *Stalin: The Court of the Red Tsar* (London: Phoenix, 2004), 186–88, 226.

122. In 1946, she complained that delivery of her special provision by Egnatashvili had been disrupted. RGASPI, f. 558, op. 11, d. 722, l. 89.

123. Khrushchev, *Vospominaniia*, 1: 48–51.

124. Timothy Blauvelt, "Abkhazia: Patronage and Power in the Stalin Era," *Nationalities Papers* 35, no. 2 (2007): 203–32.

125. Montefiore, *Stalin: The Court of the Red Tsar*, 78–79.

126. Hoover Institution Archives, "N. A. Lakoba Papers," Box 1: 60.

127. Hoover Institution Archives, "N. A. Lakoba Papers," Box 1: 26.

128. RGASPI, f. 667, op. 1, d. 16, ll. 1–8.

129. RGASPI, f. 667, op. 1, d. 17, l. 119.

130. RGASPI, f. 667, op. 1, d. 19, ll. 128–29.

131. Eteri and Tinatin Egnatashvili, interview by author. Moscow, March 23, 2008.
132. Sergo Beria, *Beria, My Father: Inside Stalin's Kremlin* (London: Duckworth, 2001), 191.
133. RGAE, f. 332, op. 4, d. 56, ll. 66–72.
134. K. Simonov, *Glazami cheloveka moego pokoleniia*, 37, cited in Service, *Stalin*, 324. The poster alluded to an ancient dispute among Slavic tribes that eventually led to the invitation of the foreign Varangians to rule over them. It revealed that factional battles between Trotsky and Stalin may have been understood as an interethnic contest between Jews and Georgians, though among Stalin's closest supporters were Lazar Kaganovich and other influential Soviet Jews.
135. Veidlinger, *Moscow State Yiddish Theater*, 7.
136. *Pavil'on Gruzinskaia SSR: Putevoditel'* (Moscow: Sel'khozgiz, 1939).
137. GARF, f. R-3316, op. 27, d. 756, l. 79.
138. GARF, f. R-3316, op. 27, d. 754; GARF f. R-3316, op. 27, d. 755, l. 175.
139. RGASPI, f. 558, op. 11, d. 728, ll. 13–14.
140. RGASPI, f. 558, op. 11, d. 730, ll. 44–186.
141. Gamsakhurdia had been imprisoned in connection with the 1924 uprising against Soviet power. His biography of Stalin was likely an attempt to seek the Soviet authorities' good graces.
142. RGASPI, f. 558, op. 11, d. 730, l. 187.
143. RGASPI, f. 558, op. 11, d. 730, l. 190.
144. See David Brandenberger, *National Bolshevism: Stalinist Mass Culture and the Formation of Modern Russian National Identity, 1931–1956* (Cambridge, MA: Harvard University Press, 2002).
145. Boris Ilizarov, *Tainaia zhizn' Stalina: po materialam ego biblioteki i arkhiva k istoriosofii stalinizma* (Moscow: Veche, 2003), 246.
146. Svetlana Allilueva, *Tol'ko odin god* (New York: Harper and Row, 1969), 337.
147. Shota Rustaveli, *The Knight in the Panthers Skin*, trans. Venera Urushadze (Tbilisi: Sabchota Sakartvelo, 1986), 139.
148. Sarah Davies, "Stalin as a Patron of Cinema: Creating Soviet Mass Culture, 1932–1936," in *Stalin: A New History*, ed. Sarah Davies and James Harris (Cambridge: Cambridge University Press, 2005), 202–25.
149. RGASPI, f. 558, op. 11, d. 159.
150. Ilizarov, *Tainaia zhizn' Stalina*, 249–53.
151. Beria, *Beria, My Father*, 283–84.
152. There is a vast literature on the Great Purges. For some representative works, see Robert Conquest, *The Great Terror: A Reassessment* (New York: Oxford University Press, 1990); J. Arch Getty and Oleg Naumov, *The Road to Terror: Stalin and the Self-Destruction of the Bolsheviks, 1932–1939* (New Haven, CT: Yale University Press, 1999); Igal Halfin, *Terror in My Soul: Communist Autobiographies on Trial* (Cambridge, MA: Harvard University Press, 2003).
153. While the purges were also driven by pressures from below, Stalin's role in guiding them appears evident when the archival record is examined. For more on how local factors played into the purges, see Wendy Z. Goldman, *Inventing the Enemy: Denunciation and Terror in Stalin's Russia* (New York: Cambridge University Press, 2011).
154. RGASPI, f. 558, op. 11, d. 779, ll. 29–33.

155. Easter goes so far as to describe Stalin's goal as the construction of a "bureaucratic absolutist state." Easter, *Reconstructing the State*, 16.
156. A. Enukidze, *Bolshevistskie nelegal'nye tipografii* (Moscow: Molodaia gvardiia, 1934).
157. RGASPI, f. 558, op. 11, d. 728, ll. 66–107.
158. RGASPI, f. 558, op. 11, d. 728, ll. 108–13. The accusations against Enukidze foreshadowed those against other Bolshevik leaders from the Caucasus, including Aghasi Khanjian, the party chief of Soviet Armenia.
159. For a carefully researched account of these events, see Getty and Naumov, *Yezhov*, 156–78.
160. Getty and Naumov, *Yezhov*, 164–65.
161. RGASPI, f. 558, op. 11, d. 728, l. 40.
162. Khlevniuk, *In Stalin's Shadow*, 76–77.
163. Khlevniuk, *In Stalin's Shadow*, 105–10.
164. Knight, *Beria*, 74–75.
165. Dubinskii-Mukhadze, *Ordzhonikidze*, 6, cited in Khlevniuk, *In Stalin's Shadow*, 148.
166. GARF, f. R-9503, op. 1, d. 43, ll. 1–3.
167. Mikoian, *Tak bylo*, 353.
168. Knight, *Beria*, 74–75.
169. Archival records show that Stalin and Beria corresponded frequently on the details of this publication. RGASPI, f. 558, op. 11, d. 704, 705.
170. Khrushchev, *Vospominaniia*, 1: 86. Translated by George Shriver in *Memoirs of Nikita Krushchev*, ed. Sergei Khrushchev (University Park: Pennsylvania State University Press, 2004), 1: 80.
171. Khrushchev, 2: 58–59, 2: 179.
172. The list is provided by Knight, *Beria*, 91. Other Georgian associates of Beria are listed in Iu. N. Afanas'ev et al, *Istoriia stalinskogo gulaga* (Moscow: Rosspen, 2004–2005).
173. See Timothy K. Blauvelt, "March of the Chekists: Beria's Secret Police Patronage Network and Soviet Crypto-Politics," *Communist and Post-Communist Studies* 44, no. 1 (2011): 73–88.
174. Oleg V. Khlevniuk argues for the political ascendancy of the police in "Stalin as Dictator: The Personalisation of Power," in *Stalin: A New History*, 108–20.
175. J. Arch Getty contrasts Old Bolshevik values with those of the "police clans" in *Practicing Stalinism*.
176. N. V. Petrov and K. V. Skorkin, eds., *Kto rukovodil NKVD, 1934–1941: spravochnik* (Moscow: Zven'ia, 1999), 495.
177. Knight, *Beria*, 176–200.
178. A similar observation is made by Blauvelt in "March of the Chekists."
179. Georgian First Party Secretary Vasili Mzhavanadze, an ally of Khrushchev, was a Politburo member from 1957 to 1972, but he never rose to a ministerial post in the center and was mainly known as a republic-level figure.

## Chapter 3

1. The description is based on the painting by M. I. Khmel'ko, *Torzhestvennyi priem v chest' predstavitelei komandovaniia Krasnoi Armii i Voenno-Morskogo Flota, uchastvovavshikh v Velikoi Otechestvennoi voine.*

2. For the transcript, see RGASPI, f. 558, op. 11, d. 1098, reprinted in V. A. Nevezhin, *Zastol'nye rechi Stalina* (Moscow: AIRO-XX, 2003), 470–72.

3. "Vystuplenie tovarishcha I. V. Stalina na prieme v kremle v chest' komandui-ushchikh voiskami krasnoi armii," *Pravda*, May 25, 1945, 1.

4. For analysis of the toast's content, see Brandenberger, *National Bolshevism*, 130–32; Erik van Ree, *The Political Thought of Joseph Stalin: A Study in Twentieth-Century Revolutionary Patriotism* (London: RoutledgeCurzon, 2003), 194–99.

5. Stalin drew on specific practices of Georgian toasting with which he was undoubtedly familiar. For a discussion of these practices, see Mary Ellen Chatwin, "Tamadoba: Drinking Social Cohesion at the Georgian Table," in *Drinking: Anthropological Approaches*, ed. Igor de Garine and Valerie de Garine (New York: Berghahn Books, 2001), 181–90.

6. The term first appeared in the Soviet dictionary for literary Russian, the *Tolkovyi slovar' russkogo iazyka*, in 1940. D. N. Ushakov and B. M. Volin, eds., *Tolkovyi slovar' russkogo iazyka* (Moscow: Sovetskaia entsiklopediia, 1940), 650.

7. For an ethnographic analysis of the qualities expected of a *tamada*, see Florian Mühlfried, "Banquets, Grant-Eaters, and the Red Intelligentsia in Post Soviet Georgia," *Central Eurasian Studies Review* 4, no. 1 (2005): 16–19.

8. For a description of the first process, see Gronow, *Caviar with Champagne*; for the second, see Terry Martin, "Modernizing or Neo-Traditionalism? Ascribed Nationality and Soviet Primordialism," in *Stalinism: New Directions*, ed. Sheila Fitzpatrick (London: Routledge, 2000), 348–67.

9. On the diffusion of Indian cuisine in Britain, see Troy Bickham, "Eating the Empire: Intersections of Food, Cookery and Imperialism in Eighteenth-Century Britain," *Past & Present*, no. 198 (2008): 71–109.

10. Carol Helstosky, *Garlic and Oil: Politics and Food in Italy* (Oxford: Berg, 2004), 63–126.

11. The tastes and sensibilities of this new middle class are described in Vera Dunham, *In Stalin's Time: Middleclass Values in Soviet Fiction* (Cambridge: Cambridge University Press, 1976).

12. Modern Georgia's most famous painter, Niko Pirosmani (1862–1918) created iconic images of the Georgian table, some of them commissioned as signboards for Tbilisi's taverns and restaurants.

13. Men not only led the toasting but also the polyphonic singing that accompanied a Georgian feast. See Nino Tsitsishvili, "'A Man Can Sing and Play Better than a Woman': Singing and Patriarchy at the Georgian *Supra* Feast," *Ethnomusicology* 50, no. 3 (1996): 452–93.

14. Norbert Elias, *The Civilizing Process: Sociogenetic and Psychogenetic Investigations*, ed. Eric Dunning, Johan Goudsblom, and Stephen Mennell, trans. Edmund Jephcott (Oxford: Basil Blackwell, 2000).

15. Pierre Bourdieu writes of the correlation of food consumption practices and class aspirations in *Distinction: A Social Critique of the Judgment of Taste*, trans. Richard Nice (Cambridge, MA: Harvard University Press, 1984), 176–200.

16. Many observers have remarked on the emergence of a Soviet middle class in the 1930s. Trotsky disparaged them as "bureaucrats" in *The Revolution Betrayed*, trans. Max Eastman (Mineola: Dover Publications, 2004); Milovan Djilas called them a "new class," in *The New Class. An Analysis of the Communist System* (New York: Praeger, 1957). Among their ranks were the *vydvizhentsy*, the professionals of working-class background whom Sheila Fitzpatrick

argued were ultimately the main stakeholders of the revolution. Fitzpatrick discusses the place of the *vydvizhentsy* in the new Soviet middle class in *The Cultural Front: Power and Culture in Revolutionary Russia* (Ithaca, NY: Cornell University Press, 1992), 1–15.

17. Sheila Fitzpatrick, "'Middle-Class Values' and Soviet Life in the 1930s," in *Soviet Society and Culture: Essays in Honor of Vera S. Dunham*, ed. Terry L. Thompson and Richard Sheldon (Boulder, CO: Westview Press, 1988), 25.

18. In 1936 Anastas Mikoian made explicit the beginnings of a corresponding shift in the state's view of alcohol, noting that "life has become more joyous, which means it is permitted to drink, though only in a way that does not cause the loss of one's intellect or damage one's health." Cited in *Kniga o vkusnoi i zdorovoi pishche* (Moscow: Pishchepromizdat, 1953), 79.

19. For a description of late imperial restaurant culture, see Louise McReynolds, *Russia at Play: Leisure Activities at the End of the Tsarist Era* (Ithaca, NY: Cornell University Press, 2003), 196–210.

20. Rusudan Gorgiladze, *Savoring Georgia: A Personal Journey Through Time and Taste* (Tbilisi: Cezanne, 2013), 86, 136–39, 141.

21. Paul Manning, *The Semiotics of Drink and Drinking* (London: Continuum Publishing Group, 2012), 175. The tendency to hold the *supra* indoors began in the late nineteenth century and became even more prevalent in the Soviet period.

22. Harsha Ram, "The Literary Origins of the Georgian Feast: The Cosmopolitan Poetics of a National Ritual" (unpublished article, 2014). Ram argues that Georgian toasts may have drawn on themes from Russian romantic literature.

23. McReynolds, *Russia at Play*, 204.

24. Halina Rothstein and Robert A. Rothstein, "The Beginnings of Soviet Culinary Arts," in *Food in Russian History and Culture*, ed. Musya Glants and Joyce Toomre (Bloomington: Indiana University Press), 177–94.

25. According to Georgian ethnographer Vakhtang Chikovani, seasonal and long-term migration by residents of western Georgia's Racha region working as bakers and cooks along Russia's railway system was fairly common by the late imperial period. Personal communication to author.

26. In this sense, Obshchepit took on the task of "civilizing" Soviet appetites, a process which, according to Stephen Mennell, occurred over the course of centuries in France and England. See his *All Manners of Food: Eating and Taste in England and France From the Middle Ages to the Present* (New York: Blackwell, 1985).

27. For a discussion of Mikoian's crucial role, see Edward Geist, "Cooking Bolshevik: Anastas Mikoian and the Making of the "Book about Delicious and Healthy Food," *Russian Review* 71, no. 2 (2012): 295–313.

28. Anton Masterovoy addresses the recurrent nature of such debates in "Eating Soviet: Food and Culture in the USSR, 1917–1991" (PhD diss., City University of New York, 2013).

29. Geist, "Cooking Bolshevik," 301.

30. See the voluminous 1956 *Kulinariia*, recently reprinted. *Kulinariia: superkniga dlia gurmanov* (Moscow: Voskresenie, 1996), 32.

31. Geist, "Cooking Bolshevik," 304. Jewish recipes were published in A. B. Gutchina, S. I. Mesropian, and V. M. Tamarkin, *50 bliud evreiskoi kukhni* (Moscow: Gostorgizdat, 1939).

32. Lenin as quoted by Leon Trotsky in "On Lenin's Testament" *New International*, July 1934.
33. Miklos Kun, *Stalin: An Unknown Portrait* (Budapest: Central European University Press, 2003), 288–89.
34. Hoover Institution Archives, "N. A. Lakoba Papers," Box 1: 43.
35. RGASPI, f. 558, op. 11, d. 765, ll. 75–76.
36. Hoover Institution Archives, "N. A. Lakoba Papers," Box 3.
37. Grapes for the production of Soviet champagne were cultivated in southern Russia, Georgia, and Crimea. See Gronow, *Caviar with Champagne*, 17–30.
38. Kandid Charkviani, *gantsdili da naazrevi, 1906–1994* (Tbilisi: merani, 2004), 410.
39. Vladimir Loginov, *Teni Stalina* (Moscow: Sovremennik, 2000), 23–27. The details of Aleksandre Egnatashvili's personal history were obtained in an interview with Eteri Egnatashvili, his daughter, and Tinatin Egnatashvili, his great niece.
40. Eteri and Tinatin Egnatashvili, interview by author.
41. Khrushchev, *Vospominaniia*, 2: 55–56.
42. Elena Osokina, *Our Daily Bread: Socialist Distribution and the Art of Survival in Stalin's Russia*, ed. Kate Transchel, trans. Greta Bucher (Armonk, NY: M. E. Sharpe, 2001), 184–88.
43. Montefiore, *Young Stalin*, 317–19.
44. Mikoian, *Tak bylo*, 353–54.
45. Mikoian, *Tak bylo*, 353.
46. Khrushchev, *Vospominaniia*, 2: 118.
47. Djilas, *Conversations with Stalin*, trans. Michael B. Petrovich (New York: Harcourt, Brace and World, 1962), 75–77.
48. Djilas, *Conversations*, 111. Georgians consider beer to be unsuitable for toasting, whereas toasting with wine and spirits is acceptable. In Georgia, one might make a toast with beer as a display of sarcasm.
49. Djilas, *Conversations*, 115.
50. Allilueva, *Tol'ko odin god*, 348–49.
51. V. V. Pokhlebkin, *Kukhnia veka* (Moscow: Polifakt, 2000), 177. The cookbooks were: Gutchina et al, *50 bliud evreiskoi kukhni* (Moscow: Gostorgizdat, 1939); V. I. Skhirtladze, *100 bliud gruzinskoi kukhni* (Moscow: Gostorgizdat, 1940); and S. I. Mesropian, *50 bliud azerbaidzhanskoi kukhni* (Moscow: Gostorgizdat, 1940).
52. *Genatsvale* was a Georgian term of endearment that became a recognizably Georgian stock term in Russian jokes about Georgians.
53. From a version of the Soviet-era joke reprinted in a retrospective article on the statue of Moscow's founder. Bogdan Stepovoi, "Iurii Dolgorukii vybral svobodu," *Izvestiia*, 7 September 2007.
54. Today, Gorky Street has reverted to its prerevolutionary name, Tverskaia Street. For more on the Stalinist reconstruction of the Soviet capital, see Timothy J. Colton, *Moscow: Governing the Socialist Metropolis* (Cambridge, MA: Harvard University Press, 1995).
55. N. S. Kiknadze, *Iz opyta moei raboty v restorane "Aragvi"* (Moscow: Gostorgizdat, 1951), 2.
56. Such occasions included events like the celebration of Lenin's one-hundredth birthday. TsGA Moskvy, OKhD, f. 429, op. 1, d. 1323, l. 50.

57. The history of the private rooms was recounted by Viacheslav Galustian, who in 2006 oversaw construction at the site of the old Aragvi restaurant. Interview by author. Moscow, July 26, 2006.

58. Darra Goldstein, *The Georgian Feast: The Vibrant Culture and Savory Food of the Republic of Georgia* (Berkeley: University of California Press, 1999), 10–11.

59. According to an interview with Natela Muntikov-Chachibaia, who grew up among an elite circle of Georgian political figures in Moscow. See "Besedy s Nateloi Muntikovoi," date of last access March 4, 2010, www.slavic-europe. eu/index.php?option=com_content&task=view&id=130&Itemid=1.

60. With Stalin's blessing, the Aragvi was also one of the only restaurants in Moscow to stay open during World War II, according to an interview with Shamil' Khadzhimuratovich Umertaev, who worked at the Aragvi from 1961 to 1996, eventually serving as Deputy Chef. Umertaev trained with Kiknadze. Interview by author. Moscow, June 30, 2008.

61. TsGA Moskvy, OKhD, f. 224, op. 1, d. 147, ll. 23–26.

62. SEAUITsA, f. 2006, op. 1, d. 403, ll. 34–49.

63. RGAE, f. 7971, op. 5, d. 448, ll. 40–41.

64. For basic autobiographical information on the Aragvi's staff, see RGAE, f. 7971, op. 5, d. 447, ll. 39–54. A profile of Kiknadze's career is given in M. Pol'skii, "Vospitanie v trude," *Obshchestvennoe pitanie* 4 (1963): 11–14.

65. RGAE, f. 7971, op. 4, d. 448, ll. 40–41.

66. On the postwar development of Soviet cuisine, see V. V. Pokhlebkin, *Kukhnia veka*, 263–84.

67. The arrests, coming when they did, were likely part of an effort to remove the Stalin-era leadership of the restaurant and re-establish central control. The case is mentioned in the *National Review*, whose American editors mourned the departure of the managers of the fine restaurant, where one could "forget the dreariness of so much of Russia in the sound of Caucasian orchestras." *National Review* 7, no. 15 (1959): 7.

68. TsGA Moskvy, OKhD, f. 224, op. 1, d. 147, ll. 23–26.

69. RGAE, f. 8546, op. 1, d. 1244, ll. 45–112.

70. TsGA Moskvy, OKhD, f. 224, op. 1, d. 147, ll. 23–26; *Obshchestvennoe pitanie v Moskve (kratkii spravochnik)*, (Moscow: Moskovskii rabochii, 1962), 21.

71. Kiknadze shared his recipe in the journal *Obshchestvennoe pitanie* 2 (1961): 28. For a Georgian-style preparation, see Goldstein, *The Georgian Feast*, 102–03.

72. TsGA Moskvy, OKhD, f. 224, op. 1, d. 147, ll. 23–26.

73. "Sotni kushanii na liubom vkuse," *Obshchestvennoe pitanie* 1 (1957): 56.

74. "Sotni kushanii na liubom vkuse," 56.

75. Sh. Kh. Umertaev, interview by author.

76. TsGA Moskvy, OKhD, f. 453, op. 1, d. 1632, ll. 145–62.

77. TsGA Moskvy, OKhD, f. 224, op. 1, d. 245, ll. 1–7.

78. Umertaev, an ethnic Tatar from Moscow, was among them. On Kiknadze's influence, see Tat'iana Tess, "Vospitanie vkusa," *Obshchestvennoe pitanie* 1 (1958): 16–21.

79. Sh. Kh. Umertaev, interview by author.

80. *Obshchestvennoe pitanie v Moskve*, 21, 28–29.

81. E. Vladimirov, "Den' v 'Kavkazskom.'" *Obshchestvennoe pitanie*, 11 (1958): 32–34.

82. TsGA Moskvy, OKhD, f. 224, op. 1, d. 277, ll. 44–45.

83. Cited by B. Anisimov, "Kak pravil'no podbirat' vina k bliudam," *Obshchestvennoe pitanie* 7 (1961): 44–46.
84. John Steinbeck, *A Russian Journal* (New York: Penguin, 1948), 208.
85. "Russia: Where to Dine," *Time*, June 12, 1950, accessed March 4, 2010, www.time.com/time/magazine/article/0,9171,812656,00.html.
86. M. Pol'skii, "Vospitanie v trude," 11–14.
87. Sh. Kh. Umertaev, interview by author.
88. The poem, later set to music, was written in 1969. Vladimir Vysotskii, *Sochineniia v dvukh tomakh: pesni*, ed. A. E. Krylov (Ekaterinburg: Krok-tsentr), 231.
89. "Refugees: Free at Last," *Time*, September 28, 1981, accessed March 4, 2010, www.time.com/time/magazine/article/0,9171,953131-1,00.html.
90. Seweryn Bialer, *The Soviet Paradox: External Expansion, Internal Decline* (New York: Knopf, 1986), 90.
91. Sh. Kh. Umertaev, interview by author.
92. For a survey of postwar trends, see Elena Zubkova, *Russia After the War: Hopes, Illusions, and Disappointments, 1945–1957*, trans. and ed. Hugh Ragsdale (Armonk, NY: M. E. Sharpe, 1998).
93. RGAE, f. 7971, op. 5, d. 452, l. 87. The Deputy Minister's mention of the specific dishes that each republic was famous for followed the formula given in *Kulinariia*, 32.
94. For a discussion of the relative merits of Chinese cuisine among Obshchepit employees, see RGAE, f. 7971, op. 5, d. 454, ll. 125–26.
95. The importance of technology and industrial production techniques is stressed in the introduction to the 1952 edition of *Kniga o vkusnoi i zdorovoi pishche* (Moscow: Pishchepromizdat, 1952).
96. RGAE, f. 7971, op. 5, d. 445, ll. 9–10.
97. Because cilantro was still in scarce supply, *kharcho* could now be made with prepared spice mixtures or sauces.
98. N. Kiknadze, "Tak gotoviat bliudo 'tsypliata-tabaka,'" *Obshchestvennoe pitanie* 2 (1961): 28.
99. "Zharovnaia i aromatizator dlia tsypliat-tabaka," *Obshchestvennoe pitanie* 12 (1961): 38.
100. "Zharovnia s pressom," *Obshchestvennoe pitanie* 12 (1963): 57.
101. RGAE, f. 7971, op. 5, d. 419, ll. 98, 120–21.
102. "Sousy kholodnye," *Obshchestvennoe pitanie* 7 (1967): 32–33.
103. Tess, "Vospitanie vkusa," 16–21.
104. N. Kiknadze, "Uchit' i vospityvat'" *Obshchestvennoe pitanie* 3 (1957): 1–3; Pol'skii, "Vospitanie v trude," 11–14.
105. The book closely reflected the tense political climate in which it was edited. Its introduction defended the culinary arts, claiming they were not "bourgeois" but important for enjoyment and nourishment. See *Kulinariia*, 1–6.
106. There were forty-three Georgian recipes in the "national dishes" section. Armenia was second in terms of national dishes, with twenty-nine recipes. The foreground of the "national dishes" cover page featured a photograph of *shashlyk*. *Kulinariia*, 942.
107. Of the forty-three Georgian recipes, ten were cross-listed and also included in the main section.
108. *Kulinariia*, 968.

109. In "Cooking Bolshevik," Geist notes that 2.5 million copies of the revised edition were printed from 1952 to 1955 and that the volume was printed in East Germany to ensure a high production quality. See Geist, 311–12.
110. "Note from the publisher" in *Kniga o vkusnoi i zdorovoi pishche*, 1952. Reprinted in the 1953 and 1961 editions.
111. For a discussion of the cookbook's intended audience, see Geist, "Cooking Bolshevik," 309.
112. Just a few of the Russian and Georgian recipes listed in *Kniga o vkusnoi i zdorovoi pishche*, 1952, 1961, and 1965 editions.
113. Based upon a reading of the tables of contents of the 1952 and 1965 editions of *Kniga o zdorovoi i vkusnoi pishche*, the number of recognizably Georgian dishes increased from 11 to 18.
114. RGAE, f. 7971, op. 5, d. 444, ll. 22–138. Georgians in particular helped run the growing network of *shashlychnye*. For an example, see R. Bikke, "Master vostochnykh bliud," *Obshchestvennoe pitanie* 8 (1963): 44–46.
115. RGAE, f. 7971, op. 5, d. 447, ll. 39–54, 250.
116. Bikke, "Master vostochnykh bliud," 44.
117. M. Khubelashvili, "Podmoskov'e obkom KPSS obsuzhdaet vopros ob uluchshenii obsluzhivaniia . . ." *Obshchestvennoe pitanie* 6 (1968): 21–22.
118. M. Finkel', "V stolovykh Kieva—gruzinskie bliuda," *Obshchestvennoe pitanie* 10 (1967): 45.
119. For details on Obshchepit's continuing problems, see RGAE, f. 465, op. 1, d. 203, ll. 1–120.
120. RGAE, f. 7971, op. 5, d. 430, ll. 150–63.
121. On the culture of the kitchen table, see Susan E. Reid, "The Khrushchev Kitchen: Domesticating the Scientific-Technological Revolution," *Journal of Contemporary History* 40, no. 2 (2005): 289–316.
122. "T" (participant wished to remain anonymous), interview by author. Moscow, July 17, 2006.
123. Dale Pesmen, *Russia and Soul: An Exploration* (Ithaca, NY: Cornell University Press, 2000), 172.
124. Evgenii Dolmatovskii, *Bylo: zapiski poeta* (Moscow: Sovetskii pisatel', 1975), 403.
125. At one such event, the stenographer recorded an array of toasts by Georgian participants—and toasts given in response by the Russian hosts. RGALI, f. 962, op. 21, d. 35, ll. 16–28.
126. Sh. Kh. Umertaev, interview by author.
127. On the development of internal Soviet tourism in the preceding period, see Anne E. Gorsuch, "'There's No Place Like Home': Soviet Tourism in Late Stalinism," *Slavic Review* 62, no. 4 (2003): 760–85.
128. See, for example, David Chiburdanidze, "50 Years of Georgia," *Travel in the USSR* 2, no. 21 (1971): 19–21.
129. The space-age statue of "Mother Georgia" was constructed in 1958 for the celebration of the 1500th anniversary of Tbilisi's founding.
130. RGAE, f. 7971, op. 5, d. 472, l. 123.
131. RGAE, f. 7971, op. 5, d. 453, l. 155.
132. "Rasskazyvaem o Gruzii," *Obshchestvennoe pitanie* 6 (1965), 1–36.
133. M. Dement'eva, "Trud i krasota: Gruzinskie vpechatleniia," *Obshchestvennoe pitanie* 7 (1965), 15–16.

134. A. Imerilishvili, "I trud i pesnia," *Obshchestvennoe pitanie* 6 (1965): 28–29.

135. *Restoran Aragvi* (Tbilisi: Ministerstvo torgovli GSSR).

136. Ol'ga Grinkrug, "Kurinaia slepota," *Bol'shoi gorod* 20, no. 192 (2007), accessed January 17, 2012, www.bg.ru/article/7072/.

137. Vasil Tsnonev, *Nedelia*, no. 533, cited in *Travel in the USSR* 2, no. 21 (1971): 20.

138. See Tsitsishvili, "'A Man Can Sing and Play Better than a Woman.'"

139. Manning writes about the "disemia" of the *supra*, noting that it could represent a supposedly "antipolitical" space or reproduce the political logic of the Soviet state. Manning, *Semiotics of Drink and Drinking*, 149–50.

140. On the struggle against "harmful traditions," see the discussions of Georgia's Central Committee in 1979. SShSSA, II, f. 14, op. 117, d. 337, ll. 104–10. For details of state-sponsored portrayals of the *supra*, see Manning, *Semiotics of Drink and Drinking*, 148–76.

141. Soviet cooks also frequently substituted ordinary chicken for scarce turkey.

## Chapter 4

1. This description is based upon footage of the Sukhishvili Georgian National Dance Company that retained the original choreography. *Georgian National Dance Company* (Tbilisi: Sukhishvili LTD, 2008).

2. *Dekada gruzinskogo iskusstva i literatury v Moskve: Sbornik materialov* (Tbilisi: Zaria vostoka, 1959), 626–27.

3. In the dance ensemble's program, the Georgian term was transliterated into Russian.

4. D. Dzhavrishvili, *Gruzinskie narodnye tantsy* (1958), cited in Avtandil Tataradze, *Piat' gruzinskikh tantsev* (Tbilisi: Khelovneba, 1981), 5.

5. G. Lebanidze and A. Nikolaev, "Krasochnyi prazdnik vesny i druzhby," *Pravda*, April 2, 1958, 1.

6. The term came from Il'ia Ehrenburg's eponymous 1954 novel *Ottepel': povest'* (Moscow, 1954). For an overview of the concept, see Stephen V. Bittner, *The Many Lives of Khrushchev's Thaw: Experience and Memory in Moscow's Arbat* (Ithaca, NY: Cornell University Press, 2008), 1–13.

7. See Christine Evans, "From *Truth* to *Time*: Soviet Central Television, 1957–1985" (PhD diss., University of California, Berkeley, 2010).

8. RGALI, f. 3162, op. 1, d. 26, l. 3.

9. *Estrada* included a broad range of popular entertainment apart from the "big stage" of classical performance. Richard Stites, *Russian Popular Culture: Entertainment and Society Since 1900* (Cambridge: Cambridge University Press, 1992), 16–22.

10. Georgian *estrada* groups played 316 concerts in Russia in 1969, more than Belarus (199 concerts), Lithuania (164), Ukraine (98), Armenia (74), and others. RGALI, f. 3170, op. 1, d. 23, ll. 1–57.

11. Sufian Zhemukhov and Charles King introduce the term "ethnokinetics" to describe forms of "human motion that are locally categorized as essential to collective belonging." Georgian dance signified belonging in this sense, but it also conveyed an important set of meanings to outsiders. See Zhemukhov and King, "Dancing the Nation in the North Caucasus," *Slavic Review* 72, no. 2 (2013): 287–305.

12. Anthropologist Susan A. Reed describes dance as a text with varied and "polysemic" meanings in "The Politics and Poetics of Dance," *Annual Review of Anthropology*, v. 27 (1998): 503–32.

13. On national representation as a form of power, see Anthony Shay, *Choreographic Politics: State Folk Dance Companies, Representation, and Power* (Middletown, CT: Wesleyan University Press, 2002).

14. K. Aimermakher et al, eds., *Doklad N. S. Khrushcheva o kul'te lichnosti Stalina na XX s"ezde KPSS: dokumenty* (Moscow: Rosspen, 2002), 97.

15. Timothy Blauvelt, "Status Shift and Ethnic Mobilisation in the March 1956 Events in Georgia," *Europe-Asia Studies* 61, no. 4 (2009): 651–68. The rumors of potential deportations were reported by a Georgian participant in the 1956 protests in an interview given in Lev Lur'e and Irina Maliarova, *1956 god: seredina veka* (Saint Petersburg: Neva, 2007), 146.

16. The precise number of civilian casualties is subject to dispute, though in a classified briefing the Georgian KGB reported twenty-one killed and fifty-four wounded. SShSSA, I, f. 6, d. 159, ll. 19–26.

17. The idea of cultural concessions is also suggested by Suny in *Making of the Georgian Nation*, 304.

18. The notion of cultural continuity with the Stalin era and even the pre-1917 past accords with some of the arguments presented in Denis Kozlov and Eleonory Gilburd, eds., *The Thaw: Soviet Society and Culture During the 1950s and 1960s* (Toronto: University of Toronto Press, 2013). Other scholars have criticized the concept of post-Stalinism itself by finding connections that spanned the late Stalinist era and the period following the leader's death. See, for example, Juliane Fürst, *Stalin's Last Generation: Soviet Post-War Youth and the Emergence of Mature Socialism* (Oxford: Oxford University Press, 2010).

19. The idea of a longer Thaw in music is suggested by Peter J. Schmelz, *Such Freedom, If Only Musical: Unofficial Soviet Music during the Thaw* (Oxford: Oxford University Press, 2009). Schmelz, however, focuses on experimental composers rather than popular musicians.

20. Russian-language press clipping collected by actor Akaki Khorava in SEAUITsA, LKh, f. 212, op. 1, d. 58.

21. Reed, "Politics and Poetics of Dance," 506–07.

22. Frolova-Walker, *Russian Music and Nationalism*, 314.

23. Armen Tigranian's *Anoush*, composed and privately staged in 1912, was the first Armenian opera performed in the Russian Empire. Donald Jay Grout and Hermine Weigel Williams, *A Short History of Opera* (New York: Columbia University Press, 2003), 672.

24. For a study of Soviet-era musical specialists in Central Asia, see Theodore Craig Levin, *The Hundred Thousand Fools of God: Musical Travels in Central Asia (and Queens, New York)* (Bloomington: Indiana University Press, 1996).

25. Mars and Altman, "Cultural Bases of Soviet Georgia's Second Economy," 548–49.

26. Soviet cultural production was dominated for many years by Ekaterina Furtseva, arguably turning the Soviet Ministry of Culture into a "woman's kingdom" against the backdrop of a male-dominated Soviet state. See Laurence Senelick, "'A Woman's Kingdom': Minister of Culture Furtseva and Censorship in the Post-Stalinist Russian Theatre," *New Theatre Quaterly* 26, no. 1 (2010): 16–24.

27. In the imperial period, Georgian singer Keto Japaridze was famous throughout Russia. In the early Soviet period, a Georgian woman, Tamara Tsereteli, was praised as "the most talented performer of gypsy songs." See David MacFayden, *Songs for Fat People: Affect, Emotion, and Celebrity in the Russian Popular Song, 1900–1955* (Montreal: McGill-Queen's University Press, 2002), 29–32.

28. Gulbat Toradze, *Kompozitory Gruzii* (Tbilisi: Khelovneba, 1973), 169–74.

29. Igor Moiseev, "Dusha naroda v tantse," *Vechernii Tbilisi*, June 12, 1967.

30. For background, see Susan Layton, *Russian Literature and Empire* (Cambridge: Cambridge University Press, 1994); Harsha Ram, *The Imperial Sublime: A Russian Poetics of Empire* (Madison: University of Wisconsin Press, 2003).

31. The "Dzhigity" dance was from a 1968 performance. RGALI, f. 3162, op. 1, d. 769, ll. 6–7.

32. In his poem "Tamara," Lermontov created an alluring image of an enchanting but dangerous Georgian princess. Il'ia Il'f and Evgenii Petrov allude to Lermontov's poem in their satirical novel, *Dvenadtsat' stul'ev* (Moscow: Izd-vo khudozhestvennoi literatury, 1959), first published in 1928. On the trope of the aristocratic Georgian woman in popular fiction, see Jeffrey Brooks, *When Russia Learned to Read: Literacy and Popular Literature, 1861–1917* (Princeton, NJ: Princeton University Press, 1985), 214–45.

33. Martin, *The Affirmative Action Empire*, 443; Frolova-Walker, *Russian Music and Nationalism*, 313–14.

34. RGALI, f. 962, op. 21, d. 35, ll. 29–30.

35. Among the press clippings collected by Khorava in SEAUITsA, LKh, f. 212, op. 1, d. 58. For more on the tour, see *Gastrol'naia poezdka 1-go gosteatra Gruzii imeni Rustaveli* (Tbilisi: Gos. izd-vo SSRG, 1930).

36. This description of Sukhishvili's life and career is based in part on his Georgian language memoir, *mogonebebi* (Tbilisi, 2008),

37. In Paris, Gudiashvili associated with the Russian modernists Natalia Goncharova and Mikhail Larionov as well as the Italian painter Amadeo Modigliani.

38. Mikeladze's production of *Keto and Kote* survived his death in the Great Purges, and the opera remained popular, enjoying a revival in the 1970s when it was restaged in Russian at Leningrad's Bolshoi Academic Theater by Tbilisi native Georgii Tovstonogov, the son of a Russian nobleman and a Georgian classical singer. Tovstonogov's reworking drew on Tsagareli's original novel, *khanuma*, and thus bore the title of the book. Anatoly Smeliansky, *The Russian Theatre After Stalin*, trans. Patrick Miles (Cambridge: Cambridge University Press, 1999), 13–15.

39. SEAUITsA, LKh, f. 2, op. 3, d. 27, l. 229.

40. Nadezhda Nadezhdina, "S beregov Kury." *Vechernaia Moskva*, February 24, 1967.

41. SShSSA, II, f. 14, op. 20, d. 177, l. 27.

42. According to Ramishvili, at a Kremlin banquet in the late 1930s, Beria remarked that all members of the Ramishvili family were "Mensheviks" who "should be shot." Sukhishvili, *mogonebebi*, 31.

43. RGALI, f. 648, op. 1, d. 3111, ll. 1–14.

44. The singing is discussed in a KGB report sent to Moscow and reprinted in Lur'e and Maliarova, *1956 god*, 156–58.

45. See Shevardnadze's interview in Lur'e and Maliarova, *1956 god*, 137–38.

46. RGANI, f. 5, op. 3, d. 60.

47. RGANI, f. 5, op. 31, d. 222, ll. 38–46.

48. SEAUITsA, LKh, f. 80, op. 1, d. 1020.

49. On Russian nationalist sentiment in the party, see Nikolai Mitrokhin, *Russkaia partiia: dvizhenie russkikh natsionalistov v SSSR, 1953–1985 gody* (Moscow: Novoe literaturnoe obozrenie, 2003).

50. On the broader context of the March 1956 events in Georgia, see Jeremy Smith, *Red Nations: The Nationalities Experience in and after the USSR* (Cambridge: Cambridge University Press, 2013), 200–04.

51. For example, the "Days of Culture and Art of Soviet Georgia in Moscow," held in 1967. "Prekrasnaia kul'tura sovetskoi Gruzii," *Vechernii Tbilisi*, June 14, 1967.

52. Moscow's importance was commented on by Georgian theater director Robert Sturua, speaking at a festival of Georgian culture in the Soviet capital in 1982. *Dni Gruzii v Mosvke* (Tbilisi: Khelovneba, 1982).

53. Shay, *Choreographic Politics*, 10.

54. Shay, *Choreographic Politics*, 59

55. On the history of the Moiseev ensemble and its repertoire, see Lidiia Shamina, *Teatr Igoria Moiseeva* (Moscow: Teatralis, 2012).

56. Igor Stravinsky, *Sovetskaia muzyka* 12 (1966), cited in a promotional booklet for the Rustavi Ensemble. SEAUITsA, LKh, f. 44, op. 3, d. 24.

57. SEAUITsA, LKh, f. 80, op. 1, d. 1020.

58. SEAUITsA, LKh, f. 80, op. 1, d. 1020.

59. SEAUITsA, LKh, f. 44, op. 3, d. 24.

60. SEAUITsA, LKh, f. 44, op. 3, d. 24. For more on his family's history, see Erkomaishvili's memoirs, *khma utsnauri* (Tbilisi: sakartvelo, 1999).

61. SEAUITsA, LKh, f. 44, op. 5, d. 16, 72.

62. RGALI, f. 3170, op. 1, d. 102, ll. 1–53.

63. On Soviet soccer in the age of television, see Robert Edelman, "Playing Catch-Up: Soviet Media and Soccer Hooliganism, 1965–75," in *The Socialist Sixties: Crossing Borders in the Second World*, ed. Anne E. Gorsuch and Diane Koenker (Bloomington: Indiana University Press, 2013), 268–86; Manfred Zeller, "'Our Own Internationale,' 1966: Dynamo Kiev Fans Between Local Identity and Transnational Imagination," *Kritika: Explorations in Russian and Eurasian History* 12, no. 1 (2011): 53–82.

64. N. Dumbadze, M. Karchava, Z. Bolkvadze, and G. Pirtskhalava, *"Dinamo" Tbilisi* (Tbilisi: Soiuz zhurnalistov Gruzii, 1960).

65. Avtandil Gogoberidze, *S miachom s trideviat' zemel'* (Tbilisi: Soiuz zhurnalistov Gruzii, 1965), 57–58.

66. *Dekada gruzinskogo iskusstva i literatury v Moskve*, 247. The term "beautiful game" entered international parlance with Brazil's victory in the 1958 World Cup, an approximation of the Portuguese *jogo bonito* ("beautiful play"). Richard Giulianotti, *Football: A Sociology of the Global Game* (Cambridge: Polity Press, 1999), 26. For many Soviet commentators, the Georgian style of play evoked the "beautiful game" as played by successful South American teams.

67. RGALI, f. 3162, op. 1, d. 297, ll. 1–72.

68. RGALI, f. 3162, op. 1, d. 33, l. 1.

69. RGALI, f. 3162, op. 1, d. 33, ll. 2–8.

70. RGALI, f. 3162, op. 1, d. 1471, ll. 1–50.
71. RGALI, f. 3162, op. 1, d. 755, ll. 16–21, d. 1675, l. 11.
72. RGALI, f. 3162, op. 2, d. 1198, ll. 1–4.
73. RGALI f. 3162, op. 2, d. 68, ll. 3–4.
74. RGALI f. 3162, op. 2, d. 68, l. 4.
75. RGALI f. 3162, op. 2, d. 68, l. 5.
76. D. Toradze, "Iarkoe muzykal'noe proizvedenie" *Vechernii Tbilisi*, October 26, 1976.
77. RGALI, f. 3162, op. 1, d. 297, l. 47.
78. RGALI, f. 3162, op. 1, d. 298, l. 17.
79. Stites distinguishes between Khrushchev's "spring" from 1953 to 1964 and the "Brezhnev culture wars" from 1964 to 1984 in *Russian Popular Culture*. Katerina Clark similarly observes that Khrushchev's ouster in October 1964 "marked the end of cultural liberalization" in *The Soviet Novel: History as Ritual* (Bloomington: Indiana University Press, 2000), 234.
80. In *The Soviet Novel*, Clark's focus is obviously on literature. Nancy Condee also argues for literature's primary importance, noting that the term "Thaw" was taken from a novel. However, when one takes the Thaw as a more general metaphor for cultural liberalization and looks at film, music, and visual art, new chronologies are needed, a point made by Schmelz in *Such Freedom, If Only Musical*. See Condee, "Cultural Codes of the Thaw," in *Nikita Khrushchev*, ed. William Taubman, Sergei Khrushchev, and Abbott Gleason (New Haven, CT: Yale University Press, 2000), 138–59.
81. Frederick S. Starr, *Red and Hot: The Fate of Jazz in the Soviet Union* (New York: Limelight Editions, 1985), 270.
82. Including Apel'sin, Karavan, Radar, Rock-Hotel, and Ruya. These bands are discussed by Artemy Troitsky, *Back in the USSR: The True Story of Rock in Russia* (London: Omnibus Press, 1987).
83. The two Moscow-based agencies repeatedly came into conflict. See, for example, TsGA Moskvy, OKhD, f. 429, op. 1, d. 2169, ll. 1–4.
84. Starr, *Red and Hot*, 229–30.
85. When the Georgian *estrada* group Iveria toured Hungary in 1972 and 1973, their leader reported that they had been warmly received by Hungarian audiences, the toughest of critics because "the best performers of the *estrada* genre regularly perform in Hungary." RGALI, f. 3162, op. 1, d. 1410, ll. 56–59.
86. The quote is from an article published in Astrakhan's *Volga* newspaper, September 15, 1965, and cited with praise in an official meeting of musical directors. RGALI, f. 3162, op. 1, d. 297, l. 16.
87. Aficionados of underground Soviet rock scoffed at much of the production of Soviet VIAs, seeing them as co-opted, politically sanctioned, and sentimental. However, Troitsky, a Soviet rock critic, admits that the albums of Stas Namin's Tsvety were the "first Soviet rock records" and "their sound and the natural quality of the vocals differed from all the VIA product coming off the conveyor." Troitsky, *Back in the USSR*, 32–33.
88. From the ensemble's website, accessed April 22, 2010, www.orera.reclama.ru/history.htm.
89. Vakhtang Kikabidze, interview by author. Tbilisi, November 26, 2008.
90. Kikabidze, interview by author.
91. Nani Bregvadze, interview by author. Tbilisi, November 5, 2008.
92. RGALI, f. 3162, d. 1411, ll. 1–13.

93.  This description comes from a performance of the band in the 1970 film *orera, sruli svlit* (*Orera, Full Speed Ahead*).

94.  RGALI, f. 3162, op. 1, d. 755, ll. 16–18. The description of the song is based on a recording made by Orera in 1967, part of the collection *VIA Orera* (Melodiia, 2008).

95.  RGALI, f. 3162, op. 1, d. 1411, l. 10.

96.  From a performance of the band in *orera, sruli svlit*.

97.  Based on a recording from 1967, *VIA Orera*.

98.  RGALI, f. 3162, op. 1, d. 529, l. 7.

99.  Based on a 1973 recording, *VIA Orera*.

100. RGALI, f. 3164, op. 1, d. 617, l. 52. The group played thirty concerts between November 25 and December 18, 1970, giving a sense of the high level of public demand and the rigors of the ensemble's tour schedule.

101. According to the group's website, accessed April 28, 2011, www.orera.rec-lama.ru/history.htm.

102. RGALI, f. 3162, op. 1, d. 529, l. 7 and d. 755, l. 16.

103. Iveria pushed the genre of Soviet multiethnic performance even further with their rock opera, *Svad'ba soek*, televised for Soviet viewers in 1984.

104. Bregvadze, interview by author.

105. According to an interview with Bregvadze available online, date of last access April 28, 2011, www.tvr.khv.ru/number/2005/14/arh.html.

106. Program archived in RGALI, f. 3055, op. 1, d. 563, ll. 1–2.

107. Bregvadze, interview by author.

108. TsGA Moskvy, OKhD, f. 429, op. 1, d. 3223, ll. 6–8, 38, 67.

109. Gurian folk songs are distinguished by their remarkably complex polyphonic structure, which can sound almost discordant to a first-time listener.

110. Bruce Grant traces the long history of the naif archetype in *The Captive and the Gift: Cultural Histories of Sovereignty in Russia and the Caucasus* (Ithaca, NY: Cornell University Press, 2009), 137–43.

111. Danelia recounts the story of his partnership with Kikabidze in his memoir, *Tostuemyi p'et do dna* (Moscow: Eksmo, 2006), 217–18.

112. According to the film's production notes. RGALI, f. 2944, op. 4, d. 3892, ll. 1–3.

113. Daneliia, *Tostuemyi p'et do dna*, 217–18.

114. Performance available online, accessed August 16, 2010, www.youtube.com/watch?v=4rlxdkFwrho.

115. RGASPI, f. 2944, op. 4, d. 4092, l. 3.

116. On Jews as the self-styled heirs of the Russian intelligentsia, see Slezkine, *Jewish Century*, 233–34. Tanny argues that a Jewish performative idiom lived on during the Thaw as part of the Yiddish inflected "myth of Old Odessa," though this myth was implicitly rather than explicitly Jewish and increasingly deployed by non-Jews. See Tanny, *City of Rogues and Schnorrers*, 131–32.

117. Official website of the Kolkhida ensemble, date of last access August 16, 2010, http://tbilisi-trip.narod.ru/Kolxida.html.

118. *Dni Gruzii v Moskve.*

119. V. Gulashvili, "'Kolkhida' rozhdena v Moskve," *Vechernii Tbilisi*, March 9, 1968, 3.

120. *Dni Gruzii v Moskve.*

121. *Dni Gruzii v Moskve.*

## Chapter 5

1. Materials on the case were collected in a report by the Georgian branch of the KGB. On the discovery of the body, see SShSSA, I, f. 6, d. 29174-74, t. 1, ll. 8–9.
2. Many residents of western Georgia are Mingrelians, considered by the Soviets as a separate nationality until 1930, when they were grouped together with the Georgians for census purposes. It is a matter of some controversy whether Mingrelian constitutes a separate language closely related to Georgian, or a dialect of Georgian. After 1938 publications in Mingrelian were all but banned, and by the time of the events described in this chapter Mingrelian would have been considered by most an informal dialect spoken at home and among acquaintances. Mingrelians can also be distinguished by their surnames, which generally end in -ia or -ava, instead of -adze ("son of") or -shvili ("child of").
3. SShSSA, I, f. 6, d. 29174-74, t. 15, ll. 109–30.
4. SShSSA, I, f. 6, d. 29174-74, t. 15, ll. 124–25.
5. SShSSA, I, f. 6, d. 29174-74, t. 2, ll. 75–76.
6. SShSSA, I, f. 6, d. 29174-74, t. 11, l. 110.
7. SShSSA, I, f. 6, d. 29174-74, t. 11, l. 112.
8. SShSSA, I, f. 6, d. 29174-74, t. 15, ll. 113, 126.
9. SShSSA, I, f. 6, d. 29174-74, t. 16, l. 71. The Ministry of Internal Affairs and the KGB were separate institutions, the former tasked primarily with ensuring domestic order, the latter concerned with state security, ideological subversion, and domestic and international espionage.
10. SShSSA, I, f. 6, d. 29174-74, t. 17, ll. 47–55.
11. SShSSA, I, f. 6, d. 29174-74, t. 15, l. 126.
12. The term "second economy" was coined by economist Gregory Grossman in his classic article, "The Second Economy of the USSR," *Problems of Communism* 25, no. 5 (1977): 25–40. Grossman uses the term to refer to economic activity conducted for private gain that was either illicit or technically legal but "ideologically alien" to the Soviet system.
13. Dunham, *In Stalin's Time.*
14. James R. Millar, "The Little Deal: Brezhnev's Contribution to Acquisitive Socialism," *Slavic Review* 44, no. 4 (1985): 694–706.
15. Small-scale trading had never completely vanished in the Soviet Union. Julie Hessler provides a history of trade during the first decades of Soviet power in *A Social History of Soviet Trade: Trade Policy, Retail Practices, and Consumption* (Princeton, NJ: Princeton University Press, 2004).
16. Millar, "The Little Deal," 694–97.
17. The term "acquisitive socialism" is Millar's. See "The Little Deal," 697.
18. For a discussion of these jokes, see Emil A. Draitser, *Taking Penguins to the Movies: Ethnic Humor in Russia* (Detroit: Wayne State University Press, 1998).
19. Perhaps more than in any other Soviet republic, Russian was a secondary language in Georgia while Georgian was the primary language of official and private life. Nevertheless, most Georgians, especially the well educated and the ambitious, spoke fluent Russian.
20. Mars and Altman describe Georgians as "gambling entrepreneurs concerned to spend and display" in "The Cultural Bases of Soviet Georgia's Second Economy," 555. The reference is to Weber's *The Protestant Ethic and the "Spirit" of Capitalism*, trans. Peter R. Baehr and Gordon C. Wells (New York: Penguin, 2002).

21. *Blat* became especially important with the growth of the second economy in the Brezhnev era. See Alena D. Ledeneva, *Russia's Economy of Favours: Blat, Networking, and Informal Exchange* (Cambridge: Cambridge University Press, 1998).

22. Mars and Altman speak of a "fusion of work life and private life" among Georgian networks in "The Cultural Bases of Soviet Georgia's Second Economy," 555.

23. Millar, "The Little Deal," 698.

24. On the colonial dimensions of the sugar industry in particular, see Sidney Mintz, *Sweetness and Power: The Place of Sugar in Modern History* (New York: Viking, 1985). For tsarist understandings of the subtropics, see the journal of the Batumi Agricultural Society, *Russkie subtropiki*, published in 1912–1913; on Soviet subtropical development in neighboring Sochi, see Johanna Conterio, "Inventing the Subtropics: An Environmental History of Sochi, 1929–36," *Kritika: Explorations in Russian and Eurasian History* 16, no. 1 (2015): 91–120.

25. Ministerstvo sel'skogo khoziastva Gruzinskoi SSR, *Gruziia—osnovnaia baza subtropicheskogo khoziastva SSSR* (Tbilisi: Sabchota Sakartvelo, 1971), 3.

26. RGAE, f. 4372, op. 15, d. 377, l. 36.

27. *Gruziia—osnovnaia baza subtropicheskogo khoziastva SSSR*, 14.

28. RGAE, f. 7486, op. 40, d. 3316, ll. 1–193.

29. A collection of Beria's reports to Stalin on Georgian agriculture are reprinted in Vakhtang Guruli and Omar Tushurashvili, eds., "Correspondence Between Lavrenty Beria and Jospeh Stalin," *Archival Bulletin* 3, appendix (2008): 4–106.

30. RGAE, f. 4372, op. 15, d. 377, l. 17.

31. Looking primarily, though not exclusively, at capitalist economies, Appadurai argues that commodities have "social lives" worthy of investigation. See Appadurai, *The Social Life of Things*.

32. See Zubkova, *Russia After the War*.

33. Tsentral'noe statisticheskoe upravlenie SSSR, *Narodnoe khoziastvo SSSR, 1972* (Moscow: Statistika, 1973), 350–52.

34. Tsentral'noe statisticheskoe upravlenie Gruzinskoi SSR, *Narodnoe khoziastvo Gruzinskoi SSR za 60 let* (Tbilisi: Sabchota Sakartvelo, 1980), 245.

35. Tsentral'noe statisticheskoe upravlenie Gruzinskoi SSR, *Gruziia v tsifrakh* (Tbilisi: Sabchota Sakartvelo, 1985), 60.

36. Tsentral'noe statisticheskoe upravlenie Gruzinskoi SSR, *Gruziia v tsifrakh* (1985), 60.

37. Tsentral'noe statisticheskoe upravlenie Gruzinskoi SSR, *Gruziia v tsifrakh* (Tbilisi: Sabchota Sakartvelo, 1969), 7

38. Tsentral'noe statisticheskoe upravlenie Gruzinskoi SSR, *Gruziia v tsifrakh* (Tbilisi: Sabchota Sakartvelo, 1965), 37

39. *Pavil'on Gruzinskaia SSR: Putevoditel'* (Moscow: Sel'khozgiz, 1939); *Vystavka Dostizhenii Narodnogo Khoziastva SSSR: Putevoditel'* (Moscow: Gos. nauchno-tekhnicheskii izd-vo mashino stroitel'noi literatury, 1959), 44–47.

40. *Vystavka Dostizhenii Narodnogo Khoziastva SSSR: Putevoditel'*, 44.

41. RGAE, f. 8546, op. 1, d. 923, l. 36.

42. *Pavil'on Gruzinskaia SSR* (Moscow: Gos. izd-vo sel'skokhoziastvennoi literatury, 1954), 5–9.

43. *Gruzinskaia Sovetskaia Sotsialisticheskaia Respublika na VDNKh SSSR* (Moscow: VDNKh SSSR, 1972), 19.

44. RGASPI, f. M-3, op. 15, d. 95, l. 53.
45. RGASPI, f. M-3, op. 15, d. 95, l. 7.
46. RGASPI, f. M-3, op. 15, d. 95, ll. 49–57.
47. RGAE, f. 8546, op. 1, d. 547, ll. 49–50.
48. RGAE, f. 8546, op. 1, d. 1244, ll. 1–11.
49. Exact production figures for flowers are hard to come by, as they were seldom listed separately in economic statistics, but instead considered as a branch of horticulture.
50. RGAE, f. 7486, op. 35, d. 60, ll. 282–83.
51. RGAE, f. 7486, op. 40, d. 3316, l. 181.
52. On the Soviet Union's car culture, see Lewis H. Siegelbaum, *Cars for Comrades: The Life of the Soviet Automobile* (Ithaca, NY: Cornell University Press, 2008).
53. Khrushchev, *Vospominaniia*, 2: 59, translated by Shriver in *Memoirs of Nikita Krushchev*, 2: 63.
54. V. P Astaf'ev, *Lovia peskarei v Gruzii* in *Sobranie sochinenii v piatnadtsati tomakh*, Tom 9 (Krasnoyarsk: Ofset, 1997), translated by Draitser in *Taking Penguins to the Movies*, 37.
55. N. S. Khrushchev, *Vospominaniia*, 2: 59, translated by Shriver in *Memoirs of Nikita Krushchev*, 2: 63.
56. Draitser, *Taking Penguins to the Movies*, 41–42.
57. V. V. Kulikov, ed., *Anekdoty ot . i do . . .* (St. Petersburg: Kristall, 1998), 476–77.
58. For a study of the influence of Soviet ideology on the historiography of the Caucasus, see Tillett, *The Great Friendship*.
59. The outmigration of Russians was part of a trend toward ethnic homogenization in the southern republics. See Brian D. Silver, "Population Redistribution and the Ethnic Balance in Transcaucasia," in *Transcaucasia: Nationalism and Social Change*, ed. Ronald Grigor Suny (Ann Arbor: Michigan Slavic Publications, 1983), 373–95.
60. As Jeremy Smith notes, between 1971 and Brezhnev's death, all of the appointees to the Politburo were Slavs: seven Russians and one Ukrainian. See Smith, *Red Nations*, 217.
61. *Kommunisticheskaia partiia Gruzii v tsifrakh (1921–1970 gg.) (Sbornik statisticheskikh materialov)* (Tbilisi, 1971), 176, 265, cited in Suny, *Making of the Georgian Nation*, 314.
62. RGANI, f. 5, op. 31, d. 60, ll. 79–85.
63. RGANI, f. 5, op. 31, d. 60, ll. 79–85.
64. For examples, see RGANI, f. 5, op. 31, d. 60, ll. 93–94; GARF, f. R-7523, op. 107, d. 185, ll. 6–7.
65. For press coverage of these lavish homes, see "Del'tsy i tuneiadtsy v kurortnykh gorodakh," *Pravda*, August 3, 1963, 3. The fact that local authorities often turned a blind eye to such excesses was discussed in a report of the Georgian Central Committee in 1964. See SShSSA, II, f. 14, op. 39, d. 265, ll. 61–87.
66. On poor state control of collective farms in general, and Georgia's farms in particular, see Grossman, "Second Economy of the USSR," 25–28.
67. RGAE, f. 7486, op. 40, d. 3316, ll. 118–22.
68. RGAE, f. 4372, op. 66, d. 185, ll. 5–6.
69. *Narodnoe khoziastvo SSSR 1922–1972: Iubileinyi statisticheskii ezhegodnik* (Moscow, 1972), 515; cited in Suny, *Making of the Georgian Nation*, 304.

70. RGANI, f. 5, op. 31, d. 222, ll. 68–69.

71. SShSSA, II, f. 14, op. 52, d. 720.

72. RGANI, f. 5, op. 31, d. 124, l. 79.

73. It is safe to say that Abkhaz standards of hospitality and traditions of wining and dining guests closely resembled those customary among Georgians and other groups in the Caucasus region.

74. "S" (participant wished to remain anonymous), interview by author. Tbilisi, November 4, 2008.

75. "D" (participant wished to remain anonymous), interview by author. Tbilisi, November 4, 2008.

76. Soviet attitudes toward corruption are described by Steven K. Staats in "Corruption in the Soviet System," *Problems of Communism*, no. 21 (1972): 40–47.

77. Konstantin Simis, *USSR: The Corrupt Society* (New York: Simon and Shuster, 1982), 23–24.

78. "Panopticism" is considered to be one of the main principles of the modern penal state. See Michel Foucault, *Discipline and Punish: The Birth of the Prison*, trans. Alan Sheridan (New York: Vintage Books, 1995), 195–228.

79. Withholding or providing false evidence or testimony were violations of articles 182 and 181 of the criminal code of the Russian SFSR, respectively. This policing technique was certainly not unique to law enforcement agents in the Soviet Union, though it was used repeatedly in the Bedia case.

80. SShSSA, I, f. 6, d. 29174-74, t. 15.

81. Items listed in several cases. See SShSSA, I, f. 6, d. 29150-72 (1971-1972); SShSSA, I, f. 6, d. 29156-72 (1972); SShSSA, I, f. 6, d. 29150-72 (1972); SShSSA, I, f. 6, d. 29195-75 (1974).

82. For example, one sailor brought back a dress purchased in Gibraltar for an associate who promised him cognac in return. See SShSSA, I, f. 6, d. 29156-72, l. 28.

83. SShSSA, I, f. 6, d. 29150-72, t. 3, l. 2.

84. Georgian Jews belong to a community that has lived in Georgia for more than two millennia. Members of this community speak Georgian as their native language, have Georgianized surnames, and share many cultural traditions with their Georgian neighbors. See Zakaria Chichinadze and Vakhtang Chikovani, *kartveli ebralebi sakartveloshi* (Tbilisi: metsniereba, 1990).

85. SShSSA, I, f. 6, d. 29150-72, t. 4, l. 47.

86. SShSSA, I, f. 6, d. 29195-75, t. 2, ll. 180–83.

87. SShSSA, II, f. 14, op. 42, d. 318, ll. 10–12.

88. SShSSA, II, f. 14, op. 42, d. 318, ll. 10–11.

89. Efraim Sevela, *Ostanovite samolet—ia slezu!* (Munich: F. Zeuner, 1977), 22–23.

90. SShSSA, II, f. 14, op. 42, d. 318, l. 12.

91. "S," interview by author.

92. For a discussion of Georgian underground entrepreneurs and the criminal world of the 1970s, see Fedor Razzakov, *Bandity semidesiatykh, 1970–1979* (Moscow: Eksmo, 2008).

93. *Del'tsy* was an unofficial term, since private business was banned. The term was, however, used in spoken language and occasionally appears in archival documents when entrepreneurs are accused of large-scale economic crime; Bonacich, "A Theory of Middleman Minorities."

94. Lazishvili's activities are discussed in Razzakov, *Bandity semidesiatykh*.

95. Cited by the journalist Hedrick Smith, who traveled to Georgia around this time. See Smith, *The Russians* (New York: Ballantine Books, 1976), 128.

96. She was also sometimes called Queen Tamar, after Georgia's famous medieval queen. William A. Clark, *Crime and Punishment in Soviet Officialdom: Combating Corruption in the Political Elite, 1965–1990* (Armonk, NY: M. E. Sharpe, 1993), 153–55.

97. Smith, *The Russians*, 129–30.

98. SShSSA, II, f. 14, op. 45, d. 457, ll. 9–14.

99. SShSSA, II, f. 14, op. 45, d. 457, l. 10.

100. SShSSA, II, f. 14, op. 45, d. 457, l. 10.

101. This account of Lazishvili's arrest is given in Clark, *Crime and Punishment*, 155.

102. Lazishvili's connections with Soviet officials are discussed in Simis, *USSR: The Corrupt Society*, 166–68.

103. RGANI, f. 2, op. 3, d. 280, l. 62.

104. Archival records of the Central Committee of the Communist Party of Georgia show that such resolutions were adopted about every five years, with resolutions passed in 1963, 1968, 1974, and 1979. See SShSSA, II, f. 14, op. 39, 44, 49, and 119. Other resolutions passed in 1972 and 1982 accompanied changes in power.

105. SShSSA, II, f. 14, op. 52, d. 720. State concern over permissive social attitudes dated back to the mid-1960s, when these trends were first mentioned in an official report. SShSSA, II, f. 14, op. 39, d. 409, ll. 132–49.

106. SShSSA, II, f. 14, op. 119, d. 1142, ll. 1–14.

107. SShSSA, II, f. 14, op. 123, d. 361, ll. 64–68.

108. SShSSA, II, f. 14, op. 123, d. 361, l. 103.

109. Draitser describes how "Georgian" was a catch-all phrase for these groups. See Draitser, 37.

110. Such an argument is put forward by Christie Davies in "Ethnic Jokes, Moral Values and Social Boundaries," *British Journal of Sociology* 33, no. 3 (1982): 383–403.

111. A. I. Ural'skii, ed., *Anekdoty. Gruziia—strana millionerov* (Moscow: Svetlana, 1996), 4. Ural'skii's collection is dedicated exclusively to jokes about Georgians.

112. Translated in Draitser, 44, from L. A. Barskii, *Eto prosto smeshno ili zerkalo krivogo korolevstva* (Moscow: Kh. G. S., 1994), 191–92. For variations, see Iosif Raskin, *Entsiklopediia khuliganstvuiushchego ortodoksa* (St. Petersburg: Ekho, 1995), 160–61, and Ural'skii, 29.

113. Irakli Iosebashvili, "Chronicles of a Soviet Capitalist (Part 1 of 2)," *Guernica*, November 1, 2009, accessed September 17, 2014, www.guernicamag.com/features/soviet_capitalist/.

114. Ural'skii, *Anekdoty*, 18; see also Raskin, *Entsiklopediia*.

115. Ural'skii, *Anekdoty*, 17.

116. SShSSA, I, f. 6, d. 29195-75, t. 1, ll. 95–98.

117. Quoted in Simis, *USSR: The Corrupt Society*, 53.

118. "S," interview by author.

119. "T," interview by author.

120. Nodar Dumbadze, *tetri bairaghebi* (Tbilisi: Merani, 1973).

121. For a study of Dumbadze's life and work, see G. A. Mitin, *On videl soltntse: chelovek i obshchestvo v romanakh i rasskazakh Nodara Dumbadze* (Moscow: IMLI RAN, 2002).

122. The thieves-in-law emerged as criminal leaders in the Soviet Gulag no later than the 1930s. Their development is chronicled in Federico Varese, "The Society of the Vory-v-Zakone, 1930s–1950s," *Cahiers du Monde Russe* 39, no. 4 (1998): 515–38.
123. Gavin Slade, *Reorganizing Crime: Mafia and Anti-Mafia in Post-Soviet Georgia* (Oxford: Oxford University Press, 2013), 49.
124. See the list of known thieves-in-law in Georgii Podlesskikh and Andrei Tereshenok, *Vory v zakone: brosok k vlasti* (Moscow: Khudozhestvennaia literatura, 1994) and the list of Georgian thieves-in-law in G. Glonti, G. Lobzhanidze, *Vory v zakone: professional'naia prestupnost' v Gruzii* (Tbilisi: Poligraf, 2004), 191–206. The expression is cited in Slade, *Reorganizing Crime*, 100.
125. Vakhtang Dzhanashiia, "Gruziia ostalas' bez poniatii," *Kommersant*, March 5, 2003, accessed September 17, 2014, www.kommersant.ru/doc/369449.
126. GARF, f. R-8131, op. 28, d. 3282, ll. 21–26.
127. He was transferred to a Georgian prison following an appeal by actors Sergo Zakariadze and Medea Japaridze, both People's Artists of the USSR.
128. In 1982, he reportedly presided over a Union-wide meeting of thieves-in-law in Tbilisi, convincing criminal leaders to abandon their traditional scorn for participation in the official economy. This contradictory individual and alleged boss of the criminal underworld went on to become the leader of the *mkhedrioni* paramilitary band and a major figure in Georgian politics in the 1990s. See G. Glonti, G. Lobzhanidze, *Vory v zakone*, 79–84.
129. Smith, *The Russians*, 126–27.
130. Bonacich, "A Theory of Middleman Minorities"; see also Slezkine, *The Jewish Century*, for a discussion of market-oriented "Mercurians" and their relationship to agriculturally-oriented "Apollonians."
131. The term was a play on the Federal Republic of Germany (FRG), the Soviet bloc's capitalist nemesis; Draitser, *Taking Penguins to the Movies*, 42.
132. Brezhnev's son-in-law, Yuri Churbanov, acting in collusion with republic-level ministers in the Uzbek SSR, enriched himself and others by selling thousands of tons of Uzbek cotton to the state that were never in fact produced. See Clark, *Crime and Punishment*, 185–87.
133. Translated in Draitser, *Taking Penguins to the Movies*, 54; for a variation, see Ural'skii, *Anekdoty*, 11.
134. "Vozrodim byluiu slavu gruzinskogo chaia," *Izvestiia*, February 5, 1982, 3.
135. "Chto za chai bez aromata," *Pravda*, March 23, 1982, 3.
136. V. V. Pokhlebkin, *Chai i vodka v istorii Rossii* (Krasnoyarsk: Krasnoiarskoe knizhnoe izd-vo, 1995). The book is based largely on Pokhlebkin's *Chai, ego istoriia, svoistva i upotreblenie* (Moscow: Pishchevaia promyshlennost', 1968), though Pokhlebkin's critique of Georgia is absent from the earlier publication and would likely have been too strident for Soviet censors.

## Chapter 6

1. This account of the hijacking attempt is based on an investigative report by the Georgian KGB. SShSSA, I, f. 6, d. 8309.
2. Photographs and footage of the group are shown in Zaza Rusadze's sympathetic 2003 documentary, *The Bandits* (*banditebi*).
3. Almost two decades later, the decision to execute the hijackers remained a point of contention between the intelligentsia and Shevardnadze. In 2001

Georgian writer Davit Turashvili wrote a play based on the event, *The Jeans Generation* (*jinsebis taoba*). Turashvili later developed the play into a novel. Turashvili, *jinsebis taoba* (Tbilisi: Bakur Sulakauri, 2008).

4. On the Soviet Russian intelligentsia, see Vladislav Zubok, *Zhivago's Children: The Last Russian Intelligentsia* (Cambridge, MA: Harvard University Press, 2009).

5. Zubok, *Zhivago's Children*, 322–23.

6. SShSSA, I, f. 6, d. 8309, ll. 189–200.

7. For a participant's account of the Leningrad hijacking attempt, see Eduard Kuznetsov, *Mordovskii marafon* (Moscow: Eksmo, 2008); on the case of the Brazinskases, see SShSSA, I, f. 6, d. 7020.

8. Georgia was officially recognized as a "Captive Nation" along with Lithuania by a resolution passed by the US Congress on July 17, 1959. However, Lithuania's diaspora beyond Soviet borders was larger, more recent, and more prevalent in the United States. As a result, it more enthusiastically embraced the label in publications like Vytautas Vaitiekunas, *A Survey of Developments in Captive Lithuania in 1965–1968* (New York: Committee for a Free Lithuania, 1969).

9. On the seemingly unchanging nature of public discourse in the late Soviet Union, see Alexei Yurchak, *Everything was Forever, Until It Was No More: The Last Soviet Generation* (Princeton, NJ: Princeton University Press, 2006).

10. The terms are from Zubok, *Zhivago's Children*, 226–58.

11. On the salience of the University of Tartu, see Beecher, "Ivory Tower of Babel."

12. On the professional success and high culture aspirations of Armenians living in Moscow in the late Soviet period, see Iu. V. Arutiunian, "Armiane-moskvichi."

13. In the introduction to the 1950 edition of Rustaveli's work, the poem was even claimed to be the first "humanistic" work of the medieval world. Shota Rustaveli, *Vitiaz' v tigrovoi shkure*, trans. N. Zabolotskii, introduction by Beso Zhgenti (Moscow: Detgiz, 1950), 9.

14. Lev Markiz, interview by author. Tbilisi, September 19, 2008.

15. Tsentral'noe statisticheskoe upravlenie SSSR, *Vysshee obrazovanie v SSSR*, 30–31.

16. *Vysshee obrazovanie v SSSR*, 60–61, 210–11. Only titular nationalities of republics were counted for this survey, so Soviet Jews were excluded.

17. Tsentral'noe statisticheskoe upravlenie Gruzinskoi SSR, *Gruzinskaia SSR v tsifrakh* (Tbilisi: Statistika, 1965), 75.

18. RGASPI, f. M-1, op. 39, d. 208, l. 18; RGASPI, f. M-1, op. 46, d. 199, l. 53.

19. N. L. Chavchanidze and K. V. Vashakidze, *Gruziny v Rossii: biograficheskie ocherki* (Saransk: Krasnyi oktiabr', 2000), 1: 39–43.

20. Rusudan Khantadze-Andronikashvili, *Nashi zemliaki v Moskve* (Tbilisi: Sakartvelo, 1990), 179–82.

21. Chavchanidze and Vashakidze, *Gruziny v Rossii*, 30–33.

22. RGASPI, f. M-1, op. 39, d. 208, l. 20.

23. Khantadze-Andronikashvili, *Nashi zemliaki v Moskve*, 179–80.

24. Chavchanidze and Vashakidze, *Gruziny v Rossii*, 30–33.

25. Zubok, *Zhivago's Children*, 51.

26. Manana Andriadze, interview by author. Tbilisi, October 27, 2008. At the time of the interview, Dr. Andriadze served as Vice-Rector of the Tbilisi Conservatory.

27. Andriadze, interview by author.

28. Neigauz recounts his personal history in *Vospominaniia Neigauza*, trans. E. R. Rikhter (Moscow: Klassika-XXI, 2007). For a collection of biographical materials on Iakov Zak, see I. I. Zak, *Stat'i, materialy, vospominaniia*, ed. M. G. Sokolov (Moscow: Sovetskii kompozitor, 1980).

29. On the Moscow Conservatory's history, see N. A. Mironov, *Moskovskaia konservatoriia. Istoki* (Moscow: Moskovskaia gos. konservatoriia im. P. I. Chaikovskogo, 1995).

30. Andriadze, interview by author.

31. A term described by Yurchak as a "state of being inside and outside at the same time." Yurchak, *Everything Was Forever*, 132.

32. Markiz, interview by author. Markiz ultimately emigrated to the Netherlands in 1981.

33. Markiz, interview by author.

34. RGALI, f. 3170, op. 2, d. 208, l. 11.

35. RGALI, f. 3170, op. 3, d. 39, ll. 63–173.

36. RGALI, f. 3170, op. 2, d. 162, ll. 1–42.

37. RGALI, f. 3170, op. 2, d. 162, ll. 1–42.

38. SEAUITsA, LKh, f. 55, op. 1, d. 511, l. 11.

39. For viewership and production figures, see Oksana Bulgakowa, "Cine-Weathers: Soviet Thaw Cinema in the International Context," in *The Thaw*, ed. Kozlov and Gilburd, 440–41.

40. For a study of early Soviet cinema, see Peter Kenez, *Cinema and Soviet Society, 1917–1953* (Cambridge: Cambridge University Press, 1992).

41. For a detailed discussion, see Bulgakowa, "Cine-Weathers."

42. Lilya Kaganovsky argues that the shift from optimism to pessimism in Soviet Cinema took place in 1966. Kaganovsky, "Postmemory, Counter-memory: Soviet Cinema of the 1960s," in *The Socialist Sixties*, 235–50.

43. For an overview of auteur theory, see John Caughie, ed., *Theories of Authorship: A Reader* (London: British Film Institute, 1981).

44. Joshua First, "Ukrainian National Cinema and the Concept of the 'Poetic,'" *Kinokultura*, no. 9 (2009), accessed September 18, 2014, www.kinokultura.com/specials/9/first.shtml.

45. For a study of this tendency in Ukrainian national cinema, see Joshua First, *Ukrainian Cinema: Belonging and Identity during the Soviet Thaw* (London: I. B. Tauris, 2015), 124–53.

46. On Parajanov's work, see James Steffen, *The Cinema of Sergei Parajanov* (Madison: University of Wisconsin Press, 2013).

47. First addresses this point in *Ukrainian Cinema*, 122–30.

48. M. Bleiman, "Arkhaisty ili novatory?" *Iskusstvo kino*, no. 7 (1970): 55–76.

49. Bleiman, "Arkhaisty ili novatory?" 73.

50. On the issue of profitability, see Joshua First, "Dovzhenko Studio in the 1960s: Between the Politics of the Auteur and the Politics of Nationality," *Canadian Slavonic Papers* 56, nos. 1–2 (2014): 57–82.

51. I. I. Ratiani, *U istokov gruzinskogo kino: vzaimosviaz' literatury, teatra i kino v kul'ture Gruzii* (Moscow: Rossiiskii institut kul'turologii, 2003). Among these directors were Aleksandre Tsuntsava, Ivane Perestiani, and the ethnic Armenian Amo Bek-Nazarov.

52. Kalatozov managed to keep this position during the turbulent period from 1946 to 1948. After the Stalinist era, Kalatozov directed a stunning series

of films that were artistically innovative and involved close collaboration with foreign artists, including *I am Cuba* (*Ia Kuba*) in 1964 and *The Red Tent* (*Krasnaia palatka*) in 1969. F. I. Betaneli, *Gruziny v Rossii (istoriograficheskoe esse)* (Tbilisi, 1996), 38–39.

53. A brief look at Kalatozov reveals a further example of this trend: Mikhail Kalatozov's son, Giorgi Kalatozishvili, and grandson, Mikheil Kalatozishvili, went on to become well-known Soviet directors.

54. Giorgi Shengelaia, interview by author. Tbilisi, December 15, 2008.

55. Nugzar Amashukeli, *Georgii Shengelaia: tvorcheskii portret* (Moscow: Soiuzinformkino, 1987), 3–4.

56. Eldar Shengelaia, interview by author. Tbilisi, December 10, 2008.

57. Giorgi Shengelaia, interview by author; Eldar Shengelaia, interview by author.

58. Giorgi Shengelaia, interview by author.

59. Giorgi Shengelaia, interview by author.

60. Giorgi Shengelaia, interview by author; Eldar Shengelaia, interview by author.

61. Eldar Shengelaia, interview by author.

62. Eldar Shengelaia, interview by author.

63. Eldar Shengelaia, interview by author.

64. Giorgi Shengelaia, interview by author.

65. Giorgi Shengelaia, interview by author.

66. RGALI, f. 2944, op. 4, d. 2286, ll. 1–16.

67. RGALI, f. 2944, op. 4, d. 2286, ll. 54–70.

68. Eldar Shengelaia, interview by author.

69. RGALI, f. 2944, op. 4, d. 6609, ll. 1–2.

70. Released from prison, Parajanov was barred from directing films on his own. Dodo Abashidze, vouching for him and offering to serve as his codirector, helped him to return with the 1984 film *Legend of Surami Fortress*.

71. *Moi drug, Otar Ioseliani* (Moscow, 2008).

72. Otar Ioseliani, "Proshchanie s nevinnym remeslom komedianta," written in 1962 and printed in *Kinotsenarii* 2–3 (2007): 10–17.

73. Andrei Plakhov, "*Enfant terrible* ukhodiashchei porody," *Kinotsenarii* 2–3 (2007): 231.

74. *Moi drug, Otar Ioseliani.*

75. *Moi drug, Otar Ioseliani.*

76. RGALI, f. 2944, op. 4, d. 710, ll. 8–14.

77. RGALI, f. 2944, op. 4, d. 710, l. 23.

78. RGALI, f. 2944, op. 4, d. 710, l. 29.

79. "Otar Ioseliani" *Kinotsenarii* 2–3 (2007): 367.

80. Bernar Eizenshits, "Zhizneradostnyi pessimist Otar Ioseliani," *Kinotsenarii* 2–3 (2007): 3.

81. RGALI, f. 2944, op. 4, d. 1677, ll. 6–15.

82. SEAUITsA, LKh, f. 52, op. 2, d. 291, ll. 24–26.

83. SEAUITsA, LKh, f. 52, op. 2, d. 291, ll. 13–21.

84. Plakhov, "*Enfant terrible* ukhodiashchei porody," 226.

85. RGALI, f. 2944, op. 4, d. 3661, ll. 1–40.

86. RGALI, f. 2944, op. 4, d. 3471, ll. 4–5.

87. RGALI, f. 2944, op. 4, d. 3471, ll. 33–34.

88. Iurii Rost, "Otar Ioseliani," *Kinotsenarii* 2–3 (2007): 237.

89. In an interview, Ioseliani thanked Raisa Zuseva, a member of Goskino's editorial board, for helping ease his films through the Goskino review process.
See "Otar Ioseliani," 363. The role of "enlightened bureaucrats" in Russian history was identified by William Bruce Lincoln. Lincoln, "Russia's 'Enlightened'
Bureaucrats and the Problem of State Reform, 1848–1856," *Cahiers du Monde
russe et soviétique* 12, no. 4 (1971): 410–21.

90. Giorgi Shengelaia, interview by author.

91. Tatiana Khlopliankina, "On the Road that Leads to the Truth," in *Russian
Critics on the Cinema of Glasnost*, ed. Michael Brashinsky and Andrew Horton
(Cambridge: Cambridge University Press, 1994), 51. Khlopliankina's article
was originally published in *Moskovskaia pravda*, February 4, 1987.

92. For a discussion of Abuladze's earlier work, see L. G. Dularidze, *Tengiz
Abuladze: portret rezhissera* (Moscow: Soiuzinformkino, 1983).

93. Josephine Woll and Denise J. Youngblood, *Repentance* (London: I. B. Tauris,
2001), 100.

94. RGALI, f. 2944, op. 4, d. 3466, l. 7.

95. Woll and Youngblood write that Abuladze was "unquestionably a Georgian
cultural nationalist" in *Repentance*, 103. Julie Christensen offers a careful
reading of the film's Georgian themes, but perhaps overstates Abuladze's
"nationalism" in an article published around the time of Georgian independence, "Tengiz Abuladze and the Georgian Nationalist Cause," *Slavic Review*
50, no. 1 (1991): 163–75.

96. Giorgi Shengelaia, interview by author.

97. Eduard Shevardnadze, *Moi vybor: v zashchitu demokratii i svobody* (Moscow:
Novosti, 1991), 55, translated in Eduard Shevardnadze, *The Future Belongs to
Freedom*, trans. Catherine A. Fitzpatrick (New York: Free Press, 1991), 21.

98. Plakhov, "*Enfant terrible* ukhodiashchei porody," 226.

99. Woll and Youngblood, *Repentance*, 90.

100. Anatolii Cherniaev, the first deputy head of the International Department
of the Central Committee, described Shevardnadze's appointment as a "bolt
from the blue" in his diary, published online by the National Security Archive
and translated by Anna Melyakova. See Svetlana Savranskaya and Thomas
Blanton, "The Shevardnadze File: Late Soviet Foreign Minister Helped End
the Cold War," accessed September 18, 2014, www2.gwu.edu/~nsarchiv/
NSAEBB/NSAEBB481/.

101. M. S. Gorbachev, *Zhizn' i reformy* (Moscow: Novosti, 1995), 1: 287, translated
in Mikhail Gorbachev, *Memoirs* (New York: Doubleday, 1996), 180.

102. Shevardnadze, *Moi vybor*, 288–90.

103. Woll and Youngblood, *Repentance*, 91.

104. RGALI, f. 2916, op. 4, d. 555, ll. 30–31.

105. Shevardnadze, *Moi vybor*, 288, translated in Shevardnadze, *The Future Belongs
to Freedom*, 172.

106. Woll and Youngblood, *Repentance*, 6.

107. Woll and Youngblood advance this interpretation and suggest a number of
allusions to Chiaureli's 1931 film in *Repentance*, 103.

108. For an authorized biography of Gamsakhurdia written by his widow, see
Manana Archvadze-Gamsakhurdia, ed., *zviad gamsakhurdia (avtorizebuli)
biograpia bibliograpiit* (Tbilisi: sakartvelos matsne, 2007).

109. Suny, *Making of the Georgian Nation*, 308–09.
110. RGALI, f. 2916, op. 4, d. 547, ll. 49–50.
111. SEAUITsA, LKh, f. 307, op. 1, d. 87, l. 2.
112. On the center's activities, see "'Mziuri' na starom Arbate," *Zaria vostoka*, December 27, 1987, 3; Georgii Gaprindashvili, "Moskvichi seli za party," *Zaria vostoka*, November 23, 1988, 4. The center provided the basis for the eventual establishment of a Georgian-language kindergarten and primary school in Moscow. Anna Kereselidze, interview by author. Moscow, July 28, 2006.
113. Visiting Mziuri in 1988, Nursultan Nazarbaev, the First Secretary of the Kazakh SSR, spoke of opening a similar center dedicated to the promotion of Kazakh culture in Moscow. Vitalii Tsereteli, "Vstrechi v stolitse," *Zaria vostoka*, June 28, 1988, 1.
114. Aleksei Glurdzhidze, "Tsentr gruzinskoi kul'tury v Iaroslavle," *Zaria vostoka*, February 18, 1989, 3.
115. The incompatibility of the Soviet Union's imperial structures with electoral democracy is discussed by Serhii Plokhy in *The Last Empire: The Final Days of the Soviet Union* (New York: Basic Books, 2014).
116. Stephen Jones, *Georgia: A Political History Since Independence* (London: I. B. Tauris, 2013), 31–34.
117. "Vchera v respublike" and "Obrashchenie k naseleniiu i trudiashchimsia goroda Tbilisi" in *Zaria vostoka*, April 11, 1989, 1.
118. Photograph by Vladimir Valishvili and Ivana Shlamova, *Zaria vostoka*, April 12, 1989, 4.
119. "Obrashchenie tovarishcha Gorbacheva M. S. k kommunistam, vsem trudiashchimsia Gruzii," *Zaria vostoka*, April 13, 1989, 1.

## Conclusion

1. There is a fairly abundant literature on the Soviet collapse, most of it written by political scientists. For a historical perspective, see Stephen Kotkin, *Armageddon Averted: The Soviet Collapse, 1970–2000* (Oxford: Oxford University Press, 2001). For an account that emphasizes the drive for Ukrainian independence, see Plokhy, *The Last Empire*.
2. Suny, *Making of the Georgian Nation*, 323.
3. N. Garifullina, "Kuda eta doroga? Interv'iu predsedatelia Verkhovnogo Soveta Gruzii Zviada Gamsakhurdia," *Zaria vostoka*, December 1, 1990, 2. Originally printed in *Sovetskaia Rossiia*, November 28, 1990.
4. Suny, *Making of the Georgian Nation*, 322.
5. SEAUITsA, LKh, f. 307, op. 1, d. 85, ll. 1–5.
6. N. Garifullina, "Kuda eta doroga?"
7. Vicken Cheterian, *War and Peace in the Caucasus: Russia's Troubled Frontier* (London: Hurst, 2008), 176–77.
8. Smith, *Red Nations*, 269; Peter Kabachnik, Joanna Regulska, and Beth Mitchneck, "Where and When is Home? The Double Displacement of Georgian IDPs from Abkhazia," *Journal of Refugee Studies* 23, no. 3 (2010): 315–36.
9. On universalism and nationalism among the Russian intelligentsia, see Zubok, *Zhivago's Children*.
10. D. L. Muskhelishvili, "Gruziia—'malaia imperiia'?!" in *Gruziia—"malaia imperia"?!*, ed. G. S. Gachechiladze (Tbilisi: Sarangi, 1990), 3–18.

11. Sergei Badurin, "Extremizmu—net!" *Pravda*, February 24, 1990, 4.

12. Liudmila Esvandzhiia "V roli podstrekatelia: redaktor zhurnala 'Druzhba narodov,'" *Zaria vostoka*, February 27, 1990, 1.

13. Guram Buadze, "Sluzhit' delu druzhby, a ne vrazhdy," *Vechernii Tbilisi*, March 13, 1990.

14. Merab Mamardashvili, "Veriu v zdravyi smysl," accessed November 17, 2010, www.iriston.ru/ru/yugooset/1101322999.php.

15. Zviad Gamsakhurdia, "sakartvelos sulieri misia," accessed November 17, 2010, www.amsi.ge/istoria/zg/missia.html.

16. Suny, *Making of the Georgian Nation*, 323.

17. Teimuraz Sturua, interview by author. Moscow, July 20, 2006.

18. Aleksandr Ebanoidze, "Perekoshennye paralleli," *Moskovskie novosti*, April 14, 1991, in *Trudnoe usilie vozrozhdeniia: iz opyta Gruzii v minuvshem desiatiletii (1989–1999 gg.)*, ed. Aleksandr Ebanoidze (Moscow: Kliuch, 1999), 4–7.

19. Ebanoidze, "Monolog tbilistsa vdali ot rodiny," *Nezavisimaia gazeta*, January 18, 1992, in *Trudnoe usilie vozrozhdenia*, 7–13.

20. For an overview of the political implications of this transformation, see Charles King, ed., *Nations Abroad: Diaspora Politics and International Relations in the Former Soviet Union* (Boulder, CO: Westview Press, 1998). For a study of post-Soviet trends in migration, see Cynthia J. Buckley, Blair A. Ruble, and Erin Trouth Hofmann, eds., *Migration, Homeland, and Belonging in Eurasia* (Baltimore, MD: Johns Hopkins University Press, 2008).

21. On Jewish emigration, see Noah Lewin-Epstein, Yaacov Ro'i, and Paul Ritterband, eds., *Russian Jews on Three Continents: Migration and Resettlement* (New York: Frank Cass, 1997); on Soviet German emigration to Germany and Canada, see Hans Werner, *Imagined Homes: Soviet German Immigrants in Two Cities* (Winnipeg: University of Manitoba Press, 2007).

22. See Tom Trier and Andrei Khanzhin, *The Meskhetian Turks at a Crossroads: Integration, Repatriation, or Resettlement?* (London: Global Book Marketing, 2007).

23. Anatol Lieven, *Chechnya: Tombstone of Russian Power* (New Haven, CT: Yale University Press, 1998), 321–23.

24. For an account of the conflict between Armenia and Azerbaijan, see Thomas de Waal, *Black Garden: Armenia and Azerbaijan through Peace and War* (New York: New York University Press, 2003).

25. See Vladimir Shlapentokh, Munir Sendich, and Emil Payin, eds., *The New Russian Diaspora: Russian Minorities in the Former Soviet Republics* (Armonk, NY: M. E. Sharpe, 1994).

26. Iu. V. Arutiunian, "On the Potential of Interethnic Integration in the Megalopolis of Moscow," *Sociological Research* 45, no. 6 (2006), 28.

27. Olga Vendina, "Social Polarization and Ethnic Segregation in Moscow," *Eurasian Geography and Economics* 43, no. 3 (2002), 228–29. Vendina's figures are for the period from 1991 to 2002.

28. Vendina, "Social Polarization," 227.

29. Siegelbaum and Moch make a similar point when discussing post-Soviet labor migration in *Broad is My Native Land*, 95–97.

30. For a comparative study, see Caroline Humphrey and Vera Skvirskaja, *Post-Cosmopolitan Cities: Explorations of Urban Coexistence* (New York: Berghahn Books, 2012).

31. Vendina, "Social Polarization," 229–34.

32. Irina Popova and Valentina Osipova, "Otnoshenie prinimaiushchei storony k migrantam," *Vestnik obshchestvennogo mneniia* 1, no. 114 (2013): 81–88; Meredith Roman, "Making Caucasians Black: Moscow since the Fall of Communism and the Racialization of Non-Russians," *Journal of Communist Studies and Transition Politics* 18, no. 2 (2002): 1–27.

33. The deportation case came before the European Court of Human Rights, which found Russia guilty of pursuing a "coordinated policy of arresting, detaining and expelling Georgian nationals." See the press release of the European Court of Human Rights, "Russia's Policy in 2006 of Arresting, Detaining and Expelling Large Number of Georgian Nationals Violated the Convention," 196 (July 3, 2014).

34. The various activities of the ministry are detailed on its website, accessed March 17, 2011, www.diaspora.gov.ge.

35. Georgian president Mikheil Saakashvili repeatedly insinuated that some of his opponents were "traitors" linked to Russia. Such rhetoric increased when Saakashvili was challenged politically by Bidzina (Boris) Ivanishvili, a Georgian billionaire who had made his fortune in Russia. See "saakashvili 'moghalateebis jgupebze' saubrobs," *Civil.ge*, June 14, 2011, accessed September 22, 2014, www.civil.ge/geo/article.php?id=24186.

36. The Museum of Occupation in Latvia was established in the building that once housed the Red Riflemen's Museum, which had commemorated the prominent group of Latvians in the early Red Army. Laura A. Lenss, "Capturing the Next Shift: The Mapping of Meaning onto the Museum of the Occupation of Latvia," *Future Anterior* 3, no. 1 (2006): 48–57.

37. An observation made by the author during his visit to the museum in July 2013.

38. According to a December 2005 poll by the Russian Public Opinion Research Center, 66 percent of Russians regretted the collapse of the Soviet Union. See the Center's report, "Ostalos' tol'ko sozhalenie," date of last access April 7, 2011, http://wciom.com/archives/thematic-archive/info-material/single/2167.html.

39. For a study of contemporary attitudes toward Stalin in Russia and Georgia that includes a discussion of the statue's removal, see Maria Lipman, Lev Gudkov, and Lasha Bakradze, *The Stalin Puzzle: Deciphering Post-Soviet Public Opinion* (Washington, DC: Carnegie Endowment for International Peace, 2013).

40. See, for example, Mikhail Oshlakov, *Genii Stalin: titan XX veka* (Moscow: Iauza-press, 2013).

41. For a discussion of the ban in the context of the international politics of food, see Darra Goldstein and E. Melanie Du Puis, "Food Politics," *Gastronomica* 7, no. 3 (2007): iii–v.

42. David-Emil Wickström, "'Drive-Ethno-Dance' and 'Hutzul Punk': Ukrainian-Associated Popular Music and (Geo)politics in a Post-Soviet Context," *Yearbook for Traditional Music*, no. 40 (2008): 60–88.

43. Bidzina Ivanishvili, the Prime Minister of Georgia from 2012 to 2013, owned two-thirds of the shares of one of Russia's largest banks, Rossiiskii Kredit, but kept a lower profile than his partner, Vitalii Malkin, who only controlled one-third of the bank's shares. Serguey Braguinsky, "Postcommunist Oligarchs in Russia: Quantitative Analysis," *Journal of Law and Economics* 52, no. 2 (2009), 313.

44. Remittances made up a crucial portion of Georgia's GDP and, according to one study, remittances from Russia composed 66 percent of all remittances sent to Georgia. Sheila Siar, ed., *Migration in Georgia: A Country Profile 2008* (Geneva: International Organization for Migration, 2008), 11.

45. For example, the French, Belgian, and Georgian production *Since Otar Left* (*Depuis qu'Otar est parti...*), released in 2003.

46. Among them, soprano Makvala Kasrashvili, tenor Badri Maisuradze, and principal dancer Nikolai Tsiskaridze. Their biographies are provided on the website of the Bolshoi Theater, accessed November 17, 2010, www.bolshoi.ru.

47. Christine Philliou, "Communities on the Verge: Unraveling the Phanariot Ascendancy in Ottoman Governance," *Comparative Studies in Society and History* 51, no. 1 (2009): 151–81. See Chapter 1 for a discussion of Parsis, Jews, and Armenians.

48. Rudolph J. Vecoli, "Are Italian Americans Just White Folks?" in *The Review of Italian American Studies*, ed. Sorrentino and Krase, 75–88.

# BIBLIOGRAPHY

## Archival Sources

GARF—Gosudarstvennyi arkhiv Rossiiskoi Federatsii (Moscow)
Fond R-3316. *Tsentral'nyi ispolnitel'nyi komitet SSSR*
Fond R-7523. *Verkhovnyi Sovet SSSR*
Fond R-7576. *Komitet fizkul'tury i sporta SSSR*
Fond R-8131. *Prokuratura SSSR*
Fond R-9503. *Kollektsiia vospominanii starykh bol'shevikov*
HIA—Hoover Institution Archives (Stanford, CA)
*Boris I. Nicolaevsky Collection*
*N. A. Lakoba Papers*
RGAE—Rossiiskii gosudarstvennyi arkhiv ekonomiki (Moscow)
Fond 195. *Gosudarstvennyi komitet Soveta Ministrov SSSR po torgovle*
Fond 332. *Kollektsiia dokumentov deiatelei metallurgicheskoi promyshlennosti*
Fond 465. *Ministerstvo torgovli SSSR*
Fond 631. *Mamatsashvili, G. A.*
Fond 4372. *Gosudarstvennyi planovyi komitet SSSR Soveta Ministrov SSSR*
Fond 6884. *Ordzhonikidze, G. K.*
Fond 7486. *Ministerstvo sel'skogo khoziastva SSSR*
Fond 7971. *Ministerstvo torgovli SSSR*
Fond 8546. *Ucherezhdeniia po rukovodstvu vinodel'cheskoi promyshlennost'iu*
RGALI—Rossiiskii gosudarstvennyi arkhiv literatury i iskusstva (Moscow)
Fond 648. *Gosudarstvennyi akademicheskii Bol'shoi teatr SSSR*
Fond 962. *Komitet po delam iskusstv pri Sovete Ministrov SSSR*
Fond 2916. *Komitet po Leninskim i Gosudarstvennym premiiam SSSR v oblasti literatury, iskusstva i arkhitektury pri Sovete Ministrov SSSR*
Fond 2944. *Gosudarstvennyi komitet Soveta Ministrov SSSR po kinematografii*
Fond 3055. *Gerasimov, S. A., Makarova, T. F.*
Fond 3162. *Gosudarstvennoe kontsertnoe ob"edinenie SSSR*
Fond 3170. *Gosudarstvennoe kontserno-gastrol'noe biuro Soiuzkontsert*
RGANI—Rossiiskii gosudarstvennyi arkhiv noveishei istorii (Moscow)
Fond 2. *Plenumy tsentral'nogo komiteta VKP(b)-KPSS*
Fond 5. *Tsentral'nyi komitet KPSS*

RGASPI—Rossiiskii gosudarstvennyi arkhiv sotsial'no-politicheskoi istorii (Moscow)

Fond 85. *Ordzhonikidze, G. K.*

Fond 124. *Vsesoiuznoe obshchestvo starykh bol'shevikov*

Fond 298. *Orakhelashvili, I. D.*

Fond 558. *Stalin, I. V.*

Fond 667. *Enukidze, A. S.*

Fond M-1. *Tsentral'nyi komitet VLKSM*

Fond M-3. *Komitet molodezhnykh organizatsii SSSR*

SEAUITsA—sakartvelos erovnuli arkivis uakhlesi istoriis tsentraluri arkivi (Tbilisi)

Fond 2006. *sakartvelos ssr vachrobis saministro*

literaturisa da khelovnebis (LKh) ganqopileba, Fond 2. *sakartvelos ministrta sabchostan arsebuli khelovnebis sakmeta sammartvelo*

LKh ganqopileba, Fond 44. *anzor davitis dze erkomaishvili*

LKh ganqopileba, Fond 52. *sakartvelos ssr ministrta sabchos kinematograpiis sakhelmtsipo komitetis leninis ordenosani kinostudia "kartuli pilmi"*

LKh ganqopileba, Fond 55. *sakartvelos ssr kulturis saministros tbilisis leninis ordenosani z. paliashvilis sakhelobis operisa da baletis sakhelmtsipo akademiuri teatri*

LKh ganqopileba, Fond 80. *sakartvelos ssr kulturis saministros sakartvelos sakhelmtsipo pilarmonia*

LKh ganqopileba, Fond 212. *akaki aleksis dze khorava*

LKh ganqopileba, Fond 307. *tengiz evgenis dze abuladze*

SShSSA—sakartvelos shinagan sakmeta saministro arkivi (Tbilisi)

I ganqopileba, Fond 6. *sakartvelos ssr sakhelmtsipo ushishroebis komitetis arkivi*

II ganqopileba, Fond 8. *sakartvelos komunisturi partiis tsentralur komitettan arsebuli partiis istoriis (marksizm-leninizmis) instituti*

II ganqopileba, Fond 14. *sakartvelos komunisturi partiis tsentraluri komitetis arkivi*

TsGA Moskvy, OKhD—Tsentral'nyi gosudarstvennyi arkhiv goroda Moskvy, Otdel khraneniia dokumentov posle 1917 goda (Moscow)

Fond 46. *Upravlenie rynkami g. Moskvy*

Fond 224. *Moskovskii trest restoranov*

Fond 429. *Glavnoe upravlenie kul'tury Mosgorispolkoma*

Fond 453. *Moskovskoe gorodskoe territorial'noe proizvodstvenno-torgovoe ob"edinenie obshchestvennogo pitaniia*

Fond 1067. *Moskovskii gorodskoi sovet "Dinamo"*

## Interviews

Andriadze, Manana. Interview by author. Tbilisi. October 27, 2008.

Arutiunov, Sergei. Interview by author. Moscow. February 19, 2008.

Bregvadze, Nani. Interview by author. Tbilisi. November 5, 2008.

"D" (participant wished to remain anonymous). Georgian man in his fifties. Interview by author. Tbilisi. November 4, 2008.

Ebanoidze, Aleksandr. Interview by author. Moscow. June 17, 2008.

Egnatashvili, Eteri, and Tinatin Egnatashvili. Interview by author. Moscow. March 23, 2008.

Galustian, Viacheslav. Interview by author. Moscow. July 26, 2006.

Kereselidze, Anna. Interview by author. Moscow. July 28, 2006.

Kikabidze, Vakhtang. Interview by author. Tbilisi. November 26, 2008.

Markiz, Lev. Interview by author. Tbilisi. September 19, 2008.

"S" (participant wished to remain anonymous). Georgian man in his fifties. Interview by author. Tbilisi. November 4, 2008.

Shengelaia, Eldar. Interview by author. Tbilisi. December 10, 2008.

Shengelaia, Giorgi. Interview by author. Tbilisi. December 15, 2008.

Sturua, Teimuraz. Interview by author. Moscow. July 20, 2006.

"T" (participant wished to remain anonymous). Georgian woman in her forties. Interview by author. Moscow. July 17, 2006.

Umertaev, Shamil'. Interview by author. Moscow. June 30, 2008.

Vartanian, Aksel'. Interview by author. Moscow. July 19, 2006.

## Newspapers and Periodicals

*Iskusstvo kino* (Moscow)

*Izvestiia* (Moscow)

*Kinotsenarii* (Moscow)

*Krokodil* (Moscow)

*Obshchestvennoe pitanie* (Moscow)

*Pravda* (Moscow)

*Russkie subtropiki* (Batumi)

*Sovetskii sport* (Moscow)

*Sportivnaia zhizn' Rossii* (Moscow)

*Travel in the USSR* (Moscow)

*Vechernaia Moskva* (Moscow)

*Vechernii Tbilisi* (Tbilisi)

*Zaria vostoka* (Tbilisi)

## Films

*ambavi suramis tsikhisa*. Directed by Sergei Parajanov and Dodo Abashidze. Tbilisi: kartuli pilmi, 1984.

*arachveulebrivi gamopena*. Directed by Eldar Shengelaia. Tbilisi: kartuli pilmi, 1968.

*Ashik Kerib*. Directed by Sergei Parajanov. Tbilisi: kartuli pilmi, 1988.

*banditebi*. Directed by Zaza Rusadze. Berlin: Credofilm, 2003.

*Depuis qu'Otar est parti* . . . Directed by Julie Bertuccelli. Paris: Les Films du Poisson, 2003.

*Dvadtsat' shest' komissarov*. Directed by Nikoloz Shengelaia. Baku: Azerkino, 1932.

*eliso*. Directed by Nikoloz Shengelaia. Tbilisi: sakhkinmretsvi, 1928.

*Georgian National Dance Company*. Tbilisi: Sukhishvili LTD, 2008.

*giorgi saakadze*. Directed by Mikheil Chiaureli. Tbilisi: tbilisis kinostudia, 1942.

*giorgobistve*. Directed by Otar Ioseliani. Tbilisi: kartuli pilmi, 1966.

*Ia Kuba*. Directed by Mikhail Kalatozov. Moscow: Mosfil'm, 1964.

*Ia shagaiu po Moskve*. Directed by Giorgi Danelia. Moscow: Mosfil'm, 1964.

*iqo shashvi mgalobeli*. Directed by Otar Ioseliani. Tbilisi: kartuli pilmi, 1971.

*jariskatsis mama*. Directed by Rezo Chkheidze. Tbilisi: kartuli pilmi, 1964.

*Kavkazskaia plennitsa, ili Novye prikliucheniia Shurika.* Directed by Leonid Gaidai. Moscow: Mosfil'm, 1967.

*khabarda!* Directed by Mikheil Chiaureli. Tbilisi: sakhkinmretsvi, 1931.

*Krasnaia palatka.* Directed by Mikhail Kalatozov. Moscow: Mosfil'm, 1969.

*Letiat zhuravli.* Directed by Mikhail Kalatozov. Moscow: Mosfil'm, 1957.

*magdanas lurja.* Directed by Tengiz Abuladze and Rezo Chkheidze. Tbilisi: kartuli pilmi, 1958.

*Mimino.* Directed by Giorgi Danelia. Moscow: Mosfil'm, 1977.

*Moi drug, Otar Ioseliani.* Directed by Andrei Pashkevich. Moscow: Kinotsenarii, 2008.

*monanieba.* Directed by Tengiz Abuladze. Tbilisi: kartuli pilmi, 1984.

*motsurave.* Directed by Irakli Kvirikadze. Tbilisi: kartuli pilmi, 1981.

*natvris khe.* Directed by Tengiz Abuladze. Tbilisi: kartuli pilmi, 1976.

*Ne goriui!* Directed by Giorgi Danelia. Moscow: Mosfil'm, 1969.

*orera, sruli svlit.* Directed by Zaal Kakabadze. Tbilisi: kartuli telepilmi, 1970.

*Osenii marafon.* Directed by Giorgi Danelia. Moscow: Mosfil'm, 1979.

*Padenie Berlina.* Directed by Mikheil Chiaureli. Moscow: Mosfil'm, 1950.

*pastorali.* Directed by Otar Ioseliani. Tbilisi: kartuli pilmi, 1975.

*pirosmani.* Directed by Giorgi Shengelaia. Tbilisi: kartuli pilmi, 1969.

*Pepo.* Directed by Amo Bek-Nazarian and Armen Gulakian. Yerevan: Armenkino, 1935.

*sherekilebi.* Directed by Eldar Shengelaia. Tbilisi: kartuli pilmi, 1973.

*Tini zabutykh predkiv.* Directed by Sergei Parajanov. Kiev: Kinostudiia im. O. Dovzhenka, 1964.

*Traktoristy.* Directed by Ivan Pyr'ev. Moscow: Mosfil'm, 1939.

*tsisperi mtebi anu daujerebeli ambavi.* Directed by Eldar Shengelaia. Tbilisi: kartuli pilmi, 1983.

*Tsvet granata.* Directed by Sergei Parajanov. Yerevan: Armenfil'm, 1968.

*vedreba.* Directed by Tengiz Abuladze. Tbilisi: kartuli pilmi, 1967.

*veris ubnis melodiebi.* Directed by Giorgi Shengelaia. Tbilisi: kartuli pilmi, 1973.

## Music and Audio Recordings

Bregvadze, Nani. *Nani Bregvadze: Grand Collection.* Moscow: Pervoe muzykal'noe izd-vo, 2007.

Iveria. *Svad'ba soek.* Moscow: Melodiia, 1986.

Kikabidze, Vakhtang. *Larisu Ivanovnu khochu.* Moscow: Soiuz, 1996.

Orera. *VIA Orera.* Moscow: Melodiia, 2008.

## Books, Articles, and Dissertations

Abdelhady, Dalia. *The Lebanese Diaspora: The Arab Immigrant Experience in Montreal, New York, and Paris.* New York: New York University Press, 2011.

Afanas'ev, Iu. N., et al. *Istoriia stalinskogo gulaga.* Moscow: Rosspen, 2004–2005.

Ahrweiler, Hélène, and Angeliki E. Laiou, eds. *Studies on the Internal Diaspora of the Byzantine Empire.* Washington, DC: Dumbarton Oaks Research Library and Collection, 1998.

Aimermakher, K., et al, eds. *Doklad N. S. Khrushcheva o kul'te lichnosti Stalina na XX s"ezde KPSS: dokumenty.* Moscow: Rosspen, 2002.

Aktürk, Şener. *Regimes of Ethnicity and Nationhood in Germany, Russia, and Turkey.* New York: Cambridge University Press, 2012.

Allen, W.E.D. *A History of the Georgian People from the Beginning down to the Russian Conquest in the Nineteenth Century.* London: K. Paul, Trench, Trubner and Co., 1932.

Allilueva, Svetlana. *Dvadtsat' pisem k drugu.* New York: Harper and Row, 1967.

Allilueva, Svetlana. *Tol'ko odin god.* New York: Harper and Row, 1969.

Allworth, Edward A. *The Modern Uzbeks: From the Fourteenth Century to the Present; A Cultural History.* Stanford, CA: Hoover Institution Press, 1990.

Amashukeli, Nugzar. *Georgii Shengelaia: tvorcheskii portret.* Moscow: Soiuzinformkino, 1987.

Anderson, Benedict. *Imagined Communities: Reflections on the Origin and Spread of Nationalism.* London: Verso, 1983.

Anufriev, V. M., N. S. Kiknadze, and G. M. Kirillova. *Sousy, spetsii.* Moscow: Gostorgizdat, 1956.

Appadurai, Arjun. *The Social Life of Things: Commodities in Cultural Perspective.* Cambridge: Cambridge University Press, 1986.

Appiah, Kwame Anthony. *Ethics of Identity.* Princeton, NJ: Princeton University Press, 2005.

Appiah, Kwame Anthony. *Cosmopolitanism: Ethics in a World Of Strangers.* New York: Norton, 2006.

Archvadze-Gamsakhurdia, Manana, ed. *zviad gamsakhurdia (avtorizebuli) biografia bibliograpiit.* Tbilisi: sakartvelos matsne, 2007.

Armstrong, John A. "Mobilized and Proletarian Diasporas." *American Political Science Review* 70, no. 2 (1976): 393–408.

Armstrong, John A. "Mobilized Diaspora in Tsarist Russia: The Case of the Baltic Germans." In *Soviet Nationality Policies and Practices,* edited by Jeremy R. Azrael, 63–104. New York: Prager, 1978.

Arutiunian, Iu. V. "Armiane-moskvichi. Sotsial'nyi portret po materialam etnosotsiologicheskogo isledovaniia." *Sovetskaia etnografiia,* no. 2 (1991): 3–16.

Arutiunian, Iu. V. "On the Potential of Interethnic Integration in the Megalopolis of Moscow." *Sociological Research* 45, no. 6 (2006): 26–50.

Baberowski, Jörg. *Der Feind ist überall: Stalinismus im Kaukasus.* Munich: Deutsche Verlags-Anstalt, 2003.

Baily, Samuel L. *Immigrants in the Lands of Promise: Italians in Buenos Aires and New York City, 1870–1914.* Ithaca, NY: Cornell University Press, 1999.

Barkey, Karen. *Bandits and Bureaucrats: The Ottoman Route to State Centralization.* Ithaca, NY: Cornell University Press, 1994.

Barkey, Karen. *Empire of Difference: The Ottomans in Comparative Perspective.* Cambridge: Cambridge University Press, 2008.

Beecher, David Ilmar. "Ivory Tower of Babel: Tartu University and the Languages of Two Empires, A Nation-State, and the Soviet Union." PhD diss., University of California, Berkeley, 2014.

Beissinger, Mark R. "Soviet Empire as 'Family Resemblance.'" *Slavic Review* 65, no. 2 (2006): 294–303.

Beria, Sergo. *Beria, My Father: Inside Stalin's Kremlin.* London: Duckworth, 2001.

Betaneli, F. I. *Gruziny v Rossii (istoriograficheskoe esse).* Tbilisi, 1996.

Bialer, Seweryn. *The Soviet Paradox: External Expansion, Internal Decline.* New York: Knopf, 1986.

Bickham, Troy. "Eating the Empire: Intersections of Food, Cookery and Imperialism in Eighteenth-Century Britain." *Past & Present,* no. 198 (2008): 71–109.

Binns, John. *An Introduction to the Christian Orthodox Churches.* Cambridge: Cambridge University Press, 2002.

Bittner, Stephen V. *The Many Lives of Khrushchev's Thaw: Experience and Memory in Moscow's Arbat.* Ithaca, NY: Cornell University Press, 2008.

Blank, Stephen. *The Sorcerer as Apprentice: Stalin as Commissar of Nationalities, 1917–1924.* Westport, CT: Greenwood, 1994.

Blauvelt, Timothy. "Abkhazia: Patronage and Power in the Stalin Era." *Nationalities Papers* 35, no. 2 (2007): 203–32.

Blauvelt, Timothy. "Status Shift and Ethnic Mobilisation in the March 1956 Events in Georgia." *Europe-Asia Studies* 61, no. 4 (2009): 651–68.

Blauvelt, Timothy. "March of the Chekists: Beria's Secret Police Patronage Network and Soviet Crypto-Politics." *Communist and Post-Communist Studies* 44, no. 1 (2011): 73–88.

Bleiere, Daina. *History of Latvia: The Twentieth Century.* Riga: Jumava, 2006.

Bodnar, John E. *The Transplanted: A History of Immigrants in Urban America.* Bloomington: Indiana University Press, 1985.

Bonacich, Edna. "A Theory of Middleman Minorities." *American Sociological Review* 38, no. 5 (1973): 583–94.

Bonacich, Phillip. "Power and Centrality: A Family of Measures." *American Journal of Sociology* 92, no. 5 (1987): 1170–82.

Bourdieu, Pierre. *Distinction: A Social Critique of the Judgment of Taste.* Translated by Richard Nice. Cambridge, MA: Harvard University Press, 1984.

Bradshaw, Michael, Phil Hanson, and Denis Shaw. "Economic Restructuring." In *The Baltic States: The National Self-Determination of Estonia, Latvia and Lithuania,* edited by Graham Smith, 158–80. New York: St. Martin's, 1994.

Braguinsky, Serguey. "Postcommunist Oligarchs in Russia: Quantitative Analysis." *Journal of Law and Economics* 52, no. 2 (2009): 307–49.

Brandenberger, David. *National Bolshevism: Stalinist Mass Culture and the Formation of Modern Russian National Identity, 1931–1956.* Cambridge, MA: Harvard University Press, 2002.

Brashinsky, Michael, and Andrew Horton, eds. *Russian Critics on the Cinema of Glasnost.* Cambridge: Cambridge University Press, 1994.

Brooks, Jeffrey. *When Russia Learned to Read: Literacy and Popular Literature, 1861–1917.* Princeton, NJ: Princeton University Press, 1985.

Brower, Daniel R. *Training the Nihilists: Education and Radicalism in Tsarist Russia.* Ithaca, NY: Cornell University Press, 1975.

Brower, Daniel R., and Edward J. Lazzerini, eds. *Russia's Orient: Imperial Borderlands and Peoples, 1700–1917.* Bloomington: Indiana University Press, 1997.

Brubaker, Rogers. "The 'Diaspora' Diaspora." *Ethnic and Racial Studies* 28, no. 1 (2005): 1–19.

Buckley, Cynthia J., Blair A. Ruble, and Erin Trouth Hofmann, eds. *Migration, Homeland, and Belonging in Eurasia.* Baltimore, MD: Johns Hopkins University Press, 2008.

Budnitskii, O. V. *Evrei i russkaia revoliutsiia: materialy i isledovaniia.* Moscow: Gesharim, 1999.

Bullock, Barbara E., and Almeida Jacqueline Toribio, eds. *The Cambridge Handbook of Linguistic Code Switching.* Cambridge: Cambridge University Press, 2009.

Burbank, Jane, and Frederick Cooper. *Empires in World History: Power and the Politics of Difference.* Princeton, NJ: Princeton University Press, 2010.

Carruthers, Susan L. *Cold War Captives: Imprisonment, Escape, and Brainwashing.* Berkeley: University of California Press, 2009.

Caughie, John, ed. *Theories of Authorship: A Reader.* London: British Film Institute, 1981.

Charkviani, Kandid. *gantsdili da naazrevi, 1906-1994.* Tbilisi: merani, 2004.

Chatwin, Mary Ellen. *Socio-Cultural Transformation and Foodways in the Republic of Georgia.* Commack, NY: Nova Science Publishers, 1997.

Chatwin, Mary Ellen. "Tamadoba: Drinking Social Cohesion at the Georgian Table." In *Drinking: Anthropological Approaches,* edited by Igor de Garine and Valerie de Garine, 181–90. New York: Berghahn Books, 2001.

Chavchanidze, N. L., and K. V. Vashakidze. *Gruziny v Rossii: biograficheskie ocherki.* 4 vols. Saransk: Krasnyi oktiabr', 2000–2004.

Cheah, Pheng, and Bruce Robbins, eds. *Cosmopolitics: Thinking and Feeling Beyond the Nation.* Minneapolis: University of Minnesota Press, 1998.

Cheterian, Vicken. *War and Peace in the Caucasus: Russia's Troubled Frontier.* London: Hurst, 2008.

Chichinadze, Zakaria, and Vakhtang Chikovani. *kartveli ebralebi sakartveloshi.* Tbilisi: metsniereba, 1990.

Christensen, Julie. "Tengiz Abuladze and the Georgian Nationalist Cause." *Slavic Review* 50, no. 1 (1991): 163–75.

CIS Committee for Statistics. *The Statistical Handbook of Social and Economic Indicators for the Former Soviet Union.* New York: Norman Ross Publishing, 1996.

Clark, Katerina. *The Soviet Novel: History as Ritual.* Bloomington: Indiana University Press, 2000.

Clark, Katerina. *Moscow, the Fourth Rome. Stalinism, Cosmopolitanism, and the Evolution of Soviet Culture, 1931-1941.* Cambridge, MA: Harvard University Press, 2011.

Clark, William A. *Crime and Punishment in Soviet Officialdom: Combating Corruption in the Political Elite, 1965-1990.* Armonk, NY: M. E. Sharpe, 1993.

Clifford, James. "Diasporas." *Cultural Anthropology* 9, no. 3 (1994): 302–38.

Cohen, Robin. *Global Diasporas: An Introduction.* Seattle: University of Washington Press, 1997.

Colton, Timothy J. *Moscow: Governing the Socialist Metropolis.* Cambridge, MA: Harvard University Press, 1995.

Conklin, Alice. "Colonialism and Human Rights, A Contradiction in Terms? The Case of France and West Africa, 1895-1914." *American Historical Review* 103, no. 2 (1998): 419–42.

Conquest, Robert. *The Great Terror: A Reassessment.* New York: Oxford University Press, 1990.

Conquest, Robert. *Stalin: Breaker of Nations.* New York: Viking. 1991.

Conterio, Johanna. "Inventing the Subtropics: An Environmental History of Sochi, 1929–36." *Kritika: Explorations in Russian and Eurasian History* 16, no. 1 (2015): 91–120.

Cooper, Frederick. *Colonialism in Question: Theory, Knowledge, History.* Berkeley: University of California Press, 2005.

Crews, Robert D. *For Prophet and Tsar: Islam and Empire in Russia and Central Asia.* Cambridge, MA: Harvard University Press, 2006.

Curtin, Philip D. *Cross-Cultural Trade in World History.* Cambridge: Cambridge University Press, 1984.

Cvetkovski, Roland, and Alexis Hofmeister. *An Empire of Others: Creating Ethnographic Knowledge in Imperial Russia and the USSR.* Budapest: Central European University Press, 2014.

Daneliia, Georgii. *Tostuemyi p'et do dna.* Moscow: Eksmo, 2006.

David-Fox, Michael. *Showcasing the Great Experiment: Cultural Diplomacy and Western Visitors to the Soviet Union, 1921–1941.* Oxford: Oxford University Press, 2012.

Davies, Christie. "Ethnic Jokes, Moral Values and Social Boundaries." *British Journal of Sociology* 33, no. 3 (1982): 383–403.

Davies, R. W. "The Syrtsov-Lominadze Affair." *Soviet Studies* 33, no. 1 (1981): 29–50.

Davies, Sarah, and James Harris, eds. *Stalin: A New History.* Cambridge: Cambridge University Press, 2005.

de Waal, Thomas. *Black Garden: Armenia and Azerbaijan through Peace and War.* New York: New York University Press, 2003.

*Dekada gruzinskogo iskusstva i literatury v Moskve: Sbornik materialov.* Tbilisi: Zaria vostoka, 1959.

Deringil, Selim. *The Well-Protected Domains: Ideology and the Legitimation of Power in the Ottoman Empire, 1876–1909.* New York: I. B. Tauris, 1998.

Deutscher, Isaac. *Stalin: A Political Biography.* New York: Oxford University Press, 1966.

Djilas, Milovan. *The New Class. An Analysis of the Communist System.* New York: Praeger, 1957.

Djilas, Milovan. *Conversations with Stalin.* Translated by Michael B. Petrovich. New York: Harcourt, Brace and World, 1962.

*Dni Gruzii v Mosvke.* Tbilisi: Khelovneba, 1982.

Dolmatovskii, Evgenii. *Bylo: zapiski poeta.* Moscow: Sovetskii pisatel', 1975.

Dragadze, Tamara. *Rural Families in Soviet Georgia: A Case Study in Ratcha Province.* London: Routledge, 1988.

Draitser, Emil A. *Taking Penguins to the Movies: Ethnic Humor in Russia.* Detroit: Wayne State University Press, 1998.

Dufoix, Stephane. *Diasporas.* Berkeley: University of California Press, 2008.

Dularidze, L. G. *Tengiz Abuladze: portret rezhissera.* Moscow: Soiuzinformkino, 1983.

Dumbadze, N., M. Karchava, Z. Bolkvadze, and G. Pirtskhalava. *"Dinamo" Tbilisi.* Tbilisi: Soiuz zhurnalistov Gruzii, 1960.

Dumbadze, Nodar. *tetri bairaghebi.* Tbilisi: Merani, 1973.

Dunham, Vera S. *In Stalin's Time: Middleclass Values in Soviet Fiction.* Cambridge: Cambridge University Press, 1976.

Dzhavakhishvili, Georgii, ed. *Iz perepiski N. A. Nikoladze s russkimi i zarubezhnymi literaturno-obshchestvennymi deiatel'iami.* Tbilisi: Izd-vo Tbilisskogo universiteta, 1980.

Easter, Gerald. *Reconstructing the State: Personal Networks and Elite Identity in Soviet Russia*. Cambridge: Cambridge University Press, 2000.

Ebanoidze, Aleksandr, ed. *Trudnoe usilie vozrozhdeniia: iz opyta Gruzii v minuvshem desiatiletii (1989–1999 gg.)*. Moscow: Kliuch, 1999.

Edgar, Adrienne Lynn. *Tribal Nation: The Making of Soviet Turkmenistan*. Princeton, NJ: Princeton University Press, 2004.

Ehrenburg, Il'ia. *Ottepel': povest'*. Moscow, 1954.

Elias, Norbert. *The Civilizing Process: Sociogenetic and Psychogenetic Investigations*. Edited by Eric Dunning, Johan Goudsblom, and Stephen Mennell. Translated by Edmund Jephcott. Oxford: Basil Blackwell, 2000.

Elliott, J. H. "A Europe of Composite Monarchies." *Past & Present*, no. 137 (1992): 48–71.

Enloe, Cynthia H. *Ethnic Soldiers: State Security in Divided Societies*. Athens: University of Georgia Press, 1980.

Enukidze, A. *Bol'shevistskie nelegal'nye tipografii*. Moscow: Molodaia gvardiia, 1930.

Enukidze, A. *Bolshevistskie nelegal'nye tipografii*. Moscow: Molodaia gvardiia, 1934.

Erkomaishvili, Anzor. *khma utsnauri*. Tbilisi: sakartvelo, 1999.

Etkind, Aleksandr. *Internal Colonization: Russia's Imperial Experience*. Cambridge: Polity Press, 2011.

European Court of Human Rights. "Russia's Policy in 2006 of Arresting, Detaining and Expelling Large Number of Georgian Nationals Violated the Convention." 196 (July 3, 2014).

Evans, Christine. "From *Truth* to *Time*: Soviet Central Television, 1957–1985." PhD diss., University of California, Berkeley, 2010.

Ezergailis, Andrew. *The 1917 Revolution in Latvia*. New York: Columbia University Press, 1974.

First, Joshua J. "Scenes of Belonging: Cinema and the Nationality Question in Soviet Ukraine During the Long 1960s." PhD diss., University of Michigan, 2008.

First, Joshua J. "Dovzhenko Studio in the 1960s: Between the Politics of the Auteur and the Politics of Nationality." *Canadian Slavonic Papers* 56, nos. 1–2 (2014): 57–82.

First, Joshua J. *Ukrainian Cinema: Belonging and Identity during the Soviet Thaw*. London: I. B. Tauris, 2015.

Fitzpatrick, Sheila. "'Middle-Class Values' and Soviet Life in the 1930s." In *Soviet Society and Culture: Essays in Honor of Vera S. Dunham*, edited by Terry L. Thompson and Richard Sheldon, 20–38. Boulder, CO: Westview Press, 1988.

Fitzpatrick, Sheila. *The Cultural Front: Power and Culture in Revolutionary Russia*. Ithaca, NY: Cornell University Press, 1992.

Fitzpatrick, Sheila. *Everyday Stalinism: Ordinary Life in Extraordinary Times: Soviet Russia in the 1930s*. New York: Oxford University Press, 1999.

Foucault, Michel. *Discipline and Punish: The Birth of the Prison*. Translated by Alan Sheridan. New York: Vintage Books, 1995.

Fowler, Mayhill C. "Mikhail Bulgakov, Mykola Kulish, and Soviet Theater: How Internal Transnationalism Remade Center and Periphery." *Kritika: Explorations in Russian and Eurasian History* 16, no. 2 (2015): 263–90.

Frankel, Jonathan. *Prophecy and Politics: Socialism, Nationalism, and the Russian Jews*. Cambridge: Cambridge University Press, 1981.

Frisby, David, and Mike Featherstone, eds. *Simmel on Culture: Selected Writings*. London: Sage Publications, 1997.

Frolova-Walker, Marina. *Russian Music and Nationalism: From Glinka to Stalin*. New Haven, CT: Yale University Press, 2007.

Fürst, Juliane. *Stalin's Last Generation: Soviet Post-War Youth and the Emergence of Mature Socialism*. Oxford: Oxford University Press, 2010.

Gabaccia, Donna R. "Is Everywhere Nowhere? Nomads, Nations, and the Immigrant Paradigm of United States History." *Journal of American History* 86, no. 3 (1999): 1115–34.

Gabaccia, Donna R. *Italy's Many Diasporas*. Seattle: University of Washington Press, 2000.

Gachechiladze, G. S., ed. *Gruziia—"malaia imperia"?!* Tbilisi: Sarangi, 1990.

Gammer, Moshe. *The Lone Wolf and the Bear: Three Centuries of Chechen Defiance of Russian Rule*. Pittsburgh: University of Pittsburgh Press, 2006.

*Gastrol'naia poezdka 1-go gosteatra Gruzii imeni Rustaveli*. Tbilisi: Gos. izd-vo SSRG, 1930.

Geist, Edward. "Cooking Bolshevik: Anastas Mikoian and the Making of the "Book about Delicious and Healthy Food." *Russian Review* 71, no. 2 (2012): 295–313.

Gellner, Ernest. *Nations and Nationalism*. Ithaca, NY: Cornell University Press, 1983.

Gerschenkron, Alexander. "Economic Backwardness in Historical Perspective." In *Economic Backwardness in Historical Perspective*, edited by Alexander Gerschenkron, 5–31. Cambridge, MA: Harvard University Press, 1966.

Getty, J. Arch. *Practicing Stalinism: Bolsheviks, Boyars, and the Persistence of Tradition*. New Haven, CT: Yale University Press, 2013.

Getty, J. Arch, and Oleg Naumov. *The Road to Terror: Stalin and the Self-Destruction of the Bolsheviks, 1932–1939*. New Haven, CT: Yale University Press, 1999.

Getty, J. Arch, and Oleg V. Naumov. *Yezhov: The Rise of Stalin's "Iron Fist."* New Haven, CT: Yale University Press, 2008.

Gilroy, Paul. *The Black Atlantic: Modernity and Double Consciousness*. Cambridge, MA: Harvard University Press, 1993.

Giulianotti, Richard. *Football: A Sociology of the Global Game*. Cambridge: Polity Press, 1999.

Glants, Musya, and Joyce Toomre, eds. *Food in Russian History and Culture*. Bloomington: Indiana University Press, 1997.

Glonti, G., and G. Lobzhanidze. *Vory v zakone: professional'naia prestupnost' v Gruzii*. Tbilisi: Poligraf, 2004.

Gogoberidze, Avtandil. *S miachom s trideviat' zemel'*. Tbilisi: Soiuz zhurnalistov Gruzii, 1965.

Goldman, Wendy Z. *Inventing the Enemy: Denunciation and Terror in Stalin's Russia*. New York: Cambridge University Press, 2011.

Goldstein, Darra. *The Georgian Feast: The Vibrant Culture and Savory Food of the Republic of Georgia*. Berkeley: University of California Press, 1999.

Goldstein, Darra, and E. Melanie Du Puis. "Food Politics." *Gastronomica* 7, no. 3 (2007): iii–v.

Gorbachev, M. S. *Zhizn' i reformy*. Moscow: Novosti, 1995.

Gorbachev, M. S. *Memoirs*. New York: Doubleday, 1996.

Gorgiladze, Rusudan. *Savoring Georgia: A Personal Journey Through Time and Taste*. Tbilisi: Cezanne, 2013.

Gorlizki, Yoram. "Ordinary Stalinism: The Council of Ministers and the Soviet Neopatrimonial State, 1946–1953." *Journal of Modern History* 74, no. 4 (2002): 699–736.

Gorlizki, Yoram, and Oleg Khlevniuk. *Cold Peace: Stalin and the Soviet Ruling Circle, 1945–1953.* Oxford: Oxford University Press, 2004.

Gorsuch, Anne E. "'There's No Place Like Home': Soviet Tourism in Late Stalinism." *Slavic Review* 62, no. 4 (2003): 760–85.

Gorsuch, Anne E., and Diane P. Koenker, eds. *The Socialist Sixties: Crossing Borders in the Second World.* Bloomington: Indiana University Press, 2013.

Grant, Bruce. *The Captive and the Gift: Cultural Histories of Sovereignty in Russia and the Caucasus.* Ithaca, NY: Cornell University Press, 2009.

Gronow, Jukka. *Caviar with Champagne: Common Luxury and the Ideals of the Good Life in Stalin's Russia.* Oxford: Berg, 2003.

Grossman, Gregory. "The Second Economy of the USSR." *Problems of Communism* 25, no. 5 (1977): 25–40.

Grout, Donald Jay, and Hermine Weigel Williams. *A Short History of Opera.* New York: Columbia University Press, 2003.

*Gruzinskaia Sovetskaia Sotsialisticheskaia Respublika na VDNKh SSSR.* Moscow: VDNKh SSSR, 1972.

Guruli, Vakhtang, and Omar Tushurashvili, eds. "Correspondence Between Lavrenty Beria and Jospeh Stalin." *Archival Bulletin* 3, appendix (2008): 4–106.

Gutchina, A. B., S. I. Mesropian, and V. M. Tamarkin. *50 bliud evreiskoi kukhni.* Moscow: Gostorgizdat, 1939.

Halfin, Igal. *Terror in My Soul: Communist Autobiographies on Trial.* Cambridge, MA: Harvard University Press, 2003.

Handlin, Oscar. *The Uprooted: The Epic Story of the Great Migrations That Made the American People.* Boston: Little, Brown, 1951.

Hanioğlu, M. Şukrü. *The Young Turks in Opposition.* New York: Oxford University Press, 1995.

Harper, Marjory, and Stephen Constantine, *Migration and Empire.* Oxford: Oxford University Press, 2010.

Hechter, Michael. *Internal Colonialism: The Celtic Fringe in British National Development, 1536–1966.* Berkeley: University of California Press, 1975.

Helstosky, Carol. *Garlic and Oil: Politics and Food in Italy.* Oxford: Berg, 2004.

Hessler, Julie. *A Social History of Soviet Trade: Trade Policy, Retail Practices, and Consumption.* Princeton, NJ: Princeton University Press, 2004.

Hirsch, Francine. *Empire of Nations: Ethnographic Knowledge and the Making of the Soviet Union.* Ithaca, NY: Cornell University Press, 2005.

Hourani, Albert, and Nadim Shehadi, eds. *The Lebanese in the World: A Century of Emigration.* London: Center for Lebanese Studies and I. B. Tauris, 1992.

Humphrey, Caroline, and Vera Skvirskaja, eds. *Post-Cosmopolitan Cities: Explorations of Urban Coexistence.* New York: Berghahn Books, 2012.

Il'f, Il'ia, and Evgenii Petrov. *Dvenadtsat' stul'ev.* Moscow: Izd-vo khudozhestvennoi literatury, 1959.

Ilizarov, Boris. *Tainaia zhizn' Stalina: po materialam ego biblioteki i arkhiva k istorio-sofii stalinizma.* Moscow: Veche, 2003.

Isupov, A. A. *Natsional'nyi sostav naseleniia SSSR (po itogam perepisi 1959 g.)*. Moscow: Statistika, 1961.

Javakhishvili, Mikheil. *tkhzulebani rva tomad*. Tbilisi: sabchota sakartvelo, 1970.

Jersild, Austin. *Orientalism and Empire: North Caucasus Mountain Peoples and the Georgian Frontier, 1845–1917*. Montreal: McGill-Queen's University Press, 2002.

Jersild, Austin, and Neli Melkadze. "The Dilemmas of Enlightenment in the Eastern Borderlands: The Theater and Library in Tbilisi." *Kritika: Explorations in Russian and Eurasian History* 3, no. 1 (2002): 27–49.

Johnson, Robert. *British Imperialism*. New York: Palgrave Macmillan, 2003.

Jones, Aled, and Bill Jones, "The Welsh World and the British Empire, c. 1851–1939: An Exploration." In *The British World: Diaspora, Culture and Identity*, edited by Carl Bridge and Kent Fedorowich, 57–81. London: Frank Cass, 2003.

Jones, Stephen F. "The Establishment of Soviet Power in Transcaucasia: The Case of Georgia, 1921–1928." *Soviet Studies* 40, no. 4 (1988): 616–39.

Jones, Stephen F. "Marxism and Peasant Revolution in the Russian Empire: the Case of the Gurian Republic." *Slavonic and East European Review* 67, no. 3 (1989): 403–34.

Jones, Stephen F. *Socialism in Georgian Colors: The European Road to Social-Democracy, 1883–1917*. Cambridge, MA: Harvard University Press, 2005.

Jones, Stephen F. *Georgia: A Political History Since Independence*. London: I. B. Tauris, 2013.

Jongerden, Joost, and Jelle Verheij, eds. *Social Relations in Ottoman Diyarbekir, 1870–1915*. Boston: Brill, 2012.

Jowitt, Ken. "Soviet Neotraditionalism: The Political Corruption of a Leninist Regime." *Europe-Asia Studies* 35, no. 3 (1983): 275–97.

Judson, Pieter M. *Exclusive Revolutionaries: Liberal Politics, Social Experience, and National Identity in the Austrian Empire, 1848–1914*. Ann Arbor: University of Michigan Press, 1996.

Jughashvili, Ekaterine. *stalinis dedis mogonebebi*. Tbilisi: Bakur Sulakauri, 2012.

Jurriens, Edwin, and Jeroen de Kloet, eds. *Cosmopatriots: On Distant Belongings and Close Encounters*. Amsterdam: Rodopi, 2007.

Kabachnik, Peter, Joanna Regulska, and Beth Mitchneck. "Where and When is Home? The Double Displacement of Georgian IDPs from Abkhazia." *Journal of Refugee Studies* 23, no. 3 (2010): 315–36.

Kalb, Judith E. *Russia's Rome: Imperial Visions, Messianic Dreams, 1890–1940*. Madison: University of Wisconsin Press, 2008.

Kappeler, Andreas. *The Russian Empire: A Multiethnic History*. Translated by Alfred Clayton. Harlow: Longman, 2001.

Kautsky, Karl. *Georgia: A Social Democratic Peasant Republic*. Translated by H. J. Stenning. London: International Bookshops, 1921.

Kenez, Peter. *Cinema and Soviet Society, 1917–1953*. Cambridge: Cambridge University Press, 1992.

Kenny, Kevin. "Diaspora and Comparison: The Global Irish as a Case Study." *Journal of American History* 90, no. 1 (2003): 134–62.

Kepley Jr., Vance. *In the Service of the State: The Cinema of Alexander Dovzhenko*. Madison: University of Wisconsin Press, 1986.

Khantadze-Andronikashvili, Rusudan. *Nashi zemliaki v Moskve*. Tbilisi: Sakartvelo, 1990.

Khater, Akram Fouad. *Inventing Home: Emigration, Gender, and the Middle Class in Lebanon*. Berkeley: University of California Press, 2001.

Khazanov, Anatoly M. *Nomads and the Outside World*. Translated by Julia Crookenden. Cambridge: Cambridge University Press, 1984.

Khlevniuk, Oleg V. *In Stalin's Shadow: The Career of "Sergo" Ordzhonikidze*. Edited by Donald J. Raleigh. Translated by David J. Nordlander. Armonk, NY: M. E. Sharpe, 1995.

Khrushchev, N. S. *Vospominaniia: vremia, liudi, vlast'*. 2 vols. Moscow: Moskovskie novosti, 1999.

Khrushchev, N. S. *Memoirs of Nikita Khrushchev*. 3 vols. Edited by Sergei Khrushchev. Translated by George Shriver. University Park: Pennsylvania State University Press, 2004.

Kiknadze, N. S. *Iz opyta moei raboty v restorane "Aragvi."* Moscow: Gostorgizdat, 1951.

Kiknadze, N. S., and G. M. Kirillova, *Spetsi i pripravy v predpriatiakh obshchestvennogo pitaniia*. Moscow: Gostorgizdat, 1954.

King, Charles, ed. *Nations Abroad: Diaspora Politics and International Relations in the Former Soviet Union*. Boulder, CO: Westview Press, 1998.

*Kniga o vkusnoi i zdorovoi pishche*. Moscow: Pishchepromizdat, 1952, 1953, 1961, and 1965.

Knight, Amy. *Beria: Stalin's First Lieutenant*. Princeton, NJ: Princeton University Press, 1993.

Kotkin, Stephen. *Magnetic Mountain: Stalinism as Civilization*. Berkeley: University of California Press, 1997.

Kotkin, Stephen. *Armageddon Averted: The Soviet Collapse, 1970–2000*. Oxford: Oxford University Press, 2001.

Kotkin, Stephen. *Stalin. Volume I, Paradoxes of Power, 1878–1928*. New York: Penguin, 2014.

Kozlov, Denis, and Eleonory Gilburd, eds. *The Thaw: Soviet Society and Culture During the 1950s and 1960s*. Toronto: University of Toronto Press, 2013.

Kramer, Paul A. "Power and Connection: Imperial Histories of the United States in the World." *American Historical Review* 116, no. 5 (2011): 1348–92.

Kulikov, V. V., ed. *Anekdoty ot... i do...* St. Petersburg: Kristall, 1998.

*Kulinariia: superkniga dlia gurmanov*. Moscow: Voskresenie, 1996.

Kun, Miklos. *Stalin: An Unknown Portrait*. Budapest: Central European University Press, 2003.

Kunt, Metin Ibrahim. "Ethnic-Regional (*Cins*) Solidarity in the Seventeenth-Century Ottoman Establishment." *International Journal of Middle East Studies* 5, no. 3 (1974): 233–39.

Kuznetsov, Eduard. *Mordovskii marafon*. Moscow: Eksmo, 2008.

Lang, David Marshall. *The Last Years of the Georgian Monarchy, 1658–1832*. New York: Columbia University Press, 1957.

Lang, David Marshall. *A Modern History of Soviet Georgia*. London: Weidenfeld and Nicolson, 1962.

Layton, Susan. "Eros and Empire in Russian Literature About Georgia." *Slavic Review* 51, no. 2 (1992): 195–213.

Layton, Susan. *Russian Literature and Empire: Conquest of the Caucasus from Pushkin to Tolstoy.* Cambridge: Cambridge University Press, 1995.

Ledeneva, Alena D. *Russia's Economy of Favours: Blat, Networking, and Informal Exchange.* Cambridge: Cambridge University Press, 1998.

Lemon, Alaina. *Between Two Fires: Gypsy Performance and Romani Memory from Pushkin to Post-Socialism.* Durham, NC: Duke University Press, 2000.

Lenin, V. I. *Polnoe sobranie sochinenii.* Moscow: Gos. izd-vo politicheskoi literatury, 1961.

Lenss, Laura A. "Capturing the Next Shift: The Mapping of Meaning onto the Museum of the Occupation of Latvia." *Future Anterior* 3, no. 1 (2006): 48–57.

Levin, Theodore Craig. *The Hundred Thousand Fools of God: Musical Travels in Central Asia (and Queens, New York).* Bloomington: Indiana University Press, 1996.

Levine, Donald N., ed. *Georg Simmel on Individuality and Social Forms: Selected Writings.* Chicago: University of Chicago Press, 1971.

Lewin-Epstein, Noah, Yaacov Ro'i, and Paul Ritterband, eds. *Russian Jews on Three Continents: Migration and Resettlement.* New York: Frank Cass, 1997.

Lieven, Anatol. *Chechnya: Tombstone of Russian Power.* New Haven, CT: Yale University Press, 1998.

Lincoln, William Bruce. "Russia's 'Enlightened' Bureaucrats and the Problem of State Reform, 1848–1856." *Cahiers du Monde russe et soviétique* 12, no. 4 (1971): 410–21.

Lipman, Jonathan N. *Familiar Strangers: A History of Muslims in Northwest China.* Seattle: University of Washington Press, 1997.

Lipman, Maria, Lev Gudkov, and Lasha Bakradze. *The Stalin Puzzle: Deciphering Post-Soviet Public Opinion.* Washington, DC: Carnegie Endowment for International Peace, 2013.

Loginov, Vladimir. *Teni Stalina: general Vlasik i ego soratniki.* Moscow: Sovremennik, 2000.

Lowry, Heath W. *The Nature of the Early Ottoman State.* Albany: State University of New York Press, 2003.

Lur'e, Lev, and Irina Maliarova. *1956 god: seredina veka.* Saint Petersburg: Neva, 2007.

MacFayden, David. *Songs for Fat People: Affect, Emotion, and Celebrity in the Russian Popular Song, 1900–1955.* Montreal: McGill-Queen's University Press, 2002.

Manchester, Laurie. *Holy Fathers, Secular Sons: Clergy, Intelligentsia, and the Modern Self in Revolutionary Russia.* DeKalb: Northern Illinois University Press, 2008.

Mandel'shtam, O. E. "Puteshestvie v Armeniiu." *Zvezda*, no. 5 (1933): 103–25.

Manning, Paul. *The Semiotics of Drink and Drinking.* London: Continuum Publishing Group, 2012.

Manning, Paul. *Strangers in a Strange Land: Occidentalist Publics and Orientalist Geographies in Nineteenth-Century Georgian Imaginaries.* Brighton: Academic Studies Press, 2012.

Mansvetashvili, Iakov. *Vospominaniia.* Tbilisi: Literatura da khelovneba, 1967.

Mars, Gerald, and Yochanan Altman. "The Cultural Bases of Soviet Georgia's Second Economy." *Soviet Studies* 35, no. 4 (1983): 546–60.

Martin, Terry. "Modernization or Neo-Traditionalism? Ascribed Nationality and Soviet Primordialism." In *Stalinism: New Directions*, edited by Sheila Fitzpatrick, 348–67. London: Routledge, 2000.

Martin, Terry. *The Affirmative Action Empire: Nations and Nationalism in the Soviet Union, 1923–1939.* Ithaca, NY: Cornell University Press, 2001.

Masterovoy, Anton. "Eating Soviet: Food and Culture in the USSR, 1917–1991." PhD diss., City University of New York, 2013.

Matthews, Mervyn. *The Passport Society: Controlling Movement in Russia and the USSR.* Boulder, CO: Westview Press, 1993.

McCabe, Ina Baghdiantz, Gelina Harlaftis, and Ioanna Pepelasis Minoglou, eds. *Diaspora Entrepreneurial Networks: Four Centuries of History.* Oxford: Berg, 2005.

McNeal, Robert Hatch. *Stalin: Man and Ruler.* New York: New York University Press, 1988.

McReynolds, Louise. *Russia at Play: Leisure Activities at the End of the Tsarist Era.* Ithaca, NY: Cornell University Press, 2003.

Mennell, Stephen. *All Manners of Food: Eating and Taste in England and France From the Middle Ages to the Present.* New York: Blackwell, 1985.

Mesropian, S. I. *50 bliud azerbaidzhanskoi kukhni.* Moscow: Gostorgizdat, 1940.

Mgeladze, Akakii. *Stalin kakim ia ego znal.* Tbilisi, 2001.

Mikoian, A. I. *Tak bylo: razmyshleniia o minuvshem.* Edited by S. A. Mikoian. Moscow: Vagrius, 1999.

Millar, James R. "The Little Deal: Brezhnev's Contribution to Acquisitive Socialism." *Slavic Review* 44, no. 4 (1985): 694–706.

Ministerstvo sel'skogo khoziastva Gruzinskoi SSR. *Gruziia—osnovnaia baza subtropicheskogo khoziastva SSSR.* Tbilisi: Sabchota Sakartvelo, 1971.

Mintz, Sidney W. *Sweetness and Power: The Place of Sugar in Modern History.* New York: Viking, 1985.

Mironov, N. A. *Moskovskaia konservatoriia. Istoki.* Moscow: Moskovskaia gos. konservatoriia im. P. I. Chaikovskogo, 1995.

Mitin, G. A. *On videl solntse: chelovek i obshchestvo v romanakh i rasskazakh Nodara Dumbadze.* Moscow: IMLI RAN, 2002.

Mitrokhin, Nikolai. *Russkaia partiia: dvizhenie russkikh natsionalistov v SSSR, 1953–1985 gody.* Moscow: Novoe literaturnoe obozrenie, 2003.

Moch, Leslie Page. *Moving Europeans: Migration in Western Europe since 1650.* Bloomington: Indiana University Press, 1992.

Montefiore, Simon Sebag. *Stalin: The Court of the Red Tsar.* London: Phoenix, 2004.

Montefiore, Simon Sebag. *Young Stalin.* New York: Knopf, 2007.

"Moscow." *National Review* 7, no. 15 (1959): 7.

Moskoff, William. *The Bread of Affliction: The Food Supply in the USSR During World War II.* Cambridge: Cambridge University Press, 1990.

Moss, Kenneth B. *Jewish Renaissance in the Russian Revolution.* Cambridge, MA: Harvard University Press, 2009.

Mühlfried, Florian. "Banquets, Grant-Eaters, and the Red Intelligentsia in Post Soviet Georgia." *Central Eurasian Studies Review* 4, no. 1 (2005): 16–19.

Mukhin, Iurii. *Stalin: khoziain Sovetskogo Soiuza.* Moscow: Algoritm, 2008.

Naimark, Norman M. *Stalin's Genocides.* Princeton, NJ: Princeton University Press, 2010.

Nathans, Benjamin. *Beyond the Pale: The Jewish Encounter with Late Imperial Russia.* Berkeley: University of California Press, 2002.

Neigauz, G. G. *Vospominaniia Neigauza.* Translated by E. R. Rikhter. Moscow: Klassika-XXI, 2007.

Nelli, Humbert S. *The Business of Crime: Italians and Syndicate Crime in the United States.* New York: Oxford University Press, 1976.

Nelli, Humbert S. *From Immigrants to Ethnics: The Italian Americans.* Oxford: Oxford University Press, 1983.

Nevezhin, V. A. *Zastol'nye rechi Stalina.* Moscow: AIRO-XX, 2003.

Nodia, Ghia. "Georgia's Identity Crisis." *Journal of Democracy* 6, no. 1 (1995): 104–16.

O'Keeffe, Brigid. *New Soviet Gypsies: Nationality, Performance, and Selfhood in the Early Soviet Union.* Toronto: University of Toronto Press, 2013.

*Obshchestvennoe pitanie v Moskve (kratkii spravochnik).* Moscow: Moskovskii rabochii, 1962.

Okudzhava, Bulat. *Chaepitie na Arbate: stikhi raznykh let.* Moscow: Korona-print, 1998.

Olcott, Martha Brill *The Kazakhs.* Stanford, CA: Hoover Institution Press, 1987.

Oshlakov, Mikhail. *Genii Stalin: titan XX veka.* Moscow: Iauza-press, 2013.

Osokina, Elena. *Our Daily Bread: Socialist Distribution and the Art of Survival in Stalin's Russia, 1927–1941.* Edited by Kate Transchel. Armonk, NY: M. E. Sharpe, 2001.

Oushakine, Serguei Alex. *Patriotism of Despair: Nation, War, and Loss in Russia.* Ithaca, NY: Cornell University Press, 2009.

Panossian, Razmik. *The Armenians: From Kings And Priests to Merchants And Commissars.* New York: Columbia University Press, 2006.

Parkes, Peter. "Milk Kinship in Southeast Europe: Alternative Social Structures and Foster Relations in the Caucasus and the Balkans." *Social Anthropology* 12, no. 3 (2004): 341–58.

Parsadanashvili, Mariam. "The Georgian Dissident Movement: The Case of Zviad Gamsakhurdia and Merab Kostava." *Archival Bulletin* 4 (2009): 34–36.

*Pavil'on Gruzinskaia SSR: Putevoditel'.* Moscow: Sel'khozgiz, 1939.

*Pavil'on Gruzinskaia SSR.* Moscow: Gos. izd-vo sel'skokhoziastvennoi literatury, 1954.

Péristiany, Jean G. *Honour and Shame: The Values of Mediterranean Society.* Chicago: University of Chicago Press, 1966.

Pesmen, Dale. *Russia and Soul: An Exploration.* Ithaca, NY: Cornell University Press, 2000.

Petrov, N. V., and K. V. Skorkin, eds. *Kto rukovodil NKVD, 1934–1941: spravochnik.* Moscow: Zven'ia, 1999.

Philliou, Christine. "Communities on the Verge: Unraveling the Phanariot Ascendancy in Ottoman Governance." *Comparative Studies in Society and History* 51, no. 1 (2009): 151–81.

Pinkus, Benjamin, and Jonathan Frankel. *The Soviet Government and the Jews, 1948–1967: A Documented Study.* Cambridge: Cambridge University Press, 1984.

Plokhy, Serhii. *The Last Empire: The Final Days of the Soviet Union.* New York: Basic Books, 2014.

Podlesskikh, Georgii, and Andrei Tereshenok. *Vory v zakone: brosok k vlasti.* Moscow: Khudozhestvennaia literatura, 1994.

Pokhlebkin, V. V. *Chai, ego istoriia, svoistva i upotreblenie.* Moscow: Pishchevaia promyshlennost', 1968.

Pokhlebkin, V. V. *Chai i vodka v istorii Rossii*. Krasnoyarsk: Krasnoiarskoe knizhnoe izd-vo, 1995.

Pokhlebkin, V. V. *Kukhnia veka*. Moscow: Polifakt, 2000.

Popova, Irina, and Valentina Osipova. "Otnoshenie prinimaiushchei storony k migrantam." *Vestnik obshchestvennogo mneniia* 1, no. 114 (2013): 81–88.

Prokhorov, A. M., et al. *Bol'shaia sovetskaia entsiklopediia*. Moscow: Sovetskaia entsiklopediia, 1970–1981.

Raeff, Marc. *Russia Abroad: A Cultural History of the Russian Emigration, 1919–1939*. New York: Oxford University Press, 1990.

Ram, Harsha. *The Imperial Sublime: A Russian Poetics of Empire*. Madison: University of Wisconsin Press, 2003.

Randolph, John, and Eugene M. Avrutin. *Russia in Motion: Cultures of Human Mobility since 1850*. Urbana: University of Illinois Press, 2012.

Raskin, Iosif. *Entsiklopediia khuliganstvuiushchego ortodoksa*. St. Petersburg: Ekho, 1995.

Ratiani, I. I. *U istokov gruzinskogo kino: vzaimosviaz' literatury, teatra i kino v kul'ture Gruzii*. Moscow: Rossiiskii institut kul'turologii, 2003.

Rayfield, Donald. *The Literature of Georgia: A History*. Surrey: Curzon Press, 2000.

Razzakov, Fedor. *Bandity semidesiatykh, 1970–1979*. Moscow: Eksmo, 2008.

Reed, Susan A. "The Politics and Poetics of Dance." *Annual Review of Anthropology*, v. 27 (1998): 503–32.

Rees, E. A. *State Control in Soviet Russia: The Rise and the Fall of the Workers' and Peasants' Inspectorate, 1920–1934*. New York: St. Martin's, 1987.

Reid, Susan E. "The Khrushchev Kitchen: Domesticating the Scientific-Technological Revolution." *Journal of Contemporary History* 40, no. 2 (2005): 289–316.

Remennick, Larissa. *Russian Jews on Three Continents*. New Brunswick, NJ: Transaction, 2007.

*Restoran Aragvi*. Tbilisi: Ministerstvo torgovli GSSR.

Rieber, Alfred J. "Stalin, Man of the Borderlands." *American Historical Review* 106, no. 5 (2001): 1651–91.

Roman, Meredith. "Making Caucasians Black: Moscow since the Fall of Communism and the Racialization of Non-Russians." *Journal of Communist Studies and Transition Politics* 18, no. 2 (2002): 1–27.

Ro'i, Yaacov. *Soviet Decision Making in Practice: The USSR and Israel, 1947–1954*. New Brunswick, NJ: Transaction Books, 1980.

Rustaveli, Shota. *Vitiaz' v tigrovoi shkure*. Translated by N. Zabolotskii. Introduction by Beso Zhgenti. Moscow: Detgiz, 1950.

Rustaveli, Shota. *The Knight in the Panthers Skin*. Translated by Venera Urushadze. Tbilisi: Sabchota Sakartvelo, 1986.

Safran, William. "Diasporas in Modern Societies: Myths of Homeland and Return." *Diaspora* 1, no. 1 (1991): 83–99.

Sahadeo, Jeff. "*Druzhba Narodov* or Second Class Citizenship? Soviet Asian Migrants in a Post-Colonial World." *Central Asian Survey* 26, no. 4 (2007): 559–79.

Sahadeo, Jeff. "Soviet 'Blacks' and Place Making in Leningrad and Moscow." *Slavic Review* 71, no. 2 (2012): 331–58.

Said, Edward W. *Orientalism*. New York: Random House, 1979.

Said, Edward W. *Culture and Imperialism*. New York: Random House, 1993.

Sanchez, George J. "Race, Nation, and Culture in Recent Immigration Studies." *Journal of American Ethnic History* 18, no. 4 (1999): 66–84.

Schmelz, Peter J. *Such Freedom, If Only Musical: Unofficial Soviet Music during the Thaw*. Oxford: Oxford University Press, 2009.

Scott, Erik R. "Ottoman Imperial Identities Between Istanbul and the Caucasus." *Journal of Associated Graduates in Near Eastern Studies* 12, no. 2 (2007): 3–29.

Scott, Erik R. "The Nineteenth-Century Gypsy Choir and the Performance of Otherness." Berkeley Program in Eurasian and Eastern European Studies (BPS) Working Paper, Fall 2008.

Scott, Erik R. "Edible Ethnicity: How Georgian Cuisine Conquered the Soviet Table." *Kritika: Explorations in Russian and Eurasian History* 13, no. 4 (2012): 831–58.

Senelick, Laurence. "'A Woman's Kingdom': Minister of Culture Furtseva and Censorship in the Post-Stalinist Russian Theatre." *New Theatre Quarterly* 26, no. 1 (2010): 16–24.

Service, Robert. *Stalin: A Biography*. London: Pan Books, 2005.

Sevela, Efraim. *Ostanovite samolet—ia slezu!* Munich: F. Zeuner, 1977.

Shamina, Lidiia. *Teatr Igoria Moiseeva*. Moscow: Teatralis, 2012.

Shay, Anthony. *Choreographic Politics: State Folk Dance Companies, Representation, and Power*. Middletown, CT: Wesleyan University Press, 2002.

Sheffer, Gabriel. *Diaspora Politics: At Home Abroad*. New York: Cambridge University Press, 2003.

Shevardnadze, Eduard. *Moi vybor: v zashchitu demokratii i svobody*. Moscow: Novosti, 1991.

Shevardnadze, Eduard. *The Future Belongs to Freedom*. Translated by Catherine A. Fitzpatrick. New York: Free Press, 1991.

Shirokii, I. V. *Tamara Khanum*. Leningrad: Iskusstvo, 1941.

Shlapentokh, Vladimir, Munir Sendich, and Emil Payin, eds. *The New Russian Diaspora: Russian Minorities in the Former Soviet Republics*. Armonk, NY: M. E. Sharpe, 1994.

Shneer, David. *Through Soviet Jewish Eyes: Photography, War, and the Holocaust*. New Brunswick, NJ: Rutgers University Press, 2011.

Siar, Sheila, ed. *Migration in Georgia: A Country Profile 2008*. Geneva: International Organization for Migration, 2008.

Siegelbaum, Lewis H. *Cars for Comrades: The Life of the Soviet Automobile*. Ithaca, NY: Cornell University Press, 2008.

Siegelbaum, Lewis H., and Leslie Page Moch. *Broad is My Native Land: Repertoires and Regimes of Migration in Russia's Twentieth Century*. Ithaca, NY: Cornell University Press, 2014.

Simis, Konstantin. *USSR: The Corrupt Society*. New York: Simon and Shuster, 1982.

Skhirtladze, V. I. *100 bliud gruzinskoi kukhni*. Moscow: Gostorgizdat, 1940.

Slade, Gavin. *Reorganizing Crime: Mafia and Anti-Mafia in Post-Soviet Georgia*. Oxford: Oxford University Press, 2013.

Slezkine, Yuri. *Arctic Mirrors: Russia and the Small Peoples of the North*. Ithaca, NY: Cornell University Press, 1994.

Slezkine, Yuri. "The USSR as a Communal Apartment, or How a Socialist State Promoted Ethnic Particularism." *Slavic Review* 53, no. 2 (1994): 414–52.

Slezkine, Yuri. *The Jewish Century*. Princeton, NJ: Princeton University Press, 2004.

Smeliansky, Anatoly. *The Russian Theatre After Stalin*. Translated by Patrick Miles. Cambridge: Cambridge University Press, 1999.

Smith, Hedrick. *The Russians*. New York: Ballantine Books, 1976.

Smith, Jeremy. "The Georgian Affair of 1922: Policy Failure, Personality Clash or Power Struggle?" *Europe-Asia Studies* 50, no. 3 (1998): 519–44.

Smith, Jeremy. *The Bolsheviks and the National Question, 1917–23*. New York: St. Martin's, 1999.

Smith, Jeremy. *Red Nations: The Nationalities Experience in and after the USSR*. Cambridge: Cambridge University Press, 2013.

Sorrentino, Frank M., and Jerome Krase, eds. *The Review of Italian American Studies*. Lanham: Lexington Books, 2000.

Staats, Steven K. "Corruption in the Soviet System." *Problems of Communism*, no. 21 (1972): 40–47.

Stalin, I. V. *Marksizm i natsional'nyi vopros*. Moscow: Gospolitizdat, 1946.

Starr, Frederick S. *Red and Hot: The Fate of Jazz in the Soviet Union*. New York: Limelight Editions, 1985.

Statisticheskii otdel TsK VKP(b). *Vsesoiuznaia partiinaia perepis' 1927 goda*. Moscow, 1927.

Steffen, James. *The Cinema of Sergei Parajanov*. Madison: University of Wisconsin Press, 2013.

Steinbeck, John. *A Russian Journal*. New York: Penguin, 1948.

Stites, Richard. *Revolutionary Dreams: Utopian Vision and Experimental Life in the Russian Revolution*. Oxford: Oxford University Press, 1989.

Stites, Richard. *Russian Popular Culture: Entertainment and Society Since 1900*. Cambridge: Cambridge University Press, 1992.

Stoianovich, Traian. "The Conquering Balkan Orthodox Merchant." *Journal of Economic History* 20, no. 2 (1960): 234–313.

Sukhishvili, Iliko. *mogonebebi*. Tbilisi, 2008.

Sunderland, Willard. *Taming the Wild Field: Colonization and Empire on the Russian Steppe*. Ithaca, NY: Cornell University Press, 2004.

Suny, Ronald Grigor. *The Baku Commune, 1917–1918: Class and Nationality in the Russian Revolution*. Princeton, NJ: Princeton University Press, 1972.

Suny, Ronald Grigor, ed. *Transcaucasia: Nationalism and Social Change*. Ann Arbor: Michigan Slavic Publications, 1983.

Suny, Ronald Grigor. *The Making of the Georgian Nation*. Bloomington: Indiana University Press, 1988, 1994.

Suny, Ronald Grigor. "Beyond Psychohistory: The Young Stalin in Georgia." *Slavic Review* 50, no. 1 (1991): 48–58.

Suny, Ronald Grigor. *Looking Toward Ararat: Armenia in Modern History*. Bloomington: Indiana University Press, 1993.

Suny, Ronald Grigor. *The Revenge of the Past: Nationalism, Revolution, and the Collapse of the Soviet Union*. Stanford, CA: Stanford University Press, 1993.

Swain, Geoffrey. "The Disillusioning of the Revolution's Praetorian Guard: The Latvian Riflemen, Summer—Autumn 1918." *Europe-Asia Studies* 51, no. 4 (1999): 667–86.

Swietochowski, Tadeusz. *Russian Azerbaijan, 1905–1920: The Shaping of a National Identity in a Muslim Community*. Cambridge: Cambridge University Press, 2004.

Tanny, Jarrod. *City of Rogues and Schnorrers: Russia's Jews and the Myth of Old Odessa.*
     Bloomington: Indiana University Press, 2011.

Tataradze, Avtandil. *Piat' gruzinskikh tantsev.* Tbilisi: Khelovneba, 1981.

Tatishvili, V. *Gruziny v Moskve: istoricheskii ocherk (1653–1722).* Tbilisi: Zaria
     vostoka, 1959.

Taubman, William, Sergei Khrushchev, and Abbott Gleason, eds. *Nikita Khrushchev.*
     New Haven, CT: Yale University Press, 2000.

Tillett, Lowell. *The Great Friendship: Soviet Historians on the Non-Russian
     Nationalities.* Chapel Hill: University of North Carolina Press, 1969.

Timasheff, Nicholas S. *The Great Retreat: The Growth and Decline of Communism in
     Russia.* New York: E. P. Dutton, 1946.

Tobias, Henry Jack. *The Jewish Bund in Russia from its Origins to 1905.* Stanford,
     CA: Stanford University Press, 1972.

Tölölyan, Khachig. "The Contemporary Discourse of Diaspora Studies." *Comparative
     Studies of South Asia, Africa and the Middle East* 27, no. 3 (2007): 647–55.

Toradze, Gulbat. *Kompozitory Gruzii.* Tbilisi: Khelovneba, 1973.

Torchinov, V. A., and A. M. Leoniuk. *Vokrug Stalina: istoriko-biograficheskii sprav-
     ochnik.* Saint Petersburg: SPbGU, 2000.

Trier, Tom, and Andrei Khanzhin. *The Meskhetian Turks at a Crossroads: Integration,
     Repatriation, or Resettlement?* London: Global Book Marketing, 2007.

Troitsky, Artemy. *Back in the USSR: The True Story of Rock in Russia.*
     London: Omnibus Press, 1987.

Trotskii, L. D. *Mezhdu imperializmom i revoliutsiei: osnovnye voprosy revoliutsii na
     chastnom primere Gruzii.* Moscow: Gos. izd-vo, 1922.

Trotskii, L. D. "On Lenin's Testament." *New International,* July 1934.

Trotskii, L. D. *The Revolution Betrayed.* Translated by Max Eastman. Mineola: Dover
     Publications, 2004.

Tsentral'noe statisticheskoe upravlenie Gruzinskoi SSR. *Gruziia v tsifrakh.*
     Tbilisi: Sabchota Sakartvelo, 1965, 1969, and 1985.

Tsentral'noe statisticheskoe upravlenie Gruzinskoi SSR. *Gruzinskaia SSR v tsifrakh.*
     Tbilisi: Statistika, 1965.

Tsentral'noe statisticheskoe upravlenie Gruzinskoi SSR. *Narodnoe khoziastvo
     Gruzinskoi SSR za 60 let.* Tbilisi: Sabchota Sakartvelo, 1980.

Tsentral'noe statisticheskoe upravlenie SSSR. *Vysshee obrazovanie v SSSR: statis-
     ticheskii sbornik.* Moscow: Gosstatizdat TsSU SSSR, 1961.

Tsentral'noe statisticheskoe upravlenie SSSR. *Narodnoe khoziastvo SSSR, 1972.*
     Moscow: Statistika, 1973.

Tsereteli, I. G. *Vospominaniia o fevral'skoi revoliutsii.* Paris: Mouton, 1963.

Tsitsishvili, Nino. "'A Man Can Sing and Play Better than a Woman': Singing
     and Patriarchy at the Georgian *Supra* Feast." *Ethnomusicology* 50, no. 3
     (1996): 452–93.

Tucker, Robert C. *Stalin as Revolutionary, 1879–1929: A Study in History and
     Personality.* New York: Norton, 1973.

Turashvili, Dato. *jinsebis taoba.* Tbilisi: Bakur Sulakauri, 2008.

Ural'skii, A. I., ed. *Anekdoty. Gruziia—strana millionerov.* Moscow: Svetlana, 1996.

Uratadze, G. I. *Vospominaniia gruzinskogo sotsial-demokrata.* Stanford, CA: Hoover
     Institution Press, 1968.

Ushakov, D. N., and B. M. Volin, eds. *Tolkovyi slovar' russkogo iazyka*. Moscow: Sovetskaia entsiklopediia, 1940.

Vaitiekunas, Vytautas. *A Survey of Developments in Captive Lithuania in 1965–1968*. New York: Committee for a Free Lithuania, 1969.

van Ree, Erik. *The Political Thought of Joseph Stalin: A Study in Twentieth-Century Revolutionary Patriotism*. London: RoutledgeCurzon, 2003.

Varese, Federico. "The Society of the Vory-v-Zakone, 1930s–1950s." *Cahiers du Monde Russe* 39, no. 4 (1998): 515–38.

Vecoli, Rudolph J. "The *Contadini* in Chicago: A Critique of *The Uprooted*." *Journal of American History* 51, no. 3 (1964): 404–17.

Vecoli, Rudolph J. "The Formation of Chicago's 'Little Italies.'" *Journal of American Ethnic History* 2, no. 2 (1983): 5–20.

Veidlinger, Jeffrey. *The Moscow State Yiddish Theater: Jewish Culture on the Soviet Stage*. Bloomington: Indiana University Press, 2000.

Vendina, Olga. "Social Polarization and Ethnic Segregation in Moscow." *Eurasian Geography and Economics* 43, no. 3 (2002): 216–43.

Verdery, Katherine. *What Was Socialism, and What Comes Next?* Princeton, NJ: Princeton University Press, 1996.

Von Hagen, Mark. "Empires, Borderlands, and Diasporas: Eurasia as Anti-Paradigm for the Post-Soviet Era." *American Historical Review* 109, no. 2 (2004): 445–68.

Vysotskii, Vladimir. *Sochineniia v dvukh tomakh: pesni*. Edited by A. E. Krylov. Ekaterinburg: Krok-tsentr, 1995.

*Vystavka Dostizhenii Narodnogo Khoziastva SSSR: Putevoditel'*. Moscow: Gos. nauchno-tekhnicheskii izd-vo mashino stroitel'noi literatury, 1959.

Weber, Max. *The Protestant Ethic and the "Spirit" of Capitalism*. Translated by Peter R. Baehr and Gordon C. Wells. New York: Penguin, 2002.

Weeks, Theodore R. *Nation and State in Late Imperial Russia: Nationalism and Russification on the Western Frontier, 1863–1914*. DeKalb: Northern Illinois University Press, 1996.

Werner, Hans. *Imagined Homes: Soviet German Immigrants in Two Cities*. Winnipeg: University of Manitoba Press, 2007.

Werth, Paul W. *The Tsar's Foreign Faiths: Toleration and the Fate of Religious Freedom in Imperial Russia*. Oxford: Oxford University Press, 2014.

Wickström, David-Emil. "'Drive-Ethno-Dance' and 'Hutzul Punk': Ukrainian-Associated Popular Music and (Geo)politics in a Post-Soviet Context." *Yearbook for Traditional Music*, no. 40 (2008): 60–88.

Willerton, John P. *Patronage and Politics in the USSR*. Cambridge: Cambridge University Press, 1992.

Williams, Brian Glyn. *The Crimean Tatars: The Diaspora Experience and the Forging of a Nation*. Leiden: Brill, 2001.

Williams, Robert Chadwell. *Culture in Exile: Russian Emigres in Germany, 1881–1941*. Ithaca, NY: Cornell University Press, 1972.

Woll, Josephine. *Real Images: Soviet Cinema and the Thaw*. London: I. B. Tauris, 2000.

Woll, Josephine, and Denise J. Youngblood. *Repentance*. London: I. B. Tauris, 2001.

Wortman, Richard S. *Scenarios of Power: Myth and Ceremony in Russian Monarchy. Vol. 2: From Alexander to the Abdication of Nicholas II*. Princeton, NJ: Princeton University Press, 2000.

Yergin, Daniel. *The Prize: The Epic Quest for Oil, Money and Power.* New York: Touchstone, 1992.

Yurchak, Alexei. *Everything was Forever, Until It Was No More: The Last Soviet Generation.* Princeton, NJ: Princeton University Press, 2006.

Zahra, Tara. "Imagined Noncommunities: National Indifference as a Category of Analysis." *Slavic Review* 61, no. 1 (2010): 93–119.

Zak, I. I. *Stat'i, materialy, vospominaniia.* Edited by M. G. Sokolov. Moscow: Sovetskii kompozitor, 1980.

Zav'ialov, Nikolai. *Istoriia obshchestvennogo pitaniia Moskvy.* Moscow: PIR, 2006.

Zdorovets, Ia. I. *Diaspory: Predstavitel'stva natsional'nostei v Moskve i ikh deiatel'nost'.* Moscow: Tsentr politicheskoi informatsii, 2003.

Zeller, Manfred. "'Our Own Internationale,' 1966: Dynamo Kiev Fans Between Local Identity and Transnational Imagination." *Kritika: Explorations in Russian and Eurasian History* 12, no. 1 (2011): 53–82.

Zhemukhov, Sufian, and Charles King. "Dancing the Nation in the North Caucasus." *Slavic Review* 72, no. 2 (2013): 287–305.

Zhordania, N. N. *Moia zhizn'.* Translated by Inna Zhordania. Stanford, CA: Hoover Institution Press, 1968.

Zimmerman, Joshua D. *Poles, Jews, and the Politics of Nationality: The Bund and the Polish Socialist Party in Late Tsarist Russia, 1892–1914.* Madison: University of Wisconsin Press, 2004.

Zolberg, Aristide R. *A Nation by Design: Immigration Policy in the Fashioning of America.* Cambridge, MA: Harvard University Press, 2006.

Zubkova, Elena. *Russia After the War: Hopes, Illusions, and Disappointments, 1945–1957.* Edited and translated by Hugh Ragsdale. Armonk, NY: M. E. Sharpe, 1998.

Zubok, Vladislav. *Zhivago's Children: The Last Russian Intelligentsia.* Cambridge, MA: Harvard University Press, 2009.

## Internet Websites and Electronic Publications

*Ansambl' Kolkhida.* Date of last access August 16, 2010. http://tbilisi-trip.narod.ru/Kolxida.html.

*Ansambl' "Orera."* Accessed April 22, 2010. www.orera.reclama.ru.

"Besedy s Nateloi Muntikovoi." *Slavianskaia Evropa.* Date of last access March 4, 2010. www.slavic-europe.eu/index.php?option=com_content&task=view&id=130&Itemid=1.

*Demoskop.* Accessed March 11, 2011. http://demoscope.ru.

Dzhanashiia, Vakhtang. "Gruziia ostalas' bez poniatii." *Kommersant,* March 5, 2003. Accessed September 17, 2014. www.kommersant.ru/doc/369449.

First, Joshua. "Ukrainian National Cinema and the Concept of the 'Poetic.'" *Kinokultura,* no. 9 (2009). Accessed September 18, 2014. www.kinokultura.com/specials/9/first.shtml.

Gamsakhurdia, Zviad. "sakartvelos sulieri misia." *AMSI.* Accessed November 17, 2010. www.amsi.ge/istoria/zg/missia.html.

Goncharova, Ol'ga. "Byt' Nani Bregvadze." *Televidenie i radio,* no. 14 (2005). Date of last access April 28, 2011. www.tvr.khv.ru/number/2005/14/arh.html.

*Gosudarstvennyi akademicheskii Bol'shoi teatr Rossii.* Accessed November 17, 2010. www.bolshoi.ru.

Grinkrug, Ol'ga. "O khitakh gruzinskoi kukhni." *Bol'shoi gorod* 20, no. 192 (2007). Accessed March 4, 2010. www.bg.ru/article/7072/.

Iaremenko, Valerii. "Kto podnial znamia nad Reikhstagom? Geroicheskaia istoriia i propagandistskii mif," *Polit.ru*, May 6, 2005. Accessed August 26, 2010. www. polit.ru/analytics/2005/05/06/banner.html.

Iosebashvili, Irakli. "Chronicles of a Soviet Capitalist (Part 1 of 2)." *Guernica*, November 1, 2009. Accessed September 17, 2014. www.guernicamag.com/features/soviet_capitalist/.

*kartuli diaspora.* Accessed March 17, 2011. www.diaspora.gov.ge.

Mamardashvili, Merab. "Veriu v zdravyi smysl." *Iriston.ru.* Accessed November 17, 2010. www.iriston.ru/ru/yugooset/1101322999.php.

"Pavil'on Gruzinskoi SSR." *Sait Vsesoiuznoi sel'skokhoziastvennoi vystavki.* Date of last access April 28, 2011. www.bcxb.ru/pavils/descriptions/018_54.htm.

"Refugees: Free at Last." *Time*, September 28, 1981. Accessed March 4, 2010. www. time.com/time/magazine/article/0,9171,953131-1,00.html.

"Russia: Where to Dine." *Time*, June 12, 1950. Accessed March 4, 2010. www.time. com/time/magazine/article/0,9171,812656,00.html.

Russian Public Opinion Research Center. "Ostalos' tol'ko sozhalenie." *Russian Public Opinion Research Center.* Date of last access April 7, 2011. http://wciom. com/archives/thematic-archive/info-material/single/2167.html.

"saakashvili 'moghalateebis jgupebze' saubrobs." *Civil.ge.* June 14, 2011. Accessed September 22, 2014. www.civil.ge/geo/article.php?id=24186.

Savranskaya, Svetlana, and Thomas Blanton. "The Shevardnadze File: Late Soviet Foreign Minister Helped End the Cold War." Accessed September 18, 2014. www2.gwu.edu/~nsarchiv/NSAEBB/NSAEBB481/.

"Vakthang Kikabidze—Chito-gvrito." *YouTube* video, 4:39. Accessed August 16, 2010. www.youtube.com/watch?v=4rlxdkFwrho.

## Unpublished Materials

Ivanauskas, Vilius. "Soviet 'Exotic' and Soviet 'West': Embodying Ethnic Particularism among Georgian and Lithuanian Writers." Unpublished article, 2013.

Manning, Paul. "Socialist supras and drinking democratically: changing images of the Georgian feast and Georgian society from Socialism to Post-socialism." Unpublished manuscript, Trent University, 2003.

Ram, Harsha. "The Literary Origins of the Georgian Feast: The Cosmopolitan Poetics of a National Ritual." Unpublished article, 2014.

# INDEX